Mind
AND
Body

Mind AND Body

PSYCHOLOGY OF EMOTION AND STRESS

George Mandler

University of California–San Diego

W·W·NORTON & COMPANY·NEW YORK·LONDON

THE TEXT OF THIS BOOK *is composed in Electra, with display type set in Caslon. Composition and Manufacturing by the Maple-Vail Book Manufacturing Group. Book design by Marjorie J. Flock.*

FIRST EDITION

Library of Congress Cataloging in Publication Data
Mandler, George.
Mind and body.
Includes bibliographical references and indexes.
1. Mind and body. 2. Emotions. 3. Emotions—Cognitive aspects. 4. Stress (Psychology) 5. Stress (Physiology) I. Title.
[DNLM: 1. Emotions. 2. Cognition. 3. Stress, Psychological, BF 311 M272m]
BF161.M36 1984 152.4 83-22139

ISBN 0-393-01855-5
ISBN 0-383-95346-7 (pbk.)

W. W. Norton & Company, Inc., 500 Fifth Avenue, New York, N.Y. 10110
W. W. Norton & Company Ltd., 37 Great Russel Street, London WC1B 3NU

1 2 3 4 5 6 7 8 9 0

For Jean, Michael, and Peter

CONTENTS

8 • DISCREPANCY AND INTERRUPTION: OCCASIONS FOR EMOTIONS, 171

9 • VALUE: SOURCE OF EMOTIONAL QUALITIES, 190

10 • ANXIETY AND EMOTION, 220

11 • STRESS AND EMOTION, 249

12 • IMPLICATIONS AND EXTENSIONS, 269

PREFACE

THIS BOOK IS WRITTEN for those general readers and students of psychology who wish to become acquainted with a comprehensive view of emotion and stress from the position of contemporary cognitive psychology. It is informed by a consistent framework about the structure of the human mind and uses these basic principles to understand human emotions as well as our peculiar human way of coping with and being affected by stress.

In addition to giving a coherent account of emotion and stress, the book reviews the history of speculations about emotions and provides an introduction to modern schema theory and the uses of consciousness in modern psychological theory. New to treatments of emotion is the extensive excursion into a theoretical and analytic treatment of the problem of value and evaluative cognitions. I have also extended the usual discussion of stress to include recent developments in the investigation of life stress and its effect on human well-being.

The book incorporates my previous *Mind and Emotion*,[1] which was an early symptom of the burgeoning influence of modern cognitive psychology on fields outside strictly "cognitive" concerns. Since that book was written, in 1971–74, the relation between cognition and emotion has become increasingly popular and populated, and our knowledge and sophistication about the human mental apparatus have significantly increased. In the intervening years, I have worked both on the more obviously immature parts of the earlier book and on additions and extensions that were published in a number of independent chapters. A sabbatical leave in 1982 made it possible to combine these new insights and developments with those parts of the earlier book that have stood the test of the intervening decade. The new volume is a quite different enterprise from its predecessor; it has incorporated some of the old, much that is new, and much that has changed.

The previous nine chapters have grown to twelve. The new chapters are Chapter 2, which includes a new discussion of emotion's history and is a revision of a chapter published in 1979;[2] Chapter 7, which addresses an approach to

1. Mandler (1975c).
2. Mandler (1979b).

biology and emotion; Chapter 9, which explores the nature and structure of evaluative cognitions and is an expansion of my contribution to the Carnegie Symposium on Affect and Cognition;[3] and Chapter 11, which is adapted from several publications on stress.[4] All of the sections that were retained from the previous book have been rewritten, either wholly or in part. Chapter 1 also incorporates an assessment of contemporary cognitive psychology, presented at the American Psychological Association meetings in 1981.[5] Chapter 3 responds to the new theoretical developmens in schema theory, and Chapter 4 represents a new departure because it incorporates A. J. Marcel's novel suggestions about consciousness. All the other chapters have also been amended to respond to the developments of the past ten years. As a result, most of this book is new, and it was decided to give it a new name without, however, denying its ancestry.

The book starts with a general discussion of psychology and emotion in its current context, paying specific attention to the bedeviling mind-body problem. Chapter 2 not only surveys the history of investigations into emotion but also summarizes currently dominant theoretical positions. Chapters 3 and 4 outline the structure of the human mind and consciousness. Chapter 5 advances the general thesis of the book on the construction and experience of emotion. This theme is developed in detail in the succeeding chapters. Chapter 6 discusses the bodily aspect, that is, the autonomic nervous system; Chapter 7 places emotional phenomena in the context of general biological considerations; Chapter 8 investigates the central occasions for arousal and emotion, that is, interruption and discrepancy; and Chapter 9 discusses the more "cognitive" evaluative aspect of emotion. The pervasive emotion of anxiety is explored in detail in Chapter 10, as is stress in Chapter 11. Chapter 12 takes up a number of ancillary and tangential problems, from development to memory and sexual emotions.

Parts of this book summarize current knowledge, others present reasonable extrapolations, and still others are optimistic anticipations of future trends. If the last decade is any indication, the prospects of an understanding of emotion that is consistent with our growing appreciation of human intellective functioning are bright indeed. I hope that this book is a useful contribution to that integration.

George Mandler

London
December 1982

3. Mandler (1982a).
4. Mandler (1979c, 1982c, 1983).
5. Mandler (1981b).

ACKNOWLEDGMENTS

THE DEVELOPMENT OF COGNITIVE PSYCHOLOGY during the past two decades made it possible for me to benefit from the seminal theoretical work of many other psychologists and to see a common basis for an understanding of the human mind enlarged and confirmed. A number of colleagues and friends have contributed to my growth and understanding, and in particular I want to thank the following who helped me directly by their contributions to mentalism and emotion and by my interactions with them: Ellen Berscheid, of the University of Minnesota; Tony Marcel, of the Applied Psychology Unit, Cambridge; Andrew Ortony, of the University of Illinois; and Roy D'Andrade, Don Norman, and David Rumelhart, from my own university. My students in both undergraduate and graduate courses helped me become more explicit about my ideas and to face some of their shortcomings. Arlene Jacobs made some of my writing comprehensible to our computer and helped in many other ways.

Two old and good friends, Jean Mandler and William Kessen, continue to be my most important supporters and critics. Our relationships do not build on indebtedness; otherwise I would be continuously in default.

I am most grateful for the hospitality of Prof. Robert Audley and the Department of Psychology at University College, London, where I found both the support and the friendship conducive to fruitful labors.

In addition to the sources of some of the materials used that are listed in the Preface, I wish to acknowledge the use in Chapter 10 of parts of my entry "Anxiety" in D. L. Sills, ed., *The international encyclopedia of the social sciences* (copyright 1968 by Crowell, Collier and Macmillan); the section on pp. 238–38 from Kessen and Mandler (1961) (copyright 1961 by the American Psychological Association), by permission of the publisher and W. Kessen; and various sections from Mandler (1972a, 1972b) and Mandler and Watson (1966) by permission of Academic Press, Inc., and D. L. Watson.

GEORGE MANDLER

Mind
AND
Body

1

MINDS, BODIES, AND EMOTIONS

HUMAN EMOTIONS have been objects of speculation for poets as well as psychologists, for painters and composers, for behaviorists and cognitive scientists. Few have adequately answered the question what emotions are or how they may be captured—in a theory, a poem, or a computer program. The emotion in the singular is often well portrayed by any who care to understand others and themselves. We seem to understand the emotion felt or displayed, but the search for the simple explanation of emotions in general seems to escape us.

Psychologists who have tried to find such general explanation have focused on some dimension of emotions, their visceral components, their apparent pervasive generality across cultures and people, the way the emotions place value on our world, or on their expressive features, interpersonal meaning, and—variously—their chaotic or adaptive features.

No such single explanation has survived, nor has William James's noble challenge "What is an emotion?" been satisfactorily answered. We understand fears and joys, the intensity and sensitivity of our passions and appreciations, and we understand—by such an enumeration—the central role of the emotions in the definition of human existence.

I shall respond to the complexity of these meanings of emotions, not by defining emotions, but by exploring the various psychological mechanisms that play a part in the emotions commonly understood. My aim is both psychological explanation and human understanding.

More than any other field of knowledge, psychology has been both the beneficiary and the prisoner of our most fascinating proclivity—to explain the world around us, to understand what surrounds us, to make up stories (i.e., myths, religions, folktales, and sciences) that explain and make comprehensible the evidence of our senses; stories that, in turn, shape that very evidence. Over the centuries the men and women who made up the most convincing stories were elevated to a special position in the life of the mind; first they were the prophets, then the philosophers, and, finally, the scientists. One built on the other, somewhere breaking through to a new way of looking at the world, a way that was somehow alien to the common language and folk beliefs, a method or structure that in the truest sense of the word "did not make sense." The growth was slow and often misunderstood. It took a Newton, not only to reach the new high ground of mathematical analysis, but also to realize that the rejection of a concept by common sense and common understanding was not relevant to the building of a system. When he postulated "attraction" in the *Principia*, he was told by his natural-philosopher colleagues that this concept was a dead end, but his answer is the important one that it might not seem reasonable but that, when he used it in a systematic sense in his axiomatic system, it did explain the data.

The pressure on psychology to "make sense," to be consistent with "common knowledge," is infinitely stronger. It may have become even more so with the advent of ordinary-language philosophy, which was aware that ordinary language produced confusion and pseudoproblems but often insisted, in unnecessary addition, that underneath the rubble—but within common sense and the ordinary language—lay the kernels of understanding human motives and actions. Unfortunately, Freud's basic insights were clouded by his system and his language; otherwise, we would not continue to look for the explanations of human actions in reasons and intentions and in the structure of the surface language. His insight was that there are forces that act like wishes, desires, reasons, and intentions but that are not available to inspection, awareness, and reason. Quite rightly, that formulation did not "make sense," because a wish or an intention is, by definition, part of the aware, sensing organism. If Freud had changed the language and showed that these forces, by some other name, had the same *consequences* as some of our conscious wishes, desires, and intentions, much of the misunderstanding of the misnamed and misrepresented unconscious might not have further muddied the waters of an objective psychology of the past fifty years. Consider, in contrast, the many-faceted "unconscious" processes and mechanisms that crowd our present theories of sensation, perception, cognition, learning, and language without drawing the slightest concern about their "scientific" status.

It is important not to fall into the trap of trying to explain what "emotion" *is*; that would be to follow the error of trying to explicate the common language. But we can, by analyzing the system of forces and processes that make up the human organism, suggest how certain behaviors, feelings, and experiences might be produced. We cannot specify all or most of these forces or their specific structures, but we can show that the outcome of these forces and processes produces behaviors and experiences that, appealing to common experience, we might consider akin to what we call emotion. Thus, I start with the aim not of *explaining* emotion but of describing a system that has as its product some of the observations that have been called "emotion" in the common language. The eventual aim is psychological theory, not an analysis of human experience expressed in phenomenal, existential, or ordinary language.

I present a psychological rather than a physiological or phenomenological view of human action and experience. As will be abundantly obvious in the following pages, I advocate a mentalistic theory in a psychologist's sense of mentalism and mind. The term *mind* implies no more and no less than the theoretical system that structures readiness, attention, and search for knowledge, transforms that information through self-correcting and self-instructing systems, and then structures its products and its actions in keeping with situation, contextual, and systematic demands. Mind is manifested when we get ready to go for a walk or try to solve a mathematical problem; whether we look out the window, search for an umbrella, leave the house, and open the umbrella to protect us; or whether we think about the proper theorem to apply to the problem, try it out on a scratch pad, look up a similar problem in a text, call a friend for help, and finally produce an answer.

The New Cognitive Psychology

During the past two decades, American psychology has turned from the rather impoverished theoretical notions of the previous decades and returned to the theoretical traditions of an earlier psychology. It has become both structural in its concern with the processes underlying the observable world of action and behavior, and constructivist in its concern with specifying how thoughts and actions could be and are derived from the processes hidden in underlying mechanisms and deep structures. If one surveys theory and practice in psychology today, one must conclude that cognitive psychology is becoming mainstream psychology. But what has happened to the other points of view that used to make up that mainstream? What about behaviorism, humanistic psychology, and psychoanalysis?

Behaviorism as a school has retreated to the study of lower animals, making few excursions into the human realm. What theory there is occasionally makes contact with cognitive constructs, though theory about underlying processes is still proscribed. The behaviorist tradition is very much alive in the applied area, but here it is primarily an innovative and imaginative technology and not a theoretical enterprise. Humanistic psychology has claimed for years to be the inheritor of the future of psychology. Unfortunately, its claims have not been substantiated with principled arguments or with a body of theory that makes interesting statements about human thought and action. Humanistic psychology is a collection of important statements about the role of interpersonal relations, moral values, and human growth. It continually reminds us about some of our unfinished business. Psychoanalytic theory, just like behaviorist theory, has become stagnant. It has—as have all successful theoretical enterprises—succumbed to its success. Only the historical and theoretical ignorance of many cognitive psychologists prevents them from seeing that much of their work is consistent with and often derives from psychoanalytic concerns. Semantic networks, theories of forgetting, models for slips of the tongue, the construction of consciousness, are all consistent with psychoanalytic theory.

On the other hand, much of social psychology was cognitive long before the new wave took hold, and it was the repository of underground cognitive wisdom during the dark ages of behaviorist sterility. What is still mising is a theoretical framework for cognitive social psychology. More than any other field, though, developmental psychology can claim cognitive priorities, particularly as it rediscovered the insights of Jean Piaget—the sage of Geneva—during the past two decades. In fact, the growth in the study of cognitive development has made developmental studies an integral part of cognitive psychology.

What is cognitive about current psychology? Why the adjective? The "new" psychology is only accidentally called cognitive. Historically, the concern with representation is a concern with the representation of *knowledge*, and hence the identification with cognition. However, the current use of representation clearly goes beyond any narrow definition of knowledge. On the other hand, there exists another tradition that identifies knowledge with conscious knowledge. Some of the older cognitive psychologies, which were part of that tradition, have become identified with a psychology of thought processes. But modern cognitive psychology is not concerned exclusively, or even primarily, with thought processes in the usual sense; rather, it claims that representations and processes can be developed to fit the full range of human thought and action.

Representation in the widest sense of the term is the central issue in cognitive psychology. The concept of representation is intimately tied to the issue of useful theory. Representational systems are theoretical constructs that are postulated as underlying (responsible for) the observable thoughts and actions of the organism. There is, of course, no one-to-one correspondence between an act and its representation; we do not use the term *representation* in the sense of a symbol that "stands for" some other event. The representation of knowledge, in other words, is the theoretical system that is constructed in order to explain, understand, and predict the behavior of organisms.[1]

If we are to have any kind of reasonable theory about human thought and action, we must have a system that represents what the organism knows. Thus, representation becomes a necessary part of any mental theory—and is neutral as to the kind of representational system one wishes to use or construct.

Representation by itself would provide only more or less static sources of cognition; it is useless without processes that shape representations, transform them, and finally construct experience and action. Another central concern of cognitive psychology, then, is the production of thoughts and acts, the specification of the processes that operate on representations. These processes include transformations, operators, search and storage mechanisms, inferential processes, and many others. Mental processes are a necessary part of knowledge, and the postulation of representation and process is only a convenient way of dividing up overlapping concepts and inextricable components of mental functioning.

Representation and process refer to the theoretical language we wish to use to talk about the operations of the mind, and the actual contents and domain of that language are the result of choices made by investigators and the consensus

1. For more extensive expositions of representational issues, see J. M. Mandler (1983) and Norman and Rumelhart (in press).

of the scientific community. I will be using primarily the notion of schema (see Chapter 3) to construct representations.

To get a sense of the variety of representation possible, just consider the distinction between declarative and procedural knowledge. I know that the capital of Austria is Vienna and I know how to tie my shoelaces, and clearly the representations involved are quite different. For example, the former can be spoken, the latter not, but it may achieve another (spoken) representation when I teach a child how to tie shoelaces. In the common language, we usually just make the distinction between "knowing that" and "knowing how." A theoretical language borrows from that usage but is also concerned with more complex and better-articulated relations between the two. We have no direct access to the representations underlying our various kinds of knowledge, but we do speak—in the common language—about our thoughts and actions. What is the relation between psychology and our common knowledge?

Psychology and the Common Language

It is futile to try to arrive at a psychologically meaningful statement about cause-effect relations in human thought and behavior merely by a reflective analysis of experience or the ordinary language. The ordinary or common language is shot through with folk wisdom and folk psychology. Such an influence is most dangerous when least obvious. It is easy to reject the contradictions of "Absence makes the heart grow fonder" and "Out of sight out of mind" as the worldly useful and scientifically useless results of folk psychology, but it is more difficult to understand that extensive analyses of ordinary-language talk about emotion, feeling, and thinking are built on similar but much less obvious foundations. Ordinary language often is an ill- or well-informed commentary on psychological processes that are not available for inspection or introspection to the thinking and behaving organism. The common language more often comments rather than explains. Such commentary includes the reasons and feelings the common language adduces for "explaining" an actor's action as well as the phenomenological reports that must be couched in ordinary language in order to be available for analysis. We cannot speak English (or any other common language) if we wish to discover the determinants of human thought and action, nor can we speak technical psychology if we wish to be poetic.

The ordinary language is, from one point of view, an extremely sensitive and highly differentiated commentary on persons and their actions, including the thoughts and behavior of the speaker. There is no reason why such a language should not be sensitive and useful, just as there is no reason why such a language and its structure should have explanatory power or causal import. The ordinary language talking about people and their behavior is, of course, not different from the ordinary language talking about physical events or biological events. However, nobody claims that a proper way to do physics is to use the ordinary-language description of physical events, although physics did start with such statements and rapidly diverged from them. Similarly, psychology did start with the discourse of the ordinary language about people and behavior but quickly discovered that ordinary discourse was not adequate to describe the causes and demonstrable antecedents of behavior and experience. The ordinary language continues to talk about physical events in a nonphysical language. We can, and do, talk about our tennis game, which deals primarily with the interaction of physical forces and their consequences, in a language that has very little to do with physics. Our folk knowledge of tennis may be very extensive and—if one is an expert—both accurate and predictive. But the generalizations about tennis and the language we use, having to with stance, follow-through, and so on, are not couched in the language of physics. One can, however, talk about tennis in physical terms and about elasticity, angles of incidence, torque, and on and on. The same game might be described extremely well in both languages, though they differ significantly in their generality. "Tennis knowledge" has limited generality; it might extend to squash and badminton, barely to table tennis. The physical description of tennis, on the other hand, has wide generality and was, of course, in the first instance not developed with reference to tennis at all.

I do not intend to preempt the concerns of philosophers to understand human discourse or their theoretical interest in structuring that discourse. But philosophers frequently are engaged in two probably incompatible tasks: first, the discussion in ordinary and philosophical language of problems of perception, morality, and knowledge and, second, the use of that language and discourse to make statements about the causes and conditions of human thought and action. The latter enterprise requires methods of verification and scientific theories; the former takes the ordinary and philosophical language as given and investigates the structure of that discourse. Thus, a philosophical system about the knowledge that people "have," a system in which people talk about what they believe they know and how they believe they know things, has no logical or psychological one-to-one correlation with theoretical attempts to build a psychological theory that explains *how* humans acquire knowledge, perceive the world, behave ethically, *and* talk about it.[2]

I distinguish between theoretical psychology and the need to understand the glosses and comments and folk models developed in the ordinary language.[3] But that language, and thereby any system that tries to structure it reasonably and comprehensibly, is not subject to the usual test and retest of scientific theories. It frequently tends to maintain intuitively obvious but factually false notions about its object. An analysis of the concept of mind, as it is used in the ordinary language, provides interesting insights into confusions that abound in that language,[4] but it is an entirely different matter when we assume that such an analysis provides any fundamental insights into the relation between psychological (mental) theories and physiological ones.

2. Piaget (1971).
3. D'Andrade (1982).
4. Ryle (1949).

None of this denies the importance of the initial insights into possible mental structures and causal sequences that arise out of the ordinary language—psychology, as all other sciences, uses the ordinary language as a starting point and, as it develops, leaves that ordinary language behind at an increasing pace.

One important pitfall that ordinary language and thought impose on us is the belief in the reality of its concepts and terms. It seems obvious that explanations generated by a recently evolved featherless biped cannot but be models of the world, convenient fictions that help our limited understanding. The tendency to take folk theories as ultimate truths must lead to holding on to distinctions and concepts that are not and cannot in principle be ultimate descriptions of the structure of reality. Such a position also vitiates the game playing that is so attractive in science—the erection and destruction of hypotheses with a claim to better and better approximations of reality, but not a claim to ultimate truth. To assert that such a truth is available by a proper examination of our phenomenal selves or by the proper analysis of language is, at least, a hindrance and, at worst, a wall that keeps us from playing that most productive game—science.

Because men and women have talked about their thoughts and emotions, both discretely and discreetly, we may assume that there may be lawful relations among events, variables, thoughts, and behaviors, but the folk psychology these thoughts express neither seeks nor cares for an unequivocal explanation. Men and women talk about specific emotions, make distinctions among discrete emotions, and individually and anecdotally assert some rational theory or some irrational defense, but these are not the necessary and sufficient building blocks of a science. Our language must be painfully built *out of* the layers of myths and insights that make up common parlance and consciousness.

Those who have looked to ordinary language as the royal road to developing a satisfactory scientific language (both syntactically and semantically) often fail to apply a fundamental distinction in the primary *function* of these two languages. Common language serves—in the first instance—as communication, and, as such, it is appropriately redundant, vague, overinclusive, and ambiguous. A common language that is nonredundant, precise, and unambiguous would require much more cognitive effort on the part of both speaker and listener than the organism usually has available. Scientific language, on the other hand, is a vehicle for description and explanation. If *it* were redundant, vague, and overinclusive, it would fail exactly on the requirements of precise definition and unequivocal explanation.

Consider the adequacy of distinguishing between heavy and light packages, loud and soft noises, and angry and joyful feelings for most communicative purposes. But the heavy-light and the loud-soft distinctions are not adequate for scientific purposes. Why, then, should we expect the angry-joyful distinction to be adequate?

Consider the following additional difficulties that would ensue if we were to permit the common language to be our guide to the emotional states and terms that a psychological theory of emotion should be able to explain. First, there is little disagreement that such a theory should account for states that are commonly termed anxiety, joy, fear, euphoria, and probably even love and disgust. But is lust an emotion—or is sexual feeling to be handled separately? Are we to be required to explain feelings of pride? Of accomplishment? Of empathy? Of dislike? Or, even worse, are we to construct national theories of emotion so that a German theory may account for *Lust* and *Unlust*, for *Gemütlichkeit*, or *ängstlich*; or a French theory for feelings of *ambience*. What are the boundaries of a theory of emotion, what terms in the ordinary language are the relevant referents to be explained? And is there even a German requirement for such a theory, since that language has no true equivalent for the English term *emotion?*

A typical reply to such claims of confusion consists of an appeal to consensual (intuitive?) judgment. After all, it is said, we all know what we are talking about when we talk about emotions, and these counterexamples are either irrelevant or esoteric. I do not believe that a serious theory of anything can be based on extensive intuitive judgment, nor do I think that the counterexamples are exotic—they are necessary and useful aspects of our flexible and redundant common language.

One of the more common ambiguities in the common language is the relation between the mind and the brain. Unfortunately, it is a confusion shared equally by many psychologists and physiologists. We need therefore to examine the relation between these two views of human functioning.

Psychology and Physiology

The use of physiological theories about the structure and the function of the human brain is an important part of contemporary psychology. However, there is no logical or empirical requirement that a psychological theory must, at this point, show a correspondence with or even make contact with neurophysiological theories. Physiological theories are concerned with developing the same complex structure of theoretical processes, although in the language of neurophysiology, that psychologists invoke for their explanatory system. Inquiries about the relation between these two systems are both important and interesting but neither necessary nor mandatory for psychologists who are developing their own theoretical structure. It is in this sense of cultivating our own garden instead of copying our neighbors' efforts that I would opt for a psychological theory that is independent, although not ignorant, of physiological hypotheses.

Psychologists have often been preoccupied with the concepts of the apparently more respectable physiologists. This tendency is still found in the remnants of reductionism and in the intellectual imperialism of the individual disciplines. As long as one accepts a hierarchical notion of the sciences and, in principle, an inevitable reduction of the higher (softer) sciences to the more basic (harder) sciences, one tends to look over one's shoulder—if soft—to make sure that one's efforts are consistent with big sister, or—if hard—to make sure that little brother keeps within the boundaries of the permissible. For example, it is conceptually constricting and empirically unsound to use the current state of one's "harder" neighbor as deterministic constraints on one's own theorizing (e.g., psychology versus linguistics or neurophysiology versus psychology). Current fashions change, and one would not want to be left high and dry because the assumptions adopted from one's neighbors have been dropped by them. Conversely, the more "basic" sciences frequently forget to look at the conceptual achievements of their "softer" neighbors. The obvious danger here is that the more basic are supposed to explain the less basic phenomena, but the latter are defined within another discipline. Reductionism is probably a mistake in principle, but it is certainly premature at the present state of the various arts. Collaboration and bridge building at the boundaries is a much more satisfying and—for the time being—more promising enterprise.

Since the theoretical concepts of modern cognitive psychology do not, in principle, seek to have physiological content, it has become (and this might seem paradoxical) much easier to envisage the bridges that need to be and will be built between psychology and physiology. Psychology is not constrained by current physiological theory and has built a data base—and a theoretical structure—that can now be related to some of the more sophisticated models and data bases in physiology. The growth of cognitive neuropsychology in the past two decades attests to this development.

The lack of independent psychological and physiological theories has also hopelessly confused the mind-body argument, though one can argue that that confusion has fueled the survival of the issue through the centuries. Specifically, the mind-body question has been posed as one concerning the relation between physical data and conscious mental data. This is somewhat like asking about the mysterious relation between the shape of a four-cylinder engine and the speed of the car it inhabits, or between the number and kinds of individual cells in the human kidney and its blood-cleansing function. It seems obvious that such questions can, in principle, be answered only by reference to inferred theoretical relations between the way engines and cells work, on the one hand, and the way cars and kidneys operate, on the other. In the absence of any mental theory to relate to physical theories about the brain, the relation remained mysterious.

There are specific, and sometimes very precise, concepts associated with the function of larger units of organs, organisms, and machines—concepts that cannot (without loss of meaning) be reduced to the constituent processes of the larger units. The speed of a car, the conserving function of the liver, and the notion of a noun phrase are not reducible to internal-combustion engines, liver cells, or neurons. Emergence is a label that has often been applied to new properties of larger assemblies. But rather than saying that the new properties emerge, one might be more parsimonious to insist that different entities have different functions. The mind has functions that are different from those of the central nervous system, just as societies function in ways that cannot be reduced to the function of individual minds. This is, of course, true even within bounded scientific fields; even physics cannot be reduced to physics, as in the case of the relation between mechanics and optics and nuclear physics.

The Mind-Body Problem—An Inconvenient Fiction

The preoccupation with the mind-body problem occurs primarily in philosophical and metapsychological writings; it has rarely bothered the psychologist working on experiments and theories.

My position is relatively simple. We are developing a psychological (i.e., mental) theory of a circumscribed set of human behavior and experience. We make no claim that the theoretical structures to be developed have any necessary correlate in the physical substratum or, specifically, in the brain. There is no doubt that we are talking about a physical system, the human organism. But we are using concepts and theories that do not claim a reduction to a physical basis. It is possible to build a psychological system that makes no claims or disclaimers about its relation to the physical structure of the organism. The question about the relation between this structure and a physical (i.e., neurological or neurophysiological) structure in the broadest sense is left entirely open. One may speculate that some physiological correlates of the structures to be developed here may someday be found. However, at the present time it is not necessary to specify what these relations are or might be. The mind-body problem will become a problem not because it can be spoken and discussed but because adequate theories of mental structures and physical structures exist that require correlation.

Much of the difficulty that has been generated by the mind-body distinction stems from the failure to consider the relation between well-developed mental and physical theories. Typically, mind and body are discussed in terms of ordinary-language definitions of one or the other. Since these descriptions are far from being well-developed theoretical systems, it is doubtful whether the problems of mind and body as developed by the philosophers are directly relevant to the scientific distinction between mental and physical systems.

Once it is agreed that the scientific mind-body problem concerns the relation between two sets of theories, the enterprise becomes theoretical and empirical, not metaphysical.[5] If, however, we restrict our discussion of the mind-body problem to the often vague and frequently contradictory speculations of ordinary language, then, as centuries of philosophical literature have shown, the morass is unavoidable and bottomless.

For example, we could, in the ordinary-language sense, ask how it is that physical systems can have "feelings." Such questions assume that we know the exact nature of the physical system and, more important, the structure of a mental system that produces "feelings." Usually, however, the question is phrased as if "feelings" were the basic characteristics of the mental system instead of one of its products. The assertion of a feeling is a complex outcome of the kind of mental system that will be espoused here. Not only is the experience of a feeling a product, but its expression, through a language system, is the result of complex mental structures that intervene between its occurrence in consciousness and its expression in language. A question regarding the relation of feelings to physical

5. Mandler and Kessen (1959) and Mandler (1969).

systems turns out to be at least premature if we agree that feelings, however defined, are the products of a complex mental system and that the "physical" observations are products of a similarly complex physiological system. But then the question about the relation (the correspondences) between physical systems and feelings requires that we know what the physical theory and the mental theory are about and that these are unequivocal in their prediction, and specified in great detail as to their structure. Until these goals are achieved, scientific questions about the mind-body problem are premature and irrelevant.

In short, there exists no special mind-body problem. It is one of many examples in which the interface between levels of explanation, theory, and conceptualization requires bridging concepts, acceptance of discontinuities, or admissions of ignorance. With the development of the explanatory systems that abut such an interface, the nature of the problem changes to the extent that, in some cases, reduction (explanation) of one level in terms of the other may become partially or even wholly possible. The mind-body problem has been the subject of special attention because it is of immediate phenomenal relevance to an active, cogitating, theory-building organism—the human being.

The emotional domain in particular has been the battleground for mind-body debates and has provided a major cottage industry for philosophers. The seventeenth-century French philosopher René Descartes made popular the question how the soul could affect the body, how ideas could cause actions. Except for anthropocentric and theological concerns, Descartes had implicitly supplied the answer when he claimed that, for lower animals, machines could be designed that would be indistinguishable from the "real thing." His test for the adequacy of such machines in the age of clockworks was the forerunner to a similar test that the mathematician Alan Turing developed for the age of computers. The modern answer is similar to Descartes's implied answer for lower animals: if we can design machines that think (aloud) and act like humans with ideas (minds, souls) and bodies, then we have solved the ancient conundrum. The answer to that conumdrum is obvious, of course—(conscious) ideas do *not* cause actions. Both ideas and actions are products of underlying representations and processes. The theory of the mind will have mechanisms that produce ideas and actions in a fashion that will give the obvious and inescapable impression that ideas cause actions. When a machine announces that it "intends to raise its third articulated limb" and if at some reasonable time thereafter that limb in fact rises, the appearance of some "intention-thought-action" sequence will be conveyed. Any reasonable knowledge of the mechanisms will reveal the sequence of underlying processes that produces all three of the components of that sequence. Even the intention to raise the limb (or the intention to announce the intention) will be identifiable in terms of underlying processes.

This line of argument restates my more general exposition of the mind-body problem. We shall understand this "interaction" when we understand the several representations and processes and the linking processes that lead from one to the other.

A *Psychology of Emotion*

A psychology of emotion directly addresses the classical questions about mind and body. How is it possible for the vegetative functions of the body to determine the intensity of emotional feelings? How does ideation about an impending embarrassment or a threatening fellow being bring about bodily reactions? How do evaluative reactions to another human being or to an environmental event combine with bodily reactions to generate a subjective emotional experience?

Questions like these face us continuously in daily life. What is the relation between our fear of a car bearing down on us at a street crossing and the pounding of our heart? Why do I sense myself flushing when I remember having inadvertently reminded a friend about a recent failure? Why do the unpleasant characteristics of an acquaintance produce both dislike and a sense of bodily unease? A reasonably successful approach to the psychology of emotion should be able to provide an understanding of these and related experiences.

I present a psychology of emotion that combines the insights of contemporary psychology with a long tradition of trying to understand the experience of emotion, the conscious contents of emotional states. My intent is to give a view of psychological mechanisms, of the workings of the mind, that provides an understanding of the variety as well as the regularity of human emotional experience.

I shall in the following chapters describe the structure and function of three important psychological systems—the evaluative aspects of the cognitive apparatus, the arousal generated by the autonomic nervous system (and its action on mental structures), and the construction of conscious contents. I shall argue that the coaction of evaluation and arousal generates states that, when represented in consciousness, produce most of the experiences that are in the common language called emotional. In the course of this exposition, I shall develop my view of the current knowledge of the mental apparatus in general, and of the specific processes that are necessary for the construction of emotional experience.

Just as the psychologies of memory, perception, or thought concentrate on processes rather than on definitions, so a psychology of emotion should stress the underlying psychological processes and mechanisms that produce the sort of events that we call emotions. Such an approach not only avoids the question "What is an emotion?" (*pace* William James) but actually denies its psychological relevance. It does not deny the historical utility of such question asking; rather, it assumes that we have achieved the kind of cumulative maturity that obviates its further pursuit.

A theory of emotion should attempt to identify those mechanisms and processes that do, in fact, generate most of the phenomena thought to be part of the family of concepts sheltered by the term *emotion*. Specifically, such a theory must state which "emotional" phenomena it will not, or cannot, address. Clearly, such an attempt will be most successful if it is catholic in the phenomena with which it deals and at the same time parsimonious in the processes and mechanisms it invokes.

It is not my intent to address other theories critically in the pages to follow, but I do want to draw attention to the limited usefulness of some current theories, incurred by their restriction of intent to highly circumscribed definitions and phenomena. Thus, a theory that stresses the subjectivity of emotional experience must deal with that subjectivity directly and empirically: we must eventually be able to predict and control, not just to describe and explain. Specifically, the conditions of the real world, as well as the personal cognitive world of the individual, must be addressed and accounted for. Or, a listing of "emotions" should, at least, be accompanied by a mechanism that accounts for the open-ended nature of emotional experience. It is an open-ended set of experiences because the number of different possible emotional experiences is at least very large, consisting of the concatenation of values on several continuous cognitive variables. As another example, the invocation of stress should address both the subjective interpretations and the external conditions that might be necessary, though not sufficient, for its occurrence. Similarly, the effects of stress and threat should be derivable from a theory of emotion rather than providing its starting point as undefined primitives, and speculations about the central nervous system should be given the same status as speculations about the conceptual nervous system (the mind).

Nearly a hundred years ago the psychologist C. Lloyd Morgan promulgated his famous canon that no action should be interpreted as the result of a "higher psychical faculty" if it can be interpreted as the outcome of a faculty lower in ontogeny or phylogeny. Morgan was battling against anthropomorphism, but today the reverse of Morgan's canon should be taken seriously and the biological and genetic causes apparent in lower animals should not be freely assigned to human actions.

A psychological theory should heed, but need not uncritically accept, a comparative, evolutionary view of behavior. The difficulty of defining or even bordering the vast, sprawling conglomerate of human behavior and feeling that is subsumed under the emotions is, surely, in part a function of its heritage, its evolutionary antecedents. Prewired, instinctual reactions to threat, sexuality, and pain are partly influenced by the autonomic nervous system and partly determined by releasing stimuli. However, the primitive reactions of our evolutionary forebears have given way to a highly refined and extensive repertory of behavior, feeling, and thought. Every now and then the archaic emotional reactions, seen very clearly in lower animals, shine through the intricate web of emotional behavior. This dim parentage has seduced some modern writers to write about and explain emotions in terms of these prehistoric antecedents. That attempt is as valid and as futile as trying to explain Rembrandt in terms of the development of the opposing thumb.

In my general view of emotional experience and behavior, I assert, with William James and the behaviorists, the importance of autonomic events, but at the same time assign these events a contributory rather than a defining role. James saw the experience of autonomic and skeletal events as *the* emotion, and the behaviorists looked at the visceral events themselves as the observables that constituted emotions. I have retained the experience of autonomic events as a central argument, but have integrated it with the cognitive evaluative functions of the mind, the continuous and automatic meaning analysis performed by the mental apparatus.

My emphasis on cognitive factors arose from an interest in the measurement and prediction of anxiety. Though not labeled as such, that approach was cognitive because it concentrated much of its effort on the determination of people's perceptions and evaluations of their internal states and the conditions under which anxiety was experienced.

Finally, seeing emotion as the confluence of experiences of autonomic activity, cognitive analyses of the current state of the world, and interactions with other cognitive processes focuses special attention on a problem that has become dominant in cognitive psychology—the analysis of the limited conscious capacity of the human processing system. The interactions of autonomic perceptions, meaning analyses, and task-relevant processes have to be seen from the vantage point of a limited conscious system.

The next chapter reviews the psychological analysis of emotion from an historical point of view and also discusses current conceptions and central issues in the field. Chapters 3 and 4 deal specifically with the structure and function of the mental apparatus and with the function and construction of consciousness. Chapter 5 investigates in some detail how emotional experiences are generated and how the mental apparatus functions in that process. Chapter 6 deals with the conditions of arousal and reviews both theoretical and empirical aspects of autonomic functioning. Chapter 7 addresses the evolution of action, with special reference to aggression and facial expression. Chapter 8 reviews the development of and evidence for the importance of interruption and cognitive discrepancy for a psychology of emotion. Chapter 9 takes up the specific issue of evaluative cognitions and develops some theoretical notions about the sources and structure of value. Chapter 10 discusses the problem of anxiety, primarily from a theoretical point of view, and Chapter 11 deals specifically with the effects of stress on thought and action. Finally, Chapter 12 considers a number of different topics that rise out of the general orientation, including such issues as the development of emotion, sexual emotions, and individual differences of emotional experience.

2

THE PSYCHOLOGY OF EMOTION: PAST AND PRESENT

THERE IS A MYTH ABROAD that writing on the history of science not only requires but also makes possible a degree of distance, objectivity, and dispassionate discussion that is rarely demanded of a theoretical paper or even an experimental report. In the latter cases we are assumed to be engaged in special pleading, defending our theories, analyzing our data in ways that conform to theoretical expectations, and attacking those whose theoretical (ideological and methodological) predilections are different from our own. These passions are supposed to disappear when we view the history of our field. We are expected to tell the story as it "really happened." Professional historians know that this is a vain hope, but unprofessional historians still vainly hope, particularly when reading somebody else's historical survey.

I do not share either these hopes or these vanities. I have some limited insight into my theoretical, ideological, and empirical prejudices, but I cannot assure the reader that I will be able to avoid the conscious ones or even to try to find the unconscious ones. I therefore do not expect that I will be unbiased or unprejudiced.

I approach the history of emotion as a movement that tends toward its current state. And I see its most promising developments as being in the mainstream of modern cognitive theory. I have culled the important milestones of the past hundred years with that goal in mind. I look backward to see what has brought us to the current state of the art. The advantage of this kind of backward look is that it permits us to consider broad trends; the disadvantage is that it may be outdated in another decade or two. In reviewing these trends, I will stress cumulative influences, believing that the history of science is a history of cumulative insights and cumulative knowledge. I shall also be talking primarily about psychological theories. With that intent, I exclude philosophical speculation and physiological theories. I also exclude the phenomenological tradition, because I can see no evidence of any cumulative insights developing out of that approach. In fact, it can be argued that phenomenological speculations are not coextensive with psychological theories at all; phenomenology cannot solve psychological problems.[1]

1. Husserl (1931).

There is another area of investigation that I do not discuss in these pages—the ethological literature. The main reason is that I have taken the experience of emotion as my frame of reference. Other work, particularly with infrahuman animals, is mentioned only as it is theoretically or empirically relevant to the main task. The ethology of emotion has produced fascinating results and fruitful theories—but primarily with and about lower animals. The extensions to human situations have typically been allusive, sometimes journalistic. Despite much talk about naked apery and territorial imperatives, the imperatives of science have too often been forgotten.

With these goals, the task becomes manageable. I focus on continuities, on what has become important in bringing us to current views of emotions. Typically, the continuities will be apparent; sometimes, as in the case of the so-called conflict theories, apparent discontinuities will be explored.

What Is Emotion?

Is there a cohesive psychology of emotion? And if there is, what is "its" history? I pursued these questions in volumes of histories, symposia, and textbooks.[2]

It may be symptomatic that the best summary was provided by Madison Bentley.[3] He knew in 1928 what too many psychologists still fail to accept today, that there is no commonly, even superficially, acceptable definition of what a psychology of emotion is about. Not even our positivistic friends have been able to construct an acceptable operational definition. Bentley lists all of the various kinds of things that psychologists do when they claim to be studying "emotion." And he concludes: "Whether emotion is today more than the heading of a chapter, I am still doubtful. Whether the term stands—in the regard of most of us—for a psychological entity upon which we are all researching I do not know. Whether it is the common subject of our varied investigations I am not sure enough to be dogmatic."

THEMES AND VARIATIONS

There exist a variety of themes that define the development of a modern approach to problems of emotion. Specifically, modern concerns with problems of emotion date from the publication of James's and Carl Lange's papers. Traces of James can be found in practically all the major modern trends.

Fundamental Emotions versus Emotions as Product • William James's major contribution in the theory of emotion really had very little to do with the problem of emotion as such. At the end of the nineteenth century, psychology was

2. For an overview of the early history of emotion, see Gardiner, Metcalf and Beebe-Center (1937); for a sampling of the last sixty years, see Reymert (1928, 1950) and Arnold (1970a).
3. In Reymert (1928).

still obsessed with its own "atomic" theory. Complex ideas, complex feelings, complex thoughts—in fact, all mental phenomena—were made up of nuclear ideas, feelings, and thoughts. We find this fundamental notion in Wundt just as much as we find it in Locke. In the beginning there are thoughts, feelings, and ideas. If anything characterizes the history of psychology in the twentieth century, it is a radical departure from that notion. It is a radical, but also a generally accepted, departure; it is a change in the fundamental approach to mental processes that characterizes practically all of the various schools, trends, and points of view. Whether psychologists are functionalists, behaviorists, modern structuralists, or modern or ancient cognitive psychologists, they would subscribe to the notion that the role of modern psychology is to describe the processes and mechanisms that produce thoughts, ideas, actions, and feelings. Whether the stress is on the production of these "mental" events or on the production of behavior and action is irrelevant; the important point is that the basic building blocks are mechanisms and processes rather than atomic, undefined mental contents.

Although others had moved in the same direction, it was William James who promoted the change from the content to a process approach. It becomes important, therefore, to note his insistence[4] that emotional consciousness is "not a primary feeling, directly aroused by the exciting object or thought, but a secondary feeling indirectly aroused." The only parts of the sequence that James is still willing to call "primary" are the "organic changes . . . which are immediate reflexes following upon the presence of the object." He contrasts his position with that of Wundt, who insisted that a feeling (*Gefühl*) was an unanalyzable and simple process corresponding to a sensation.

It is this fundamental distinction between feeling or emotion as a secondary, derivative process and the nineteenth-century view that feelings are unanalyzable and simple that provides one of the main themes running through the history of the psychology of emotion.

It is somewhat puzzling that the stress on process fathered by William James has taken hold more firmly in every area of psychology other than emotion, even though he initiated it in that field. Nearly a hundred years later, we still find psychologists insisting on a search for "fundamental" emotions and their correlates. And if one asks what these unanalyzable primary feelings or fundamental emotions might be, one usually finds the answer in the common language and subtle linguistic distinctions among feelings, emotions, and affects. James properly considered such attempts purely "verbal." The fundamental, unanalyzable view versus the derivative, secondary view is a watershed that has divided psychologists of emotion.

What Does a Psychology of Emotion Explain? • It was not difficult for William James to insist that his and Lange's theories were theories of "an emotional consciousness." After all, the analysis of consciousness was everybody's business in the nineteenth century. The idea that this analysis was either impossible or

4. James (1894).

unscientific—or, as Watson would have it, both—did not really become an important issue until later. But by the middle of the twentieth century, the notion had become dominant in the United States that only emotional behavior could be the subject of a psychology of emotion. Unfortunately, the dominance of behaviorist doctrine in the United States effectively ruled out the analysis of emotional experience and consicousness. As a result, much of the criticism of James's theory was not just misplaced but wide of the mark. One cannot possibly use the Jamesian theory to explain emotional behavior, particularly because, as we shall see later, emotional "behaviors" (visceral reactions and the autonomic processes in general) were the antecedents for the events in consciousness that he tried to explain.

Only in the last two decades has it become possible again in the United States to concentrate on problems of emotional experience apart from emotional behavior. European psychology, in contrast, which was relatively untouched by the behaviorist interlude, had continued to focus on the structure of the inferred experience rather than on the observable behaviors. Except for the psychoanalytic movement, however, these efforts were generally not in the tradition of systematic theory.

One important step toward the psychology of experience was the rejection of the assumption that introspective reports stand in a one-to-one relation with conscious (emotional) experience. Thus, we can use and look at introspective reports, adjective checklists, verbal protocols, and similar devices successfully and extensively. We use them as indices of emotional experience, knowing full well that they reflect a postulated process just as other overt behaviors are indices of theoretical entities like instincts, habits, and drives.

Thus, another theme that runs through a history of emotion in the twentieth century is the distinction between theories that address only emotional behavior, including visceral "behavior," and theories that wish to address emotional experience as well. Given that James was particularly interested in visceral events as one of the precursors of emotional experience, and that he wrote just before an era in which conscious experience was to be ignored, it is not at all surprising that much subsequent research focused on the "acceptable" part of the sequence—the visceral events.

THE NEW CENTURY

Apart from the themes of disagreement that run through the history of emotion, there are also some fundamental changes and new emphases that are not in dispute. The first change has to do with the realm of psychological theory. By the end of the nineteenth century, there was evident some reluctance to write complex, intricate theories, and only the Gestalt theorists some decades later were willing to be so adventurous. Psychologists believed that they were examining "real" contents of consciousness that mirrored "real" psychological phenomena. What there was by way of theory was addressed to the shuffling of the basic building blocks of this consciousness, but even these were subject to direct inspection. With the advent of behaviorism (and the functionalist bridge from James to behaviorism) came a prejudice against theory in general. I am referring here primarily to theory in the sense of the postulation of theoretical processes, mechanisms, and entities. Functionalism, with its concern with finding relations among observables, and behaviorism were true children of American society and its pragmatic emphases. Complex theory and the postulation of useful fictions arrived in the 1950s, in psychophysics and in the psychology of memory and of cognitive processes; they were welcomed in mathematical psychology and in the social psychologies that were derived from some of the Gestalt locutions. But in the 1980s theory has arrived and been made welcome, and even radical behaviorists are willing to write theoretical models.

The second shift has taken place within cognitive psychology as such. The modern cognitive psychologist knows that the contents of consciousness are products and not the processes of thought. Thought, cognition, and mind all refer to the family of postulated mechanisms and processes that form the bases of cognitive theory.

The third change that has occurred is one that is shared by cognitive psychologists and behaviorists. Specifically, it refers to the definition of *stimulus* and *response*. To the extent that cognitive psychologists use those terms, or their cognates, they refer to constructed, inferred entities. The stimulus in the environment and the observed response are indices to effective "stimuli" and to action systems. The physical characteristics of stimuli and responses do not define stimuli and responses. Luckily, the surviving behaviorist tradition, Skinner's approach, essentially shares this point of view. A stimulus is defined as whatever it is in the environment that controls a particular behavior; it can be defined in physical terms, but it is not theoretically so defined. Similarly, though a response may be topographically described, its important theoretical function is stated in terms of the consequences it produces in the environment; in short, a response class is defined in terms of consequences and not of its physical characteristics.

THE TWO ASPECTS OF EMOTION

There are two major traditions in the study of emotion. The distinction between them can be found in the relative emphasis on central as against peripheral theories, the former being concerned with central-nervous-system mechanisms, the latter with peripheral reactions and particularly autonomic nervous system (ANS) responses.[5] A similar distinction, and one that I prefer, is essentially a Cartesian one between mental and organic causes of emotion. Paul Fraisse[6] discusses this distinction convincingly and calls it "les deux faces de l'emotion"—the two aspects, or actually Janus-like faces, of emotion.

One face is mental and intellectual—the organic events are seen as consequences of psychic events. While much of this line of thinking is tied to a belief in fundamental unanalyzable feelings, it is also the forerunner of another series

5. Schachter (1970).
6. Fraisse (1968).

of developments that we shall examine in more detail. It is a line of thought that has a long history, going back at least 150 years, to Johann Friedrich Herbart,[7] who suggested that emotion is a mental disorder based on discrepancies (or what we would call today "conflicts") among perceptions or ideas.

The other face of emotion is organic. It also has a long history, being popular primarily among the sensualists of the eighteenth century. They insisted on the influence of organic reaction on mental emotional consequences. In contrast to the "mentalists," the organic theorists insisted that physiological events, rather than thoughts, are the precursors of emotion.

In the rest of this chapter, I follow Fraisse's distinctions and argument. I start with William James, who was an effective defender or organic theory and a successful antagonist of the notion of the unanalyzable feeling. I shall return to the mentalist position in the guise of the "conflict" theories of emotion. Eventually, I consider the possibility of joining the two "faces" in a common view of emotional phenomena.

The Organic Tradition

JAMES—AND LANGE, AND OTHERS

We start with James's bald statement in his 1884 article in *Mind*: "*My thesis is . . . that the bodily changes follow directly the PERCEPTION of the exciting fact, and that our feeling of the same changes as they occur IS the emotion.*"[8] His emphasis on subjective experience is illustrated when he notes that we might see a bear and decide it would be best to run away, or receive an insult and consider it appropriate to strike back, but "we would not actually feel afraid or angry." One other aspect of James's theory must be emphasized: he is talking about all "bodily changes" and not about exclusively visceral ones. The bodily changes he wants to consider include running, crying, facial expressions, and even more complicated actions such as striking out. The emphasis is important because it serves to remind us of two historically relevant consequences. First, James has frequently been interpreted as having said that particular emotional experiences follow certain visceral patterns and nothing more. He did say that certain emotions were tied to specific visceral patterns, but he certainly did not confine himself to them. By the time of Walter B. Cannon's critique, the notion was generally abroad that James was talking primarily about visceral antecedents of emotional experience and even emotional behavior—a statement James never made, and in fact rejected. Second, his general commitment to "bodily" changes sets James apart from Lange. In fact, Lange had insisted that emotions were the consequences of certain "vaso-motor effects." In 1894, James specifically rejected that position when he noted that "Lange has laid far too great stress on the vaso-motor factor in his explanation."[9]

7. Herbart (1816).
8. James (1884).
9. James (1894).

James's insistence that his theory was about "emotional consciousness" is best illustrated by the difficulties he encountered when he tried to answer his own question as to how to test it experimentally. He knew that the only way one could disprove it would be to show that for some emotions certain qualities of feelings could be shown to exist that would be "demonstrably additional to all those which could possibly be derived from the organs affected at the time."[10] However, he knew that to detect such "purely spiritual qualities" was not within the realm of science. So much for the possibility of falsifying the theory. But how about positive tests? His favorite hope was that he could demonstrate the theory with those few individuals who show complete anesthesia, subsequently known as congenital analgesia. However, all the cases that he found in the literature had failed to ascertain the individual's subjective state, or, as James called it, their "emotional condition." Cases that showed "emotional behavior," such as crying, did not concern him. He dismissed them as irrelevant to his theory and explained their behavioral manifestations as being perhaps purely intellective or reactive or situationally induced. His was the theory of "emotional consciousness."

Although these concerns with falsifiability, testability, and specification of theoretical consequences have a modern ring to them, they are all in the realm of the scientific Zeitgeist of the nineteenth century. More surprising to the modern reader is James's and Lange's obvious awareness of the linguistic and verbal traps in the specification and investigation of emotion. He says that if one were to try to name each one of the emotions, then:

> It is plain that the limit to their number would lie in the introspective vocabulary of the seeker, each race of man having found names for some shade of feeling which other races have left undiscriminated. If then we should seek to break the emotions, thus enumerated, into groups, according to their affinities, it is again plain that all sorts of groupings would be possible, according as we choose this character or that as a basis, and that all groupings would be equally real and true. The only question would be, does this grouping or that suit our purpose best? The reader may then class the emotions as he will.[11]

In modern language: any classification of emotions is possible, and it depends on the kinds of ideology or theory one wishes to serve when one chooses one or the other. Furthermore, the ability to find certain culturally agreed-upon groupings among men and women would simply demonstrate that there are indeed culturally agreed-upon groupings. Such a finding does not, by itself, produce theoretical advance. Lange said very much the same thing at about the same time, the result being that the general theory is called the James-Lange theory. Lange's theory held that "the various emotional disturbances are due to disturbances in the vascular innervation. . . ."[12,13]

In understanding the James-Lange "theory," we face a problem of interpre-

10. James (1890).
11. James (1890, 485).
12. In Dunlap (1922), which contains the first English translation of Lange's 1885 book.
13. Others presented very similar views about emotion at roughly the same time, including the Italian Sergi (1896) and the Australian Sutherland (1898). See also Ruckmick (1936).

tation of James's and Lange's "perceptual" antecedent of visceral disturbance. We are told repeatedly that particular perceptions produce certain bodily effects, which in turn are perceived and experienced as "emotions." What we are not told, except possibly by indirection, is how these perceptions of external events produce the bodily effects. The indirection, puzzling because of the behaviorist flavor in the midst of "cognitive" theory, is found in James's insistence that external events can give rise to bodily, visceral changes without any awareness of the meaning of these environmental events and without any interpretation of them. For the modern reader, who sees nothing strange or surprising in complex perceptual, cognitive processes occurring in response to environmental events without conscious accompaniment, the central argument about the visceral-emotional sequence that James and Lange asserted seems to fall apart at that point. If complex cognitive processes intervene between some "stimulus event" and a subsequent visceral or even "emotional" reaction, then the felt emotion is not just the product of the perceived bodily reaction, but rather results in part from some interpretive event that generates the bodily (visceral) response. Such reconsiderations in the light of modern insights undo the classical James-Lange position. Instead we arrive, as we surely do by the end of this chapter, at a complex of cognitive-physiological interactions.

James might have been surprised that one is willing to talk "cognition" about unconscious events. But these cognitive interpretations or perceptions are not the unanalyzable feelings that James was attacking—those were conscious and introspectable. Nearly a hundred years later, the James-Lange theory may seem irrelevant and superficial, but it was necessary in order to bring us to this recursive point in history.

THE JAMESIAN CRITICS

For purposes of understanding the general tenor of the times, it is useful to look at Wundt's critique of the James-Lange theory.[14] Dealing essentially with Lange's theory, Wundt called it a psychological pseudo-explanation that tries to explain away psychic facts with physiological observations. Parenthetically, we recall that it is exactly the psychic fact of the unanalyzable feeling that James and Lange were trying to get rid of. What did Wundt offer in its stead? He starts off with the unanalyzable feeling, akin to a sensation. These feelings then alter the stream of ideas. For example, the unanalyzable feelings of "fear" or "joy" can influence the current stream of ideation, encouraging some ideas, discouraging others, or inhibiting still others. In any case, this altered stream of ideas produces a secondary feeling as well well as organic reactions. And the organic reactions produce sensory feelings that are added to or fused with the preceding feeling (or sensation) and thus intensify the volume of conscious feeling. This Wundtian train of thought still has its modern counterparts.[15]

14. Wundt (1891).
15. A typical contemporary example of primary feelings can be found in Arnold (1960), who argues for the initial primitive appraisal of events as "good" or "bad."

The American critique from the old guard was stated by its dean, E. B. Titchener. He started off with the same notion of the fundamental feeling, although he described it in somewhat more complex form and gave it somewhat less of the Wundtian unanalyzable quality. The feeling is seen as similar to the perception or the idea, but, according to Titchener, "it is in reality a complex process, composed of a perception or idea and affection, in which affection plays the principal part." As far as the formation of an emotion is concerned, Titchener saw it in three essential parts:

> One, that a train of ideas shall be interrupted by a vivid feeling; two, that this feeling shall mirror the situation or incident in the outside world; and three, that the feeling shall be enriched by organic sensations, set up in the course of bodily adjustment to the incident. The emotion itself, as experienced, consists of a strong affection, and the stimulus association of ideas, some of the part processes in which are always organic sensations.[16]

Here is a recurring theme: there is some accompaniment by organic response. For Titchener, the accompaniment is always present. How does Titchener handle the definition of the external world, which, as we have seen, produces serious problems for James? Surprisingly, for Titchener these definitions are truly external and not "cognitive." For example, he notes that emotions occur in the presence of particular situations, conflicts, and predicaments. And he holds out the hope that if we could know all the "typical" situations that an individual must encounter, we could then determine the "fundamental" emotions.

Cannon Roars • None of the criticisms of James, piecemeal as they were, had much of an effect. The important and devastating attack came from Walter B. Cannon,[17] who assailed the James-Lange theory with a mixture of experimental findings and logical analyses. Cannon used the attack on James in order to further his own neurophysiological theory of emotion, which had relatively little impact. What had more impact was his criticism, and it set the tone for the succeeding fifty years of psychological evaluation of the James-Lange theory. Cannon's major points were really addressed to the question of visceral feedback as the basis for emotional behavior. In that sense he attacked Lange in the first instance and somehow missed James in the second, because James was concerned with emotional consciousness rather than emotional behavior. However, those niceties were forgotten in the light of the devastating and elegant content of Cannon's attack. It consisted essentially of five major points:

1 • Even when the viscera are separated from the central nervous system, some emotional behavior may still be present. Thus, in cases of sympathectomy or vagotomy, where no visceral response can occur, emotions may still be observed.

2 • There does not seem to be any reasonable way to specify visceral changes that differ from emotion to emotion. If James were correct, rather sharp and well-differentiated patterns of visceral actions would have to be found.

3 • The perception and feedback from autonomic nervous system (ANS) dis-

16. Titchener (1896, 214, 220–21).
17. Cannon (1914, 1927, 1929).

charge is so diffuse and indistinct that one must assume that the viscera are essentially insensitive and could not possibly serve the differentiation function that James's position requires.

4 • ANS responses are very slow, and their slow onset, on the order of one to two seconds, would suggest that emotion should not occur within shorter intervals. Introspection and some observations seem to indicate that such long latencies are not typical of emotional reactions.

5 • When visceral changes are produced by artificial means—for example, by the injection of adrenalin—emotional states do not seem to follow as a matter of course.

History has been kinder to Cannon than to James. Cannon's first point turned out to be essentially correct. However, as we shall see later, there is evidence that separating the visceral from the central nervous system significantly interferes with at least the acquisition of emotional behavior. Arguments have also been made that even in the absence of the viscera there are other, including skeletal, systems that may subserve the Jamesian functions.

Cannon was quite right as far as points 2 and 3 are concerned; there is no evidence that different emotional states or behaviors are antecedentally caused by different visceral states. As we shall see, much heat has been generated by this argument in subsequent years, but still no causal evidence is available. Evidence about the differential conditioning of various autonomic functions, or even differential responding in different parts of the autonomic system, is not relevant to this argument. We are talking about different causally implicated patterns of the autonomic system.

As far as point 4 is concerned, its argument is somewhat similar to that of point 1. Cannon is right in general, but other mechanisms such as conditioned skeletal responses and autonomic imagery may serve to bridge the gap and explain the kind of phenomena that the subjective evidence suggests.

As for Cannon's fifth point, the evidence will show that visceral changes produced by artificial means are not sufficient to produce emotional states, but that their presence certainly is an important condition for emotional experience in conjunction with other, cognitive factors.

In any case, Cannon's five criticisms were important enough to generate extensive research on the points of disputation between James-Lange and Cannon. Their historical importance is not so much that they destroyed the James-Lange theory but rather that they were influential in producing an extensive research tradition in the psychophysiology of emotion.

VISCERA AND COGNITION

The next crossroads after Cannon's critique were marked by the work of Stanley Schachter's group in the 1960s. A new era of investigation and theory was opened up. Again, it is possible to see a position similar to Schachter's in a variety of different earlier writers, including James. But Schachter's contribution stands out as a major turning point, just as James's did seventy years earlier. The contribution was less the ingenious experiments, though they were the basis for acceptance of the theory, than the straightforward statement of a visceral-cognitive theory.[18] Visceral action was necessary, setting the stage for emotional experience, but so was a cognitive evaluation, and emotion was the product of the two. Perhaps more important was the bald statement that general autonomic arousal, rather than a specific pattern or an emotion-specific arousal, was the visceral concomitant of emotional experience. The consequences of this position have been a large number of experimental studies showing the influence of visceral and cognitive factors, ranging from the instigation of aggressive behavior to the occurrence of romantic love.

The major antecedent of Schachter's work was an essentially anecdotal study by G. Marañon.[19] Marañon found that when he injected a large number of patients with adrenalin, approximately one-third of them responded with a quasi-emotional state. The rest reported little or no emotional response and simply described their physiological state of arousal. However, the patients who gave emotional reactions typically reported what has now become the classical description of the "as if" emotion. They would report that they felt "as if" they were afraid or "as if" something very good were about to happen. In other words, they did not report the full range of emotional experience, but something closely akin to it. Marañon discussed a recent emotional experience, such as a death in the family, with a few subjects; and in these cases patients reported full rather than "as if" or "cold" emotion. Thus, there appeared to be three kinds of reactions in Marañon's experiment: a description of the physiological arousal, an "as if" emotion, and a full emotion, if appropriate cognitive support was available.

Considering these and other data, Schachter[20] put forward three general propositions:

> *1* • Given a state of physiological arousal for which an individual has no immediate explanation, he will "label" this state and describe his feelings in terms of the cognitions available to him. . . .
>
> 2 • Given a state of physiological arousal for which an individual has a completely appropriate explanation . . . , no evaluative needs will arise and the individual is unlikely to label his feelings in terms of [any] alternative cognitions available. . . .
>
> 3 • Given the same cognitive circumstances, the individual will react emotionally or describe his feelings as emotions only to the extent that he experiences a state of physiological arousal.

In other words, both physiological arousal and cognitive evaluation are necessary, but neither is a sufficient condition for the production of emotional states. In addition, it is assumed that physiological arousal produces an evaluative need,

18. See also Ruckmick (1936) and Hunt, Cole, and Reis (1958) for similar views about the interaction of cognitive and visceral factors.
19. Marañon (1924).
20. Schachter (1971, 4).

such that the individual seeks an appropriate explanation. In the first set of experiments, Schachter and Singer[21] gave subjects injections of adrenalin under the cover story that these were vitamin compounds that would affect visual skills. After they got the injection, subjects were either informed of the consequences of the injection (i.e., they were given correct information about the effects of adrenalin, but not told that they had been given an adrenalin injection), or they were not given any information about the effects of adrenalin, or they were misinformed.

In the informed condition, they were told that they would feel symptoms of sympathetic nervous system (SNS) discharge. In the misinformed condition, they were given a description of parasympathetic symptoms, none of which would be expected as a "sympathetic" result of the adrenalin injection.

Following the injection and the various types of information, the subject was left in a waiting room together with another person who was ostensibly another experimental subject, but who was actually a "stooge" of the experimenters. Then, depending on whether the subjects were in a euphoria or an anger condition, the stooge would engage either in euphoric behavior (playing with paper airplanes, playing basketball with the wastebasket, and engaging in other happy behavior) or in angry behavior (becoming more and more insulting, asking personal and insulting questions, and eventually leaving the room in anger).

The results were essentially in keeping with the two-factor theory, coupled with an evaluative-need hypothesis. The degree of information about the physiological consequences of the injection was negatively correlated with the degree of self-reported emotional state and with the degree of emotional behavior induced by the stooge's behavior. Thus, those in the misinformed group, which presumably had the highest evaluative need while under the influence of adrenalin, because the information they had been given about the physiological effects and their actual experiences were completely uncorrelated, showed the greatest degree of self-reported euphoria as well as behavioral signs of the "appropriate" emotion.

At the other extreme, the informed group, which had no "evaluative need," showed the lowest degree either of self-report or of behavioral euphoria. The ignorant group fell in between. Similar differences were found in the anger condition.

The data suggested that if a state of physiological arousal is induced, and if the individual has no immediate explanation for it, he will then describe his state in terms of the environmental-cognitive information available at the time. Conversely, if the state of physiological arousal is completely explained in terms of antecedents such as an injection, then the individual will not use other environmental-cognitive information to describe his internal state.

As I noted earlier, the impact of these experiments was theoretical rather than empirical. In fact, a variety of misgivings have been aired about them. For example, autonomic measurement was restricted to pulse rate; possible interac-

21. Schachter and Singer (1962).

tions between the effects of the adrenalin and the experimental situations were left unexplored; and some of the conclusions depended on post hoc analyses of the data.

With the Schachter experiments the organic tradition came to an end, at least for the time being. Once it had been shown that visceral response alone was not sufficient to produce an emotion and that the same visceral background can in fact lead to different emotions, purely organic theories had played out their role. The line from James and Lange was switched to a cognitive, or at least situational, track.

However, even if purely organic theories seemed untenable, the stress on visceral-cognitive interactions still involved visceral response. I turn now to the role of the viscera, specifically the role of the autonomic nervous system in the production and maintenance of emotions. These investigations are, of course, consonant with, and in part derive from, the James-Lange tradition. This research area has generally been subsumed under the rubric of psychophysiology—the psychological relevance of peripheral physiological response.

PSYCHOPHYSIOLOGY

There are five general areas of research that, under the umbrella of psychophysiology, are relevant to problems of emotion. One involves the artificial removal of autonomic events or autonomic feedback—summarized under the topic of sympathectomies. The next two areas of research investigate the degree to which specific or nonspecific visceral patterns are associated with specific emotions. The fourth area examines the effect of variations in visceral feedback on emotional experience, and the fifth looks more generally at the role and function of the autonomic nervous system.

Sympathectomy • An experiment important to an understanding of the role of the autonomic nervous system in emotional behavior was published by Lyman Wynne and Richard Solomon in 1955. Even though the study did not address problems of emotion directly and though it examined lower animals rather than humans, it is frequently cited as relevant to the James-Cannon controversy. The genesis of the problem that Wynne and Solomon consider is found in a two-stage theory of fear conditioning, which proposed that the avoidance of noxious stimuli is mediated by a visceral response conditioned to a particular situation that is associated with some noxious stimulus—for example, shock. On subsequent occasions the situation elicits the visceral conditioned response, which then acts as a signal for the animals to escape from the situation and thus to avoid the shock. Wynne and Solomon argued that if peripheral autonomic nervous system (ANS) functioning were significantly impaired, then avoidance learning should also be difficult, if not impossible.

Wynne and Solomon's study involved the use of surgical procedures (sympathectomy) and drugs that blocked the ANS in order to eliminate, or at least significantly reduce, feedback from the ANS. Their general conclusion was that such intervention impaired the acquisition of the avoidance response in dogs, but did not, in the two cases studied, interfere with an avoidance response that had been acquired prior to the surgical and drug intervention. The mediating function of the ANS has been considered to be one of the functions of an "emotional" response system. In consequence, the experiment becomes relevant to a Jamesian view that emotion is dependent on the perception of visceral response.

A more modern and promising technique for investigating the role of the sympathetic nervous system (SNS) is the procedure known as immunosympathectomy. Following the discovery of a nerve growth factor by Levi-Montalcini, an antiserum derived from the nerve-growth-factor protein, which removes significant portions of the SNS, became available.[22] Typically, the antiserum is injected into newborn animals (usually mice) and destroys from 80 to 90 percent of the SNS, apparently without affecting other aspects of the animals' functioning. As far as total activity is concerned, immunosympathectomy seems to have little effect. However, emotionality in an open field test, as measured by defecation, does seem to be decreased. The intervention also retards learning to avoid shock, whether the animals are active or passive in the situation. The "immunosympathectomized animal . . . [is] somewaht less reactive to threatened aversive stimuli, . . . but also somewhat overreactive to certain actual stimuli. . . . The results obtained . . . are compatible with the hypothesis that sympathetically innervated responses may play a mediational role in avoidance learning."[23] In other words, acquisition of "emotional" avoidance behavior apparently requires the operation of an intact SNS.

There remain two difficulties with all of these experiments. First, it is somewhat doubtful whether either the surgical or the immune intervention completely removes all possible feedback mechanisms from the visceral system. One could thus argue that even a small percentage of such remaining feedback might be adequate to perform the signaling or visceral-feedback function. More important is an argument, made already by Wynne and Solomon, that the ANS is only one part of several feedback systems, including skeletal responses (in keeping with a Jamesian interpretation). We do know, as a result of these experiments, that emotional behavior is to some degree dependent on visceral feedback. The relevance of these findings for human emotional experience is not as clear.

Visceral Patterning • Once James had intimated and Lange had insisted that for every discrete emotion there existed a discrete pattern of visceral response, the hunt was on for specifying these discrete visceral antecedents of emotion. Unfortunately, years of search have proved to be fruitless. Before examining one or two of the purportedly positive pieces of evidence, we must have a clear understanding of the theoretical position involved. Specifically, it must be shown that some specific emotional experience (or even behavior) is the consequence of (is caused by) a specific pattern of visceral response. Any experiment claiming to support that position must show at least that the visceral pattern occurs before

22. Levi-Montalcini and Angeletti (1961).
23. Wenzel (1972).

the emotion does. Mere demonstrations of a correlation between emotion and visceral response do not address the issue.

The most widely cited study purported to support the physiological specificity notion is an experiment by Albert Ax.[24] Ax exposed subjects either to a fear-provoking or to an anger-provoking situation, and measured patterns of physiological response to these two experimental "stimuli." Both situations produced elevated levels of SNS response, with some significant differences on a number of visceral indicators. This does not show any causal effects of visceral patterns on emotional response or experience. The question is, What does it show? We do not even really know, in the absence of extensive internal analyses and subjects' reports, what specific "emotion" the subjects experienced.

But we must put the study in the proper historical perspective. It was done thirty years ago, when psychology was still in the grip of functionalist and behaviorist approaches to emotion. All too often, "fear" and "anger" were defined by what was done to the subjects, not by what the subjects experienced. Similarly, the difference in visceral patterning was shown as the average pattern of response for the two groups of subjects. It was not until some years later that it became methodologically more appropriate to show effects of this sort for individual subjects. In fact, the kind of patterns that Ax found could have been a combination of a variety of different patterns from each individual subject. Thus, with hindsight, we cannot even come to any correlational conclusion about this study. More important, the succeeding years have failed to provide any independent replication of this finding. S. Wolf and H. G. Wolff[25] did report a single patient's response to a large number of different stimuli. They were able to study his visceral reactions through a fistula, which permitted inspection of the stomach lining. In a wide variety of situations tested, they found only two distinct physiological patterns; but again, the data are correlational and permit no causal conclusion.

There is no doubt that the fulfillment of the James-Lange dream would have provided a very pleasant outcome to the search for specific emotions. But, although the hope remained, it was not to be. For example, a recent authoritative survey of the field concludes: "Investigators have been unable to find an identifiable physiological change that corresponds to changes from one specific emotion to another," but they have consistently found that "there is an unspecific relation between the emotional state and physiological state."[26] A footnote does add that "there are a number of studies that show differentiation of emotion as a function of the physiological state"; but the studies cited are all correlational at best, and none of them show the production of an emotion as a function of a physiological state. Dreams die hard.

Current evidence suggests that there are no specific visceral antecedents for the various emotions. It would be exciting and important if somebody could demonstrate such a relation. For the time being we are left with Bertrand Rus-

24. Ax (1953).
25. Wolf and Wolff (1943).
26. Candland, Fell, Keen, Leshner, Plutchik, and Tarpy (1977).

sell's probably apocryphal response to the question of how he would react to being confronted with God after his death: "Lord, you did not give us enough evidence!"

Autonomic Generality • What about an "unspecific relation" between viscera and emotion? Schachter's studies provided one piece of evidence. The same physiological antecedent potentiated different emotions.

It is also true that widely different emotions show relatively little difference in physiological patterns. Here we need not go into the question of whether these patterns are antecedent to the emotional expression. If, with very different emotions, the patterns are similar, the argument can be made that it is highly unlikely the different emotions depend on different patterns. The autonomic patterns are unlikely, in this case, to have been differential antecedents to the emotional response. If the subsequent patterns show great similarity, it is unlikely that there were large differences between them prior to the onset of the emotional behavior and experience.

In 1969, Averill showed that both sadness and mirth are associated with measurable visceral responses and that both of them seem to involve primarily SNS patterns. Averill found few visceral differences between sadness and mirth, and obtained the more interesting result that two such divergent emotional states, not typically investigated by psychologists, produce highly similar sympathetic states of arousal.[27]

Another study suggested, from the point of psychophysiological research, the ubiquity of general SNS discharge. P. Pàtkai started with the Funkenstein hypothesis that habitual reaction patterns in anxious and aggressive states may be differentiated by the selective release of adrenalin and noradrenalin, respectively.[28] Although there had been previous evidence that the Funkenstein generalization might not hold,[29] Pàtkai tested the notion that the magnitude of adrenalin release may be an "indicator of general activation rather than being related to a specific emotional reaction." In her study, Pàtkai exposed subjects to situations with different emotional content and found that adrenalin excretion increased in both pleasant and unpleasant situations when compared with a neutral one. The highest value of adrenalin excretion was found for the situation described by the subjects as most positive. Pàtkai concludes that her results "support the hypothesis that adrenalin release is related to the level of general activation rather than being associated with a specific emotional reaction. The quality of emotions elicited is probably determined by the characteristics of the individual subject."

Marianne Frankenhaeuser's laboratory[30] has produced additional evidence relevant to the question of whether adrenalin and noradrenalin energize different emotional responses. Frankenhaeuser concludes:

27. Averill (1969).
28. Funkenstein (1956).
29. See, e.g., Frankenhaeuser and Pàtkai (1965).
30. E.g., Frankenhaeuser (1975).

[The] results indicate that adrenalin is secreted in a variety of emotional states, including both anger and fear. Similarly, a rise in noradrenalin secretion may occur in different emotional states, but the threshold for noradrenalin release in response to psychosocial stimulation is generally much higher than for adrenalin secretion

Variations in Visceral Perception • For William James the *experimentum crucis* for his theory was a natural experiment: an individual who would have no visceral perception, no feedback from his visceral responses—the anaesthetic person. (Parenthetically, we might note that this is a peculiar retreat from James's position, which stressed any bodily reaction, to the position of Lange, which emphasized visceral response.) In any case, James insisted that these people would provide the crucial evidence for his theory—namely, they should be devoid of, or at least deficient in, their emotional consciousness. In that sense, James initiated the study of biofeedback. He thought then, as many psychologists believe now, that variations in the perception of visceral response are central to the emotional life of the individual and that control over such variations would provide fundamental insights into the causes of emotions.

The sources of the biofeedback movement in modern times are varied, but one can distinguish three lines of research that have addressed James's problem. One of them involved individuals who were victims of an even crueler natural experiment than congenital anaesthesia: people with spinal injuries that had cut off the feedback from their visceral systems. The second approach has assumed that individuals may differ in the degree to which they perceive and can respond to their own visceral responses. The third approach is in the direct tradition of what is today commonly called biofeedback, and has involved teaching individuals to control their autonomic level of response and thereby to vary the feedback available.

The first area of research, the "anatomical restriction" of autonomic feedback, is related to several animal studies.[31] These experiments were inevitably concerned with emotional behavior. An important study by G. W. Hohmann[32] looked at the problem of "experienced" emotion. Hohmann dealt with patients who had suffered spinal-cord lesions. He divided these patients into subgroups depending on the level of their lesions, the assumption being that the higher the lesion, the less the autonomic feedback. He collected reports from his patients about the decrease in experienced emotion associated with situations of anger, fear, and sexual stimulation. His finding, in support of a Jamesian and all other visceral-feedback positions, was that the higher the level of the spinal-cord lesion, the greater the reported decrease in emotion between the preinjury and the postinjury levels. A subsequent study[33] also investigated a group of patients with spinal-cord lesions, classified into three categories on the basis of lesion level—from cervical to thoracic and lumbar. They were presented with slides of either

31. See, e.g., Sherrington (1900) and Wynne and Solomon (1955).
32. Hohmann (1966).
33. Jasnos and Hakmiller (1975).

clothed or nude females and asked to give their thoughts and feelings in reaction to these slides. Despite the fact that the measurable visceral response (heart rate) did not differ among the three groups, there was a significantly greater reported level of emotion the lower the level of spinal lesion. To the extent that the level of spinal lesion controlled the degree of visceral feedback, less feedback (but not a lower level of visceral response) produced less intense emotional reactions.

As far as the second approach (individual responsiveness) to studying variations in autonomic feedback is concerned, several studies are available that use the "Autonomic Perception Questionnaire" (APQ).[34] The APQ measures the degree of subjective awareness of a variety of visceral states. The initial findings were that autonomic perception was related to autonomic reactivity and that autonomic perception was inversely related to quality of performance; individuals with a high degree of perceived autonomic activity performed more poorly in an intellective task.[35]

Since then a series of studies[36] has suggested that individuals who show a high degree of autonomic awareness generally are more reactive to stress stimuli and are more affected by anxiety-producing situations. The APQ dimension measures individuals' variations in their ability to detect autonomic events.[37] We can conclude that the perception of autonomic events does play a role in emotional reactivity.

The final set of studies has examined the effect of experimental manipulation of visceral responses. Because our concern here is not with visceral response as such, but rather with some emotional, and particularly experiential, consequences of such response, we need not go into the history of the controversy concerning the possibilities of the experimental control of "autonomic behavior." The pioneering work in this area was performed by Neal Miller[38] and his colleagues, who demonstrated that reinforcement procedures could affect the acquisition of visceral and glandular responses. By teaching animals to increase or decrease their heart rate, one could significantly affect their subsequent ability to avoid electric shock. More relevant to our present purposes are two studies that showed that subjects could be taught to control their heart rate and that voluntarily slowing of the rate led to a reduction in the perceived noxiousness of painful shock. The results "lend further credence to the notion that subjects can be trained to control anxiety and / or pain by learning to control relevant physiological responses."[39]

There is a variant of the biofeedback method that entails "feedback" but is not really "bio." Specifically, there exists some evidence that people can be led to believe that arousal has occurred when it actually has not. Stuart Valins[40] presented subjects with purported feedback of their heart rates. These rates were

34. Mandler, Mandler, and Uviller (1958).
35. Mandler and Kremen (1958).
36. Borkovec (1976).
37. Borkovec and O'Brien (1977).
38. Miller (1969).
39. Sirota, Schwartz, and Shapiro (1974, 1976).
40. Valins (1966, 1970).

actually prerecorded, and under various conditions the heart rate was either at a normal level or was accelerated. Valins showed that when subjects believed that they were experiencing an accelerated heart rate in response to certain stimuli, their evaluation of those stimuli differed significantly from their evaluation of stimuli (pictures) that were not presented with the increased-heart-rate feedback. Valins noted that the actual heart rates of the subject did not differ as a function of this false feedback but that it was the cognitive evaluation of their arousal that affected their judgmental behavior. In related work, simulated-heart-rate feedback changed subjects' reactions to feared stimuli.[41] When subjects were "shown" that their heart rates changed in response to shock, but not in response to pictures of snakes, which they feared, they subsequently showed more approach reaction to snakes than did control subjects, who had been given no information about any differential heart rate response to the two kinds of stimuli.

All the work on variations of autonomic feedback, whether due to anatomical variation, individual variation, or learned variation, indicates that autonomic feedback—the perception of autonomic or visceral activity—is in fact an extremely powerful variable in manipulating emotional response. Such autonomic feedback may be the result of actual visceral response, or merely autonomic "perception" without actual visceral response. The important modern insight is that what is subjectively registered by the experiencing individual influences emotional experience. In that sense, James and Lange have been partially vindicated: the perception of visceral events is an important part of emotional experience.

Beyond Homeostasis • Considering the increasing popularity of speculations about the adaptive and evolutionary significance of phenomena ranging from aggression to crowding and marriage, the attention given the uses and function of the autonomic nervous system has occurred relatively late in the game. The traditional nineteenth-century view considered the organic reactions as bothersome, interfering, and at best playing some incidental mediating role. However, the past two decades have produced increasing evidence that neither that old position nor the modern emphasis on homeostasis adequately describes the functions of the visceral reactions. Visceral response may, in addition to its vegetative functions, color and qualitatively change other ongoing actions, it may serve as a signal for action and attention, and it may select events and actions that are important for the survival of the organism. That position will be developed in greater detail in Chapter 6.

The currently dominant notion about the function and evolution of the sympathetic nervous system has been the concept of homeostasis, primarily linked with W. B. Cannon. In a summary statement in 1930, he asserted: "In order that the constancy of the internal environment may be assured, therefore, every considerable change in the outer world and every considerable move in relation to the outer world must be attended by a rectifying process in the hidden world of the organism. The chief agency of this rectifying process . . . is the sympa-

41. Valins and Ray (1967).

thetic division of the autonomic system."[42] In order to remove terms with "psychological implications" from physiology, Cannon suggested that the distinction between voluntary and involuntary systems be replaced by the terms *exterofective* system (for the somatic, striped-muscle, and skeletal functions) and *interofective* system (for functions of the heart, smooth muscles, and glands). The latter keeps "the internal environment constant and fit for continued exterofective action."

While Cannon credits the central nervous system with the role of altering the external environment by "laboring, running, or fighting," he still leaves us with the impression of a passive organism adjusting its internal environment to external events, just like a physical thermostat. But the organism often reacts to the requirement for internal adjustment by action on the environment. These actions may change external stimulation to the point where the internal environment is restored to its previous "normal" level. Homeostatic action by the SNS may also mobilize the "exterofective" system to act on the environment.

The arguments and evidence that the autonomic nervous system may play an active role in information processing will be discussed in Chapter 6. Suffice it to say here that arousal as expressed in autonomic activity acts on processing, as much as it reacts to environmental demands.

We have now completed the review of developments from the point of view of the organic or peripheral face of emotion. In the course of this survey, I have wandered far from a purely organic point of view and have probably even done violence to some who see themselves as cognitive centralists rather than organic peripheralists. However, the line of succession seemed clear, and the line of development was cumulative.

Neither the succession nor the cumulation will be apparent when we look at the other face of emotion—the mental tradition.

The Mental Tradition

Historically, this tradition started with the unanalyzable feeling, but its main thrust was its insistence on the priority of psychological processes in the causal chain of the emotions. Whether these processes were couched in terms of mental events, habits, conditioning mechanisms, or sensations and feelings, it was these kinds of events that received priority and theoretical attention. I summarize these processes as mental ones. This tradition sees organic visceral events as being the result of these processes, not—as the Jamesian organic tradition would have it—the other way around.

FUNDAMENTAL-EMOTION THEORIES

The most persistent tradition in the mentalistic camp has postulated one or more fundamental, innate processes from which emotional expression and expe-

42. Cannon (1930).

rience emerge. Fundamental emotions are usually ascribed to innate (neural) patterns that have arisen from the evolutionary history of the organism. Given these fundamental emotions, other emotional states are then seen as the product of some combination of fundamental states together with cognitive, perceptual, and visceral attenuating and accenting influences.

The most influential of the current positions is that of Sylvan Tomkins.[43] Since I cannot possibly do justice to this very rich and complex proposal, I shall confine myself to those aspects of the theories that describe the kinds of emotions they wish to consider and the processes that elicit them.

Tomkins postulates distinct programs for each affect, which are stored subcortically. When activated, these programs affect the structure of the face, autonomic blood flow, and respiratory and vocal responses[44] and impose on them "a specific pattern of correlated response."[45] There are nine distinct innate affects: three positive—interest, enjoyment, and surprise—and six negative—distress, fear, shame, contempt, disgust, and anger. These emotions are activated by increasing, decreasing, or unchanging levels of stimulation. Differentiation within these three kinds of activators depends on the suddenness of increase or on the level of stimulation that is maintained. For example, the suddenness of increase differentiates among startle, fear, and interest. With its emphasis on stimulus intensity, this is the only influential position that does not explicitly or implicitly require the existence of some kind of analytic mechanism before the evocation of emotional states.

The most prolific writer on fundamental emotions has been Carroll Izard,[46] whose work derives from Tomkins's earlier formulations. Fundamental emotions are defined as "complex motivational phenomen[a], with characteristic neurophysiological, expressive, and experiential components."[47] Feedback from these various sources "is transformed into conscious form, [and] the result is a discrete fundamental emotion."[48] The ten fundamental emotions produce the experiences of interest, joy, surprise, sadness, anger, disgust, contempt, fear, shame/shyness, and guilt. Emotion is continually present in consciousness, and the activation of a new emotion is occasioned by some internal or external event (e.g., memory, image, or personal interaction) which "changes the pattern of electrochemical activity in the nervous system."[49] The change in the level or pattern of neural activity determines some (innately defined) facial expression that generates the subjective experience of an emotion and subsequently activates cardiovascular, glandular, and other biological systems. The neural pattern that sets off this train of events is some interpreted environmental event, such as threat or restraint. Izard is quite unequivacal about the unalterable nature of the fundamental emotions. They are distinct throughout the life span, are subserved

43. Tomkins (1962, 1963, 1980).
44. Tomkins (1981).
45. Tomkins (1980).
46. Izard (1971, 1977) and Izard and Buechler (1980).
47. Izard and Buechler (1980).
48. Izard (1971).
49. Izard and Buechler (1980).

by distinct innately programmed neural mechanisms, and emerge "according to an innate maturational pattern."[50] Autonomic arousal is a secondary process that occurs after the sensory feedback from the face and that serves to sustain the emotion.

Robert Plutchik[51] shifted from an early scheme in which all of human evolution was implicated in the production of unanalyzable primary emotion to a position that leads from a specified set of stimulus events to cognitive evaluations, and thence to feelings, behavior, and an overall evolutionarily significant emotional product. The system produces eight primary emotions: fear, anger, joy, sadness, acceptance, disgust, anticipation, and surprise.

These three positions are reasonably representative of one that reaches back, by way of Darwin, to the Greeks and prehistory.[52] Given such an eminent ancestry, it is somewhat surprising that no agreement is found on either the number or the kinds of fundamental emotions. In fact, agreement exists for only six: fear, anger, joy, disgust, interest, and surprise. The last two seem intutively to be out of place; surprise and interest can, under different conditions, lead to a number of different emotional states. And one can be at least puzzled that theories that have strong evolutionary emphases do not give lust (or sexual emotionality) a fundamental rank. The following table illustrates both the overlap and the disagreements among these positions.

Fundamental or Primary Emotions
Listed by Three Leading Theorists

TOMKINS	IZARD	PLUTCHIK
Fear	Fear	Fear
Anger	Anger	Anger
Enjoyment	Joy	Joy
Disgust	Disgust	Disgust
Interest	Interest	Anticipation
Surprise	Surprise	Surprise
Contempt	Contempt	
Shame	Shame	
	Sadness	Sadness
Distress		
	Guilt	
		Acceptance

With the exception of Tomkins's, all of these theories require some cognitive analysis before the initiation of the fundamental, innate train of events. This

50. Izard and Buechler (1980).
51. Plutchik (1962, 1977).
52. Among other fundamental-emotion theorists, Leventhal (1979) assigns eight basic emotions to facial motor mechanisms, and Bower and Cohen (1982) invoke basic feeling "nodes" that are activated by emotional-interpretation rules. Leventhal also suggests that a discrepancy between "spontaneous and . . . intentional expressive activity" is the "basis of emotion."

prior processing of information makes them not only mental theories but also cognitive ones in the modern sense. Complex cognitive analysis, involving current and prior knowledge and expectation, seems to be required in order for us to gain access to the fundamental, primary states. And the process becomes even more complex when secondary emotions are said to result from some combination of the fundamental ones.

Tomkins's position, which follows more clearly a principled approach to fundamental emotions, suffers from its insistence on the simple mechanisms of increasing and decreasing levels of stimulation. It is not only difficult to determine a priori which events will in fact be responsible for different kinds of stimulation (or density of neural firing); it is also difficult to place the secondary emotions in this context, and the translation of complex cognitive events into neural stimulation is at least obsecure, and crosses currently opaque boundaries between physiological and psychological discourse.

One can also ask whether the fundamental emotions are to be found in the organism or whether they describe environmental regularities that in turn produce regularities in thought and action. Moreover, they may represent regularities in action, as in aggressive behavior, which is defined in terms of specific actions toward other individuals. Regularities in action and in the environment may in fact produce regularities in human cognition, across societal and cultural lines. All humans may at one time be threatened, achieve some desired goal, withdraw from some unpleasant event, or be blocked from carrying out some important goal-directed activity. The nature of the cognitive representations that underlie these perception-action sequences needs to be investigated; the theorists whom I shall discuss in greater detail in Chapter 9 have made a start.

The placement of the fundamental emotions "inside" the organism, into ready-to-act neural patterns, may be the reflection of the cultural view of human nature that characterizes social theories in industrial societies of the nineteenth century. The human being, in this view, is independent of external forces, autonomous, "free," and world shaping. It is only when the individual is exposed to the emotions that that freedom seems to be limited, when humans react passively (as in their passions). An alternative view of human nature, which has replaced the nineteenth-century view to some extent, holds that human nature is to a large extent socially and situationally determined and functions as an expression of its history and its social significance.[53]

Finally, a word about facial expression. The majority of the fundamental-emotion theories, as well as many others, place great emphasis on the role the face plays in the expression and experience of emotion. The most extreme position is Tomkins's, which claims that "each affect is mediated by specific sensory receptors in the skin of the face."[54] I shall address these claims in Chapter 7, where I shall also argue that facial expressions are communicative devices, often correlated with but, in principle, independent of any separate emotional system.

Distinct from the fundamental-emotion theories, there is another line of

53. Averill (1980).
54. Tomkins (1981).

thought in the mental tradition; it is embodied in the conflict theories, which have a tattered history stretching back at least 150 years.

CONFLICT—NOW YOU SEE IT, NOW YOU DON'T

The conflict theories have a history of noncumulativeness and isolation. Their continued existence is well recognized, but rarely do they find wide acceptance. For example, over forty years ago the generally accepted working definition of emotion involved some emergency situation of biological importance during which "current behavior is suspended" and responses appear that are directed toward a resolution of the emergency. These "classical" theories "concern themselves with specific mechanisms whereby current behavior is interrupted and 'emotional' responses are substituted." Little novelty was seen in formulations that followed the old idea that "when an important activity of the organism is blocked, emotion follows."[55] Over the past century that same old "theme" has been refurbished time and time again.

One of its major exponents was the French psychologist Frédéric Paulhan. Paulhan's main thesis is that whenever any affective phenomena take place, we observe the same fact: the arrest of tendency. Arrested tendency is a "more or less complicated reflex action which cannot terminate as it would if the organization of the phenomena were complete, if there were full harmony between the organism or its parts and their conditions of existence, if the system formed in the first place by man, and afterwards by man and the external world, were perfect."[56] However, though that statement rehearses some themes that were present before his time, Paulhan must be given credit for what, as far as I can tell, was a first. He did not confine himself to the usual "negative" emotions but made a general case that even positive, pleasant, joyful, aesthetic emotions are the result of some arrested tendencies—or, as we might say, of disconfirmed expectations or interrupted actions. And he avoided the temptation to provide us with a taxonomy of emotions, but rather noted that no two emotions are alike, that the particular emotional experience is a function of the tendency that is arrested and the conditions under which that "arrest" occurs.[57]

In 1894 and 1895, John Dewey published two papers on his theory of emotion. In 1927, John Angier attempted to resurrect Dewey's views.[58] Dewey's conflict theory can best be stated in Angier's words:

> Whenever a series of reactions required by an organism's total "set" run their course to the consummatory reaction which will bring "satisfaction" unimpeded by other reactions . . . there is no emotion. Emotion arises only when these other reactions (implicit or

55. Hunt (1941).
56. Paulhan (1930, 17).
57. Paulhan's original book (1887) was not translated into English until 1930, when his translator C. K. Ogden complained that too little attention had been paid to Paulhan's basic thesis.
58. See Dewey (1894, 1895) and Angier (1927). Angier issued a plaint about the silence following the publication of Dewey's theory that sounds just like Ogden's expressions of disappointment about the reception received by Paulhan.

overt) are so irrelevant as to resist ready integration with those already in orderly progress towards fruition. Such resistance means actual tensions, checking, interference, inhibition, or conflict. . . . [Such] conflict constitutes the emotion . . . without such conflict there is no emotion; with it there is.[59]

Conflict theories have appeared and reappeared throughout the history of speculations about emotion. They seem destined to be reinvented every fifty years or so. I shall return to their current status shortly.

Behaviorism and Psychoanalysis • I must pause in the recital of the conflict theories in order to place two theoretical traditions in the proper context. Both behaviorist and psychoanalytic theories of emotion are conflict theories, and both had relatively little effect on the mainstream of emotional theory—the former because it generally avoided a theoretical approach to emotion, the latter because all of psychoanalytic theory is a theory of emotion as well as a theory of cognition. Behaviorists had their chief impact on theories of motivation, and the majority of their work relevant to emotion addressed animal behavior and the conditioning of visceral states. The behaviorists' failure to address the problem of emotional experience meant that they simply did not make contact with many of the issues that have concerned psychologists of emotion since William James. However, behaviorist approaches do fall under the rubric of mental theories, as defined here. In general, I use the term *mental* to apply to psychological, as opposed to physiological, processes. In their approach to emotion, behaviorists stress the primacy of psychological mechanisms; and in that sense they can be distinguished from those who take the organic approach, and be said to belong to the mental tradition.

There is another reason to consider behaviorism and psychoanalysis under a single heading. Particularly in the area of emotion, these two classes of theories exhibited most clearly the effects of sociocultural-historical factors on psychological theories. Both, in their own idiosyncratic ways, were the products of nineteenth-century moral philosophy and theology, just as the unanalyzable feeling was congruent with nineteenth-century idealism. The influence of moral and religious attitudes finds a direct expression in a theory of emotion, which implies pleasure and unpleasure, the good and the bad, rewards and punishments. A classical example of the behaviorist attitude toward emotion decries emotional consequences: they are chaotic and disturb the ongoing stream of behavior; they produce conflict.[60]

In the sense of the American Protestant ethic, behaviorist dogma is the dogma of fundamentalism. Behaviorism enthrones its fundamentalist scriptures, it raises the improvability of the human condition to a basic theorem, it decries emotion as interfering with the "normal" (and presumably rational) progress of behavior. It opposes "fanciness" with respect to theory, and it budges not in the face of competing positions; its most dangerous competitor is eclecticism. Behaviorism departs from classical Calvinism in that it does not see outward success as a sign

59. Angier (1927).
60. Kantor (1921).

of inward grace. Rather, in the tradition of the nineteenth-century American frontier, it espouses a Protestant pragmatism that sees outward success as the result of the "proper" environment; grace is out in the world. Conflict is to be avoided, but when it occurs it is indicative of some failure in the way in which we have arranged our environment.

The best examples of these attitudes can be found when the psychologist moves his theories to the real world, as John B. Watson did when he counseled on the raising of children.[61] While quite content to build some fears into the child in order to establish a "certain kind of conformity with group standards," Watson was much more uncertain about the need for any "positive" emotions. He was sure that "mother love is a dangerous instrument": children should never be hugged or kissed, never be allowed to sit in a mother's lap; shaking hands with them is all that is necessary or desirable. In contrast, B. F. Skinner[62] noted the emotional consequences that occur during extinction; he understood the conflict engendered by punishment, and his fundamentalism went the other way—avoid the use of punishment; build a society based on positive reinforcement. Certainly an admirable position, much to be preferred to the stern Dr. Watson's. But it is fundamentalist just the same.

I have discussed the classical behaviorists here for a serious as well as a whimsical reason. The serious one is that underneath classical behaviorist enquiries into emotion lies a conflict theory; it is obvious in J. R. Kantor, and implied in Watson and Skinner. But there is another aspect of conflict in behaviorist approaches to emotion—namely, the conflict between an underlying rational pragmatism and the necessity of dealing with emotional phenomena, which are frequently seen as unnecessary nuisances in the development and explanation of behavior. There is no implication that emotions may be adaptively useful. For example, apart from mediating avoidance behavior, visceral responses are rarely conceived of as entering the stream of adaptive and useful behavior.

One of the major aspirations of the behaviorist movement was that the laws of conditioning would provide us with laws about the acquisition, maintenance, and extinction of emotional states. Pavlovian (respondent, classical) procedures in particular held out high hopes that they might produce insights into how emotions are "learned." It was generally assumed that emotional conditioning, by studying the shift in stimulus control from unconditioned to conditioned stimuli, would provide one set of answers. However, the endeavor has produced only half an answer. We know much today—and we know it often elegantly—about the laws of conditioning, particularly of visceral responses. On the other hand, we have learned relatively little from this line of inquiry about the determinants, acquisition, or loss of human emotional experience. The most active attempt to move from the animal laboratory to the human stituation, in the area of therapy and behavior modification, is increasingly being faced with "cognitive" incursions. Apparently, we need to understand how the human patient knows, evaluates, and categorizes his world in order to be able to apply methods

61. Watson (1928).
62. Skinner (1938).

derived from the conditioning laboratory. We have gained no further insight into the class of events that are unlearned, unconditioned, primitive evokers of ANS activity. And we find that the results of conditioning procedures often produce much more complex results than the theories would lead us to expect (e.g., the conclusion that inescapable trauma leads to helplessness and depression).[63] We know now that even in the laboratory the animal's phylogeny and ontogeny will determine what situations and conditions are likely to lend themselves to the application of conditioning procedures.

None of this denies the importance, or the intrinsic elegance and scientific appeal, of the insights and generalizations gained in the investigation of learning and conditioning. The degree of control achieved over behavior and action is a model for the psychological community.

There are two single contributions from the behaviorist tradition that have had significant consequences for a psychology of emotion. One was O. Hobart Mowrer's analysis of common concepts in terms of the conditioning paradigm.[64] He suggested, for example, that fear was the conditioned form of the pain response and that hope was the conditioned form of positive reinforcement. The utility of these suggestions is not at issue; what is important is the insistence that psychological explanations must be couched in psychological language. The other contribution that influenced psychologists in important ways was Skinner's analysis of the conditions under which we acquire emotional words—words whose referents (to use a non-Skinnerian term) are not observable or available to the reinforcing (teaching) community.[65]

One of the most influential examples of neobehaviorist conflict theories is Abram Amsel's[66] theory of frustration. Amsel asserted, and a large number of studies (primarily in the area of animal behavior) confirmed, that the withdrawal of reward has motivational consequences. These consequences occur only after a particular sequence leading to consummatory behavior has been well learned. Behavior following such blocking or frustration exhibits increased vigor, on which is based the primary claim for a motivational effect. The motivational focus of Amsel's theory and research is the reason why this theory has not been put into the framework of general approaches to emotion, although Amsel himself noted that fractional anticipatory frustration behaves in many respects like fear. In any case, this approach is the most sophisticated development of the early behaviorists' observations that extinction (nonreward) has emotional consequences.

Another quasi-behaviorist approach to emotion, one in the tradition of conflict theory, is represented by the concept of "learned helplessness."[67] While it is not presented as a theory of emotion, the term *learned helplessness* is used to refer to a cognitive state that follows the perception that the onset or offset of a noxious event (e.g., electric shock) is not controllable. Given such independence

63. Seligman (1975).
64. Mowrer (1939, 1960).
65. Skinner (1957).
66. Amsel (1958, 1962).
67. Seligman (1975).

of behavior and external events, the subject will show "apathy" and passivity and will often fail to learn simple avoidance and escape responses. Generalizing from animal experiments, Martin Seligman opined that this "learned helplessness" is at the basis of human depression. In general, this position fits a variety of different "conflict" theories that deduce emotional consequences from the inaccessibility of appropriate and useful responses in a particular situation.

Psychoanalytic theory was not a child of puritanism, but it was in part a product of the nineteenth century's interpretation of the Judeo-Christian ethic. The great regulator is the concept of unpleasure (Unlust); Eros joins the scenario decades later. At the heart of the theory lies the control of unacceptable instinctive impulses: to be constrained, channeled, coped with. Freud did not deny these impulses; he brought them out into the open, to be wondered at, controlled—and sometimes even liberated. However, at the base of the theory was sinning humanity, which could achieve pleasure mainly by avoiding unpleasure.

Psychoanalytic theory thus qualifies as one of the major conflict theories of emotion. There are two reasons why I have chosen not to describe psychoanalytic theory in great detail. First, as far as the mainstream of psychological theories of emotion is concerned, Freud has had a general rather than a specific impact. Second, all of psychoanalytic theory, as several writers have noted, presents a general theory of emotion. To do anything like full justice to the theory would require a separate chapter.

It is easy, however, to describe Freud's theory as a conflict theory. In fact, it is one of the few precursors of more modern conceptions, which combine conflict notions with Jamesian concerns. Curiously, after rejecting psychological theories and particularly the James-Lange theory of emotion, Freud characterizes affect, and specifically anxiety, by a formulation that is hardly different from James's. Freud talks about specific feelings, such as unpleasantness, efferent or discharge phenomena (primarily visceral), and the organism's perception of these discharge phenomena.[68] However, in general, affect is seen as a result of the organism's inability to discharge certain "instinctive reactions." The best description of the psychoanalytic theory in terms of its conflict implications talks about three stages that are implicit in the psychoanalytic theory of emotion:[69] first, the arousal of energy (libido) in connection with some instinctual tendency; second, manifestations of this energy in behavior or conscious thought if that tendency is blocked; and, third, manifestations of the energy as felt emotion or affect if behavior and conscious thoughts are also blocked and inhibited. Psychoanalytic theory of emotion concerns itself primarily with the conditions under which energy becomes blocked and redirected. An important aspect of that redirection is the way the individual copes with conflict.

With this excursion into two traditions that have shaped many currents of contemporary psychology, we can now return to modern conflict theories.

68. Freud ([1926] 1975).
69. MacCurdy (1925).

CONTEMPORARY CONFLICT THEORIES

A highly developed position that takes a cognitive view of the emotions and that is in the tradition of the psychoanalytic concerns with coping mechanisms is the one developed by Lazarus and his associates.[70] I briefly review the position in light of more extensive comments elsewhere. Emotions are defined as "complex, organized states . . . consisting of cognitive appraisals, action impulses and patterned somatic reactions."[71] Each discernible, discrete emotion is thus associated with a particular appraisal, an action impulse appropriate to this appraisal that may or not be carried out, and a patterned somatic reaction, a physiological-response profile that is unique for each different emotion. Appraisal is the central cognitive element, and it reflects perceived threats or dangers, senses of security or mastery, or a desired relation among individuals.[72] Appraisal first evaluates the situation in terms of the individual's well-being; then secondary appraisal evaluates coping resources and behavioral and cognitive options. Reappraisal is the ongoing process in which appraisals, actions, and thoughts may change as a result of new evaluations. The initial appraisals include evaluations of outcome, the extent to which the individual can cope with the situation. Coping influences the emotional complex because it affects appraisals of past, present, and future relations with the environment. The relation to other conflict theories is shown in the way appraisal is viewed. For example, in reappraisal the individual "takes in information about his or her changing relationship with the environment and evaluates its significance" or "the evaluative judgment represents an intrapsychic effort of coping with stress."[73] Thus, competing and conflicting situations and actions are responded to by direct action or intrapsychic changes, and these efforts and their appraisal enter into the current emotional state.

I have started the discussion of current "conflict theories" with the position of Lazarus, which has discernible antecedents, particularly in psychoanalytic theory. However, the noncumulative development of conflict theories continued at the same time.

We last left these theories with Paulhan and Dewey. Nothing much had happened by 1941, when a commentator barely suppressed a yawn at the reemergence of another conflict theory.[74] But within the next decade, another one had appeared, and this one with much more of a splash. It was put forward by Donald O. Hebb,[75] who came to his conflict theory following the observations of rather startling emotional behavior. Hebb restricted his discussion of emotion to what he called "violent and unpleasant emotions" and to "the transient irritabilities and anxieties of ordinary persons as well as to neurotic or psychotic disorder."[76] He specifically did not deal with subtle emotional experiences

70. See, e.g., Lazarus, Averill, and Opton (1970) and Lazarus, Kanner, and Folkman (1980).
71. Lazarus, Kanner, and Folkman (1980).
72. Lazarus, Averill, and Opton (1970).
73. Lazarus, Kanner, and Folkman (1980).
74. Hunt (1941).
75. Hebb (1946, 1949).
76. Hebb (1949).

or with the positive pleasurable emotions. Hebb's theoretical work flowed from his observations of rage and fear in chimpanzees. He first discovered that the animals would have a paroxysm of terror at being shown a head detached from the body, that this terror was a function of increasing age, and that various other unusual stimuli, such as other isolated parts of the body, produced excitation. Such excitation was apparently not tied to a particular emotion; instead, it was followed sometimes by avoidance, sometimes by aggression, and sometimes even by friendliness. Hebb assumed that the innate disruptive response that characterizes the emotional disturbance is the result of an interference with a phase sequence, a central neural structure that is built up as a result of previous experience and learning. Hebb's insistence that phase sequences must first be established before they can be interfered with, and that the particular emotional disturbance follows such interference and the disruptive response, identifies his theory with the conflict tradition. The theory does not postulate any specific physiological pattern, but does require an acquired pattern of response that occurs as a result of the disruption of a phase sequence. Such disruption may take place because two phase sequences are in conflict. Although Hebb did not implicate specific physiological antecedents for specific emotions, neither did he put any great emphasis on the physiological consequences of disruption.

Leonard B. Meyer was a conflict theorist who, in contrast to many other such theorists, had read and understood the literature. He properly credited his predecessors and significantly advanced theoretical thinking. More important, he showed the application of conflict theory not in the usual area of fear or anxiety or flight but in respect to the emotional phenomena associated with musical appreciation. None of that helped a bit. It may well be that because he worked in an area not usually explored by psychologists, his work had no influence on any psychological developments in the field of emotion.

In his 1956 book, Meyer started by saying that emotion is "aroused when a tendency to respond is arrested or inhibited." He immediately gave John Dewey credit for having fathered the conflict theory of emotion, and he recognized that it applies even to the behaviorist formulations that stress the disruptive behavioral consequences of emotion. Moreover, Meyer noted that Paulhan's "brilliant work" predates Dewey's, and he credited Paulhan with having stated that emotion is aroused not only by opposed tendencies but also when "for some reason, whether physical or mental, [a tendency] cannot reach completion."

So much for Meyer's awareness of historical antecedents. Even more impressive is his anticipation of the next twenty years of development in emotional theory. For example, he cited the conclusion[77] that there is no evidence that each affect has its own peculiar physiological composition. And given that conclusion, he immediately proceeded to the corollary that physiological "reactions are essentially undifferentiated, and become characteristic only in certain stimulus situations." Or, to put it another way, "affective experience is differentiated because it involves awareness and cognition of the stimulus situation which itself

77. In Woodworth (1938).

is necessarily differentiated." For the reader for whom this is not yet familiar enough, let me restate Meyer's conclusion: an undifferentiated organic reaction becomes differentiated into a specific emotional experience as a result of certain cognitions. As an example, Meyer noted that the sensation of falling through space might be highly unpleasant but that a similar experience, in the course of a parachute jump in an amusement park, may become very pleasurable. In short, Meyer anticipated the development of the cognitive and physiological interactions that were to become the mainstays of explanations of emotions in the 1960s and 1970s (e.g., Schachter). Most of Meyer's book is concerned with the perception of emotional states during the analysis and the appreciation of music. His major concern is to show that felt emotion occurs when an expectation is activated by a musical event and then temporarily inhibited or permanently blocked.

Another discussion of emotion within the context of "conflict" was provided by George Miller, Eugene Galanter, and Karl Pribram in their influential 1960 book, which provided some of the overtures for modern mentalism and cognitive psychology.[78] Miller, Galanter, and Pribram treat the problem of emotion relatively briefly, as might be expected from authors concerned primarily with cognitive structures, but they do suggest that emotional behavior and experience are related to the disruption or interruption of Plans. For example, they note that when "a successful Plan suddenly becomes useless, the reluctant desertion of that Plan is accompanied by strong emotions." This phrase suggests that emotionality accompanies the desertion of Plans, but it does not directly ascribe emotional consequences to the interruption or disruption of Plans. However, in another context, they say that "the [emotional] activation appears to result directly from the suddenness in the alternation of Plans. . . ." Here they do appear to ascribe the emotional experience at least to the degree of interruption of an existing Plan. Miller, Galanter, and Pribram are thus precursors of the current position on the importance of interruption as a condition for emotional behavior. Since they were primarily concerned with cognitive structure, it is not surprising that they do not consider the problem of emotional experiences other than negative or disruptive ones or that they do not deal with the interaction between arousal and cognitive structures.

Miller, Galanter, and Pribram do describe briefly three possible consequences of an interrupted or disrupted Plan. One of them is the reinstatement of the old Plan and the perseverance, against environmental evidence, in maintaining existing cognitive structures. The extreme such case would be a paranoid state. The second possibility is to maintain the general structure of the Plan, the strategy, but to change the tactics. Thus the underlying, unconscious, and often irrational structure would be maintained, but different behavior would be employed in its service. The extreme case would be a schizophrenic reaction. Finally, they note the possibility that the strategy may be given up (i.e., the central structure may be changed) but that the individual may hang on to the tactics, in which

78. Miller, Galanter, and Pribram (1960).

case isolated bits of behavior, without adequate central structural support, are maintained—which is, in the extreme case, seen in the occurrence of compulsive and obsessional behavior.

The last variant of the "conflict" theme to be considered has all the stigmata of its predecessors: the emotional consequences of competition or conflict are newly discovered, previous cognate theories are not acknowledged, and well-trodden ground is covered once again. The name is Mandler, and the year is 1964. The theory is one of conflicting actions, blocked tendencies, and erroneous expectations. But there is no mention of Dewey, of Paulhan, and certainly not of Meyer. The basic proposition[79] was that the interruption of an integrated or organized response sequence produces a state of arousal, which is followed by emotional behavior or experience. This theme was expanded in 1975 to include the interruption of cognitive events and plans.

However, in all fairness it must be said that there are differences between the interruption position, as Mandler's theory has been labeled, and the previous conflict positions, with the exception of Meyer's synthesis. The claims are that interruption is a sufficient and possibly necessary condition for the occurrence of ANS arousal, that such interruption sets the stage for many of the changes that occur in cognitive and action systems, and, finally, that interruption has important adaptive properties in that it signals important changes in the environment. Compared with previous approaches, the major changes in this proposal are due to the influence of Schachter's work. In contrast to Dewey and Paulhan, it is not assumed that conflict, interruption, or inhibition have specific emotional consequences, but rather that they have undifferentiated visceral consequences. The emotional content—the quality of the emotion that follows—is set by specific cognitive circumstances of the interruption and possibly its consequences. Thus, both positive and negative emotions are seen as following interruption, and the same interruptive event may indeed produce different emotional states or consequences, depending on the surrounding situational and intrapsychic cognitive context.

In a sense, this approach built the bridge between the conflict theories and the organic theories. It extended the importance of conflict in the more general sense of interruption, but it also saw visceral events as a necessary, though not a sufficient, condition for emotional experience and behavior. Thus, whereas Schachter had made his major contribution by disengaging emotion from specific patterns of visceral behavior and conjoined the visceral and cognitive components, interruption theory merely added the idea that conflict or interruption produced the visceral arousal in the natural state.

I raised the question earlier whether there was such a thing as a coherent psychology of emotion. The answer is yes, in the sense that important work illuminated and changed the direction of dominant theories. But the psychology of emotion is clearly different from the psychology of learning or of memory or of motivation. In the latter cases, the experiments led the way, and theories were the by-products. That was the dominant characteristic of psychology, and particularly of American psychology, between 1880 and 1950. The psychology of emotion has always been much more of a theory-dominated area, as the entire field of psychology has become.

In part the interest in theory was a result of William James's question "What is an emotion?" It was not the sort of question asked in other fields in psychology, and answering it demands theory rather than experiments.

Another salutary trend is discernible in the past ten to twenty years. Psychologists have once again become interested in the positive emotions. In part this development is to be welcomed because the preoccupation with anxiety, dread, and fear had become somewhat depressing; it is really more rewarding to talk and think about happy people than about anxious ones. More important, the trend suggests that psychologists of emotion have accepted the task to address all emotions. As a result most of the recent work talks about joy as frequently as about dread. Contemporary theories of emotion seem to have lost the bipolarity characteristic of their predecessors. We no longer ask whether an emotion is the result of "nothing but" organic response, or the consequence of certain mental, often "conflicting," events. The two traditions seem to have merged into a more general view that conflicting interruptive (mental and environmental) events play an important role in emotion and perhaps even in generating the visceral substratum. Conversely, it is recognized that a mere visceral response is not a sufficient condition for emotional phenomena, though it may be necessary; other, mental or cognitive, events are also required.

The same blurring has occurred with respect to the central-peripheral distinction, and in the same way. Both central and peripheral events contribute to the production of emotional experience and emotional behavior.

But did we not know all of that before? Were not many psychologists aware that James's notion of the perception of the threatening event implied central cognitive components, no matter how much he insisted on the organic antecedents of emotion? And, as it turns out, even Darwin, the grandfather of the psychology of emotion, knew that emotional feelings per se were not enough, that arousal was also necessary. In 1872, Darwin had this to say:

> Most of our emotions are so closely connected with their expression that they hardly exist if the body remains passive—the nature of the expression depending in chief part on the nature of the actions which have been habitually performed under this particular state of mind. A man, for instance, may know that his life is in the extremest peril, and may strongly desire to save it; yet, as Louis XVI said, when surrounded by a fierce mob, "Am I afraid? Feel my pulse." So a man may intensely hate another, but until his bodily frame is affected, he cannot be said to be enraged.[80]

If psychologists of emotion seem to be circling the central issues, reaching new ground but returning to old issues in a Hegelian spiral, then possibly some of the concepts discarded here and elsewhere will return to the study of emotion. Although some frown on speculations about primary or fundamental emotions,

79. Mandler (1964a).
80. Darwin (1872).

or about definable causal patterns of autonomic or skeletal response, the future may bring us back to these notions in a new guise. Luckily, the search for first causes and final words is always fruitless. In the meantime we are still hunting for some reasonable representation of the events that produce emotional experience.

Finally, there may be another useful way of looking at the classical problems. The two traditions assume either that a perception was followed by a feeling followed by a state of arousal or that the perception was followed by arousal, which in turn led to the feeling—the cognition. It is obvious that neither of those two sequences is satisfactory today. The "continuous loop model" recognizes that certain stimuli elicit both "cognitive and physiological components of the emotional experience concurrently. Neither cognitive nor physiological factors are antecedents. . . . [They] are viewed as feeding back upon and modifying both continuing emotional experiences and future emotional responses.[81]

81. Candland, Fell, Keen, Leshner, Plutchik, and Tarpy (1977).

3

THE HUMAN MIND

I SHALL OUTLINE a general view of processing systems that best represent the variety of actions, thoughts, experiences, and feelings and the organizations, transformations, plans, and programs that characterize the human organism. The intent is not to present a general theory. The analysis is programmatic rather than theoretical, structural rather than specific. The development of system analyses—in the broad sense—has misled many readers to mistake a programmatic picture of the system for a theoretical position. A theory for all of *psychology* is, in principle, as impossible as the endeavor to attain such a theory is misled. It is no more possible to develop a general psychological theory than to develop a general chemical theory or a general biological theory or a general astronomical theory. Psychologists have learned that minitheories provide the best approach toward an understanding of the system as a whole. It is subsequently required to show how transfers of information take place between one such subsystem and others.

In that sense, theories of perception, learning, sensation, psychopathology, attitude formation, and so forth need not be deducible from a general theory of learning or perception or whatever. Instead, these subsystems and minitheories can exist in their own right, and it is not even encumbent on the theorist to show how his minitheory of acoustic information processing, for example, is parallel to or tied in with a theory of speech production. Such an outcome is highly desirable, but it is not necessary, and the last several decades have shown the utility of this approach.

The outline of a general information-processing system is important, and the label one applies to it also seems to be of some consequence, particularly to psychologists who tend to be jealous of their ideological identities. From my point of view the system represents what psychologists mean by the concept *mind*. It is the complex of organizations and structures ascribed to an individual that processes information (including information from its own actions and experiences) and generates information to various subsystems. The intricacies of that system suggest something as complicated as the surplus meaning of the term *mind* implies. In the interface between psychology and neurophysiology, mind could be equivalent to the neurological mechanisms that are ascribed to the brain and its elaborations. Thus, if we wanted to do neurophysiology, we would say that the psychologists' mind is capable of processes that should find their parallel in neurological, physiological mechanisms. Since it is likely that any mechanism manufactured by the psychologist is capable of being represented by some known neurological mechanisms, there are no psychological constraints on the kind of processing mechanisms and structures that we may ascribe to the mind. Similarly, the psychologist who, perhaps for reasons of childhood trauma, is opposed to any terms that contain words like *mind* or *mental* may find comfort in the fact that mind is also the system that contains the past history of the individual; it encompasses structures that operate as a result of past history and, of course, as a result of prewired, innate structures. Finally, it is unlikely the system is the same one that the philosopher refers to, since the mentalism of the contemporary philosopher is frequently a set of processes that is available to inspection. The system that we wish to use is not available to inspection; it is a convenient device to encompass the structures that have been developed to explain observable and experienced events. Thus mind contains generative grammars, neural counters, the unconscious, and all other explanatory devices that have been useful to psychologists. Whether it also contains the "true" structure of the mental apparatus is, of course, unknown to mere humans.

So far I have indicated only a general metapsychological position for the use of the concept *mind*, but, since it encompasses all the systems involved in psychological functioning, for present purposes, some restriction to less inclusive subsystems becomes necessary. I shall refer to the *cognitive-interpretive system* to summarize many of the functions of primary interest to the analysis of emotion and mind. Its name indicates that the system is cognitive in that it is concerned with knowledge, and it is interpretive in that it transforms information into functional units.

In addition to the cognitive-interpretive system, I shall be concerned in particular with structures that organize and structure action, arousal, and consciousness. I shall discuss consciousness and arousal in later chapters; the structure of action will be discussed later in this chapter and in Chapter 8.

The cognitive-interpretive system is involved at all stages of processing. Not only does it receive input from the environment and distribute it as functional signals to other systems, but it also takes the product of arousal and action systems and, as part of this feedback, may change the functional signal or generate perceptions of actions and arousals. The perception of arousal is particularly important in the further development of the "emotional" structures with which I shall deal later.

The Structure of Mind

ORGANIZATION AND STRUCTURE

When talking about organizations and structures, I intend to carry along such notions as complexity and relatedness. For example, physical events measured in physical terms such as the amplitude and frequency of soundwaves are transformed by structures into the functional units that are acted on by the organism. People do not hear amplitude; they hear loudness—and complex transformations are needed to go from amplitude to the experience of reported loudness. If there were in fact a one-to-one relation between physical measurement and human experience or response, we should gladly forego any such complex notions as structures—or theories. The relation between a "physical" giant panda and one's cognitive-interpretive experience of it is immensely more complex. But how I see, hear, feel, like, or examine that particular large patch of black and white is fashioned by my biological limitations and my past experience represented in cognitive structures.

Structures are organized. Organization is defined by stable relations among elements. These elements may be sensations, perceptions, phonemes, words, action sequences, behaviors, syntactic units, or the elements themselves organized into groupings, categories, and concepts. Organized sets of relations form structures that, in turn, determine what is perceivable, sayable, or doable. The cognitive structures determine what is selected from the environment—events that cannot be organized in a structure cannot, in the first instance, be perceived. Actions that are not organized are at best chaotic (i.e., ineffectual).

The origin of cognitive structures is primarily experiential, sometimes genetic, and typically the result of an interaction of the two. Structures organize experience. In that function they integrate present events with the representation and generation of past history. A heuristic distinction can be made between intrinsic and extrinsic structures.[1] Intrinsic structure "is inherent in the stimulus itself," whereas extrinsic structure "occurs when the stimulus denotes or signifies something other than itself." Although the distinction has heuristic value, it does not easily survive more intensive analysis. Any property of the stimulus must perforce be analyzed and processed by the organism. Thus, intrinsic structure would not be perceived if the organism did not have certain appropriate structures that made the analysis of these properties possible. Color is not perceivable by a color-blind organism. But the general dimension of the distinction is useful, since it arranges structures from those that permit little or no individual variabilities to those that show great variability and idiosyncrasies among individuals.

Meaning is equated with structure. Thus, a set of events on which we cannot impose any relations is meaningless. Meaning is not some sum of meanings of individual elements but, instead, "the structure itself is meaningful."[2]

At the action side, similar arguments need to be invoked. I prefer the term *action* to that of *behavior*. Action implies and asserts the organization of behavior. Action is organized and is dependent on the invocation of action structures. Actions are represented internally and may be the antecedent conditions for structures or schemas that organize the world.

By talking about action rather than behavior, the speaker is drawing the line between behaviorism and contemporary psychology. Behavior—at least as viewed

1. Garner (1974).
2. Garner (1962).

by the behaviorist movement—was seen largely as the passive response of the organism to stimulating events in the environment. Its regularities were controlled in large part by the consistencies of stimuli and the predictability of reinforcement, all primarily characteristics of the environment that shaped the organism. Action in contrast implies an agent, usually an agent that intends some goal. Instead of the passive organism implied by the behaviorist locutions, the cognitive psychologist invokes an active organism shaping the environment as well as being shaped by it. The term *action* is used primarily to talk about some observable and usually intentional movement of the organism that is not verbal.

MENTAL STRUCTURE—CONSCIOUS AND UNCONSCIOUS

The minimal requirements of mental structure that we need for later descriptions of emotional functions are the registration of environmental events, a system of structures that interprets such events and performs complex transformations, and two productive systems, one of them an action system and the other one a physiological-arousal system. In addition, there must be provision for feedback, in the one case to provide for the perception of arousal, in the other for the monitoring of action. Some of these functions are conscious, and the notion of consciousness will be developed more fully in the next chapter. For now, the function of consciousness is best left underdefined. It is often useful not to define any particular construct too precisely but, instead, to rely on its development as well as an appeal to plausibility to define its operations.

Mind includes all the inferred events that are ascribed to the human mental system. It includes notions of how external events are transformed by appropriate structures and then executed in observable action and arousal systems. Included within that body of mechanisms are the transducers that operate on energy inputs (the sense organs), the hypothetical neural events that transform these analyzed and transduced inputs—all the major systems that provide transformational mechanisms prior to action. These systems include the perceptual and sensory systems and their transformations, systems that may very often be self-starting.

My major purpose is to present a way of looking at mental organization. This system represents the most important, necessary, and also desirable features of human mental organization. It has some evocative use in that, without being a theory, it implies certain consequences about the relation between events and action, and between action and consciousness. It makes it possible to understand the restricted sense in which some psychologists and most philosophers have talked about mentalism—by referring to that part of the mental organization that is coextensive with consciousness and partly accessible through language. However, that part of the mental organization is only a very small cross section, constrained by the vast number of organizations and structures that are not represented in consciousness and constrained as well by some of the hypotheses that may exist in consciousness but that are not, in fact, representations of actual transformations or structures.

The cognitive-interpretive system is an organized system of structures that operates on the information from the external world. These organizations and structures interpret the world—broadly defined, including any and all perceptible events, whether they take place inside or outside the skin of the actor. The system provides the effective, interpreted cues for action, arousal, and, most important, interpretations and characterizations of the surround. The system is, by definition, different from individual to individual in its content and effects, but it is, in principle, identical from individual to individual when we are concerned with the form of its structures, with the way in which they may be modified, and with the structures that are innate or prewired (i.e., existing at birth or developing during the process of maturation). The system processes inputs from the sense organs, but it is also self-generating in that it contains programs and transformations that, under given circumstances, will seek information and add information when such is lacking from the external world.

The operation of the cognitive-interpretive system is inferred from its actions and thoughts. It is only after it has produced some consequence that the system is observable—by its effects. In that sense it is equivalent to Freud's notion of the unconscious that "in its innermost nature . . . is as much unknown to us as the reality of the external world, and . . . is as incompletely presented by the data of consciousness as is the external world by the communications of our sense organs."[3]

Thus most of mind is unavailable to introspection. Self-awareness reflects the conscious consequences of mental operations; introspection deals with the conscious *results* of the cognitive-interpretive system. Furthermore, since this system does have self-referential instructions—for example, to be self-consistent or "rational"—its outputs may reveal not the operations of its structures alone but the operations of structures that, in effect, conceal the work of other components. Thus, awareness and introspection are just as much products of the mind to be explained by its underlying representation and process, as are other actions, percepts, emotions, and feelings.

The Structure of a Cognitive-Interpretive System

The external world is structured, and the human mind also imposes structure on that world. It is the nature of the human enterprise, including the scientific enterprise, that these structures can never be completely disentangled. Scientists, of course, try to determine what the structure of the world is, but *qua* scientists and humans, they can do that only within the limit of the structures of the mental organization. That organization, that structure of the mind, is shaped in three ways—by the evolutionary history of the species, by the historical and social constraints that operate on a particular culture or class, and by the specific life experiences of the individual.

The activities of the psychologist in trying to arrive at reasonable theoretical

3. Freud ([1900] 1975).

constructions of the human mind have often been seen by many philosophers and psychologists to be somehow different and differently constrained from the activity of other scientists. There is no logical justification for that assertion. Presumably, the theoretical structures that we can build up about an observed set of events (in this case the actions and experiences of other human beings) are no more or less constrained by the mental structure of the observer than are the observations of physical, biological, or astronomical events. There is no doubt that the limitations of human mental organization constrain what we can experience and what we can think about (anything else would elevate man into the place of a god). However, there is nothing in that constraint to say that the kinds of theories we can make up about mental structures are peculiarly influenced by our own mental structures *any more* so than our theories about the structure of the atom are. To say that only part of the "real" world is knowable is to make an empty statement, since, by definition, we do not know what is not knowable. This limitation should be recognized, but we can and do enlarge our knowledge of the world. Some of our methodological and technological extensions have made both structures and events of the world knowable that were unthought of before these advances. We need only think about the extensions of the electromagnetic spectrum beyond the visible limits or the contributions of the microscope or the discovery of subatomic particles or the operation of unconscious structures.

The notion that mental structure is influenced by the evolutionary history of the species is a truism at this point in scientific history. Consider the special characteristics of the sensory apparatus and the analytical systems that support it; we need not even go into complex behavioral structures. The notion that mental processes are subject to historical and social constraints is less popular in the recent positivistic history of Western science, but the evidence is fairly conclusive that sociohistorical processes influence at least the distribution of various kinds of thought processes.[4] Finally, even with the current return of nativism, there is little doubt that many of the mental structures operating in everyday life are a function of the particular cultural, social, and individual experience of the individual and the group. Even the most ardent defender of a nativist position on language will admit the importance of individual experiences in developing the structures that are specific to a particular language. Cultural influences and individual experiences assume great importance as they affect the structures that underlie the business of daily living. Somebody brought up in a rural environment views the bustle of city traffic as much more threatening and confusing than a city dweller does, and a native of a Swiss mountain village values the cows in her dairy herd very differently from the way a devout Hindu regards the cows in his village. We will have occasion to discuss these differences at greater length in the chapter on value.

How can we describe the structures that store the knowledge of the world in which we live? In order to know what something means, we need to know what

4. Luria (1971).

its relation is to other events and propositions that represent our past experience. The knowledge and relation must be represented by some sort of structural system.

SCHEMAS: THE BASIC UNITS OF MIND

Cognitive structures organize knowledge and information, but they also have transformational functions and processing duties to perform. It is therefore useful to make some distinctions among cognitive structures, and in particular I want to make use of the concept of the *schema*.

I use the term *schema* in order to conform with current usage but also to evoke similarities with Frederic Bartlett's and Jean Piaget's usage. My previous preference was to refer to cognitive structures, but I now reserve that concept for a more general notion. Schemas are included under cognitive structures. The latter also include such devices as logical structures, syntactic structures, and strictly procedural mechanisms. Schemas are used primarily to organize experience, and in that role they overlap with some aspects of concepts like "plans" and "images."[5] In current usage, cognate concepts are those of scripts[6] and frames.[7] The concept of the schema goes back at least to Kant, who viewed schemas as directing our experience. For example, in the case of the schema of a dog, it is a mental pattern that "can delineate the figure of a four-footed animal in a general manner, without limitation to any single determinate figure as experience, or any possible image that I can represent *in concreto*, actually presents."[8]

A schema is a bounded, distinct, and unitary representation. For reasons to be spelled out in some detail below, activation of parts of a schema implies the activation of the whole, distinct from other structures and other schemas.

Schemas are built up in the course of interaction with the environment.[9] They are available at increasing levels of generality and abstraction. Thus, schemas may represent organized experience ranging from discrete features to general categories. For example, one schema may represent a horse's head, and another one facilitates the perception of a particular animal as a horse because of the concatenation of certain features (variables of a schema) such as a head, a tail, a mane, a certain size, or a range of colors. That same horse is categorized as an animal because of the occurrence of certain defining characteristics of that class of events.

The schema that is developed as a result of prior experiences with a particular kind of event is not a carbon copy of that event; schemas are abstract representations of environmental regularities.[10] Schemas vary from the most concrete to the most abstract; they are available for the perceptual elements of an event as

5. Miller, Galanter, and Pribram (1960).
6. Schank and Abelson (1977).
7. Minsky (1975).
8. Kant ([1781] 1929).
9. See J. M. Mandler (1979), Rumelhart and Ortony (1978), and Rumelhart (1980) for more detailed discussions of schema theory.
10. See, e.g., Franks and Bransford (1971).

well as for the abstract representation of its "meaning" or gist.[11] We comprehend events in terms of the schemas they activate, though we have different ways of talking about different kinds of comprehension. Perception is "comprehension of sensory input";[12] one sense of understanding involves comprehension of semantic relations; and some value judgments are based on the comprehension of structural relations. Finally, it should be noted that generic schemas have modal (or even canonic) values of variables. This property responds to the notion of schematic prototypes[13] that affect the likely congruity of specific instances of objects and events.

Schemas operate interactively, that is, input from the environment is coded selectively in keeping with the schemas currently operating while that input also selects relevant schemas.[14] Whenever some event in the environment produces "data" for the schematic analysis, the activation process proceeds automatically (and interactively) to the highest (most abstract) relevant schema. Evidence from the environment activates potential schemas, and active schemas produce an increased readiness for certain evidence and decreased readiness (inhibition) for other evidence. The particular interaction between the contextual environmental evidence and the organism's available schemas constricts perception and conception to specific hypotheses and schemas.

Schemas are also processing mechanisms; they are active in selecting evidence, in parsing the data provided by our environment, and in providing appropriate general or specific hypotheses.[15]

Most, if not all, of the activation processes occur automatically and without awareness on the part of the perceiver-comprehender. When and under what circumstances we become aware of any part of the processing steps will be examined later.

I have alluded to the distinction between concrete and generic schemas. The schema for the living room of my house is more specific than the schema I have for living rooms in general. The latter has such variables as coffee tables, couches, chairs, and TV sets. The former is populated with a specific tan leather couch, but also with a piano. I expect these objects to be present when I enter my living room, that is, the living-room schema activated when I come home has certain specific values of living-room variables. On the other hand, when visiting somebody whose home I have not seen before, I would not be surprised to see two couches, no piano, and a TV set (which is not part of my home living-room schema). But, I would be surprised if on returning home I found two couches in my living room or if on visiting someone I found a kitchen range in the living

11. I am using the terms *concrete* and *abstract* as essentially equivalent to *specific* and *general*. Though the distinction between these two sets of terms is potentially important, it does not interact significantly with my theme. For example, I have a concrete-specific schema for my wristwatch and an abstract-general schema for wristwatches, watches, clocks.

12. Rumelhart and Ortony (1978).

13. See Rosch and Mervis (1975) and Rosch (1975).

14. McClelland and Rumelhart (1981) and Marcel (1983b).

15. Rumelhart (1980).

room. The expectations are important because they define in part the problem of discrepancy and interruption that is central to my tale of emotion.

Another aspect of schemas concerns the development of specific expectations by generic schemas. In the case of prototypes this role is played by the specific values of features, attributes, or variables that constitute the prototypical animal or fruit or piece of furniture. These instantiations of schemas in the absence of environmental evidence are referred to as their default values. For example, if asked to describe the typical kitchen or living room or baseball game, we are quite willing and able to describe specific instantiations—that is, the default values for ranges, refrigerators, couches, TV sets, pitchers, and home runs.

The distinction between our generic expectations (and their default values when called for) and specific instantiations of schemas when we are presented with evidence in our surrounds has been described as a distinction between top-down and bottom-up processes.[16] Top-down processes are expectations, variables and values of variables, that have been built up as the result of our past experiences with the relevant events and objects. Top-down determinants of experience are the stored cumulative result of our past experience; bottom-up processes use the schemas in order to make sense of the actual world in which we live, from location to location and from instance to instance.

Preoccupations with top-down processes, with the power of expectations that are driven by schemas and scripts, and with the notion that schemas and similar structures determine what is perceivable have led to arguments and talmudic explorations about the limits of human experience. Does a schema define exhaustively what may be experienced in a familiar situation? For example, if I walk into my kitchen, open the cupboard, and am faced with a lion charging across the desert sand, do I actually not see the lion? Is an event that bears no relation to my current schema and its possible default values not perceivable at all? It is exactly that kind of internal view of the organism that has sometimes given cognitive psychology a bad name. Schemas are interactive products of expectations and external evidence, and experience depends primarily on the activated schemas that are driven by a world that is assumed to be real and palpable. Lions charging across desert sands activate schemas about wild animals and about lions in particular; they will be quite perceivable. What will be difficult for me is to "make sense" of this particular occurrence in my kitchen cupboard. I will not be able to construct a sensible structural relation between my kitchen and the charging lion, my conscious experience will be confused, and I will panic not only because of the threat of the lion but also because of the extreme discrepancy of the various activated schemas. Events that do not "fit" into active schemas are perceivable; in fact, they demand cognitive processing.[17] The power of discrepant perceptions and their relevance to adaptation and to emotional constructions will be discussed in detail in Chapter 8.

A related approach to perceptual processes distinguishes among three com-

16. Norman and Bobrow (1975).
17. Friedman (1979).

ponents of perception.[18] The first consists of the regularities of the physical world that result in patterns of stimulation; the second comprises channels of specific nerve energies that are the results of physical stimulation and that constrain what we can discover in the world; and the third is made up of the mental structures that are patterns of expectation that have been learned from the patterns of the physical world by way of specific preconscious stimulation. The result is that "we perceive that object or event which would, under normal seeing conditions, be most likely to produce the pattern of sensations that we receive."[19]

The traditional representation of schemas has been in terms of distinct structures that are activated—structures that can, for example, be illustrated in terms of some graphic analogue of nodes of features connected by relational, directed ties or bonds. An alternative, and useful, way of looking at schemas is in terms of distributed features,[20] where features are not conceived as belonging to single schemas, but where instead features and attributes have relations that determine specific schemas. In that sense, schemas are distributed across a population of features. For example, consider a set of features (f_1 to f_n) that represents all possible features of a particular event. Whenever the surround produces an activation of a particular set of features, these features and their relations are activated, and repeated exposure to these concatenations and conjunctions will define a specific schema. As a result whenever any subset of these features is activated, they will activate the other features with which they have been associated in the past. The features that are most likely to occur consistently in conjunction with each other and that are likely to maintain their particular relations to each other are usually referred to as the perceptual aspects of an event or object. Cherries are usually of a particular size, red, joined in pairs or triplets, round, and so forth. Thus, whenever we are exposed to some or most of the features that are usually part of the cherry experience, all the features that are present in the environment will be activated. In addition, because of their past conjunction, these features will also activate one another. This kind of reverberation among the constant (perceptual) features of a schema will not only define the bounded schema of a cherry but also bring about a high level of activation of the particular "cherry" set, rather than the apple set, which is also partially activated by the round and red features but in which the other features are missing. As a result the apple schema will be barely activated, certainly much less so than the very vivid experience of the cherries. Note, though, that there is enough activation and similarity among the activated features for us to be able to say that apples are more like cherries than like bananas. Other aspects of the cherry schema will co-occur much less frequently with the perceptual features—for example, the fact that they have pits, are fruits, taste very good with ice cream, or are frequently eaten by birds. While these additional features will also be activated, as is obvious in the ease of elicitation of these characteristics, they do not benefit

18. Hochberg (1981).
19. Hochberg (1981).
20. Hinton and Anderson (1981) and Rumelhart, Hinton, and McClelland (in preparation).

from the intense mutual activation that is characteristic of the perceptual features that are always, or usually, present.

In other words, features of a schema produce mutual activation, and the greater the prior probability of relational ties among the features, the greater the likelihood that the representation as a whole will be activated. One of the consequences of such activation is that features that are not part of the current evidence will be activated—missing features will be "filled in." The conceptual features (e.g., fruit and dessert features of the cherry) are frequently not part of the immediately activated set of features, but they will be activated because part of the schema has been activated. This is one mechanism whereby default values may well be brought into an activated state and may eventually become conscious. Conversely, given the existence of a mutually connected set of cherry features, not only the perceptual but also the conceptual features may serve as pathways to gain access to the schema as a whole. Thus, cues about a fruit that is red and is used on ice cream provide one way of retrieving the cherry schema.[21]

Whenever we see a particular object or event the relation among the features as well as the specific features themselves (or instantiations of generic variables) are activated. Experiences with such events or objects renew the activation of that particular schema, a mechanism I have called the integration of the structure.[22] On the other hand, focusing on the relation between the object or event and other mental contents or environmental events constitutes the elaboration of the event or object.

It might be noted that integration and schematic activation are not distinguishable from elaboration unless one specifies a particular target event or object. For example, a window consists of such features as frames and glass, while a house includes windows as one of its features. Attending to a house will integrate the window as a feature, but windows can also be seen as elaborations of the concept of a house. Similarly, a particular street and house number may serve as an elaborated cue for a house we are visiting for the first time, but these may well become integrated features of that house after we have moved into it.[23]

Integration and activation in general are also relevant to the experience of familiarity. Well-established and integrated schemas would be assumed to be a characteristic of a familiar event.

However, there are two aspects of the notion of familiarity that need to be distinguished, both in terms of their phenomenal differences and as represented in underlying processes. The commonsense notion of familiarity implies that there exists a representation (a schema) that "fits" the encoded event. The phenomenal counterpart of that conjunction is the experience of "knowing that" or "having seen (heard, etc.) that before." I shall refer to this sense of familiarity as familiarity$_1$, which also includes variations in degree of familiarity. The British

21. For related discussions of priming and activation, see Collins and Loftus (1975), Meyer and Schvaneveldt (1976), and Neely (1977).
22. Mandler (1979a).
23. Mandler (1982b).

flag is more familiar to me than that of Belgium; the word *table* seems more familiar than the word *gnu*. However, I "know" both flags and both words; they are all $familiar_1$.

In addition to the experience of familiarity, and degrees of familiarity, there exists the experience of recency. The judgment of having recently encountered an event, regardless of its value of $familiarity_1$, is also related to the state of the event's schema. I have suggested[24] that the phenomenal sense of recency is derived from the integration, the compactness, or the clarity of the representation of the event. Repeated encounters increase that integration and give rise to the sense of familiarity embodied in judgments of recency, which I call $familiarity_2$. The distinction is captured in our ability to distinguish recently encountered instances from among familiar groups of objects (such as books, faces, clothes).

Both kinds of familiarity are properties of the representation of an event; they are context independent. The fact that familiarity experiences are independent of context is illustrated by the well-known phenomenon of "recognizing" a face or a scene without being able to determine where, when, or how we encountered it before, or knowing who the person is. On the basis only of information contained within the representation of the event itself, it is possible to make the familiarity judgments. Other judgments of familiarity may, of course, be based on primarily contextual information.

AUTOMATICITY AND ACTIVATION

Although the detailed discussion of consciousness will be presented in the next chapter, there is an aspect of activation that interacts with consciousness and that needs to be explored here. If it is true that activation is an automatic, ballistic process that takes advantage of all previously established connections and relations among features and structures, then it must be puzzling that some activities do in fact follow such activation and run off automatically, whereas others seem to require some awareness, some conscious capacity, in order to be executed.[25] Knowing that an apple is a fruit, using a series of keys to open a well-known sequence of locks, using the appropriate commands on a computer, and recalling our own telephone number are all activities that seem to run off automatically, that require no "thought." In contrast, deciding when we last saw a polar bear, finding our way in an unfamiliar house, using some new command on a computer program, and recalling a friend's telephone number all seem to require some awareness, some conscious activity. Similarly, storing information about food to be bought on the way home from work, learning a new colleague's and her spouse's names, and other feats of memory also require conscious activity. Yet, most of the memory activity of everyday life involves no such deliberate effort. Contrary to the psychologist's preoccupation with memory experiments in which specific material is to be remembered, most of our daily memorial activity

24. Mandler (1979a, 1980a).
25. See, e.g., Hasher and Zacks (1979) and Posner and Boies (1971).

is done automatically. We are frequently "reminded" by particular contexts and situations that we are supposed to bring home some milk, that a paper has to be revised, that it is time to change the sheets on our bed, or that our typewriter needs an overhaul.

As a first approximation, I assume that actions and thoughts that issue from automatic processes require no intentions or choice. Nonautomatic actions and thoughts are "conscious"—they may have equivocal outcomes, they sometimes require intentions, and, in particular, they usually require choices, decisions, and selections. The specific role of consciousness in these processes will be discussed in detail in the next chapter.

While there is little limitation on the number of structures, schemas, and features that are activated, in the automatic case there is generally no serious competition between the particular outcome and other candidates for thought and action in the particular situation or task. This does not imply that we do not make mistakes, that automaticity results in errorless behavior; errors, too, can result from automatic activation. However, there is usually only one primary outcome. The well-known phenomenon that skills are conscious when first acquired but become unconscious once they are well practiced describes the availability of choices in the former and the inevitability of outcomes in the latter kind of performance.

It should be obvious that selective-search mechanisms require access to schemas that are activated. Activation is thus a necessary condition for selective retrieval, but it is both necessary and sufficient for the occurrence of automatic thoughts and actions.

Another way of distinguishing automatic and nonautomatic processes is to refer to them as nondeliberate versus deliberate. Deliberate retrieval implies that the target or goal state is not immediately available, that choices need to be made and searches and selections initiated. In the case of actions, deliberate ones are often referred to as voluntary (rather than as mechanical or automatic). In other words, a large part of the meaning of voluntariness is taken up by the initiation and exercise of decisions and choices—these are always necessary when automatic processes do not provide the target state.

ATTENTION

We do need to consider the function of attentional processes in this scheme of things. The common usage frequently coalesces attention, analytic processes, and consciousness. It is said, for example, that one attends to the theme of a musical composition, to the message in a speech, to the use of colors in a painting. In contrast, a simple use of the attention concept need claim only that one focuses on the spatiotemporal source of the music, the speech, or the painting—that is, on general locations in one's environment.

Most current theories of attention fall into two broad classes—early-selection theories and late-selection theories. Early-selection theories claim that top-down processes, sometimes called attentional mechanisms, select only parts of the perceptual continuum and inhibit or filter (exclude) others.[26] Late-selection theories admit all the available evidence to analytic (activational) processes and then select relevant aspects of the available unconscious evidence.[27] In both kinds of theories there is frequently some confounding of the selection process and implied entry into conscious states.

I wish to define attention as being independent of consciousness and to restrict it to the potential intake of formation. Attention is the process whereby a specific part of the space-time continuum is automatically made available for further processing. As a result, the information potentially available in the spatiotemporal section that is scanned is accessible to all relevant analytic processes. However, conceptual (top-down) processes will select the analyses-syntheses to be performed, and under some circumstances the nature of the information scanned may command certain analytic processes. As a result of spatiotemporal attention and the subsequent activation of selected cognitive representations (schemas), a subset of activated schemas constructs the unified phenomenal conscious experience. When the part of the spatiotemporal continuum that is selected by attention is very narrow and when the consequent activated schemas are determined primarily by the information scanned and by a (small) number of relevant schemas, the conscious contents will be determined and generally invariant from situation to situation and person to person (e.g., in the psychophysical experiment, the demands of a loud noise or of a familiar word).

There is no selection in this view, except for the inclusion or exclusion of parts of the spatiotemporal flux. All gating or selection phenomena and attentional priorities are determined at the next level of analysis, beyond the mere intake of the "physical" information from the spatiotemporal flux. For example, the request to "look for a red object in this room" does *not* involve a peripheral looking for red objects; what does happen is that the whole room becomes the domain of the spatiotemporal continuum that is scanned. Independently of this directive process, another top-down process will then select the evidence that fits the "red" criterion. Relevant evidence on this purely spatiotemporal selection by attentive processes has been developed in recent work on the "size" of the attentional spotlight.[28]

In a sense, this is a combination of the early- and late-selection views. The early selection, however, is neutral with respect to conceptual or semantic features, and does not involve any inhibition of perceptual evidence. Most of the work that is appealed to by the general notion of attention is done by late-selection mechanisms, particularly by the functions of constructive consciousness to which I shall return in the next chapter.

SCHEMA COMPLEXITY AND CHANGE

Not only are there generic schemas and very concrete ones, but schemas are also embedded in other schemas. I have indicated how the schema of a window

26. Broadbent (1958) and Treisman (1964, 1969).
27. Deutsch and Deutsch (1963) and Shiffrin and Schneider (1977).
28. LaBerge (1982).

becomes a feature of the schema of a house, and that the elaboration of one of the schemas (by establishing relations to others) may—from a different point of view—be seen as the integration of the larger schema. Furthermore, some schemas incorporate specific spatial and temporal features, whereas others are devoid of any specific reference to personal time and space. Thus, there exists a schema for physician's offices that tells me what to expect when visiting an internist, obstetrician, or pediatrician and a very specific schema, an instantiation of the generic one, for my last visit to my family doctor. In addition to specific features of time and place, there will be instantiations of the nurse, the kinds of magazines, and—if stressful—some of the emotional overlay of the visit.

The difference between generic and instantiated schemas also illustrates in part the development and growth of schemas. Any specific experience with a particular event not only establishes a sometimes transitory schema of its own but also contributes to the expected values of the variables of a more generic schema. Consider the story of the father and son who were involved in an accident. The father dies, and the son is brought to the hospital emergency unit, where the surgeon exclaims: "My God, that's my son." The story is surprising because our traditional surgeon schemas identify surgeons as being male. Changing that value of the surgeon variable to being gender neutral is a long process, brought about in part by hearing a story like this one.

The most widely accepted concepts about the change of schemas are Piaget's notions of accommodation and assimilation.[29] *Accommodation* refers to the case in which a new experience is such that existing structures (schemas) cannot accept the new information; structures must be changed in order to take account of it. As a result our view of the world is changed as it includes the novel experience as a legitimate part of a new perceptual or conceptual structure or adapts existing action structures to accommodate the new demands and information. Accommodation typically takes place in the young child as accumulating experiences build up a model of its world. Even for the adult, however, accommodation takes place as we learn something new. For example, when we learn to drive a car with a clutch (having previously used only automatic transmission), our schema for driving is changed, and when we switch from a dial to a push-button telephone, our telephoning schema changes. In the case of *assimilation*, on the other hand, existing structures remain unchanged, but the interpretation of the world is changed in order to deal adequately with a slightly changed situation—for example, when meeting somebody at a party and finding the initial conversation about a painting puzzling because the other person talks about shadings when we see brilliant color. We might accommodate these new opinions to a new structure, but simply assimilate when we discover that the other person is colorblind—no change in our existing mental organization is needed. Most cases of categorization and stereotyping are cases of assimilation.

Accommodation and assimilation are obviously extremes of a continuum of potential change in mental structures. But what about the case in which an event

29. Piaget (1970).

(conceptual, perceptual, or action demanding) cannot be handled by accommodation or assimilation? Events that cannot be assimilated or accommodated present a special problem for mental theory. In principle, they should not be registered. However, as we have seen in the case of the lion appearing in a kitchen cupboard, such a conclusion would be both foolish and theoretically sterile. The adaptability of the mental system handles such situations in a variety of ways, in the first instance by searching for hypotheses and schemas that *can* handle the new evidence. These immediate attempts often produce relatively unstructured results, as in the identification of a vague shadow, an unfamiliar noise, or an unidentifiable taste or smell. In fact, as we shall see in Chapters 8 and 9, the cognitive processing of interruptions and discrepancies plays a major role in the construction of emotion.

Schemas change, spin off new ones, are incorporated into others, and develop superordinate and subordinate relations to each other. Such hierarchical relations and organization seem to be a natural choice for the larger organization of schematic structures. These organizations support our general proclivity to see things not only as "part of" others but also as examples of more general or abstract notions. Shinbones are not only connected to kneebones, which are connected to thighbones, all to the greater glory of the whole human body, but toes are parts of feet, are parts of legs, are parts of human bodies, are parts of animal organisms, are parts of living things. Similarly, apples are fruit, are plants, are organic things. Or, in a more emotional context, one might think of professors as part of an educational system, which is part of a system that preempts what we should think and believe.

Structures are not as neatly ordered as a simple hierarchy may indicate; a better expression is found in the notion of heterarchy, where superordinate and subordinate relations exist but where these relations may shift from requirement to requirement and where within a particular concept there may be assembled a number of equivalent, unordered features, attributes, or schemas. As an example of the development of schemas, consider a child learning about dogs. The schema about "dogs" will develop out of the early instances and the early discriminations. Assume that the first experience a child has is with a large, black dog that barks frequently. The unspoken, prelinguistic meaning[30] of this concept thus involves something moving, something black, and also something that, because of sudden barking noises, may have attached to it a degree of autonomic arousal. This initial experience is elaborated on subsequent occasions. However, the initial "dog" schema has connections to a structure, presumably present before the first experience with a dog, that makes distinctions between large and small moving objects. As experience with dogs increases, the schema of dog is discriminated into both generic and embedded schemas of small ones, nonblack ones, ones that do not bark, and also ones that lick your hand, that fetch things, and so forth. At the same time, there are characteristics of dogs (e.g., they are self-propelled objects) that will produce generalizations and coordination with high-

30. Macnamara (1972).

level schemas, including those relating to living things, or, for example, the common schema between cats and dogs, which refers to them as tame domestic animals usually found in the home. We thus assume that "lower" and "higher" schemas develop from initial schemas in a hierarchical system. But if the initial instance is extensively processed, then despite the development of the schema and its generalization and discrimination, reference will frequently return to that initial schema. If the child's attention has been particularly drawn to the initial large, black, barking dog, then what will, to a very large extent, characterize its schema of dogs and even the general meaning of pets.

We have seen how the contents of specific schemas may lead to autonomic arousal. However, the use of schemas as one of the basic units of the mental armamentarium has other implications for the construction of emotion. In the first instance, the notion of interruption or discrepancy to be developed in later pages is intimately tied to the discrepancy between a particular event and the expectancy engendered by already existing schemas. Second, some of the sources of evaluative cognitions will be seen to depend to a certain extent on the nature and structure of schemas representing object and events.

BEYOND THE SCHEMA

I have used the concept of schema to represent the organization of environmental regularities. Schemas are the primary representations of our physical world. In that function, they are the mental counterpart of all events and objects that we regularly encounter. This is a somewhat broader meaning of schema than other theorists use, some of whom restrict the concept to spatial and temporal regularities, as represented in objects, event sequences, stories, layouts, and so forth.[31] I also include the representation of categories, such that the concepts of furniture, of fruit, of friendly people, and of dangerous situations are all represented schematically. The facts that apples, pears, and cherries occur together in supermarkets, that they occur in conjunction with the label "fruit," and that they are claimants to certain dietary advantages are all regularities that are represented in the fruit schema. Such categorical schemas also display the characteristic of mutual activation (whether directly or via the conceptual relation) and the "filling-in" characteristics of schemas. If I go to market to buy some apples, but remember only fruit, then I may well return with pears instead.

The existence of prototypes also suggests the operation of schematic representations; a prototypical fruit is that fruit which combines the optimal concatenation of the default features of fruit. Whether a particular "concept" (to use a rather vague term) displays these characteristics depends on how it is acquired and used. Schemas are the result of experienced combinations. For example, it is not surprising that the notion of oddness has schematic characteristics; the number 937 seems more "odd" than 9, which is more odd than 4, and so forth.[32]

31. J. M. Mandler (1979).
32. Armstrong, Gleitman, and Gleitman (1983).

A question of "oddness" responds to the *degree* of activation, as the question whether or not "4 is odd" does not. The latter is rule governed.

Structures that embody formal rules and definitions are, of course, quite different from schemas, even in their wider definition. Such rules are not important to emotional phenomena, nor is their structure well known or generally accepted. They range from simple structures like those that determine whether a number is odd to very complex ones like those involved in problem solving.[33] However, it should be remembered that even some apparently complex reasoning problems are solved on the basis of prior activation. The availability heuristic is one such example, and it has been applied to quite complex reasoning.[34]

A large number of the rule-governed structures refer to a conditional set of actions and processes that are performed subject to the prior satisfaction of other conditions, events, or actions. If I want to learn either abstract or concrete rules—for example, "When winning stay with a particular choice, when losing shift to an alternative one," "In French, the position of the adjective relative to the noun depends on the required emphasis," or "Don't stop at a diner unless there are a lot of trucks parked outside of it"—I have to know the proper conditions under which these rules apply, which in turn have a structure of the appropriate acts to be performed.[35]

It is not my purpose to discuss in detail different kinds of cognitive models and cognitive structures. However, I draw attention to the two dominant models of cognitive development: first, Piaget's, because it is the only well-worked-out system of cognitive development at the present time; and, second, Freud's, because it pays special attention to the problem of emotional development. It should be obvious by now that most workable theories are consistent with the kind of approach advocated here. There is no reason why both Piaget's notions of cognitive development and Freud's notions of emotional development cannot be included within this view of mental organization. Under different conditions and for different reasons, different kinds of these structures will be used and will be expressed in behavior and experience.

I shall not at this time deal with the development of emotionally relevant structures, such as Freud's notions of infantile preoccupations. How cognitive structures may be influenced and molded by specific infantile experiences, will be discussed more properly in Chapter 12.

COGNITION AND CONDITIONING

The shift from behaviorism to cognitive concerns also brought with it an abrupt change of interests in research paradigms. In the period up to the 1960s, American psychology was preoccupied with several variations of classical (Pavlovian) and instrumental (operant) conditioning, but that interest has waned and given way to research on more complex human thought and action. However,

33. See, e.g., Newell and Simon (1972).
34. Pollard (1982) and Tversky and Kahneman (1973).
35. Norman (1973).

one of the curiosities of cognitive theory is that it has essentially ignored the wealth of information about the conditioning process that was amassed in previous decades. I shall make an attempt to remedy that oversight in the following pages, particularly because classical conditioning has frequently been brought into play as a descriptive mechanism for our understanding of emotions like anxiety.

I shall essentially ignore the literature on operant, instrumental learning, because the kind of contingencies with which it is concerned are readily assimilated into cognitive theory. The following description of operant behavior is easily read from a cognitive, information-processing perspective: "What unites all examples of operant behavior is that they are activities of the whole organism that have effects on the environment; and the central thesis of behavior theory is that it is these environmental effects that control the occurrence of the activities."[36] In our language, situations and schemas interact in determining action.

Cognitive psychologists are concerned with the representation of the environment, with actions on the environment, with changes in our perceptions and knowledge about that environment, and in the way in which these representations and the manner in which they are processed control our activities. The main difference is that we want to know, or postulate, not simply that this system works but how it works.

I turn, therefore, to the Pavlovian (classical, respondent) paradigm, which does not immediately evoke appropriate processing models.

The conditioning paradigm most relevant to problems of emotion involves an unconditioned stimulus such as shock that is preceded by the conditioned stimulus (e.g., a tone). The conditioned response, typically described as autonomic nervous system (ANS) activation, eventually appears in some changed (attenuated) form when the conditioned stimulus alone is presented. The shock and tone may be presented simultaneously, or the tone may precede the shock, but the time interval must be short. Whether we interpret the shock as an innate elicitor of the ANS or whether we wish to interpret shock (and other painful events) as maximally interruptive of ongoing processing activity is not immediately relevant. Whatever the resolution of that question, shock and other painful events are clearly to be classed as events that are (at least in the adult) classified as bad—that is, they are the occasion for a negative evaluative cognition. What is the underlying representation of that course of events? The tone and the shock are organized as a repeated sequence, as a schema. Since schemas, by definition, describe our expectations about the world, the conditioning schema defines the sequence and also contains information about the negative evaluation of that sequence. But why does the tone eventually come to be followed by ANS activation? To say that conditioning has taken place obviously begs the question. We want to explain the occurrence of the conditioning sequence. One interpretation is that the tone signals the occurrence of the shock, which is an inescapable noxious event. The inability to have available some action that copes with

36. Schwartz and Lacey (1982).

that event is a discrepant, interruptive event. In other words, I would argue that the reason why the tone evokes the ANS reaction is not that the shock, which has followed it in the past does so, but rather that the tone is a signal for the inability of the organism to recruit some behavior that will avoid the noxious events; it is a sign of helplessness. Thus, in contrast to conditioning explanations that claim that the conditioned response is the prototype of anxiety—that is, that anxiety is the conditioned form of pain or fear,[37]—my argument holds that "anxiety" is the emotional anticipation of the inescapable pain. In other words, what happens in this situation is not the transfer of the autonomic response to the conditioned stimulus but the recruitment of a novel response.

One might query this account and suppose that a schema consisting of the conditional stimulus and the ANS response could be established. In fact, there is no evidence that the ANS response can be simply transferred at all; it always requires its usual eliciting conditions (as discussed in Chapter 6). What will happen is that the *perception* of ANS arousal can become part of a new schema, though in a rather shadowy form. This process produces the phenomenon of autonomic imagery (see Chapter 6). Thus, the conditioned stimulus may remind the organism of the impending ANS reaction, but it does not reproduce it.

But what happens when the shock is not inescapable, when it can be avoided? Experiments on avoidance learning, in which the organism can make a response that avoids the occurrence of the shock after the onset of the signal tone, show that the avoidance response is learned very rapidly. Such a response, like moving to another part of the cage, occurs typically as soon as the tone sounds—that is, animals do not wait until just before the expected occurrence of the shock. More important, however, is the well-known fact that avoidance responses like this are very difficult to extinguish. They persist for hundreds of trials even though the animal has not experienced any more shocks.[38] This effect seems quite reasonable from a cognitive point of view. The information about the tone-shock sequence has not been changed; it just so happens that the animal is not in the situation in which shock usually occurs after it has learned the avoidance response. Evidence also suggests that fear or autonomic responses disappear during the course of the "extinction" trials. The situation represented by the tone initiates the schema that leads to the avoidance response, and this is a stable, unchanging world. However, avoidance responses *can* be extinguished, just as the conditioned ANS response can be extinguished. In the latter case, following the establishment of the contingency between tone and shock, the elimination of the shock *in the same situation* changes the expectations for that situation, and the tone ceases to be a reliable precursor of shock. In the avoidance case, extinction can be accomplished if the animal is blocked from executing the avoidance response.[39] Under those circumstances, for example, if the animal is prevented from crossing the cage, it is kept in the same situation, and the environmental regularities that have been previously established are now changed. Tone can no longer be fol-

37. Mowrer (1947) and Rescorla and Solomon (1967).
38. Annau and Kamin (1961).
39. Baum (1970).

lowed by the avoidance response and is not followed by shock. Both the tone-shock schema and the tone-response schema are replaced by a tone-no-shock schema. Staying on the original side of the cage no longer presents the problem of the uncontrollable shock, and animals stop jumping to the other side when given the opportunity. Even then, however, occasional avoidance responses tend to occur. I assume their occurrence depends on the aspect of the situation that is attended to and on whether the representation of tone-no-shock is activated and becomes dominant or whether the tone-jumping sequence is the dominant representation that produces actions.

Other aspects of the conditioning paradigm are conducive to this kind of analysis. It has now been generally accepted that the likelihood that a conditioned response will be established depends on the contingency between the conditioned and the unconditioned stimuli. Despite the prior behaviorist view that conditioning occurs when the conditioned and unconditioned stimuli occur contiguously, it is true that the conditioned stimulus must tell the organism something about the occurrence of the unconditioned stimulus.[40] In other words, the conditioned stimulus must provide some degree of predictability. One of the major functions of schemas is to provide reliable expectations about environmental consistencies. That is exactly what the conditioned stimulus provides. When such a stimulus is occasionally paired with the unconditioned stimulus, but does not make possible any consistent expectations (predictions), conditioning will not take place.

Blocking and overshadowing effects in conditioning refer to the fact that stimulus compounds (e.g., a light and a tone) can have differential effects.[41] If a response is conditioned to one stimulus and if later on a compound stimulus including the old stimulus and a new one is used, the newly introduced stimulus will not, by itself, show any conditioned effects in later tests. Similarly, a compound stimulus consisting of two stimuli that differ greatly in their discriminability or intensity will produce conditioning. However, in subsequent tests the "weaker" of the two stimuli will be shown to be ineffective. This contrasts with compound conditioning with equally attention-demanding stimuli, which will produce conditioning effects for each of the two components alone. These effects illustrate the highly selective nature of schema formation. Information must be informative; assimilation of new information will not take place (in blocking) if the new information does not provide or require a new organization of the serial structure. Similarly, "attentional" mechanisms will focus on and select the more discriminable of two stimuli when the information provided by two stimuli is the same.

Our example of tone-shock conditioning has suggested that the autonomic response to the tone is not just an unconditioned response that has been shifted to the conditioned stimulus, but rather a different response altogether, though similar in form to the unconditioned response. In the latter case, it is a response to a noxious event; in the former, it is the response to the unavailability of appro-

40. Rescorla (1967).
41. Kamin (1969).

priate coping behavior. The fact that the conditioned and the unconditioned responses are not simply the same response that has been shifted from one stimulus to another has been known for quite some time. In fact, the conditioned response may change its character altogether, and in the case of autonomic tone-shock conditioning it seems to do just that. If animals have been exposed to a long series of conditioning trials, the sympathetic response to the tone shifts to a parasympathetic response—that is, heart rate decreases rather than increases, even though the response to the shock is still an *increasing* heart rate.[42] As we shall see in Chapter 6, heart-rate decreases are associated with greater attention to environmental demands. In this case, the tone that at first signals an insoluble problem becomes a signal for greater attention to the environment and to possible novel problem-solving strategies.

This line of reasoning also suggests that different kinds of conditioning paradigms require different kinds of analyses. In the case of eyelid conditioning, the unconditioned stimulus is a puff of air and the unconditioned response is an eye blink. The latter is obviously a well-established (probably innate) defensive response. The schema of tone–air puff is one in which the tone signals a noxious, negatively evaluated event that is not inescapable, and the action schema of tone–eye-blink–air puff is established. Here the tone is the signal not for an unsolvable but for a solvable problem. In the case of salivary conditioning, meat powder produces salivation, as does a tone paired with the meat powder. Here again, the anticipation is different. The meat powder signals ingestive, eating behavior that elicits the preparatory salivation. The schema of tone–salivation–meat powder embodies the expectation of the (organized) eating activity.

I have not done full justice to the conditioning literature; rather, I have only highlighted some well-known phenomena. My purpose was to show the generality of a cognitive approach that seeks to understand the underlying representations for observable organismic actions. The wealth of knowledge available through the conditioning paradigm remains to be mined by cognitive psychologists. For example, the available information about the effect of CS-US intervals should provide much needed information about the temporal organization of schemas.

Meaning Analysis

Only in unusual circumstances do we live in a meaningless world. Typically, we know where we are, what we are doing, and why we are doing it, even though these insights may be unavailable to an uninitiated observer. We are more or less continually aware of these facts of life. How does a schema-driven view of the mind account for this dominant aspect of human existence?

In order to discuss the issue at all, I must briefly indicate here some conclusions about consciousness that the next chapter will discuss in detail. Our awareness is constructed out of activated schemas. The current contents of consciousness

42. Obrist, Sutterer, and Howard (1972).

are primarily constructed out of abstract schematic representations but become less abstract and very concrete depending on the requirements of the task, situation, and occasion. The question to be addressed next is therefore what is available for such construction, for making sense of the environment by the use of the schemas and structures that have been activated.

In a sense the analysis of the current situation depends on the choices made by the constructive consciousness. But the available meanings of the world must first be available in the underlying representation.

It is one of the axiomatic characteristics of the mental system that all evidence coming in, whether from the surround or from other mental structures, is accepted to the extent that it fits into available structures. It is in that sense that we continually "examine" the world around us and that we experience the relations between the current evidence and past experiences.

I assume that all evidence presented to the mind undergoes such meaning analysis. The system takes an event and, locating it in terms of its particular characteristics, attributes, and features, activates the relations of that particular object to other structures and sets of events. The relation of a particular event to existing structures thus gives us an organization that is specific to that event and gives us its organization within the existing structures or its meaning. Remember, however, that objects, events, and situations are not taken in isolation; of particular interest are many of the relations to other events at the same time. A good example is the meaning analysis of polysemous words.

For example, the word *table* undergoes entirely different meaning analyses in the sentences "I put it in the table" and "I put it on the table." The relational characteristics in the former case have to do with tables in books and papers, while the latter have to do with tables that are found in rooms and houses.

There exist any number of pieces of information that seem to be almost immediately available to us. There is a real difference between the knowledge available to me about the path taken from my home to my office in California and the path I have *just* taken from my home in London to my office. Similarly, I seem to have available in some preconscious state all sorts of information about a friend who just visited us that seems different from the information about friends whom I have not seen in a couple of years. The distinction I wish to make is one between general knowledge and what I have called state-of-the-world knowledge.

PRECONSCIOUS STATE-OF-THE-WORLD KNOWLEDGE

At present we know very little about the course of feature and schema activation. It seems that activation spreads in an essentially uncontrolled fashion from the immediate evidence to all related (and connected) mental structures. Whether the "strength" of such activation decreases as it spreads to farther (more derivative) reaches of the mental realm is unclear. An alternative argument is that the more abstract and derivative schemas are activated less intensely because they receive only partial information, not less strong activations. Thus, a schema about ice cream will be only weakly activated by the sight of cherries, simply because the ice-cream schema may receive an activation from one or two common features with the cherry complex. However, if I go to the local coffee shop and look over its menu, which contains ice cream, the activation of the schematic representation will be more extensive.

We are also uncertain about the decay of activation. After what period of time does the level of activation return to the baseline, in the absence of other activations? Certainly the decay takes place over hours rather than days or weeks, but whether it takes half an hour or ten hours is not certain at present. It is difficult to determine that value in part because we know very little about the degree of activation received at any one time and because we cannot be certain that some uncontrolled events in the intervening time period might not have reactivated the relevant schema or parts thereof.

Thus, while the degree of activation is certainly a continuum, one can for purposes of exposition make a distinction between mental structures that were activated during the immediate past (spanning at most a few hours) and other knowledge represented in mental structures. It is the former that represent the current state of the world. Another way of conceptualizing this process is to note that our ongoing experiences in the world—and our mental operations while we traverse that world—update the values of variables within both specific and general schemas. For instance, seeing one's family at breakfast reactivates the schemas that represent them (specific schemas), whereas a visit to a doctor's office updates specific instantiations of my generic schema (script) about such offices.

In any case, there will exist at any one point in time a set of schemas or representations that were recently activated and updated and that, being in some state of current activation above resting level, can be distinguished from other inactive mental contents. This subset defines the current state of the world. It has the specific characteristic of being available to conscious construction. As we shall see in the next chapter, consciousness requires one or more activated schemas for the construction of our current awareness. We can become instantly aware of any construction that addresses currently active schemas. No subconscious search processes are needed to determine where I am or what I am doing or approximately what time it is or what I am currently writing about—unless there are some temporary lapses of conscious efficiency because of alcohol consumption, for example. We arrive at a distinction among unconscious, preconscious, and conscious mental structures (see below), the state of the world being represented in the preconscious realm.

The state-of-the-world set of schemas and instantiated variables helps us not only to locate ourselves in time and space but also to define the expected state of the current situation. This becomes important with respect to discrepancy and interruption, which are central to the initation of emotional states. I not only know where I am and what I am doing but I also "know," without necessarily thinking (being conscious) of it at the moment, that it is not likely to snow on this July day, that there is no other person in this room with me. If I were to be confronted with a snowbank on leaving the building or with another person as I turned from my desk, I would certainly be surprised—that is, there would be rather distinct discrepancies between my current knowledge of the state of the world and the evidence presented to my mind. The preconscious state-of-the-world part of mental representations is, of course, being continuously updated. Sitting in the library, I may or may not update myself as to who is sitting at the table opposite me. If I do attend to that temporal-spatial region whenever somebody new arrives, then I will expect—as I look up—the evidence to be consistent with my most recent update. At the same time, information about those who departed remains available in a preconscious state. Upon seeing somebody later that day, I can be expected to note that I saw that person earlier in the library.

Activation of unconscious structures to the readily available preconscious state is overdetermined. Mental structures that become active usually gain activation from more than one source; both the external world and the mental activity as such have immediate ramifications for a large number of different mental structures. The most active ones, and the ones most likely to participate in conscious constructions, are multi- or overdetermined. This particular insight of Freud's is often ignored by psychologists who would prefer to deal with simple, linear causal chains. I should also note that the term *preconscious* as defined here is isomorphic with Freud's use of it—when, for example, he says that preconscious processes can enter into consciousness "without further impediment" and that unconscious contents have "no access to consciousness *except via the preconscious*."[43]

We carry with us a state-of-the-world activation that provides us with our currently active knowledge of the world, that is, of its meaning. However, at any one time, an analysis of the meaning of the current situation, of our current state, will depend on two general considerations: first, on the mental structure of the individual at the time, considering both the structure of the whole mental apparatus (conscious and otherwise) and the particular character of the mental structures that are currently in a state of activation; second, on the requirements, demands, and structure of the situation, context, problems, and tasks that are defined by our surround and by our mental activations prior to the event in question.

The more complex the mental structures, the more complex the meaning analysis, the "richer" the meaning, and the larger the number of implications a particular event will have for a variety of different past experiences. We may assume that the meaning analyses a rat performs between a black and a white cue will activate a relatively narrow range of relations, specifically the structures that have previously been established involving the relation of "black leading to food" and "white leading to no food." For human subjects a distinction between "black" and "white" may have similar implications (particularly if they have recently been subjects in a psychological experiment), but other relations involve

43. Freud ([1900] 1975).

the event "black" at various levels of the semantic hierarchy, and such an analysis may range from simple brightness discrimination to the symbolic meaning of black.

The assertion that all incoming evidence undergoes some meaning analysis may be true, but the degree of analysis can obviously differ. For example, if I were to ask somebody whether a cow is a domestic animal, the degree of analysis would be relatively poor as compared with a question that requires the individual to tell me everything he knows about cows. The second question will elicit all the information that the first one does, but not vice versa. The complexity of response and the degree of analysis will be affected by the question. In short, it is highly likely that the system has a stop rule that goes into effect whenever the requirements of the tasks are apparently fulfilled. For example, in the process of recognizing a particular object or event—that is, making the judgment that it has been experienced before—we are usually presented with some copy of the original event. It appears that the presentation of that event, a film we saw or a person we met before, initiates two processes. One is the judgment of sheer familiarity, that we saw or heard it before; the other is a search for retrieval routes in our mental representation, routes that might lead to the original representation and encoding of the event. Depending on the task involved, we might well stop if an adequate representation of its familiarity (its structural representation by itself) can be found, but if we are asked to determine not only that it was experienced before but also who or what it is and where it was previously encountered, the analysis proceeds until the retrieval and search processes have either succeeded or failed. Thus, a person's face may be very familiar, but we continue our mental activity until we determine who that person is.[44] Similarly, the degree of deliberate (that is, conscious and elaborative) activity with a particular event will depend on our interpretation of what might be required in the future. A telephone number needed to inquire what is playing at the local movie theater is barely held in consciousness until we have completed the call, whereas the number of an attractive new acquaintance may be elaboratively encoded in order to make later recall more likely. In psychological experimentation this degree of elaboration and subsequent recall can be manipulated by instructions.[45]

Stating the requirement of the task specifies what range of events is to be attended to as well as what subsequent analyses are required. In the process of inspecting a scene, a large number of representations of the features are activated. Instructions to search for certain objects will bring about increases in activation as top-down processes that are sensitive to the appearance of certain objects are brought into play. Scanning for a dandelion in the picture invokes dandelion schemas, which are then further activated when "dandelion evidence" is in fact in the picture. Meaning analysis and overt behavior are not necessarily correlated. It is not necessary to show some product in order to be able to say that a particular set of stimuli has been attended to. Low levels of meaning

44. Mandler (1981a).
45. Craik and Lockhart (1972) and Craik and Tulving (1975).

analysis go on continuously without any immediate reflection in action or experience.[46]

A structural view of "meaning" leaves us somewhat at a loss in trying to make any rigid distinction between connotative and denotative meaning or between sense and reference. It has generally been assumed that denotative or extensional meaning relates the perceptual world to the linguistic code, whereas connotative meaning is a more personal, frequently affective, or internal, intensional use of the term *meaning*. Denotative meaning is considered to be consensual, whereas connotative meaning is more individual and therefore more variable. The difficulty of making any strict distinction between connotation and denotation within a structural view should be obvious. While there will be structures that primarily relate perceptual events to language codes, there may also be structures that can be described without any reference to perceptual events. The "meaning" of a sentence or word will frequently involve the full range of structural relations of the concept addressed; there may be no "pure" denotations or connotations. If we accept the notion that many meaning relations involve imagery and the quasi-visual structures associated with it, then the "meaning" of *table* will involve not only its relation to superordinate schemas such as "furniture" and "useful objects" but also perceptual features involved in the imagery of tables. Although it is quite possible, of course, to restrict ourselves, particularly in the laboratory, to purely connotative judgments[47] by asking an individual how "good" or "bad" the "murderer" is, in daily functioning it is highly unlikely that these evaluative judgments are made in the absence of other analyses relating to perceptual, categorical, and other aspects of the word or sentence. I shall elaborate on the relation between description and evaluation in Chapter 9.

While I have referred to meaning analysis primarily in terms of the verbal mode and within language codes, I do not mean to imply that cognitive and linguistic structures are isomorphic. On the contrary, I believe—as do most psychologists today—that language-free cognitive structures precede language, particularly during the early years of life.[48] They continue to exist jointly in later years, often with rather complex relations. For purposes of communication, the verbal mode is a useful simplifying device, both for exposition and as the primary communicative device available to adults who wish to relate their experiences.

I use the term *meaning analysis* in the widest possible sense and prefer it to terms like *appraisal*.[49] Meaning analysis does not imply or invoke notions of goodness or badness.[50] Meanings can range over a wide variety of values and experiences; things may be awe inspiring, sexy, funny, or just unexpectedly novel. Meanings arise out of our continuing experience and interactions with our surrounds, and they need to be used and integrated in their own right. And, as we

46. The notion that attentional mechanisms involve continual analyses of the environment can also be found in theories of discrimination learning (e.g., Sutherland and Mackintosh 1971).
47. Osgood, Suci, and Tannenbaum (1957).
48. Bruner (1975).
49. Arnold (1970b), Bowlby (1969), and Lazarus, Averill, and Opton (1970).
50. Arnold (1960).

shall see in Chapter 9, evaluative meanings in particular play a special role in the construction of emotion, and meaning analyses are crucial in determining what particular emotion will be experienced in any specific situation.

Action Systems and Their Structures

Actions involve all the behaviors that act on the environment, social or not. Actions are activated by particular schemas and structures (action systems) within the mental organization, and they have consequences that, in turn, feed back into the system of organizations and structures and modify them. The output of these action systems has been of particular interest to psychologists of learning and motivation. The representation of structures that underlie these action systems is of immediate interest. These structures may be ordered according to, on the one hand, the degree to which they are developed as a result of evolutionary and genetic history and, on the other hand, the extent to which they have been built up as a result of interactions and transactions with the environment and its response to actions. The intent is not to imply a dichotomy between "innate" and "learned" structures but to indicate an awareness that many action systems depend, for both their initiation and their effectiveness, on the evolutionary history of the species. Thus, there are species-specific action systems,[51] situationally appropriate systems,[52] situation-specific adaptations,[53] and many other structures that demonstrate the intricate interaction between the preparedness of the organism for certain situations and environmental pressures and demands.[54]

We can assume that, whether a structure is preprogrammed or whether it is primarily influenced by the individual history of the organism, the functions of the central structure are essentially the same for well-developed behaviors. With extensive experience the structure that leads to the well-organized and highly integrated behavior known as "writing" is probably similar in its structure and functions to those that may be much less dependent on interactions with the environment, such as "walking" or "eating."

THE ORGANIZATION OF ACTION

The notion that even simple behaviors are not just chains of reflexes has occupied psychologists and biologists for some decades. In the following section, I borrow heavily from C. R. Gallistel,[55] who has presented the psychological-biological evidence for the pivotal idea that action sequences are centrally programmed (i.e., structured). Building on previous work,[56] Gallistel emphasizes the need to consider higher processes that manage the direction of behavior. The

51. Bolles (1970).
52. Staddon and Simmelhag (1971).
53. Rozin and Kalat (1971).
54. Bowlby (1969) has discussed some of the possible characteristics of these interactions in humans.
55. Gallistel (1974, 1980).
56. Tinbergen (1951), Von Holst (1939), and Weiss (1941).

hierarchy of actions and behaviors start with the "reflexes, endogenous oscillators, taxes, and other functional units of behavior." Nodes at succeeding higher levels control combinations of structures or coordinations represented at the next-lower level. This control is generated by appropriate inhibitory and disinhibitory signals. Organized actions controlled by a particular node have functional significance, but they do not necessarily, or even usually, involve the serial firing of the behavioral constituents. The nodal organization "uses" the appropriate lower constituents so that a particular reflex, for example, may precede another under one organization and follow it under another. The apexes of these hierarchical organizations of actions are equivalent to the psychologist's use of the term *motive.* Stimuli may be received at any level of the hierarchy, but those that activate the apex of a hierarchy are generally equivalent to motivational stimuli. Although Gallistel and others do not use the term *schema* in this context, their locutions can easily be understood in terms of schema theory.

There are two distinct issues in the organization of actions: the structure of action and the representation of action. The first addresses the structure of action as presented by Gallistel. Leaving aside for the moment the class of preprogrammed, "innate" structures, we note that in the course of its transactions with the environment the organism acquires new complex action structures. These are typically built out of existing units, at the lowest level of reflexes and taxes, but more generally out of any existing organized action units. The conditions under which these new action systems develop are, at least, complex and, to a large extent, unknown in their specifics. For example, (primary) reinforcers may function by inducing or generating the appearance of previously established systems under new "motivational" contexts. New sensory-motor structures may develop on the basis of cognitive maps and explorations of new environments.[57] The distinction seems forced, and the extensive literature on operant shaping suggests that new action systems may as readily be generated by "reinforcement" as by the information-seeking explorations of the organism. As we shall see shortly, "primary" reinforcement is often the occasion for the occurrence of highly organized responses, and the system that is being organized develops out of the extension of these existing "primary" systems. In any case, it may be assumed that the continuing exercise (execution) of an action system generates a more tightly organized and invariant structure. For example, a rat learning a maze or a human learning to drive from his office to his new home both eventually develop well-organized action systems that at first are constituted of individual and unrelated subsystems. In the course of development much hypothesis testing (or so-called trial-and-error behavior) occurs. Potential subsystems may be tested behaviorally or cognitively before a particular combination is found and used. As it is used consecutively, with less and less variation (error), it establishes its own general structure and organization. But how do we acquire the analogues of subsystems that can be cognitively or behaviorally tried out? This question brings us to the second issue in the organization of action. The distinction here is, for example,

57. Gallistel (1974).

between the action system that organizes my use of knives and forks in eating a steak and the fuzzy cognitive representation I have of those actions.

Once an action is executed, it becomes represented in a second sense in a cognitive structure.[58] In other words, actions, typically efferent motor systems, are represented in two distinct ways: first, in the underlying representation of the action structure itself, the action system just discussed; second, in the representation of our perceptual (primarily visual and kinesthetic) registration of that action. For the sake of brevity, we might call the former *action structures* and the latter *cognitive structures*. Action systems themselves are primarily automatic and not even subject to conscious representation in many cases. Thus, we know how to walk and talk, eat and speak, laugh and love. The knowledge for the execution of the hierarchies of actions involved in these acts is represented in the action system. We have no direct insight into the sequence of muscle movements and limb and body coordinations that are involved in these complex acts.[59] Nonetheless, we can, in a more general sense, talk about these actions. Our ability to do so depends on schemas that arise out of the execution of the actions themselves. There are, at present, no well-defined, definite relations between the action structures and their secondary schematic representation. Not only can the latter initiate action structures (as in my decision to type this sentence) but they can also be used to interface with and modify existing action systems, as every novice tennis player and coach knows.

The importance of the distinction between the two kinds of action structures for the topic of emotional experience will become obvious in later chapters. I do want to note here that our secondary representations of actions make possible evaluative cognitions about our own actions. Whether the action is aggressive or helping, our schema about that action will determine how we evaluate it and will in turn become important in the construction of emotional experiences that accompany it.

Many of our cognitive structures represent this secondary internalization of action. Although much of this representation seems to be in the form of images (tactual and visual), there is no need to restrict the formal character of these structures to one modality or another. We have demonstrated the development of the representation of complex response patterns.[60] During early stages of training, people could not reproduce the pattern in the absence of external stimulus support; after moderate training, however, they reported tactual imagery, and after extended overtraining they reported visual imagery of the overt pattern. So-called analogic structures of actions follow the elimination of errors. After the action systems that generate the structures have stabilized and performance is essentially asymptotic, the representation of the action will be essentially identical from occurrence to occurrence, and stable schemas will develop.[61]

58. Piaget (1953) and Piaget and Inhelder (1969).
59. For an example of how one might approach these problems, see Gentner, Grudin, Larochelle, Norman, and Rumelhart (1982).
60. Mandler and Kuhlman (1961).
61. Mandler (1962a).

Once such a structure of action has been developed, these cognitive structures can be used for the elaborate choice and decision processes prior to output. What is manipulated is the secondary representation of action and not the action structures directly. As a matter of fact, much cognitive activity is involved in the constructions of new action systems. During that phase, various separate action units are inspected and tested before they are incorporated into the new action system. Thus, the construction of new systems is characterized by consciousness (e.g., when we consider various alternatives in learning a new skill). Once it has been established, the action runs off without cognitive intervention (i.e., by the activation of the appropriate action system). These new integrated actions will, in turn, become represented as secondary schemas.

What is the relation between existing actions systems and the secondary schemas that represent them? In the first instance, I assume that the mental organization always establishes a relation between any two or more structures that are active at a given time. For example, a relation will exist between old memories of past meetings that are retrieved when one sees an old friend and the perceptual structure that is operative in constructing the physical conditions of the current meeting with that friend. Given that assumption, a relation will necessarily exist between an action system and its secondary representation, since the action system is by definition active when the representational structure is being established. Furthermore, that relation is unique in that only a particular action system and its cognitive structure have this relation, which might be called a pseudo-isomorphism. Clearly, the two structures are not isomorphic—typically, the cognitive structure will be a degraded, abbreviated version of the action system itself. While verbal labels offer only a poor approximation, they do convey the flavor of this abbreviated isomorphism. Consider the relation between "driving home," "making love," "preparing beef Wellington," "writing my name," and the appropriate action systems. What remains obscure is the mechanism whereby the system goes from a cognitive consideration of a possible action system to its execution. Despite the lack of isomorphic structures, a single action system may occur after only some partial activation of its cognitive representation or even in response to just a summary label (e.g., "Draw a dog" or "Tie your shoelaces"). To say that such a sequence involves the relation between an action structure and a (secondary) cognitive structure is only to restate the hoary problem about the relation between thought and action. It still needs to be spelled out how changes in one of them affect changes in the other. Clearly, we do learn about changing our action systems via the cognitive structures—for example, when we are instructed to execute a tennis serve as if we were swatting a fly, or a gymnastic exercise by imagining that our feet are cemented to the floor.

The relation between action structures and their secondary representation in cognitive ones finds its parallel in the mental models that we construct about our environment, its technology, artifacts, and science.[62] These mental models have a function similar to the mental models we construct about ourselves; their "major

62. Gentner and Stevens (1982).

purpose . . . is to enable [us] to predict the operation of the target system."[63] As our cognitive schemas are adjusted and changed, we become better able to understand how our body works and why and how we do the things we do.

Another parallel exists between action schemas and their secondary representation, on the one hand, and the distinction between procedural and declarative knowledge alluded to earlier, on the other. Actions are procedures, practically by definition, and procedural knowledge, just like an action system, is frequently not accessible to conscious knowledge, for it cannot—in contrast to declarative knowledge—be spoken. Secondary schemas, as discussed here, have the advantage of providing declarative access to procedural knowledge. I can speak and think about the fact that I know how to tie my shoelaces, double-clutch my car, or prepare an excellent omelet without having access to the detailed procedures involved.

ORGANIZED ACTION SEQUENCES

I wish to stress my rejection of the emphasis on energies and drives, which was so popular in the first half of the century. I share with others the hope that a psychology without an economical substratum or energy concept might be possible and should be attempted. Motives can be defined as nonenergetic; "motivation is an internally patterned *signal*" that facilitates or inhibits the activity of lower behavioral units.[64]

In addition to rejecting an energy model, I also believe that despite their universal utility, concepts such as expectancies are sometimes overused. An expectancy may often be a construction that the human animal puts on his behavior but that can be explained without such concepts.[65] This does not lead to a psychology without ends or goals, but the attempt is to talk about some of these "goals" without a necessary appeal to *conscious* expectations. Similarly, variations in the intensity of behavior do not require energy concepts; we may talk instead about distributions of responses with different characteristics.

The development of new behavioral structures proceeds largely by response integration, the process whereby new response units are built out of previously discrete units.

The single most important feature of an organized sequence is its unitary nature. It is elicited or emitted as a whole, as a single unit: it is not simply a chain of responses. Consider an example: single letters or phonemes of a language are single units, but so are well-practiced words in that language. The letter *c* is just as unitary as the word *cat*, and there is good evidence that they function as equivalent units.[66] To stay in the context of language, well-practiced phrases are also unitary (e.g., "How do you do" or "I love you"). Similarly, starting a car, unlocking a familiar door, and drinking out of a glass are single

63. Norman (1982).
64. Gallistel (1974).
65. Cf. Skinner (1957).
66. Murdock (1961).

behavioral units. Now, it is obvious that such units may be built into imposing proportions, such as driving home from the office. At the same time, some organized sequences are not rigid with respect to the units composing them; the organism may have some element of choice at various times. Obvious examples that come to mind are taking a walk around the block or giving a prepared lecture.

In the discussion to follow, I shall address rather hoary issues in the psychology of action. They center on the organization of behavior and the use of such organized action systems.

The concept of goals has received increasing attention in cognitive psychology, in part because cognate activities by the artificial-intelligence community have found it to be useful.[67] However, we need to distinguish among action structures and cognitive structures and representations, which subsume both of these. It is the latter kind of schema that often contains goal concepts. The notion that one wishes to reach a particular subjective state or to create some specific constellation of the environment is frequently derived from a schema, a plan, at a high level of abstraction. These goals certainly are psychologically real; the question is whether they are necessarily causal in the initiation of a particular behavioral sequence.

I shall concentrate on those cases in which an explanation alternative to "goals" might be useful, and even correct. This does not preempt those cases in which goals in fact determine ensuing actions and thoughts. Much of human problem solving is goal determined and goal driven. If I am visiting friends at some other university and wish to have a cup of coffee, I need to explore possible paths that might lead to the fulfillment of that wish. Once I have decided on an appropriate path, the initiation will depend as much on current local conditions as on the goal that generated my plans for future action. Goals are thus important cognitive precursors of action, but frequently they cannot be said to "drive" the actions themselves. Actions have expected outcomes that might be seen as subgoals, but they are not necessarily determined by them, in the sense of a direct causal link.

Psychologists, in general, have not bothered too much with the definition of action, and some influential theorists have taken it for granted that we know intuitively what the response units, innate or acquired, may be. Others, like Skinner, have demonstrated a curious ambiguity in first talking at length about the acquisition of a topographically unique response but then, once it is acquired, defining it solely in terms of its consequences.

Among the several variables that might determine organization, there is one convincing antecedent condition for the development of organized sequences. It is the frequency of the use of a sequence, with organization or integration developing gradually.[68]

I do not consider an organized response a chain of constituent units with goal gradients, anticipatory goal responses, or expectancies within it busily driv-

67. Wilensky (1982).
68. Mandler (1962a).

ing the organism toward a goal. On the contrary, once started, any organized response has the same inevitability of completion that we readily accept in short, organized responses like swallowing, lever pressing, kicking, or speaking a word. They are acquired in much the same way. There is no qualitative difference between learning how to write and learning how to strike a single typewriter key. There are, though, very potent organized sequences in an organism's repertory that are not acquired in this sense at all. These are preoprogrammed organizations and unlearned actions, such as sucking, and the consummatory facets of eating, drinking, copulation, and so forth.

Within the performance of an organized pattern there will, of course, be minor variations from occasion to occasion. The important point is that the band of variability around an organized sequence will be not only fairly stable but also much narrower than that around an as yet unorganized one. Similarly, there may also be quantitative differences, especially among sequences that differ in length, in the sense that longer ones are more apt to be interrupted and may be less well organized (i.e., their band of variability may be wider).

I want to emphasize that the organization or integration of an action occurs after it has been "learned" in the traditional sense of the term (i.e., after errorless performance has been attained). The organization of the units that make up the new sequence—and that are themselves previously organized responses—cannot take place when errors still interfere with smooth performance.

GOALS

In saying that these organized actions are not simply a bundle of means leading to an end, I am stressing that in the world of integrated responses there are no pure goals, no goals without means. There is often no need for invoking end states that are desired or anticipated; we may need only to specify behavior sequences that are performed. There are no differential goals and paths to them, only goal paths functioning as units. And what may be intended or anticipated are the organized sequences, not the pure goals.

Contrary to the intuitive and phenomenological view that all acts are goal directed, that expectancies and goal anticipations are involved in the performance of an approach, we could argue equally intuitively that the phenomenal goal is never the pure consummatory act but always involves at least a small part of a complete goal path.[69] It can hardly be argued that the phenomenal goal of going to a restaurant is the consummatory act of swallowing or digestive activity, or that the goal of riches is the folding of money into a billfold. What is envisaged as the goal always involves much more complex acts than that, sequences in which the "goal" represents only a minor part. But it is these apparent goals that are the goal paths, the organizations and plans that do—in contrast to the "goals"—play important cognitive roles.

John Bowlby[70] has discussed the difficulties inherent in the concept of "goal"

69. Simon (1967).
70. Bowlby (1969).

and has suggested that for behavioral systems like the ones I have discussed here, other terms might be more appropriate. For example, he compares two kinds of such systems that have predictable outcomes; we might talk about a "goal" for one, but not for the other. Thus, a system that through continuous feedback adjusts itself to environmental input—for example, a ball player running to catch a ball—may be said to have a "goal," whereas another system in which a particular organized set of responses runs off smoothly (e.g., eating a meal) may not be said to have a goal. It is interesting to note in the last example that the "goal" of eating cannot possibly be just one of its constituents, such as restoring the blood-sugar level, which is not discriminable as part of the action system, or finishing the meal, which is not always done, or any other number of other possibilities. This difference is also related to the distinction between the cause and the function of a particular set of behaviors, a distinction that I will discuss below.

Bowlby prefers to use the term *set-goal,* by which he means "either a time-limited event or an ongoing condition either of which is brought about by the action of behavioral systems that are structured to take account of discrepancies between instruction and performance. . . . A set goal is *not* an object in the environment but is either a specified motor performance, e.g. singing a song, or the achievement of a specified relation, of short or long duration, between the animal and some object in or component of the environment."[71]

I believe that a withdrawal from an indiscriminate use of the concept of "goal" is most appropriate. We will still use it in some contexts, such as the notion of goal correction. When an organism uses many different sequences to achieve some particular outcome, we might talk about that outcome as correcting the sequences that are used in order to complete the overall plan. One can then talk about the execution of a higher-order plan and its latter stages. A term like *plan-directed* correction might be appropriate. This is in keeping with the use of the plan as the overall structure that serves as the umbrella or executive organizer of a hierarchy of subsystems or schemas.[72]

TELEOLOGY

The mental system and its products and actions act on the environment in order to create conditions that are adaptive, pleasurable, or generally sought by the organism. In this connection a discussion[73] of the function of instinctive behavior is illuminating and instructive with respect to this apparently teleological sequence. Bowlby summarizes the general notion of *function* and its distinction from that of *causation* and concludes that "functions are the special consequences that arise from the way a system is constructed; causes are the factors that lead the system to become active or inactive on any one occasion." He goes on to note that for the individual organism, instinctive behavior is inde-

71. Bowlby (1969).
72. Miller, Galanter, and Pribram (1960).
73. Bowlby (1969).

pendent of function, while for a population of individuals the functions of a particular system must be fulfilled at least some of the time. Thus, though a particular system will have a predictable outcome for *individuals*, its adaptive function is a property of that system for the *population*, not for the individual.

Since we are here concerned primarily with acquired instead of preprogrammed or instinctive systems, the notion of adaptive function has to be interpreted in a wider and somewhat different sense. However, Bowlby's distinctions may be used to indicate that events like goals, outcomes, and consequences occur as a result of the way a system is constructed, while the factors that lead a system to become active are conceptually different and may be considered to be the causal factors. As a matter of fact, Bowlby's distinction between individual and population aspects of instinctual systems can be generalized to acquired systems in looking at their specific occurrence and their general function. Thus, for a specific, unique action, the activation of the underlying structure is independent of its consequences or goals; it is "caused" by the initiating conditions. On the other hand, for a "population" of actions, these goals and consequences must be fulfilled at least part of the time.

Thus, just as instinctive behavior is maintained for the population, so the structure for a particular sequence of behavior is maintained for the individual, but the individual act is independent of its consequence for the organism and only dependent on the conditions that are necessary for its initiation. Getting into one's car and driving home from work form a single instance of a structure that is maintained because it has the "function" of spanning the distance between work and home. However, the organized behavior at any one time may be independent of the function but initiated by such factors as that it is five o'clock. The concept that consequences maintain a system is, of course, similar to the notion of reinforcement in Skinner's system, although in a less restricted sense. Generally, it is a set of consequences that establishes the behavior, but it is the controlling event that initiates the specific action.

Just as teleological discussions in the literature of biological systems have often mistaken the population characteristics of particular behavior for characteristics in the single individual, so the function of a particular structure in an individual leads us to make teleological comments about a specific act. The acting individual may, on the initiation of the particular organized behavior, comment on that behavior as if the characteristics displayed were the characteristics of the population of acts instead of the unique action about to be performed. Since consciousness may have access to the structure of a particular act, output from the system may be of the form "I am engaging in this act in order to reach a particular goal." In contrast we would say that though the function of the structure is, when completed, to have certain adaptive consequences, the only thing that can be said about the individual expression of that structure (the present and immediate action) is that it has been initiated and has certain predictable behavioral outcomes, but consequences that are probabilistic and *not* strictly predictable. Here again, we are faced with the difficulty of making theoretical statements on the basis of the commentary that consciousness and language systems provide about ongoing behavior and the selection of structures. The teleological expression of a goal—for example, "I'm going to leave now to go home and have dinner"—is a commentary on the general secondary structure but not, in any case, a "motivating" condition for the initiation of a particular set of behaviors. Presumably, certain internal and external conditions (including blood-sugar level and the sight of a clock) start a specific set of organized actions; the "goal" is often phenomenally perceived in terms of the class of behaviors of which this is an instance. In Bowlby's terms, the behavioral system is constructed in such a way that it has the consequence of leading one home and to food; the system is activated by factors that are present at this particular occasion. The gloss provided by introspection is interesting but not causally relevant. Finally, the phenomenal experience of "goals" may be related to the general operation of stop rules, including Bowlby's set-goals. Since most, if not all, organized action systems include a stop rule, the registration of such a rule may, in the common language and in phenomenal experience, be identified as the goal of the action. Stop rules terminate actions, as do "goals." But neither motivates or "causes" the initiation or performance of the act.

In this chapter, I have ranged over a number of issues in the interests of defining the vast apparatus called the human mind and of specifying some of the structures and processes that operate within the mental sphere. At various points, I have made reference to the relation between mental structures and conscious experience. Since it is in conscious experience that these mental processes have some of their most important effects, in particular with relation to the experience of emotion, the next chapter deals in detail with the problem of human consciousness.

4

THE CONSTRUCTION OF CONSCIOUSNESS

THE CONCEPT OF CONSCIOUSNESS was abandoned as a proper object of experimental study about seventy years ago for a variety of reasons. The introspective method erred in assuming that consciousness could be made the datum of psychology or that a verbal report was a royal road to its exploration. The failure of introspection engendered behaviorism and failed to provide any viable alternatives. Others, like the Gestalt school and the French and English enclaves, successfully defended their views of the conscious organism but had, for theoretical reasons, little basis for mounting a major analytic attack. The return of American psychology to a theory-rich as well as experimentally rigorous stance has given us the opportunity to develop the appropriate theoretical tools to return consciousness to its proper place in a theory of thought, mind, and actions.

Apart from its phenomenal insistence, consciousness ties together many disparate but obviously related mental concepts, including attention, perceptual elaboration, and limited-capacity notions.

William James stressed the selective functions of consciousness, and selection also became a theme of the postbehaviorist investigation of consciousness. G. A. Miller, one of the prophets of the new mentalism, reemphasized that only some part of all possible experience is available to consciousness at any one point in time and space. He made the further point that "the selective function of consciousness and the limited span of attention are complementary ways of talking about the same thing," an insight still receiving some opposition. Finally, he reminded us that it "is the *result* of thinking, not the process of thinking, that appears spontaneously in consciousness."[1]

Consciousness has meant many things to different people—an epiphenomenon, an inference, introspective awareness, focal attention, and so on. Hence, the present view and the relevant evidence form only part of the topic covered by consciousness writ large, and other interpretations, meanings, and functions still need to be explored.[2]

1. Miller (1962). See also Lashley (1923).
2. Natsoulas (1970, 1977).

In his influential *Cognitive Psychology*, Ulric Neisser[3] is circumspect in dealing with the problem of consciousness. Not that Neisser avoids the subject; he clearly talks about consciousness, although in circuitous ways. In the final chapter he comes to consciousness through the attentive processes in visual perception and memory. He notes that the constructive processes in memory "themselves never appear in consciousness, their products do." And, in rational problem solving, the executive processes "share many of the properties of focal attention in vision and of analysis-by-synthesis in hearing." Noting the distinction between primary and secondary processes,[4] he asserts that rational, conscious thought operates as a secondary process—elaborating often unconscious, probably unlearned primary-process operations in the Freudian sense. The products of the primary process alone, preceding consciousness and attention, are only "fleetingly" conscious unless elaborated by secondary processes. By implication the elaboration by secondary processes is what produces fully conscious events.

Neisser uses the term *focal attention.*[5] "Attention . . . is an allotment of analyzing mechanisms to a limited region of the field." On the other hand, preattentive processes (i.e., processes that are not in attention but that precede it) form the objects of attention. Some of these preattentive processes are innate. Many actions, such as walking and driving are "made without the use of focal attention." Some processes run off outside of consciousness (unconsciously); others do not. "More permanent storage of information requires an act of attention." Transfer to permanent storage requires consciousness, as some decisional processes apparently also do.

In summary, Neisser's interpretation is consistent with much of the modern speculations about consciousness. It is a limited-capacity mechanism, often synonymous with the notion of attentional mechanisms. Conscious processes are secondary in elaboration and time to primary, preattentive processes that are unconscious, sometimes innate, and often the result of automatization. Consciousness permits decision processes of some types to operate; it makes it possible for the products of different systems to be integrated and for permanent storage to take place.[6]

The limited evidence from experimental studies confirms the operation of extensive preconscious processing that is, under some circumstances, followed by conscious states. Much of human information processing, however, is automatic and does not require attention. Such processes are typically called habitual, automatic, or preprogrammed.

I have already discussed the distinction between automatic and nonautomatic processes in Chapter 3. *Deliberate*, *selective*, and *voluntary* are the adjec-

3. Neisser (1967).
4. Cf. also Garner (1974).
5. See Schachtel (1959).
6. Among the important contributors to the ongoing discussions about consciousness have been Posner and his associates (Posner and Keele 1970; Posner and Boies 1971; Posner and Snyder 1975; Posner and Klein 1973), who have argued that the limited-capacity mechanism is related to the unity of consciousness and that attention is related to conscious mental operations. Shallice (1972) assigned consciousness to the identification of the dominant action system and its goals.

tives frequently used to describe nonautomatic processes. Another way to approach the distinction is to ask which processes and mechanisms require conscious participation—that is, to pose questions about the functions of consciousness. One can then decide, in a principled way, which processes are automatic and run off without conscious representation and which require some conscious capacity. The latter are in common parlance called voluntary, selective, and deliberate.

In the arena of perceptual events the topic of automatic processing confronts us repeatedly as the converse of conscious processing. Generally, what is automatic is very much like what Neisser calls preattentive, parallel processes. In contrast, conscious processes are more variable, and constructions in consciousness provide the elaborative devices needed to store material in long-term representations. It is here that we face the conclusion that new encodings for long-term storage depend on a functioning conscious system.

David LaBerge[7] has addressed the issue of automatization in a novel way—asking not only about the relation between automatization and attention but also about the process whereby certain coding systems become automatized. He concludes that during postcriterial performance a gradual withdrawal of attention from the components of a task occurs. Under this process of decreasing attention (consciousness?), the part of the processing involved in coding the perceptual material is being made automatic. Eventually, much of the perceptual processing can "be carried out automatically, that is prior to the focussing of attention on the processing." This postcriterial, overlearning process produces the integration of new, higher-order units or chunks, and "one cannot prevent the processing once it starts."[8]

The fact that well-practiced, invariant behavioral units eventually run off automatically and without conscious intervention is well known to psychologists and pianists, athletes and typists. The notion is abroad that there exist essentially two kinds of unconscious structures: those that are innate and part of the organism's initial armamentarium and those that develop out of interactions with the environment into well-bounded units of action and thought and eventually also run off without conscious initiation or maintenance. At present it is difficult to describe the boundary between the two. Some action systems are clearly unlearned (e.g., swallowing), whereas some are clearly acquired (e.g., typing). At the perceptual level the distinction becomes more difficult and is certainly beyond my present scope. But there are some borderline cases, for example, in linguistics, where some argue for a prewired structure while others see the intervention of organism-environment interactions in the development of unconscious representations. If an activity competes for the limited capacity of consciousness, it is assumed to be nonautomatic. If it is automatic, it should not compete with the allocation of capacity. In the context of syntax acquisition, it has been argued that syntactic rules that operate without access to consciousness in the adult do in fact require limited-capacity resources at the time of acquisition. The acquisition of specific syntactic forms competes with other aspects of sentence produc-

7. Posner and Warren (1972).
8. LaBerge (1974).

tion that are also in the process of formation. Only when the new forms become automatized do they cease such competition for limited capacity and, at the same time, become "unconscious."[9]

In summary, current thought has concentrated on consciousness and the perceptual and encoding aspects of information flow. Some attention has been given to its functions in memory storage and retrieval. Current notions have focused on the functions of consciousness in selecting encoded sensory information and preparing choices among appropriate actions or responses.

Conscious Contents and Processes

In common usage one frequently talks about consciousness as a space, a place, or even a homunculus. I do not want to imply any of these, but I will often use common expressions that may convey the wrong impression. Thus does the common language make liars of us all. What I do want to say, as a preliminary approach to an understanding of consciousness, is that consciousness is a mode of processing. Given that conscious mode, the "contents" of consciousness are mental products that are in the conscious state. Consciousness is limited in capacity because of the limitations on the conscious-processing mode. But consciousness is not a special place or space or area of the mind.

My own interest in consciousness arose partly from some considerations of the limits of attention and consciousness.[10] I argued for a direct translation between focal attention and consciousness. I suggested that some of the so-called short-term-memory phenomena are best assigned to the limited-capacity mechanism of consciousness and that the limitations, in terms of dimensional analyses, may serve to illuminate the puzzling aspects of the similar limitations for short-term memory and absolute judgment.[11]

The limited capacity of "short-term" memory, the immediate-memory span, and the limitation in absolute judgment tasks to some seven values or categories can be ascribed usefully to the limited capacity of conscious content. The limitation refers to the limited number of values on any single dimension (be it physical, acoustic, semantic, or whatever) that can be kept in the conscious state.

The main points of the argument relevant to the present topic concern certain distinctions among the concepts of attention, consciousness, and short-term memory. In the first instance, I want to restrict the concept of consciousness to events and operations within a limited-capacity state, the limitation referring to the number of functional units or chunks that can be kept in the conscious state at any one time. Attentional processes are the mechanisms that deal with the selection of objects or events that occur in the conscious state. Second, I want to assert a distinction between short-term memory and consciousness. The insight that consciousness has a limited reach has a respectable history, going back at

9. Knapp (1979).
10. Mandler (1975a).
11. Miller (1956).

least 200 years.[12] But it is not a memory system—it does not involve any retrieval. What is in the momentary field of consciousness is not remembered; it does not have to be recalled. Other short-term memory phenomena that do not involve immediate consciousness can remain under the rubric of a *memory* concept.

None of the foregoing denies the utility of the conception of different memory systems, whether long-term, working, or operational. Different types of analyses require different processing strategies and processing times. But the information that can, so to speak, be "read off" the contents of consciousness is not memorial as such. Variations in processing determine how we remember and what we can remember. If processing time is short or encoding "superficial," and if the code decays rapidly, it will be "shallow"; if processing is extended or if encoding is "complex," information adequate for long-term retrieval or reconstruction will be stored. Within certain limits, the storage processes—at whatever depths—can work only on conscious material; conversely, retrieval implies retrieval into the conscious field. But the memory *mechanisms* and the process that generates consciousness are two very distinct kinds of mental events.[13] The confounding of these two systems in early investigations and theories is understandable, given the very brief duration of some memory processes and the rapid changes in the focus of consciousness (attention).

Structures, or schemas, combine to construct a conscious state. Limited capacity refers to the number of such unitary structures that may be conscious at any one time. Conditions of personal and social development determine what can and what cannot be represented in consciousness. Depending on these conditions, different individuals, groups, and cultures will have different conscious contents—different social and cultural consciousness, different realities.

Finally, conscious contents can be spoken about. I shall discuss later the lack of any one-to-one correspondence between consciousness and language, but this should not obscure the important relation between private conscious events and language. It is by the use of the latter that we primarily communicate our own private view of reality; it is, in turn, by the use of language that—in the adult, at least—many conscious structures are manipulated and changed.

A *Constructivist View of Consciousness*

The history of consciousness is strewn with philosophical, theological, and pedestrian semantic debris; the history of unconscious concepts has, by inherited contrast, suffered similarly. Having made the decision to recall the concept of consciousness to service, I find it useful to start baldly with the distinction between conscious and unconscious processes. In particular, I want to distinguish among three kinds of mental contents: conscious ones, activated but not conscious structures, and unconscious structures not available to conscious construction. This partition maps directly onto my previous discussion of schemas and the state of

12. See Mandler (1975a).
13. Posner (1967).

the world system. Generally speaking, schemas and other structures are quiescent until activated by environmental evidence or by access from other mental structures. The set of activated schemas and structures—remaining in a state of activation for some time after the initial input is received—is available for the formation or construction of conscious structures. Unactivated structures are not available to consciousness. This partition is the same as Freud's distinction among the unconscious, preconscious, and conscious. I shall use the term *preconscious* with the understanding that it refers to all currently active schemas and structures.

My current view of consciousness is derived from two arguments recently advanced by Anthony Marcel.[14] The first—the rejection of the *identity assumption*—directly engenders the second—the *constructive view of consciousness*.

The identity assumption has dominated our view of consciousness throughout the history of psychology. It states that the shift from the preconscious to the conscious state maintains the identity of the structure. The shift is said to be due to an increase in the strength of a structure, or it is accomplished when a preconscious event is selected for consciousness, or it occurs when a structure is pushed or pulled into consciousness or illuminated by consciousness.[15] Another view, closer to a constructivist position, states that only the results of mental processes are conscious.[16] However, this view often seems to hold that conscious contents are the unchanged results of preconscious activities that still mirror the structure of the preconscious.

Freud's use of the unconscious is also marked by the identity assumption. Preconscious contents "become" conscious, impulses "force their way through to consciousness," and consciousness is a sense organ that "perceives psychical qualities." There is a hint that conscious contents may be different from unconscious and preconscious contents, when Freud suggests, without elaboration, that "memory and the quality that characterizes consciousness are mutually exclusive."[17]

Another forerunner of Marcel's interpretation noted that in consciousness "information about multiple individual modalities of sensation and perception is combined into a unified multidimensional representation," that is, that "consciousness itself is a representational system."[18]

By rejecting such an assumption of identity between preconscious and con-

14. Marcel (1983a, 1983b). I have adopted Marcel's position primarily with respect to these two innovations. Beyond the rejection of the identity assumption and the adoption of a constructivist view, I have also been persuaded by his argument that schema activation and conscious construction proceed in opposite directions, the former from the concrete to the abstract, the latter from the abstract to the particular. I have not adopted Marcel's terminology and take responsibility for the discussion of the source of the structures that make up conscious experience, a topic that Marcel has left open. Other arguments—for example, for the cases in which consciousness does reflect single schemas and the speculations on dreaming—should also not be identified with his exposition.

15. E.g., Dixon (1971), Freud ([1900] 1975), Norman and Shallice (1980), Posner and Snyder (1975), and Shallice (1972).

16. E.g., Lashley (1923), Mandler (1975b), and Miller (1962).

17. Freud ([1900] 1975).

18. John, in Thatcher and John (1977).

scious events, we are *nolens volens* pushed to a constructivist position—that is, to the view that between the preconscious automatic activiations and the conscious contents another transformation must take place. We thus assert that consciousness is a construction of phenomenal experience out of one or more of the available preconscious events, schemas, and structures. I shall argue that the active mechanism in such construction is the most general or abstract schema relevant to the current motives and goals of the individual. This abstract representation seeks the relevant evidence in the preconscious state and constructs the conscious state. Conscious constructions are our usual views of the world; they contain our expectation of the stable world that is represented in abstract schemas. It is the failure of such an abstract schema to find relevant evidence that often leads to discrepancy and interruption when we cannot make sense of the world around us.

In summary, the identity assumption implies that what we are conscious of is some picture of external or internal reality, seen as a direct representation in consciousness of external events or of some activated preconscious structure. The constructivist position, in contrast, denies any such "pass through" from the world to consciousness; rather, it insists that consciousness uses some higher-order structure that incorporates but does not necessarily mirror the original events. This position is coextensive with the consensus that memory, perception, and conception are all constructive, but it makes the more pervasive point that consciousness in general is constructive.[19]

THE CONSTRUCTION OF CONSCIOUSNESS

Up to now I have talked about the contents of consciousness without indicating how these contents are formed, except to say that they are not as a rule merely currently dominant preconscious structures in a different state. I now turn to the construction of conscious contents.

We start with the schemas and structures and their activation as outlined in Chapter 3. With any evidence given by the environment, or generated intrapsychically, the hierarchy of possible structures receives activation and also facilitation from other activated structures and features. Beyond the concrete and specific schemas that are activated, generic and abstract schemas that function as hypotheses about the pattern of external events are activated, as are appropriate co-occuring action structures. The important structures in the process of constructing conscious contents are those that are fully active—namely, schemas that have received sufficient activation from evidence and/or from other activated schemas and features to be available as bounded units.

In the normal course of events, any set of (sensory) evidence will activate more than one (generic) hypothesis or schema. A conscious content is constructed by the selection of a particular abstract, generic schema (hypothesis) that can assimilate the evidence. Obviously, even a partially activated generic schema

19. Bartlett (1932), Hochberg (1981), and J. M. Mandler (1983).

will not contribute to conscious contents unless it accounts for a substantial part of the available evidence. The white color of the building that is outside my window may activate some of the features of my schema for a bridal gown, but the latter is an unlikely candidate for the construction of my consciousness of the external world. The selection of the appropriate hypothesis will depend not only on the evidence available but also on previous activation (e.g., I am inside a building and not in an open field). It will depend above all on the activation of generic schemas that reflect the demands of the immediate situation, defined by appropriate actions, by instructions and conversations, and by search processes. Just "looking for something" activates relevant higher-order structures.

Conscious construction is a "late stage" in processing. A mass of activations is available when the constructions take place and only the relevant ones are selected, relevance being determined by previous activations and current demands.

What kinds of conscious contents are constructed? One can reasonably claim that "phenomenal experience is an attempt to make sense of as much data as possible at the highest and most functional useful level possible."[20] But clearly what makes sense in one situation may not in another, and what is functionally useful may not be very abstract. The system is not left to follow its whims but is determined by its history, context, and situation. It is the current content in particular that determines what level of generality is required and which specific structure will be called into play to construct the phenomenal experience. The constructed representation of a main dinner course will be different at a fast-food restaurant from that at a three-star restaurant. Different structures are required for these different evaluations. This last level of mental construction into consciousness is represented by intentionality, which is described by the motives (high-order schemas), instructions, and contexts that dominate the here and now. The color of my steak will be schematically registered at the gourmet restaurant and at the dinner, but the construction will use this information in the world-renowned restaurant; it will not be relevant at the diner (or at least has been found to be useless there).

The abstract or general structures that represent the final step into conscious construction are, of course, not outside the mental system; they are part of it. Do they differ at all, then, from other higher-order structures that are part of schematic representation, such as scenes and categories? At this point I can only suggest some possible theoretical notions.

In the first instance, structures that represent situational demands and intentions are activated primarily "top down"; they depend on prior evaluations and activations of situational identifications and interpretations, of current needs and goals. They do not, therefore, receive activation from the physical evidence of our surrounds directly. But it is not at all certain that these structures do not receive some activation as activation spreads through the system. If they do, and if they are active for the same reason that other structures have become active, then the identity assumption requires some modification. Consciousness will

20. Marcel (1983b).

have to be said to be the conscious equivalent of these high-order structures that tell us where we are, what we are doing, and what we want to do.

For the time being I can only suggest that the structures that participate in the actual construction of consciousness are different from those lower down in the hierarchy. Their special role is the selection of relevant knowledge in order to satisfy situational and intentional demands—or, in another locution, motivational requirements. I would prefer to think of them as separate from the schemas discussed up to now. To be sure, they too are children of our lives and experience, but their role is more selective and directive. And, as we shall see shortly, they become active in a flow from the most general to most specific, which is quite different from—in fact, opposite to—that usually assigned to schema activation. We are aware of the most general sense of our surrounds and activities unless contextual and task demands require a more detailed or specific construction.

The difference between these directive and other structures is obvious when we perceive the Gestalt quality of an object or its components; but the constructed representation of the whole is in fact different from the sum of its parts. The two cannot coexist; we construct one or the other conscious representation and, given some additional guidance, we can make the system switch from one to another such representation.[21] Perception, like all other conscious phenomena, is constructive.[22]

If we are just "sense making" in a most general mode, as we gaze out the window, walk along the street, or eat a meal, then the most abstract construction will be imposed on the available evidence. It is often in this mode that the unexpected event disturbs the dominant schemas and requires troubleshooting, that is, the conscious construction that takes the discrepant event into account. The attentional phenomena that select information either early or late[23] in the processing sequence will enter into the picture and make available both activated (preconscious) structures and higher-order structures that will now construct the best current sense of the world. And the new construction will usually move from the abstract to the concrete, from a sense of significance to a sense of detail, in order to make maximal sense of the world.

For example, we may be walking along a street admiring the gardens on either side when a fire truck appears and we are instantly aware of it. In contrast, expected events, such as passenger cars driving by, may not be noticed at all in the sense that they enter the current conscious construction that is preoccupied with roses and camellias. Activations not entering into a conscious construction but clearly available for such at a later time are exemplified in the double-take phenomenon. As we walk along, we may pass several people, but in one case we may some seconds or even minutes later come up with "Oh, that was neighbor Gundelfinger."

Our ongoing perception and meaning analysis of the world around us pro-

21. Hinton (1981).
22. Hochberg (1981).
23. Treisman and Gelade (1980).

ceeds with the simple goal of making sense of our surrounds. Unless some other construction is selected for specific reasons, we have a general (abstract) sense of where we are and what we are doing. It is only when a specific selection is made to construct the sound of my typewriter that a conscious percept of that sound, still at a general level, enters my conscious contents.

Which schemas are used in the process of construction? The system usually combines evidence from more than one activated schema. We certainly have the subjective sense of the phenomenal unity of our experiences. Whether it is always true that evidence from more than one separate schema is represented in consciousness[24] or whether we deal with a high-level schema that has embedded in it other schemas is not certain. It is certain that if only a single unidimensional source of evidence is represented in consciousness, the model reduces to an identity model—a particular preconscious schema directly forms the contents of consciousness. We shall see that this does sometimes happen, but not usually.

It is important to note this significant asymmetry between activation and conscious construction: activation proceeds from external evidence to features to concrete schemas and then to general and abstract structures; conscious construction proceeds in the opposite direction, being built out of the most general, abstract structure consistent with the evidence and the situational demands.[25] This alone would argue against a simple identity or isomorphism between preconscious and conscious contents.

MEANING ANALYSIS AND CONSCIOUSNESS

The above analysis also permits us to be more specific and helpful about the concept of meaning analysis. In the preceding chapter, I suggested that meaning analysis is fairly automatic; that the world is interpreted and that appropriate higher-order structures are activated *automatically*, as a matter of course. However, there are clearly two different ways in which a meaning analysis can proceed. First, it can be a purely automatic result of activation, the most activated general schemas providing the materials for conscious contents. This occurs when we wander through an essentially uneventful environment that requires no choices or decisions. It is also apparent when we are able, and permit ourselves, to associate freely. We say, think, or do whatever happens to come to mind. If we are able to disengage from environmental or internal demands on the stream of mental activity, we follow the paths of the preconscious activated mental apparatus. It is therefore not surprising that psychoanalytic method demands special training and special conditions for the free-associative stream to work unhindered (except for repressions) in order to provide clues to the structure of the unconscious. The activation that provides this kind of meaning is automatic and, at least to a large extent, independent of conscious controls and intentions.

The second kind of meaning analysis proceeds when we use conscious constructions to put specific questions to our representation of knowledge. This sort

24. Marcel (1983b).
25. Marcel (1983b).

of analysis is a relatively slow process; products do not automatically come to mind. Specific hypotheses that may not have been previously activated are put into play and evidence is sought for their validity. The focus is generally quite specific and inhibits other mental structures in this intentional, conscious process of selection and search. Most problem solving in the general sense follows this kind of analysis.

The distinction is intuitively obvious. We are automatically able to produce our own telephone number, but we need to generate and choose when asked for the number of a friend or some government office. We may order a hamburger automatically at the local diner but choose deliberately in an elegant restaurant. We think automatically about the path from home to office but use conscious representations for a rarely traversed route. We may automatically interpret a barking dog as dangerous but need conscious interpretation to understand that our friend's apparently quiescent parrot may peck rather viciously. The meanings of paths and fears, as well as of good and evil, may occur via either route, but the processing machinery is quite different.

An example of these two kinds of knowledge can be found in some symptoms of anterograde amnesic patients. The dominant characteristic of these patients is their inability to learn new things, to remember what has just been presented to them. For example, given a list of nouns to recall, they will be able to retrieve only about 5 percent of them, in contrast to about 30 percent for normal people. However, if they are given the initial three letters of the words on the list and asked to complete these stems with the first word that comes to mind, their performance is as good as that of the normals.[26] The same effect can be obtained with normal individuals if they are not permitted to process the words on the list in any elaborate, semantically relevant way.[27] The deficit of the amnesics is rooted in the need to establish new structural combinations for the retrieval of the words, a conscious process; but they have no difficulty in completing a task that requires them only to take advantage of the initial activation of the words and the activation provided by the letter stem. Then the target words become highly activated and available to conscious representation in response to the request to say whatever comes to mind. What comes to mind is what is highly activated.

The notion that our initial conscious analysis of our world is in terms of its significance—that is, in fairly abstract and general terms—is intuitively appealing. It usually occurs in everyday situations, and meaning analyses shift to less abstract aspects of the world as the situation demands different and new information. Conscious contents become obviously selective with respect to situation, context, and task.

The constructive process can be demonstrated in the laboratory under conditions of minimal significance and importance. Conscious contents will vary with the task presented, with the activated structures available for conscious constructions, and with the unavailability of other structures because of inadequate activation or confusing and interfering activations. There is evidence that, under

26. Graf, Squire, and Mandler (in press).
27. Graf, Mandler, and Haden (1982).

some conditions of minimal attention to or exposure of instances of verbal or visual categories, people "know" (consciously) to which category a specific event belongs (e.g., furniture, landscape) without being able to identify which particular item (piece of furniture or specific scenes) they witnessed or even whether anything was presented at all.[28] Similarly, semantic incongruity in a visual display is recognized (peripherally) even before the direct fixation of the incongruous object.[29] In a clinical context, we have reports of patients who were unable to retrieve the identity (name) of an object but were able to give its category membership.[30]

Similar evidence relevant to the construction of conscious experience has demonstrated that conjunctions of the separable features of objects are synthesized when objects are attended serially.[31] Under conditions of directing resources to an irrelevant task or an overload of processing resources, features of objects may be wrongly recombined, giving rise to "illusory conjunctions."[32] A similar demonstration exists in the auditory mode.[33]

The constructive approach argues that the "spotlight" metaphor of focal attention (or consciousness) is misleading because we do not normally realize that at any instant "we are attending at just one level" of representation. It is not some "area" of the mind that is spotlighted; rather, the level of analysis determines what it is we see. Introspection "is of little use for deciding what is in our minds at one brief instance"; for example, "shape representations are generated . . . the moment we ask ourselves whether they are there."[34]

Certain constructions seem to reach consciousness rapidly and apparently without selection or intention. This fact suggests an amendment to the constructivist position. The best way to achieve such an accommodation is to consider construction on a dimension of complexity. Some conscious contents, particularly in complex perceptual situations, require a lot of work—that is, interactive selective processes. Others will require practically no selection. The manner in which some ideas and solutions "pop" into the mind is a good example. However, even the latter use some guiding intention or goal that requires or seeks relevant information. The phenomena of solutions to problems or responses to tip-of-the-tongue feelings that suddenly appear in consciousness at some later time are presumably a function of continuing activation of the task-defining structures. Continuing mutual activations finally produce some structure that is active enough and that satisfies the set goal to bring about the construction without any obvious current conscious intention.

Intentions are not necessarily conscious states. Sometimes they are, and even then they may be epiphenomenal descriptions of ongoing retrieval processes, just as the secondary schemas in the realm of action are *about* the required action

28. Fowler, Wolford, Slade, and Tassinary (1981) and Intraub (1981).
29. Parker (1977).
30. Warrington (1975).
31. Treisman and Gelade (1980).
32. Treisman and Schmidt (1982).
33. Deutsch (1981).
34. Hinton (1981).

but are not representations of the action itself. Task setting, contexts, and situations all determine intentions, that is, they activate structures that require certain outcomes in order to be fully active and available for conscious construction.

On the other hand, and truly at the extreme of the constructivist continuum, there are certain stimuli and situations that demand immediate conscious constructions, regardless of the current set, intention, or context. The most obvious are intense sensory stimuli—of sound, sight, pain, heat, or cold. It is difficult not to be conscious of a cannon going off in the next room, or of a flash of intense light in the night sky. Not only do such events demand conscious capacity but they are also instances of single schemas (and even features) determining conscious content. Actually, the immediate reaction (consciousness) to some of these events suggests that the constructive process has been short-circuited. We often do not immediately "know" the source of such intense stimulation, or entertain hypotheses as to its nature. The question, and subsequent conscious meaning analysis, frequently is "What was that?" or "Where did it come from?"

This phenomenon is in part related to my later argument for the adaptive property of discrepancy and interruption. Highly discrepant (unexpected) events are likely to be important, and they immediately demand conscious capacity. I shall return to this function of consciousness shortly, but it is important to remember these events as conscious-capacity-demanding ones that define one endpoint of the constructive continuum.

THE LIMITED CAPACITY OF CONSCIOUSNESS

We are apparently never conscious of all the available evidence that surrounds us, but only of a small subset. What is the nature of that limitation? There is nothing in the constructivist position that limits the possible contents of consciousness, and we have to look elsewhere for the source of the limitation.

One of the earliest references to the limitation of human attention was made by Charles Bonnet (1720–1793); Antoine Louis Claude Destutt de Tracy (1754–1836) first elaborated on the notion that the mind can apprehend only six "objects" at any one time. William Hamilton[35] brought the notion into the modern era and noted that it applied both to single objects and to groupings of objects. By 1890, William James had firmly established the limited-capacity concept as a cornerstone of our knowledge about consciousness-attention. G. A. Miller made the magical number 7 ± 2 central to modern approaches to human information processing.[36]

As a pervasive characteristic of human beings, the limited capacity of attention should be an excellent candidate for an evolutionary analysis. Our colleagues who are often overly eager to ascribe evolutionary and genetic origins to a variety of human characteristics and differences might well focus on limited conscious capacity, which knows no boundary of group, society, race, or even

35. Hamilton (1859).
36. Miller (1956).

age. At present, the generalization holds, and "there is little or no evidence of either individual or developmental differences in [attentional] capacity."[37]

So general a characteristic of human functioning as limited attentional capacity must have a rather important role to play in thought and action. I assume in the first place that the limited-capacity characteristic of consciousness serves to reduce further the information overload that the physical world potentially presents to the organism. Just as sensory end organs and central transducers radically reduce and categorize the world of physical stimuli to the functional stimuli that are in fact registered, so the conscious process further reduces the available information to a small and manageable subset. Similarly, I assume, somewhat circularly, that the limitation of conscious capacity defines what is in fact cognitively manageable. While we do not know why the reduction is of the magnitude that we observe, it is reasonable to assume that some reduction is necessary. Just consider the process of pairwise comparisons (in a choice situation) among *n* chunks in consciousness; clearly the number *n* must be limited if the organism is to make a choice within some reasonable time span.

Some psychologists have noted that the "limited-capacity mechanism may serve an important inhibitory function . . . [by] giving priority to a particular pathway. . . ."[38] Others have elaborated the function of attention in the execution of action; they restrict attention to the central aspects of action selection and execution. The limitation of capacity prevents other structures and schemas from competing overtly with the selected process.[39]

We have seen that there are occasions and stimuli that demand conscious capacity and construction almost automatically. Among these are intense stimuli and internal physiological events like unusual autonomic nervous system (ANS) activity. Whenever such events claim and preoccupy some part of the limited-capacity system, other cognitive functions will suffer, that is, they will be displaced from conscious processing and problem-solving activities will be impaired. Particularly in the case of the interruption or failure of ongoing conscious (and especially unconscious) intercourse with the world, signals from both the external and the internal world will require conscious representation.

The question arises whether we are really "conscious" of five or six discrete events. The arguments for a constructive view of consciousness seem to counsel against taking such a view. If we consider consciousness as an integrated construction of the available evidence—a construction that seems to be phenomenally "whole"—then it is more likely that the limitation to a certain number of items or objects or events or chunks refers to the limitation of these elements *within* the constructed holistic conscious experience. I would argue, therefore, that whatever schema guides the conscious experience is necessarily restricted to a certain number of features or relations. Cognitive "chunks"—organized clusters of knowledge—can operate as units of such constructed experience, just as the experience itself acts as a constructed holistic chunk. For example, as I look

37. Dempster (1981, 87).
38. Posner and Snyder (1975).
39. Norman and Shallice (1980) and Shallice (1972).

out my window, I am aware of the presence of trees and roads and people—individual organized schemas. I may switch my attention (reconstruct my conscious experience) to focus on one of these events and note that some of the people are on bicycles, that others walk, that some are male, some female. Switching attention again, I see a friend and note that he is limping, carrying a briefcase, and talking with a person walking next to him. In each case a new experiential whole enters the conscious state and consists itself of new and different organized chunks.

In arguing that the limited capacity of consciousness is represented by the number of events that can be organized within a single constructed conscious experience, I respond to the intuitively appealing notion that we are both aware of some unitary "scene" and have available within it a limited number of constituent chunks.

The effects of limited capacity can be demonstrated in deliberate memory retrieval and encoding, processes that require conscious participation. We have shown in a variety of studies that retrieval from natural cateogries, such as animals, occupations, and kitchen utensils, is subject to capacity limitation. When people are asked to name all the members of these categories that come to mind, they produce them in clusters that are defined by related instances (e.g., small reptiles), by fast bursts of production, and by a limitation in size to about five instances.[40] In fact it appears that only entry *into* such a cluster is sometimes deliberate; once a cluster is retrieved, it is produced in full and without hesitation. When these categories are very large, it is because there are many different chunks in them, but the size of the chunks is the same for both large and small categories. In other words, only a related set of about five members can reach consciousness at any one time.

One of the most convincing demonstrations of the limited capacity of conscious perception is the phenomenon of subitizing, which has long been a mainstay in the definition of the limited-capacity phenomenon.[41] The term *subitizing* refers to the rapid, confident, and accurate report of the numerosity of arrays of elements presented for very brief exposures. The phenomenon is restricted to arrays of six or fewer elements (usually simple dots). It is an extension of the long-known limitation that the immediate apprehension of the numerosity of a random array of objects or events is restricted to arrays of six or fewer objects. Our experiments showed that subjects give very fast responses to canonical patterns of one to three elements, engage in mental counting for arrays consisting of four to six elements, and estimate the numerosity of the array if there are more than six or seven elements.[42] It appears that after exposures of the arrays as short as 200 msec subjects are able to hold the array in consciousness and to count the elements in it. The temporal slope for mental counting, in the absence of physical evidence, is identical with the counting slope for physically present arrays

40. Dean (1971) and Graesser and Mandler (1978).
41. The subitizing phenomenon was baptized and explored by Kaufman, Lord, Reese, and Volkmann (1949).
42. Mandler and Shebo (1982).

that are presented for unlimited exposures. However, people apparently cannot hold more than six elements in their mind's eye; arrays larger than seven that are presented for brief periods cannot subsequently be counted. This finding suggests that a perceptual field, such as an array of elements, can be organized for conscious construction but that the number of elements that can be consciously constructed is limited. This supports my initial argument that the limited capacity of consciousness may well be the number of related chunks or constituents that can be accommodated in a single organized construction.

One of the difficulties of the experimental investigation of human consciousness is the fact that the very act of inspection interacts with the contents of the conscious construction. In our subitizing study, we were able to take one step toward circumventing this problem. In one of our experiments, we asked subjects not to give the number of elements they saw displayed but rather to indicate whether they thought they *could* give such a number judgment if required. In other words, the subject does not count or estimate the mental arrays but rather reports on its cognitive clarity. In contrast to the numerosity judgments, which show significant positive temporal slopes as the array size increases, these judgments of the apprehensibility of the arrays produce essentially flat slopes for array size from one to five, that is those that produce accurate numerosity responses. The conscious construction of these arrays makes them "look countable," and the judgment provides a more direct access to the phenomenal appearance of the array when it is not distorted by the requirement of mental counting. The speed of the response is essentially unaffected by the number of elements. On the other hand, whether or not a clear percept of the countable array *can* be constructed is determined by a limitation of the number of elements (or chunks) that can be organized.

Consciousness—A Special Problem for Mental Theory

The individual experiences feelings, attitudes, thoughts, images, ideas, beliefs, and other contents of consciousness, but these contents are not accessible to anyone else. Briefly stated, it is not possible to build a phenomenal psychology that is shared. A *theory* of phenomena may be shared, but the private consciousness—once it is expressed in words, gestures, or in any way externalized—is necessarily a transformation of the private experience. No theory external to the individual (i.e., one that treats the organism as the object of observation, description, and explanation) can, at the same time, be a theory that uses private experiences, feelings, and attitudes as data.[43] Events and objects in consciousness can never be available to the observer without having been restructured, reinterpreted, and appropriately modified. The content of consciousness, as philosophers and psychologists have told us for centuries, is not directly available as a datum in psychology.

43. Gray (1971a).

Can the perennial problem of private datum and public inference at least be stated concisely in order to indicate the magnitude of the problem?

We are faced with a phenomenon that might be called the uncertainty principle of psychology: "The particular difficulty that the questioner may influence the answer recalls the uncertainty principle in physics, which limits the knowledge we can gain about any individual particle."[44]

There are two related problems in the study of consciousness. First, not only may the nature of the interrogation affect the reported content of consciousness but, more basically, the act of examination itself may affect the individually observable conscious contents, since the conscious act of interrogating one's conscious content must occupy some part of the limited capacity. As a result, the available content is altered by the process of interrogation.

The second problem to be faced is the fact that the contents of consciousness are not simply reproducible by some one-to-one mapping onto verbal report. Even if these contents were always couched in language—which they surely are not—some theory of transmission would be required. As a result, we are faced, on the one hand, with the individual's awareness of the conscious state and, on the other, with the psychologist's theoretical inference about those contents, on the basis of whatever data, including introspective reports, are available. Both sorts of knowledge may be used as relevant to the construction of a psychology of cognition, although it may in principle be impossible to determine, in any exact sense, the relation between these two interpretations of consciousness.

Private experiences are important aspects of the fully functioning mental system. It is possible to get transformed reports about those events, and it should be possible to develop appropriate theories that relate the contents of consciousness, their transformations, and their report. However, it is not possible to build a viable theory that makes direct predictions about private experience, since the outcome of those predictions cannot be tested by the psychologist-observer.

This position does admit the development of private theories, by individuals, about themselves. To the individual, one's experience *is* a datum, and, as a consequence, personal theories about one's own structures are, within limits, testable by direct experience. These individual, personal theories of the self are both pervasive and significant in explaining human action, but they cannot—without peril—be generalized to others or to the race as a whole.[45]

The fact that people develop representations not only *of* their perceptions, thoughts, and actions but also *about* these products is by now well established. I have discussed these secondary structures in particular with respect to action systems, which often remain permanently inaccessible to conscious construction. These secondary schemas are quite pervasive, and what is available to consciousness is frequently such a secondary schema about our thoughts and actions, represented in personal theories and beliefs. What is represented in consciousness, and available for introspective reports, often is not a reflection of the operating processes and structures at all.[46]

44. Adrian (1966).
45. Mandler and Mandler (1974).
46. Nisbett and Wilson (1977).

Even principled attempts at determining the conditions for introspective accounts often beg the question. For example, one may give an account of the relations between the contents of short-term memory and verbalized information.[47] In such an account, short-term memory seems to operate as a (more respectable?) substitute for consciousness. Recently attended information is supposed to be kept in short-term memory and is "directly accessible" for the production of verbal reports. In contrast, automatic processes make their products unavailable to short-term memory. In this account, "attended to," "heeded," and "stored in short-term memory" are used synonymously. The question of what it is that is available in short-term memory (consciousness) is never specifically addressed, but it is implied that this information somehow directly represents cognitive processes. In contrast, I would argue that these "available" contents are themselves the product of constructive processes. A theory of introspection needs to specify how "heeding" and "attending" operate, and also how such processes determine (construct) specific conscious contents.

I do not mean to imply that these secondary schemas, these beliefs and constructions about the workings of our mind, are useless by-products of the mental system. I have already indicated how they provide shortcuts to the underlying representations and possibly to the addresses of those structures in the case of action systems. They may also be related to the "descriptions" of memories that have been shown to be an important route of access to stored events.[48] More generally, secondary schemas can be seen as an independent system that contains our knowledge about ourselves, however faulty it may be at times. Such a system could be assigned the function of the "self"—the representation of our thoughts and actions, our body and mind, our beliefs and theories and perceptions of ourselves. When we refer to them as delusions and rationalizations, they often perform the function of making us conscious of ourselves in ways that may protect us from being conscious of more "real" but also more threatening and unpleasant constructions. The process of psychotherapy is often concerned with the task of bringing these secondary schemas into line with more realistic evidence.

The Uses and Adaptive Functions of Consciousness

Given that conscious contents are constructed and that they are usually constructed in the service of making sense of the world around us, when does the constructive process take place and with reference to what is it constructed? Quite obviously, there are a large number of possible constructions that could take place at any one time; there are even likely to be several candidates that would satisfy the current state of the world, intentions, and the context in which we operate. As I noted earlier, nonautomatic processes seem to be particularly in evidence when choices have to be made, when selectivity is required. I suggest

47. Ericsson and Simon (1980).
48. Norman and Bobrow (1975).
49. See Dillon and Person (1981).

that conscious states are constructed when the demands of context and situations are such that decisions must be made, that choices are indicated among two or more possible actions or cognitive paths or outcomes.

It is unreasonable to postulate that a conscious state exists only when selections are required. How do we account for our continuous consciousness of the surround? I suggest, as a first approximation, that a state of consciousness exists that is constructed out of the most general structures currently being activated by the environmental requirements. It provides, in consciousness, a specification in rather abstract terms of where we are and what we are doing there. Changes in that very general state of consciousness are then a function of the choice and selectivity process.

This second, more important part of the use of consciousness occurs whenever there is a change in the state of the world, defined as any change in the sensory evidence—in intentions, instructions, context, or situation. It is well known that spatiotemporal attentional adjustments take place whenever there is movement in the environment, when there is a change in the current state of the world. These changes can be indexed by changes in the conscious state or by adjustments to the locus of changes (e.g., in eye movements).[49] Although I shall concentrate on this second kind of mechanism, I should say that the first kind of mechanism, the general state-of-the-world consciousness, may also be constructed in response to the same kinds of demands and variables. It can be argued that the world is always in a state of flux and change and that such changes always demand new conscious constructions. The results of such activity will always be the most abstract, general kind of representation, unless some specific change is so intense and relevant to current functioning that it requires more concrete, special focusing and new conscious constructions. From that point of view, the continuous state of consciousness is simply a reflection of a dynamic, changing environment.

Much of what is often considered to be the commonsense meaning of the term *thinking* refers to what takes place in consciousness when the outcome of different constructions are evaluated and decisions are made. It is possible for the cognitive system to call for the testing of specific outcomes while temporarily blocking output from the system as a whole, to compare the consequences of different outcomes, and to choose outcomes that produce one or another desired alternative. The notion of choice would be entirely within the context of choice theories,[50] and the choice itself, of course, would go through some "unconscious" cognitive structures before a "decision" was made. However, consciousness permits the comparison and inspection of various outcomes.

It appears that one of the functions of the conscious construction is to bring two or more (previously unconscious) mental contents into direct juxtaposition. The phenomenal experience of choice seems to demand exactly such an occurrence. We usually do not refer to a choice unless there is a "conscious" choice between two or more alternatives. The attribute of "choosing" is applied to a

50. Luce (1959) and Tversky (1972).

decision process regarding two items on a menu, several possible television programs, or two or more careers, but not to the decision process that decides whether to start walking across a street with the right or the left foot, whether to scratch one's ear with a finger or with the ball of the hand, or whether to take one or two sips from a cup of hot coffee. The former cases involve the necessity of deciding between two or more alternatives, whereas the latter involve only the situationally predominant action. However, given a hot cup of coffee, I may "choose" to take one very small sip, or I may "choose" to start with my right foot in a 100-meter race, given certain information that it will improve my time for the distance. In other words, consequences and social relevance determine which choices are conscious.

Final "choices" are carried out by complex unconscious mechanisms that have direct connections with and relations to action systems and other executive systems. Consciousness permits the redistribution of activations, so that the choice mechanism operates on the basis of new values of schemas and structures that have been produced (activated) in the conscious state. Choices are not made consciously, but the conditions for new choices are created consciously, thus giving the appearance of conscious free choices and operations of the will.[51] What consciousness does permit is the running through of potential actions and choices, the coexistence of alternative outcomes, the changing of weightings of currently active schemas in the direction of one that promises greater likelihood of success, and so forth. The simultaneity of consciousness, within the structures that have been realized in consciousness, makes possible the occurrence of new associations, of previously quiescent cognitive structures, now activated by the conscious structures. In problem-solving activities, our consciousness of various alternatives, of trying out solutions, is often taken for the process that determines the final outcome. Although these conscious activities are no doubt related to the unconscious activations and processing that they influence, they are not the forces that directly determine actions. Their similarity, in many situations, to those unconscious ones leads one to conclude that thought determines actions directly, but thought—defined as conscious mental contents—is in one sense truly epiphenomenal and in another determinative of action. It determines further unconscious processes but is several steps removed from the actual processes that pervade our mental life. Conscious thoughts are good first approximations, in fact the best available, but they are no substitute for the representations and processes that need to be postulated for an eventual understanding of human action—and thought.

So-called mnemonic devices, which restructure our mental contents in order to make later retrieval possible, fall into the same category. They are conscious shorthand devices, often a reflection of secondary schemas, that will access the to-be-remembered material and encourage a particular restructuring of the target information. All such activity requires consciousness, if for no other reason than the absence, usually, of an automatic organization that will tell us which of

51. See Norman and Shallice (1980).

many different relations to encourage and reinforce. If I am given a telephone number that I wish to remember, the activation of that number will spread to other, similar numbers, and possibly even to old mnemonic devices linking a number to a face, a person, a place. But this activation will not relate the new number to a specific person and place. That work, that new elaboration, needs to be done in consciousness, where a variety of different devices can be activated and where a few can then be selected and activated for future use. The expectation is that the work is effective enough to produce the automatic activation of the number when the person is given as a starting point for retrieval in the future.

Schemas are built up slowly as a result of the concatenation of features and activations. However, with the intervention of conscious construction some of the activations can be established quickly and in a saltatory fashion—new juxtapositions create new activations. The normal course of learning is slow and cumulative, but new demands can create conscious constructions and new rapid learning.

Practically all novel relational orderings require that events to be ordered must be simultaneously present in the conscious field. This applies to choice as well as to relational concepts stored in memory. Needless to say, there are many relational judgments that do not require conscious comparisons. The statement "A dog is an animal" makes use of established structures and does not require a new relational operation. However, the statement "Rex looks like a cross between a dachshund and a spaniel" might require conscious juxtaposition.

In summary, when a situation demands conscious representations, the conscious state includes a selection and concatenation of available preconscious evidence, a selective construction of potentially available thoughts and perceptions. The demand for *conscious* evidence arises out of requirements for comprehension, selection, choice, or judgments. Such demands come from intra- or extrapsychic sources, that is, they may be bottom-up or top-down requirements. In the case of extrapsychic instigation, conscious construction will follow unexpected changes in the environment (e.g., unprepared for movement, schema-discrepant events, evidence competing for activation of more than one schema). Intrapsychic instigation will depend on demands for evidence by higher-order schemas of some generality (e.g., search processes) and by the activation of such schemas by the interpretation of current situational, contextual requirements (e.g., intentions).

Relatively little has been said about the adaptive functions of consciousness except in very general terms. Consciousness may perform various functions, all of which may be said to have adaptive significance and all of which have varying degrees of evidence for their utility. Most of these were mentioned in the preceding section, on the uses of consciousness. I shall briefly summarize their possible adaptive significance.[52]

1. The most widely addressed function of consciousness is its role in choice and in the selection of action systems. This function permits the organism more

52. For a general discussion, see Gray (1971a) and Miller (1962).

complex considerations of action-outcome contingencies, which alter the probability of one or another set of actions. It also permits the consideration of possible actions that the organism has never before performed, thus eliminating the overt testing of possible harmful alternatives.[53]

Consciousness makes possible the modification and interrogation of long-range plans rather than of immediate-action alternatives. In the hierarchy of actions and plans, this makes it possible to organize disparate action systems in the service of a higher plan. For example, in planning a drive to some new destination, we might consider subsets of the route, or, in devising a new recipe, the creative chef considers the interactions of several known culinary achievements. Within the same realm, consciousness makes it possible to retrieve and consider modifications in long-range planning activities. These, in turn, might be modified in light of other evidence, either from the immediate environment or from long-term storage.

2. In considering actions and plans, consciousness participates in retrieval from long-term memory, even though the retrieval strategies themselves are usually not conscious. Thus, frequently, although not always, the retrieval of information from long-term storage is initiated by relatively simple commands. These may be simple instructions like "What is his name?" or "Where did I read about that?" or more complex instructions like "What is the relation between this situation and previous ones I have encountered?" This process serves the adaptive function of using simple addresses to complex structures.

3. Current activities are represented in consciousness and use available cognitive structures to construct storable representations. Many investigators have suggested that these new codings and representations always take place in the conscious state. Processes such as mnemonic devices and storage strategies apparently require the intervention of conscious structures. Once this new organization of information is stored, it may be retrieved for a variety of purposes.

First, in the social process, prior problem solutions and other memories may be brought into the conscious state and, together with an adequate system of communication, such as human language, generate the benefits of cooperative social efforts. Other members of the species may receive solutions to problems, thus saving time, if nothing else; they may be apprised of unsuccessful alternatives or may, more generally, participate in the cultural inheritance of the group. This process requires selection and comparison among alternatives retrieved from long-term storage, all of which apparently takes place in consciousness.

Second, both general information and specific sensory inputs may be stored. The rerepresentation at some future time makes possible decision processes that depend on comparisons between current and past events and on the retrieval of relevant or irrelevant information for current problem solving.

4. Consciousness provides a "troubleshooting" function for structures normally not represented in consciousness. There are many systems that cannot be brought into consciousness; most systems that analyze the environment in the

53. Mandler and Kessen (1974).

first place probably have that characteristic. In most of these cases, only the product of cognitive and mental activities is available to consciousness. In contrast, many systems are generated and built with the cooperation of conscious processes, but later become nonconscious or automatic. The latter systems may apparently be brought into consciousness, particularly when they are defective in their particular function.[54] We all have had experiences of automatically driving a car, typing a letter, or even handling a cocktail party conversation, and of being suddenly brought up short by some failure such as a defective brake, a stuck key, or a "You aren't listening to me." At that time the particular representations of actions and memories involved are brought into play in consciousness, and repair work gets under way.

Many of these functions permit the organism to react reflectively instead of automatically, a distinction that has frequently been made between humans and lower animals. All of them permit more adaptive transactions between the organism and its environment. Also, in general, the functions of consciousness permit a focusing on the most important and species-relevant aspects of the environment. The processes that define such relevance are generally unknown, although we can assume that an adaptive function of construction into consciousness exists.

The Limitation of Conscious Capacity and the Flow of Consciousness

One of the most perplexing results of experimental studies of consciousness has been the counterintuitive notion that mental contents of the conscious state seem to be discrete, relatively short-lived, and quite transient. How does this contrast with consciousness in the common discourse? There it is described as continuous, flowing, and extending without break throughout our waking hours—and just as flowing and continuous in our dreams. William James aptly called it "the stream of thought, of consciousness, or of subjective life." How can we reconcile these two impressions?

Before we tackle that particular problem, consider the role of consciousness in our perception of time or, better, duration. For this purpose I shall adopt a model of duration proposed by Robert Ornstein,[55] which relates the time experience to "the mechanisms of attention, coding, and storage." The central thesis is that storage size is the basis for the construction of the duration of an interval. The more different, unrelated units there are, the greater the storage size; the more highly organized the units, objects, or events are, the fewer units or chunks, the smaller the storage size. As storage size of the material in consciousness increases, the duration experience lengthens. What changes storage size are increases or decreases in the amount of information received and changes in the

54. See also Vygotsky (1962).
55. Ornstein (1969).

coding or chunking of input. "The more organized . . . the memory . . . the shorter the experience of duration."[56]

The experience of duration (in consciousness) is a construction drawing on immediately pressing factors (such as attentiveness) but primarily on our stored long-term memory. Duration is constructed, first, in momentary consciousness and, second, in the retrieval of events and codes that are recalled during the construction of a past interval. The contents of consciousness thus determine the experience of duration. Restricting these contents shortens duration; expanding them—by, for example, increasing the complexity of an experience—lengthens duration. Vigilance, which increases expectancy of some event, lengthens duration, as in the example of the "watched pot." By contrast, condensing some experience into a very brief code ("I made breakfast") shortens the duration. The concatenation of limited conscious capacity, on the one hand, and of the same consciousness serving as a vehicle for constructing experience of duration, on the other, brings us back to the disjunction between discrete consciousness and the flow of consciousness.

There is, in principle, no objection to constructing a flow model of consciousness out of discrete units. The metaphor that comes to mind is a simplistic view of modern conceptions of light, which may be described either in terms of particles or in terms of waves. We then may metaphorically speak of the quantum of consciousness, on the one hand, and the flow of consciousness, on the other. Another possible metaphor is that of the illusion of moving pictures, which consist of individual frames. Neither metaphor probably does justice to the phenomenon, as no metaphor ever does. In particular, it is likely that instead of individual quanta or frames, the flow of consciousness may frequently involve the successive sampling of materials across a continuous retrieval of connected material from long-term storage. In the case of consciousness of externally generated events (e.g., somebody else's speech), the overlapping moving model may be the most appropriate, whereas in the attempt to retrieve a specific chunk of knowledge, the retrieval may be discontinuous. Because of the limited-capacity characteristics of discrete consciousness, I shall use the metaphor of the conscious frame, the momentary structure that constructs conscious contents.

CONSCIOUS STOPPING

One special reason why the view of the conscious frame is useful is that it permits a consideration of special conditions; when the flow of consciousness stops, single frames enter into consciousness and remain there. Experimental psychologists have paid some attention to this phenomenon, as in the concept of maintaining or primary rehearsal, in which material is repeated but does not enter into long-term storage.[57] However, the major source of knowledge of this phenomenon comes from esoteric psychologies and meditative methods.

56. Ornstein (1972).
57. Craik and Watkins (1973) and Woodward, Bjork, and Jongeward (1973).

The best objective presentation of these methods is again provided by Robert Ornstein,[58] in whose work a recurrent theme may be discerned. The achievement of the special kinds of conscious states that are claimed to occur seem to depend, without exception, on the unique attempt to stop the flow of ordinary consciousness—to concentrate on the frame, to hold it fixed in the focus of consciousness. The very difficulty of achieving the initial, apparently trivial, exercises of these techniques suggests the difficulty of stopping the flow. It requires total attention to a single, restricted set of limited thoughts or perceptions. In Zen, the exercises start with counting breaths and then go on to concentrate on the process of breathing. Yogic meditation uses the mantra, "sonorous, flowing words which repeat easily." Some of the Sufi practices are seen as an "exercise for the brain based on repetition." The Christian mystic St. John of the Cross says: "Of all these forms and manners of knowledge the soul must strip and void itself and it must strive to lose the imaginary apprehension of them, so that there may be left in it no kind of impression of knowledge, nor trace of thought. . . . This cannot happen unless the memory can be annihilated in all its forms. . . ."[59] Many prayers are monotonous, repetitive chants. In summary, the "common element in these diverse practices seems to be the active restriction of awareness to one single, unchanging process, and the withdrawal of attention from ordinary thought."[60] And again: "The specific object used for meditation is much less important than the maintenance of the object as the single focus of awareness during a long period of time. . . ."

I suggest that the "object of the single focus" must be no more than a frame of consciousness; in fact, it is restricted by the very limits that the limited-capacity mechanism has been shown to exhibit. We could not meditate on an event that, at first, contains more than five to seven chunks. The observations that Ornstein and many others have reported suggest that it is possible to stop the flow of consciousness to keep a single frame of consciousness in focus for extended periods of time. However, such an experience should be a very *different* form of consciousness; the normal form is the flow. We thus experience this new consciousness only after the extensive practice it requires. But we must also experience a very different content of consciousness. Given that the single "object" is held in consciousness, many new and different aspects of it may then be discovered; new constructions of a limited amount of material can be attempted.

Consider the possibility that at first any such object consists of several related qualities (or chunks). Presumably, as these various attributes are related one to the other, the new relations form a more compact perception, and the number of chunks, as it were, is reduced. This opens up the possibility for new chunks or attributes to enter into the single frame. New relations are discovered and again coalesce. Under these circumstances we may go through a process of structuring and restructuring, of discovering aspects of objects or events that would not normally be available during the flow of consciousness. Once this ability has

58. Ornstein (1972).
59. Ornstein (1972).
60. Ornstein (1972).

been achieved, we should, in principle, be able to use the special consciousness to stop the flow of events, examine new nuances, and then continue. Thus, a limited set of attributes within a single frame is available at first; then new aspects enter, and old ones drop away. The complexities of a rose, a face, or a cake "become conscious." This seems to be taking place in the "opening up" of awareness, which follows the "turning off" phase and provides the individual with a different state of comprehension of ongoing actions and events. "The concentrative form turns off the normal mode of operation and allows a sensitivity to subtle stimuli which often go unnoticed in the normal mode. . . . It also produces an *after-effect* of 'fresh' perception when the practitioner returns to his usual surroundings."[61] Meditative techniques provide us, in this fashion, with new insights into a mechanism that otherwise seems mundane and restrictive. There need not be anything mysterious about meditation, or anything pedestrian about an information-processing analysis of consciousness.

The enriching of knowledge through meditative experiences or conscious stopping should be put into the proper context of the ordinary, normal means of enriching experience. Without doubt, we enrich our experience and knowledge about the world around us without resorting to meditation. We can, without special preparation, perceive new facets of the world, of other people, and even of ourselves as we gain new perspectives, new ways of structuring and constructing our experience. A main difference between the normal and the meditative enrichment is that the former deals with an open system and the latter with a closed one. Our enrichment in knowledge and appreciation of a lover, a novel, a science, an occupation, always occurs in new contexts, sometimes widely different, sometimes only minutely so. But the relation between the object or event and ourselves is changed continuously by our mutual relations with the rest of the world. The new information is, in a way, always acquired in new contexts. What seems to distinguish this usual accretion from the meditative one is that in the latter we are restricted to those relations among qualities and attributes that are given in that object or situation. This restriction of possible relations presumably provides not only the illusion but possibly also the reality of the depth of perception that the special experience provides. In contrast, artists and scientists, for example, apparently achieve the same depth of perception of special objects or events without the meditative experience.

The notion that the experience of duration is constructed from the storage size of the cognitive structures that constitute an interval may be applied directly to the flow and frame aspects of consciousness. Time experience is constructed across frames out of cognitive structures that will, to varying degrees, occupy the limited-capacity frame. Consider listening to a lecture on difficult but interesting material. As the speaker proceeds, information is transmitted at a great rate, taking up the full capacity of each frame of consciousness. The storage of information is near a maximum. A redundant speaker makes fewer demands on each frame; the very ability to approach a difficult subject slowly and cumulatively

61. Ornstein (1972).

permits us to use less of the full capacity of the frame, or—another possibility—the capacity is filled less frequently in physical time and fewer frames are expected. In the extreme, the boring lecturer produces little information, the amount of material in each frame is minimal, and the storage "size" is small and the time experience long.

The storage metaphor may be directly translated into the frame locution. Since consciousness is necessary for the transfer of information to long-term storage, complex information (comprising many chunks and relations) requires more frames for the transfer function, as does rapidly presented information (more chunks per unit of physical time). It appears that the storage metaphor is quite consistent with the frame-flow notion of consciousness. In the latter mode the construction of time depends on the sheer number of frames of consciousness activated or utilized during a specific interval. Parenthetically, we may note that this position also indicates the independence of the conscious frame from physical time. The specious present, the limited-capacity mechanism, does not have a time constant. Frames are replaced under a variety of conditions, all of which seem to depend on using up their capacity; a new perceptual dimension, another class of stimulation, a sudden demand for focusing (attention), and many others will demand a shift to another conscious construction, which is perceived as another *moment* of consciousness.

Finally, I note the drastic changes in time perception that take place as a result of meditative experience. Given that the flow of frames is radically altered, we would naturally expect a similar and unusual change in duration experiences. The change can be in either direction. Holding a single unit of consciousness and impeding the flow may collapse the duration experience, whereas the eventual ability to manipulate the flow of consciousness may change the usual duration experience with its apparently rather constant rate of change into a more variable ebb and flow of "short" and "long" durations. In contrast to the flow of frames during normal states, during meditation the change from one conscious content to another occurs infrequently in physical time. The slow changes in perceptual structures that I suggested earlier for the meditative phase thus produce unusual duration experiences.

It is intriguing to speculate that the action of hallucinogenic or "mind-expanding" drugs has a similar locus and effect. Changes in perceptual processes coexist with changes in the experience of duration. It has been argued that these drugs often produce in an instant the experiences that meditative methods generate with extensive practice. It is possible that some drugs actually slow the flow of conscious frames, and that some of the lasting effects of these drugs may be due to structural changes in the control of the flow of consciousness.

Dreaming

The most unusual conscious constructions occur in dreams. Traces of real-world evidence mix with ancient and contemporary themes and with current conscious contents that, while often weird and novel, are still highly structured and certainly not random. Something constructs the consciousness that we dream. The mechanism that does the constructing and the material that is used are not different from the representations and processes that are responsible for consciousness in the waking state.

In the latter the evidence that arrives at the mental frontier, that activates schemas and structures, that generates and validates hypotheses, is itself structured by the reality and lawfulness of the external world. Both concrete and abstract schemas, generic ones and their instantiations, depend to a large extent on the current activation by the imperatives of a real world, peopled by real problems and real situations. There is something out there that demands attention, thought, and action. No doubt, these thoughts and actions are determined and modified in part by previous activations, by schemas and structures that are still active as a result of our continuing transactions with the world; otherwise our actions would be ahistorical. In fact they are context bound.

In dreams, however, present activations are of no great importance. Although there is no doubt that some current activations (such as alarm clocks, sexual arousal, bladder pressure, and smells) activate their respective structures and enter into dreams, these occurrences do not make up the major part of our dream world. Dreams are constructed out of the remnant activations of the preceding hours and days. These activations are of two kinds—generic schemas that have received activation from one or more sources and instantiated schemas (perceptions and thoughts) that are the result of specific experiences and thoughts in the preceding hours. But these active schemas are not organized by the structure of the world; they are the haphazard activations of a variety of experiences, some of them quite unrelated or even incompatible. They are available in varying degrees of activation for conscious constructions and, in many cases, will be activated structures that were not used in conscious constructions during the waking state at all. Without the guiding structures of the real world, these structures are now "free"; combinations of them that were not coacting in the face of evidence may now seek (activate) higher and more abstract structures that themselves may have been quiescent. Whereas my breakfast thoughts and my afternoon lecturing thoughts are not likely to have activated similar or overlapping features or structures, their remnants, residues that are still active[62] as I sleep, may find a higher-order schema or hypothesis that combines Rice Crispies and the noisy student reading his newspaper in the last row. Similarly, abstract structures that have not been used for daytime constructions, because they produce unpleasant, conflicting consequences, may now well find conscious expression because the instantiations that they find are "disconnected" and unlikely to lead to conflict.

Another mechanism that makes some unpleasant consequences more acceptable is that dreams by definition do not lead to actions that may have unpleasant consequences. Thus, the repressed structure is not repressed when its use in a conscious construction leads to little or no real conflict. Dreams may

62. Rosenbaum (1972).

avoid real-world conflict. This is not to deny that in many cases dreams, that is, some abstract structure and the residue activations available for its instantiation, lead to real affect. Just like the waking state, a dream may produce discrepancies, arousal, and negative evaluations. It is just that previously shunned schemas may sometimes be able to find conscious expressions without their dreaded consequences. I should note, however, that even this bypassing of action depends on the fact that in dreams the consequences of conscious constructions are not channeled by a real world, just as the structure of available instantiations is not determined by the current structure of the world.

Dreams are therefore determined by two sources—activated remnants of the waking life and abstract structures that may or may not have been activated during the day or that are activated during dreaming. Dreams, too, are thus the product of top-down and bottom-up processes.

The major sources of the waking residue are schemas and structures that have not been brought to a halt by a stop rule; loops of activation still exist. These include actions that have accidentally not been brought to a conclusion, unsolved problems, rejected or suppressed thoughts, top-down activations that have not been "used" in consciousness, and mundane occurrences that have been prevented from being selected by the pressure of other business.[63] The generic abstract structures that will be effective in dreams are those that have been activated during the waking state as well as those that now become activated by new concatenations of the active residue.

Modern cognitive psychology has the tools to determine the nature of the residues that bring about strange dream combinations;[64] it is less able to determine the themes of our dreams, the underlying major schemas that are used by, and that use, these remnants. The approach to the former might be similar to that used in the explanation of human error, but even that analysis still leaves open the question of why some potential errors and slips occur whereas others do not. That is the function of unconscious generic themes and schemas.[65]

Consciousness and Emotion

One of the directing themes of my speculations about emotions has been the notion that emotional experience is constructed out of autonomic arousal and evaluative cognitions. In the past I was unable to give a principled account of how these disparate events combine into a single, unitary phenomenal experi-

63. Freud ([1900] 1975).
64. Foulkes (1966).
65. My interpretation of dreams obviously owes much to Freud's analysis ([1900] 1975, esp. chap. 7), particularly in the distinction between top-down and bottom-up processes in dreams, in the listing of the sources of residues (and in the use of the term in the first place), and in his use of "repression." My suggestion that the structure of the world is left out of the construction of dreams is related to Freud's notion of regression, that is, that dreams, in contrast to our consciousness of reality, are initiated by unconscious structures rather than by perceptual elements.

ence. The proposal for a constructivist view of consciousness provides that mechanism. Subjective experiences of emotional states are conscious constructions that combine evaluative and arousal structures into a single construction, which itself is an abstract structure. The kinds of evaluations that are used in such constructions will be discussed at length later, as will the nature of the arousal that is incorporated in the experienced emotional structure. But whatever these components are, it is a well-accepted view that emotional states do in fact lend significance to situations; they have the same abstract status as the cognitive structures that produce complex meanings and significances.

The high-level structures that participate in this construction of emotion will to some degree be similar in different individuals, at least to the extent that we share a world and a biology common to human beings that dictate fears, angers, joys, and lusts. Other integrative emotional structures will be highly idiosyncratic, at least in so far as we experience different loves, hates, and anxieties. Most important, the nature of the specific emotional experience will depend, as all conscious constructions do, on two general sources. The first will be the generic, abstract schemas that represent the abstractions that we have acquired in our lifetime—shaped by common human, cultural, social, and personal experiences. The second source will be the evidence from schemas that evaluate the current surround, from cognitive states that represent value schemas, and from the autonomic nervous system.

The constructivist view of consciousness and particularly its sensitivity to intentional, situational factors is well demonstrated in experiments in which arousal is paired with values generated by environmental displays. In the Schachter and Singer experiments, for example,[66] the instructions to subjects that they should expect certain physiological symptoms preempted any sensitivity to the social induction of emotion; the structure in which the arousal system participated, that is, the expectations about the values of other open variables, did not leave any room for further construction—there were no expectations about arousal and value concatenations. However, when the symptoms were not expected, the structure that was activated was probably one or more emotional schemas with instantiation for evaluations still left to be filled. Under those conditions, subjective emotional states were induced. This is far from a labeling notion of emotional states; rather, it considers the structure of the variety of activations to which the individual mind is exposed. Experiments showing that under conditions of arousal, and in the (apparent) absence of emotion-inducing cues, subjects will still report slightly negative subjective states, are not at all relevant to this position.[67] Not only is it possible that states of high arousal can be negatively evaluated by some people or populations but it will also be necessary to know what the current state of the experimental subjects is and what kinds of schemas are likely to have been activated as a result of their immediate preceding experiences in the laboratory and just before coming there. Any remaining negative activa-

66. Schachter and Singer (1962).
67. Maslach (1979).

tions before the experiment would, of course, be used in the construction of an emotional state.

In any case, the constructivist approach does provide a principled account not only of how emotions are constructed but also of how the specific emotional experience arises out of the general characteristics of consciousness.

5

MIND AND EMOTION

IN THIS CHAPTER I SHALL DESCRIBE those aspects of mental organization that are responsible for the production of the experiences often called "emotional." Specifically, I shall discuss those interactions between arousal and the mental system that produce a set of behavior and experiences that overlaps with the concept of emotion. Having given that warning and having bounded my interest, I shall use the term *emotion* fairly freely, with the understanding that I am primarily interested in certain specifiable outcomes of our mental apparatus.

I shall avoid saying two things: first, that this is a theory of emotion and, second, that conscious mental states are unanalyzable events. Conscious states are to be explained like any other part of the mental system; they have no special status. This is my main point of contention with psychologists and philosophers who often are entranced by their own and others people's minds—when they admit their existence.

My first disavowal is obvious. I do not claim to have a prescriptive, quantitative theory of emotion, but I do believe that many of the parameters discussed below are, in fact, operative when we talk about "emotions." My efforts are impervious to examples of experiences and behaviors that are "emotion" in common parlance but do not fit the system. What follows is a summary statement about arousal, cognition, and consciousness, all of them active in the generation of the experiences and actions that I want to subsume under the term emotion.[1]

Mental Organization and Emotion

AROUSAL

The particular human behaviors and experiences of interest to us occur concurrently with the activities of the autonomic nervous system, particularly its

1. I have presented models of the production of emotion over the past twenty years in Mandler (1962b, 1964a, 1975c, 1980b). The present treatment is a descendant, but not a copy, of those previous statements. The original motivation for my theoretical notions derived from the insights developed by Stanley Schachter, whose influence on current views of emotion I discussed in Chapter 2.

sympathetic division. I shall refer to this activity as arousal. The ANS acts on visceral receptors. The resulting effective event is the perception of autonomic activity, which—except for some special states such as sexual arousal—is registered as undifferentiated arousal, varying primarily in intensity.

Some of the conditions that lead to autonomic arousal are known in detail but not in principle. Many of these conditions depend on cognitive transformations. A broad category of such conditions that also appear to have reasonable adaptive and evolutionary backing can be found in the interruption of ongoing plans and actions and in the discrepancy between the expected and the actual. Interruption refers to the blocking of or interference with any well-established action sequence or cognitive plan. One of the consequences of discrepancy and interruption is autonomic arousal.

Autonomic arousal has two main adaptive functions. One is embodied in the principle of homeostasis and the physiological readiness of the organism. The other is a signal to the mental organization for attention, alertness, and scanning of the environment. The latter function demands interpretation and analysis of the environment by the various sensory and cognitive systems. This information-seeking activity may inquire either about the sources of autonomic arousal or generally about the present state of the environment and the organism.

MEANING ANALYSIS AND COGNITIVE EVALUATION

Part of the emotional complex is the ongoing meaning analysis and the resulting cognitive interpretations that are relevant to the evaluative part of the emotion experienced. Meaning analyses deal both with events in the external world and with the organism's own actions and behaviors. Some of these actions are prewired, and many of them involve some evaluative cognition, sometimes just asserting the goodness or badness of a situation, but most frequently resulting in very subtle and finely differentiated judgments of value. These in turn define the qualitative aspect of the experienced emotion.

Among the reactions to the environment that are reevaluated and subjected to meaning analyses are expressive movements, which are most profitably seen as evaluative reactions arising out of the species's history (see Chapter 7). Another set of pervasive evaluations consists of those that determine the appropriateness or inappropriateness of actions in response to the demands of the environment and the self. The evaluation of inappropriateness and particularly of the unavailability of appropriate actions issues in a cognition of helplessness, which is often coextensive with the commonsense experience and description of anxiety.

Evaluations and meaning analyses are self-correcting and reflexive. As the situation changes, often as a result of the individual's actions, reevaluations change the current evaluative state. Thus, evaluation and interpretation of the situation and self may change continuously and provide new and different evaluative states.[2]

2. Lazarus, Kanner, Folkman (1980).

CONSCIOUSNESS

Emotional *experience* is by definition conscious. Both the perception of arousal and the results of cognitive-interpretive activities are registered and integrated before or in consciousness. Conscious experience is frequently coded by our language systems into socially sanctioned and culturally determined categories. These categories subsume relatively large subsets of these "emotional" experiences; their usage is determined by conscious content as well as by the initial interpretation of the surround. In other words, verbal expressions of emotion depend on prior mental states, on direct environmental categorization, and on conscious structures.

The Construction of Emotion

We assume that the two major systems involved in emotional behavior are arousal and meaning analysis. Many of the processes involved will be elaborated in Chapters 6 and 9, but the major assumption will be discussed here. Emotional experience has as one of its necessary concomitants the production of autonomic nervous system (ANS) arousal. This arousal is nonspecific and merely sets the quantitative specifications for emotional behavior and experience; the particular quality of the emotion is determined entirely by the meaning analysis, which may be engendered by the arousal but which is, more important, determined by the general situation and current cognitive states. The joint products of both of these systems, arousal and meaning analysis, construct consciousness and also determine action. Arousal provides the intensity of the emotional state, and cognition provides its quality.

Specific events relevant to emotional experiences have two functions: they set off arousal, and they induce a particular meaning analysis of the situation. Events may produce arousal under one of two possible conditions. First, there may be a preprogrammed, automatic release of ANS arousal. Second, that arousal may be mediated by a meaning analysis that transforms an otherwise innocuous stimulus into a functional releaser of the ANS. Thus, there are some classes of stimuli, for example, tissue injury and interruption of ongoing plans and actions, that produce an immediate reaction. On the other hand, there are objects and events, such as animals, radiators, and guns, that are initially innocuous but that on the basis of past experience are transformed into functional autonomic releasers. The complexity of the human mental organization suggests that this dichotomy is not as simple as it sounds—that there is, rather, a continuum from innate to experiential factors, which are needed to produce arousal. For example, we know that tissue injury by itself may sometimes not be a releaser for autonomic arousal.[3]

Only perceived arousal has psychological consequences, although we will

3. See Melzack (1973).

note some effects of arousal on attention in Chapter 6. Arousal feeds back into the mental system, which registers the state of arousal and together with a meaning analysis constructs a conscious state. However, the perceptual system may be nonoperative because instructions or past experience have raised the threshold, or the system may be turned off by pharmacological means.

Meaning analysis takes place automatically for any event that is attended. The perception of arousal may set the stage for additional analyses, for example, "search" for a structure that can assimilate both the meaning analysis and the perception of arousal. When such a structure has been found, a stop rule goes into effect, the search terminates, and a conscious content is constructed. Many different stop rules are in operation in our mental organization. In the case of instinctive behavior,[4] some of the various stopping and starting conditions have been explored. These include many hormonal as well as environmental factors that are involved in starting a particular instinctive sequence. The conditions that terminate these instinctual-behavior sequences may come from a variety of sources, most frequently from the completion of a particular sequence, as in the execution of a consummatory act. However, there are other terminating stimuli or stop rules that may be extraneous to the behavior observed. Some of these stop rules may be changes in the current context and situation, which then terminate the search for an appropriate structure.

Action systems may involve the automatic release of particular actions, as in the case of sexual behavior or defensive aggression actions that are executed as a result of deliberate processing. In any event, central structures ("motives") will activate actions, which vary in the degree to which they have been influenced by past experience.

Since the emphasis in these pages is on emotional experience, we need to explore the relation between it and emotional behavior. The latter has been, particularly under the aegis of behaviorist assumptions, the focus of one important tradition in the study of emotion. From that point of view, the important aspects of emotion are to be explored by an extensive analysis of the relations between environmental events and observable actions of the individual. One of the reactions to that position has been the tendency to assert the converse—that is, that all emotional behavior is the outcome of some cognitive state, usually a prior conscious emotional state. I shall argue for a greater complexity.

There are conditions under which so-called emotional behaviors occur as automatic consequences of some environmental event. I have already alluded to sexual behavior and defensive aggression, but the potential for such occurrences is much broader than that, particularly when we take into account acquired action patterns that have bypassed the deliberate stage and occur as a direct consequence of schematic activation by environmental events. No conscious experience intervenes between their instigators and their occurrence. Under some social conditions, we may learn to lash out at real or imagined aggressors, or we may reach out toward an object of love (or chocolates), or we may cringe at the

4. Bowlby (1969).

appearance of spiders (or symbols of authority). These actions, often occur rapidly and sometimes long before autonomic arousal can be activated or an evaluative analysis performed. Under these conditions, the evaluated (perceived) actions themselves become objects of a meaning analysis and determine the evaluative state. In other words, the emotional "behavior" determines the evaluative state that, subsequently, defines the subjective emotional experience.

This may sound like a Jamesian model for the induction of emotion—and it is indeed that. There are some conditions under which the immediate actions determine the emotional state. The behavior itself, however, is not to be considered emotional within the context of this model. Rather, actions, as well as cognitions, may be the contributing events to cognitive evaluations, which in turn determine the phenomenal experience of the emotion.

In contrast, there are many more emotional states that determine action; situations where arousal and evaluation induce the emotional experience, which in turn becomes the occasion for actions. Anger as a precursor of hostile action, lust as a stimulus for sexual approaches, and joy as an initiator of ecstatic behavior are all instances of this type of sequence. And, as we shall see later, the effects of anxiety and stress on behavior and action are prime examples of the experience-action sequence.

In summary, emotional behavior may precede (cause) emotional experience or it may be preceded (caused) by it. In either case, one cannot substitute the behavior for the experience. At best, emotional behavior serves an index function, suggesting the likelihood that emotional experiences have been or will be occurring.

This index function is well served by the external evidence for autonomic arousal. Here again the evidence suggests, but does not confirm, emotional experience, since arousal can occur in the absence of emotional experience. A classic example of external evidence is found in the startle response to extreme interruption and stimulation, in which a stable action pattern, including head movements, widening of the mouth, and muscle contractions,[5] are reliably associated with a particular class of external events. Other indices of arousal include blushing, rapid eye blinks, and even failure to control elimination.

As far as emotional language is concerned, we must deal with statements such as "I feel . . ." and frequently make reference to the unobservable private events that we have summarized as conscious. Emotional verbal behavior varies from highly specific references to ANS reactions such as "I can feel my heart racing" or "My stomach feels tight" to analogical discussions about the state of one's internal economy. The conditions under which we learn to make these referential statements are complex, since the events that control this kind of behavior and its consequences are not as available to the social environment as, for example, the contingency between the visual appearance of red objects and learning to refer to them as "red."[6] Thus, emotional statements that make references to unobserved events can be expected to be vague and to show large

5. Landis and Hunt (1939) and Ekman, Friesen, and Ellsworth (1972).
6. Skinner (1957).

variance from individual to individual and even within individuals from situation to situation.

Verbal emotional behavior that is not directly descriptive typically involves a classification or interpretation of the environment or the behavior of the individual. In the first class are statements such as "I feel so good the world looks beautiful to me today" or "I feel as if everybody is after me." The second type is often related to referential statements, but it also describes one's own behavior—for example, "I have never been so happy in my life" or "I must look terrible" or "I wish I could stop running away from this situation." All of these tend to be either descriptions of one's behavior (i.e., feedback from action systems) or descriptions of tendencies or structures that may or may not be completely realized. In the area of psychotherapy, extensive work has been done on the analysis of verbal behavior, and the analysis of the emotional utterances of patients is an important potential source of insight into the classification of emotional experience.

The most important aspect of the *quale* of an emotional experience and its accompanying behavior is the interpretation of the environment, the events that occasion particular emotions. Some environmental events may automatically produce arousal and may also be subject to very little in the way of complex meaning analysis. These "unlearned" emotional stimuli will be discussed again in Chapter 6, where I consider the particular characteristics of arousal. When a stimulus has an invariant effect on the autonomic nervous system, its interpretation by the meaning system may also be constant and invariant. Thus, for lower animals, the instinctual response to species specific "fear" stimuli involves the interpretation of the stimulus as threatening, which may be just as automatic as the arousal occurring at the same time. In many human cases some releasers also have fairly invariant interpretations. Consider, for example, the feeling of loss of support or sudden intense stimulation (which sets off the startle response).

However, even here the action of the interpretive system may be important. For example, loss of support has been considered an instinctive condition for an essentially negative emotional reaction, yet it is a condition for euphoria for many people when it is experienced on a roller coaster. The interpretation of the roller coaster as a positive event and the autonomic reaction that takes place at the same time produce a positive emotional response in this particular case.

The roller-coaster effect illustrates again the "meaning" of a particular situation for our own behavior. If we see ourselves in control of a given situation, the emotional reaction is more likely to be positive than negative. Thus, the seeking of autonomic stimulation, as in the case of the roller coaster, is a condition for positive rather than negative evaluation. Contrast this with the child that does not want to go on a roller coaster but is forced to do so; the reaction is likely to be negative. With the increasing observation of the child's control of the situation, that it can "choose" to go on the roller coaster, the situation changes from negative to positive. I shall discuss this question of "control" further when dealing with the problem of anxiety and the question of value.

I have made repeated reference to the fact that one of the sources for interpretive evaluations is the person's own behavior and actions. This point of view fits well into self-attribution theories of social behavior[7] and more behaviorist analyses that call attention to the control of a person's action by his or her own behavior.[8] These theories usually assume that some automatically engendered actions form the basis of evaluations by the actor. Our attitudes may be judged by observing our own behavior under certain conditions. These formulations fit well into the present schema, but two reservations must be entered with respect to those theories that *require* action prior to evaluation. First, not all, or even most, evaluations are based on self-attribution. If they were, we would always be dealing with actions that have to be generated automatically and that are then evaluated by the organism and form the basis of conscious self-perceptions and attributions. In contrast, many self-attributions are not the product of actions but may well be generated directly by structures of the "self." In other words, *one* of the sources of interpretive evaluations is the analysis of our own actions. It is an important source, particularly in emotional behavior, but not the only one. Second, it is important to note that only those actions of the agent that are, in fact, processed and perceived form the basis of these self-evaluations. We need to attend to and be conscious of our own actions in order for them to be the basis of evaluations. The clinical and theoretical literature of psychoanalysis is full of examples of individuals who are not conscious of their own actions or their meaning. In the course of therapy, these persons often learn appropriate self-attribution. Before such "insight," these individuals attribute or misattribute characteristics to themselves that are often directly derived from their existing long-term self-images.

Continuous feedback characterizes self-perception and emotion. Some cognitive interpretation of the environment produces arousal, and the perception of that arousal together with some cognition of the situation generates emotional experience. But then the evaluation and perception of our own new "emotional" states changes and colors the original interpretation. It should be obvious by now that neither particular situations nor sequences of situations determine emotional experience. Arousal and evaluation must occur, but not in any one sequence or confined to any one source.

MASTERY AND THE APPRAISAL LOOP

Continuous changes in perceptions and self-perceptions have effects on evaluations and even on the potential for arousal. In many cases these changes involve a sense of mastery. If we are able to change a threatening event into an innocuous one, and if we thereby change its evaluation from negative to positive and also avoid autonomic arousal, we have thereby mastered the situation. However, the more common sense of the term *mastery* implies that we become the masters of the situation, that we can encounter its demands and by meeting them adequately render them manageable. Rising to the challenge of a previously unen-

7. See, e.g., Heider (1958) and Kelley (1967).
8. Bem (1967).

countered or unconquered situation, we determine its course and master it. The evaluative implications of these locutions are obvious: a mastered situation is a good one, an unconquered one is bad.

An event may be differently appreciated depending on whether we believe that the outcome of one's transactions with it are going to be positive or negative. Specifically, the sense of control, whether or not the onset and offset of a particular event is under the individual's control, may be of special importance. This variable determines our positive response to the roller coaster (and the negative response to the loss of support), the control of masochistic behavior (and the fear of pain), and generally the child's developing sense of mastery. Mastery is a generalized concept indicating that events may be controlled and therefore may sometimes stop being unexpected. It colors the way in which a particular emotional situation is interpreted. Thus, what may be frightening at one point may become amusing, not because there has been an objective change in the situation but because a sense of mastery has drastically changed its cognitive interpretation.

Sense of control is only the anticipatory part of self-observation; it says that the individual will be able to control a situation. Sometimes the cognitive consequences of *ongoing* mastery are more important without our necessarily having anticipated it. In a new situation we frequently find that we may not expect to be able to avert bad consequences but cannot escape being in the situation. As the events unfold and actual mastery (i.e., control over the events) is observed, the experience of changing emotional tone, merely as a result of changing self-observation, is often dramatic. The euphoria of the underdog as she overcomes the favorite in sports, the soldier's joy at surviving a battle, and the child's delight at mastering a new task are all relevant examples.

The discussion of mastery raises a related issue of baseline levels of autonomic activity. I have assumed that the intensity of emotional experience varies with the degree of autonomic activity. However, some degree of arousal is present in all living human beings at all times. It is necessary, therefore, to assume a species-wide or individual threshold before arousal becomes "emotionally" functional. Some related issues will be discussed in connection with psychopathy in Chapter 12. The issue of mastery is relevant because, in a sense different from that used above, mastery is also related to the ability to manage or tolerate high degrees of arousal. Thus, individual differences in the functional threshold of arousal may be related to such mastery. By not reacting emotionally to even high levels of arousal, individuals may differ in their ability to manage (master) different situations.

I shall have occasion to return to the problem of mastery in connection with my discussion of the management of stress in Chapter 11. For present purposes, however, the more general notion of mastery associated with the concepts of appraisal and coping needs further attention. I turn here to the work of Richard Lazarus.[9] Lazarus's concept of appraisal refers to the restructuring of environ-

9. E.g., Lazarus (1968).

mental inputs into functional stimuli. The consequences of appraisal are divided into two categories: benign appraisal and threat appraisal. This dichotomy is a little unwieldy, since it is highly likely that appraisal is continuous from extreme threat to extreme positive or benign evaluations. More important, however, is the fact that judgments of whether a particular situation is benign or threatening are complex and require some theoretical basis, not an intuitive appreciation of what is benign or threatening, or good or bad.

Lazarus suggests some important variables to be considered in the outcome of appraisal. As far as benign appraisal is concerned, he first deals with automatized coping, which is a handling of the situation that does not bring emotion into play. In our terms this means that a particular response occurs often without conscious participation, and without arousal. The second outcome of the benign appraisal is so-called reappraisal, which restructures the stimulus and makes a potentially threatening, unpleasant, or unwanted situation more positive and produces essentially benign perceptions. The third class of benign appraisals comprises the positive emotions, such as elation, and Lazarus suggests that when these occur there is usually an implied mastery of danger. Although it is likely that the mastery of danger is involved in some of the positive emotions, many of them do not involve the mastery of danger. We need not have escaped a threat in order to be joyful or elated. This notion that some of the positive emotions are necessarily tied up with the avoidance of noxious events is a recurring theme in psychological writing and somewhat puzzling, since it can be found all the way from the writings of psychoanalysts to those of behavior therapists. It seems to be a last remnant of the notion that anxiety and fear are the fundamental emotions.

The consequences of threat appraisal are twofold in Lazarus's view. First, there is direct action and negative emotion, which presumably includes the typical flight-fight reaction and the appearance of aggression and anxiety. The second possibility is benign reappraisal, which changes the situation into a benign one and thus eliminates the negative emotional experience in action. It is this benign reappraisal of the threatening stimulus that may, under conditions of arousal, produce some of the positive emotions that involve the mastery of danger. Danger can be mastered both in the real world and in the mind.

Finally, psychoanalytic notions of denial and repression are considered as mechanisms of appraisal and reappraisal, and Lazarus has shown experimentally the importance of these reappraisals in objectively handling threatening situations. Similarly, the degree to which people are able to cope with threatening material by recoding it also determines the degree of their arousal. Recoding the threatening material, by changing its meaning to something innocuous or by rationalizing it (by making its implications innocuous), significantly decreases the degree of visceral arousal. However, making the content of a communication personally relevant or trying to avoid its implications, although acknowledging the meaning, tends to increase visceral arousal.[10]

10. Mandler, Mandler, Kremen, and Sholiton (1961).

Meaning Analysis and Emotion

As was indicated in Chapter 3, the ongoing meaning analysis refers to the activation and accessibility of those schematic representations that best fit the available evidence; it tells us where we are and what the meanings of our surrounds are. The very complexity of emotional situations will, as a result, produce complex meaning analysis and complex emotional experiences. Apart from the analysis of our surrounds, social and otherwise, and of our current mental states, the full meaning analysis in the case of the emotions must also take into account activations caused by autonomic arousal.

Given the active nature of hypothesis testing that takes place in the activation and use of schemas,[11] we are not simply assuming that activations occur and schemas are activated. On the contrary, partially activated schemas exhibit the nature of hypotheses that seek relevant additional information. This kind of hypothesis testing may lead to emotional consequences. When there is a noticeable discrepancy between the evidence available and the expectations produced by existing schemas, arousal will occur and an emotional synthesis will be produced.

Consider listening to a favorite piece of music that is played very badly. The schema for the music is activated, but the discrepancy between the way we expect it to be played and the way it actually sounds will produce arousal. The negative evaluation of the performance (not the music) will join with the arousal to produce an emotional state of annoyance or some similar negative emotion. If, however, the misplaying is done deliberately—as a musical joke—other schemas (e.g., about such musical jokes) will come into play and thereby modify expectations, discrepancies, and arousal.

Even though in the adult we assume active participations of schematic structures, passive meaning analysis (without hypothesis testing and search processes) can occur—for example, when the evidence is unequivocal or during the early stages of the development of schemas.

There may be a developmental shift from the passive to the active system. Thus, a particular schema is organized through a concatenation of circumstance, and a new structure is developed. On subsequent occasions any of the components of this passively established system may occur in the life of the individual. The previously laid down "passive" organization now is activated and becomes a possible way to organize experience and may work as an active system. It is difficult to specify, although easy to speculate about, the experiences that produce new structures out of these passive concatenations. The sheer frequency of similar experiences provides the process whereby passive organizations become autonomous within the mental system and can work as active schemas. The malleability and variability of the young child in emotional expression and experience suggest that the fortuitous concatenation of events produces variable emotional structures in the child.

Is there any a priori way of predicting specific passive evaluations of "objec-

11. Rumelhart (1980).

tive" situations? Except for some life-sustaining and life-threatening situations, the individual structures, on the basis of past experience, vary widely. There is one pragmatically useful categorization of emotional situations. This purely operational solution lies in the area of social induction. There is good reason to believe that the most powerful environment for the induction of certain kinds of behavior is to have that behavior exhibited by others. The Schachter experiments show quite clearly that people tend to be euphoric in the presence of a euphoric model or angry in the presence of an angry model. Experiments on mood[12] demonstrate the general point that the mood exhibited by the majority of a social group influences the mood of all its members. The source and structure of evaluative cognitions represent a special challenge to psychologists, worthy of a separate chapter. I can anticipate some of its conclusions by noting that they will surely be more complex than the argument, advanced by some philosophers[13] and psychologists,[14] that emotions follow an initial appraisal of an object as "good" or "bad."

Given the general hierarchical structure of mental organization, meaning analyses may move upward or downward within that structure. In addition, some analyses may occur automatically and inevitably, whereas others will require deliberate elaboration. Meaning analyses are often not complete in the sense of exploring all possible and potential activations and connections. They are more likely to be terminated when they meet the general requirements of the situation and task.

In the course of a meaning analysis, schemas that trigger autonomic arousal may or may not be reached. Whether arousal will occur depends on the structure of the situation (likely evidence that will activate the relevant schemas and paths to them) and on the accessibility of these trigger schemas. For example, some higher-order schema might produce arousal because of the conflict it engenders, but such a schema might be blocked as a result of repression, to be discussed below.

Since analytic requirements may be ambiguous, the same event may lead to arousal under some conditions and not others. Consider the alternative analysis in a very simple case, the definition of a dog. It might simply be considered an animal, or it might be defined as the generic terms for poodles, Alsatians, and so on. If some early experience with black poodles provides a link to arousal, the latter analysis will produce a negative reaction to dogs but the more general analysis will not.

Consider a parent who recently lost a child. Thinking about a two-year-old child may be painful (conflictual), but a remark about preschoolers in the context of a discussion of education will produce an analysis in the direction of "children" and no emotional consequence. The same remark in the context of relating examples of preschool behavior may lead to the "two-year-old" schema and emotional consequences.

In summary, whether a particular situation will lead to some emotional expe-

12. E.g., Nowlis and Nowlis (1956).
13. Peters (1969).
14. Arnold (1960).

rience will depend on whether arousal has been triggered, which in turn depends in part on the meaning analysis that the input has undergone. If a schema that leads to arousal is involved in the meaning analysis, then arousal and emotional experience will presumably take place. However, arousal may also arise from other sources—unrelated to the currently observed scene—and still contribute to "emotion."

Consciousness and Emotion

I am obviously more concerned with the expression of emotion in private experience or consciousness than with behavioral indices of the emotional complex. Some special aspects of consciousness and emotion deserve specific attention. Once again, the examination of consciousness is a theoretical enterprise, and it is not a high road to the raw constituents of feeling and emotion. Nobody has ever had access to the "raw experience" of another individual, and it is impossible in principle. Language and nonverbal communication, in gestures and bodily attitudes, cannot possibly give full expression to the felt emotional experience. Our language and action systems are crude instruments when it comes to describing the fine distinctions among emotions that we can "feel" in consciousness. This does not deny that, because of the essential identity of mental structures (but not their content) from individual to individual, much of private experience is made of the same stuff in different individuals, but it does suggest that similarities may be due to similarities in language and action that are to a very large extent molded by the social community.

One of the functions of consciousness is to make it possible to evaluate environmental conditions and action alternatives more effectively. But these evaluations and decisions often occur prior to any observable behavior. There may be conditions under which there are no direct behavioral "observable" consequences of these "emotions" at all; their primary function is to be experienced, to contribute to the evaluation of the current state of the organism, and to influence a final set of decisions as to actions and behaviors. From a behavioral point of view, however, they may not be expressed at all. At the subjective level, we are often well aware of the "emotional" reactions that enter into the complex determination of much of our behavior but are never expressed directly.

In a sense this position comes full circle in the context of my rejection of the nineteenth-century position that placed feelings and ideas before actions. Under some conditions, emotional states occur prior to action or inaction. There is, however, one important difference; the emotional contents of consciousness that I espouse do not posit feelings and ideas as primitives. On the contrary, emotional consciousness is seen as developing out of more basic and more general processes involving arousal and cognitive structures. Just as some action may be a prior condition for some other behavior in the flow of human acts, so may some conscious state. This analysis pushes the building blocks of emotional consciousness back to the same constituents as those that control other aspects of human action, and eventually to the individual and social conditions of development.

In the preceding chapter, I noted that the constructive nature of consciousness permits an understanding of the process whereby arousal and cognition are combined to produce a phenomenally unified experience of emotion. Since the evaluative processes that issue into mental structures are complex and since they also need to be combined with some representation of arousal, the structures that construct conscious emotional experiences are themselves at a fairly high level of generality. They do not usually involve some simple combination of a sensory schema and arousal. Most emotional experiences are delicately colored, complexly shifting experiences. In Chapter 9, I shall discuss in detail the nature of the evaluative structures. For present purposes I consider them as given. The constructed conscious structures use these evaluative schemas in combination with arousal schemas or structures to develop a new, more complex structure.

The first question that arises is whether these complex, high-level structures eventually develop their own independent existence, just as schemas for horses, friends, apples, and well-known cities do. Are there fear schemas, anger schemas, and joy schemas that await instantiation, both from evaluative and from arousal structures? If so, have we come full circle to the postulation of a set of primary emotions?

I believe that at a very abstract level some few such emotional structures do develop. But they cannot be directly accessed; just try to think of joy or fear or anger in the abstract. What is always needed is some specific instantiation; we need to think about a particular situation in which we felt fear or joy or anxiety. More important, even such ideational instantiations do not produce the full-fledged emotion; they are more like images of them, just as I am not mistaken that my thought of an apple or of Paris or of a friend produces a direct experience of that event or object. In other words, there will be an abstract representation of emotional states that share certain characteristics. As I will illustrate again later, some conditions of human existence that are similar enough in different situations, and even in different societies and cultures, repeat the same theme. Whether it is a situation that is threatening to existence or well-being, or the unattainability of some goal, or the unavailability of appropriate actions, they share enough similarities that repeated experiences will develop some abstract representation of fears, angers, or anxieties. Note well, however, that the specific experience will be determined by the unique instantiation, and will depend on actual evidence, both in terms of value-laden events and physiological arousal. However, there are rather few generalities in emotional experience. Most of our emotional experience tends to be constructed out of specific valuations and situational arousal. I should add that the abstract representation of arousal, the image of arousal, will become important again in our discussion of arousal, when autonomic imagery will play an important role. And the existence of abstract representation of emotional experiences is also relevant to the interplay between memory and arousal, to be discussed in Chapter 12. The important point is that abstract emotional representations are reflections of our interactions with a real world. It is the nature of the human organism and the conditions of our lives in a world with a limited repertory of possible situations in which we can act that produce internal representations. Our mental life—in cognition and in emotion—reflects our activity in our real and social world.

Why is it that emotions seem so obviously to demand conscious capacity? One interesting link is between the condition of arousal and the conditions for conscious constructions. In the preceding chapter, I indicated that consciousness is particularly evident when we are faced with choices, alternatives, and decisions. I also suggested, and will develop in successive chapters, that conditions of interruption and discrepancy are at least one of the most important determinants of autonomic arousal. In other words, both arousal and consciousness arise out of similar mental conditions—the need to select, to choose, to alter the current stream of action. It is therefore not surprising that those conditions that generate arousal also tend to lead to conscious constructions.

The construction of emotion is in the service of making optimal sense of the world, of presenting us with the most general picture of the world that is consistent with current needs, intentions, and situations. What is it about emotional states that they seem to demand priority in the process of emotional construction? Why is it that we seem unable to avoid our emotional experiences? In the first place, we need to question the generality of such assertions. Frequently, we do not register emotional states consciously. Psychotherapists and other observant people know of instances in which individuals were in states of intense arousal and barely hidden evaluative attitudes but were unable to report any conscious accompaniment of these indices. This is a case in which a repression-like effect blocks consciousness from constructing the relevant experience; other—often seemingly irrelevant—events and objects are reported to be in command of consciousness.

In most cases conscious construction does respond to the conditions that produce emotional states. These conditions are important events in the life of the individual; they are either unexpected events or meanings that lead to the memory of the significant events. Emotions occur at the choice points of actions, of lives, and of intentions. The dominance of conscious emotions reflects the role that evaluations and arousal play in our lives in general. We live in a world of values and of ordered and normative expectations; when the former are invoked and the latter violated, the scenario is one of central relevance to the individual. Emotions reflect these guideposts of human existence. Conscious constructions of emotions are the experiences that exemplify the centrality of these processes.

Repression

One other important interaction between emotion, consciousness, and actions needs to be explored—the concept of repression. As classically used, it refers to the absence from consciousness of important memories. The relation between memory models and emotional activity goes back to fundamental principles first systematically specified by Freud.[15]

First, recall Freud's notion of affect, which is a "process of discharge, a final expression of which is perceived as feeling." More specifically, "affectivity manifests itself essentially in motor (i.e., secretory and circulatory) discharge resulting in an (internal) alteration of the subject's own body."[16]

For Freud, affects cannot be unconscious; they are, by definition, represented in consciousness, even though their source may not be known to the individual (i.e., they are unconscious). Freud never taught that the disagreeable is forgotten. This is of central importance for a cognitive model. Semantic (memory) representations are not disagreeable as such; it is only if they lead to conflict, arousal, and interpretation that they may become disagreeable. "What Freud discovered was the function preventing the emergence into consciousness of an unconscious idea, which if it became conscious, would give rise to conflict."[17]

Repression, with its essential "function of rejecting and keeping something out of consciousness,"[18] operates to prevent retrieval, not of unhappiness, but of mental contents that would produce conflict in consciousness. Among these conflicts are reality situations that prevent the execution of actions, or conflicts between different cognitions—for example, between a particular mental content and its social unacceptability. In brief, "if the course of ideas in the [unconscious] were left to itself, it would generate an affect."[19]

Repression keeps out of consciousness those meaning analyses whose presence would produce interruption in either actions or plans. And, as we shall see in discussing the major mechanisms of interruption, the mental mechanisms that Freud proposed for "screen memories" that may be "allowed" into consciousness are not that different. When we consider substitution or alternative response sequences in action, we can easily see their cognitive parallels in the psychoanalytic concepts of displacement, condensation, and symbolization.

Feelings, Moods, and other Uncertainties

If emotions can be subsumed under the concatenation of autonomic arousal and evaluative cognitions, what then are feelings, affective states, and moods? I have already alluded to the dead end that William James's question "What is emotion?" presents; the problem is even more complicated for these emotional outliers. It would surely be unprofitable to try to construct what it is, exactly, that the common language conveys with these terms. Is the use by psychologists any more exact? Has it been refined and defined? Generally speaking, the term *feelings* has been used to refer to "little emotions," but even that usage is uncer-

15. See Rapaport (1942) for an excellent summary.
16. Freud ([1915] 1975).
17. Rapaport (1942).
18. Freud ([1915] 1975).
19. Freud ([1900] 1975).

tain, since little emotions are sometimes thought to be just like emotions but with less intense arousal, and since at other times they are just the evaluative states without any arousal whatsoever. In the latter case, they would be very much like cognitive evaluations. The problem arises when one wants to understand people's statements about their emotions and feelings, since the latter will sometimes be used like the former and sometimes only to refer to evaluations.[20] The same is true of the term *affect*, though psychologists tend to use it fairly consistently to refer to evaluative, "cold" emotional states.[21]

One possible solution is to refer to all incomplete "emotional" states as feelings, which would include conditions when evaluations are unaccompanied by arousal or the perception of arousal, when there is arousal but not a relevant evaluative state, and when there is an evaluative state but only the perception (image) of arousal without actual arousal.[22] A similar argument could then be made for the use of the terms *affect* and *affective states*.

Moods also seem to be little emotions, but persistent rather than transitory ones. In general, the term *mood* seems to refer to fairly persisting evaluative states that affect the character (evaluation) of all other ongoing evaluations—and emotions.[23]

I shall not try to be restrictive in the use of these terms. When they occur in these pages, they will usually be interpreted in the commonsense fashion dictated by the context.

I must enter a general disclaimer about a class of emotional experiences that, though mentioned at various places in the chapters to follow, are beyond the treatment offered here—the aesthetic emotions in general. Although I hint every now and then how I may want to go about understanding the emotional force of music and art, I am neither theoretically ready nor artistically competent to deal with them in any depth. I still wonder at the impact that some Puccini arias, Beethoven quartets, and Billie Holiday renditions have on my viscera.

As I have suggested earlier, the refusal to enter into an exegesis on what is and what is not an emotion inevitably raises question about the way one would deal with such things as pride, boredom, and patriotism or with such incomprehensible attractions as TV serials and repetitive cheap novels. In the long run, we must hope to understand all of these human strengths and weaknesses, whether or not we call them emotional. But that enterprise lies beyond my present goals.

With the conclusion of this chapter, I have presented the broad outlines of the mechanisms of the human mind and consciousness and the manner in which these processes contribute to the construction of emotional experience. In the chapters to follow, my discussion will repeatedly return to the nature of the mental structures (and in particular of schemas), the constructive nature of consciousness, and the manner in which schemas, arousal, and consciousness contribute to emotion.

20. Berscheid (1983).
21. Zajonc (1980).
22. Berscheid (1983).
23. Nowlis and Nowlis (1956).

6

AUTONOMIC AROUSAL: ITS USES AND FUNCTIONS

THIS CHAPTER DEALS WITH AROUSAL and its ramifications. It is specific and measurable arousal that, combined with the cognitive-interpretive system, lends the special "emotional" quality to certain experiences and actions. I shall first briefly describe the autonomic nervous system, which provides the physiological background of psychologically perceived arousal. I shall then present some speculations about the evolutionary role and current significance of the autonomic system, primarily within the context of its interaction with an acting, adjusting, and thinking organism. I shall further discuss the specific stimulation from the autonomic nervous system that is psychologically functional, and consider current knowledge about the stimuli that produce autonomic arousal.

I use the concept of arousal differently than most arousal theorists have employed it. The term *arousal*, as used here, refers to specific measurable events that occur outside the mental system; arousal is stimulation. Although the arousal system is responsible for producing that stimulation, which is, in turn, perceived by the mental apparatus, arousal is external to the system, just as other environmental events that receive cognitive interpretation are external.

The difference between this environmental-cognitive use of the concept of arousal and previous applications[1] is that the former endorses a psychological system that does not rely on energy concepts. The belief that the actions of organisms require some economy of energy in order to spring alive or, in a larger sense, to be motivationally justified, is relatively recent. Notions of energy flow did not become central to psychological theories until the late nineteenth century and, in particular, with Freud's primary insistence on an energy economy. After that, concepts of arousal, drives, motives, and their cognates became indispensable in the explanation of action. Although biologists tended to be wary of these constructs, which have so little empirical grounding,[2] the necessity for such mechanisms seemed to be self-evident. However, recent years have seen a questioning of this necessity, and it now seems worthwhile to proceed with an

1. E.g., Berlyne (1960) and Duffy (1962).
2. See Hinde (1956).

energyless psychology that relies a little bit more on autonomic functions and less on hydraulic fictions.[3]

The Autonomic Nervous System

The autonomic nervous system and the somatic nervous system may be roughly differentiated by their respective functions. The ANS is generally concerned with those functions that may loosely be called visceral, with the muscles of the heart, with the smooth muscles of the intestines, blood vessels, stomach, and the genito-urinary tract, and with the glands that are activated by the nervous system. In contrast, the somatic system includes among its functions the conveyance of information from sense receptors, their transformation, and the conveyance of information to the striped musculature of the body and limbs. And, though the pathways of the two systems can often be easily differentiated in the peripheral system, in the central nervous system both the autonomic and the somatic systems are closely interrelated and, at the present state of knowledge, frequently cannot be distinguished.

My major focus here is the peripheral autonomic system, primarily because I am concerned with the actions of the ANS that are discriminable by the psychological system (i.e., that are psychologically functional). The action of the peripheral ANS provides direct input to receptors, thence to the central nervous system, and generally to mental organization. The ANS tends to act in a more or less total fashion; its output is less differentiated than that of the somatic system, so that it is less usual—as is obviously often true in the somatic system—that only specific parts of the ANS will react to stimulation.

However, there is a division of the ANS that is separable and that does show generally differentiated but not wholly separate action. That is the distinction between the sympathetic and the parasympathetic divisions of the ANS. Again, I am concerned not with the neurophysiological distinction (whether anatomic or functional) between these two divisions but with the differences in their perceptually differentiable products.

Generally, the sympathetic system is concerned with bodily mobilization and the expenditure of energy, whereas the parasympathetic system is concerned with the conservation of bodily energy and resources. The two systems are antagonistic but not independent, and, depending on the demands of particular environmental and internal situations, they will be in varying degrees of balance.

Because of the mobilization aspect of the sympathetic system, it is often considered to be the emergency system that reacts to bodily threat and danger—for example, in flight or fight. Visceral blood vessels are constricted, thus channeling the blood supply to the muscles and the brain; the heart rate is increased; stomach and intestinal activity is slowed down; the pupils of the eyes widen; the rate of metabolism is increased; and the sugar content of the blood is raised. The

3. See also Kessen (1971).

function that most of these effects have in preparing the organism for immediate and alert reaction is obvious.

The parasympathetic system, by contrast, renews and conserves bodily resources. Blood vessels are dilated, and, as a result, blood pressure is lowered; heart rate is inhibited; stomach and intestinal activity is increased, as is salivary secretion; waste materials are disposed of by action of the bladder and colon; the pupils of the eyes are constricted; and the rate of metabolism decreases. The parasympathetic system is also effective in the reproductive system, as in lubrication and tumescence, although it should be noted that the sexual response is a prime example of the interaction of the two systems. For example, the contraction of the prostate before and during ejaculation is sympathetically innervated.

The evolution of the two systems suggests that the parasympathetic system is the earlier one.[4] The emergence of the sympathetic system, devoted to mobilizing and spending energies, is a "comparatively late acquisition in the evolution" of the ANS. In fact, when stimulation is excessive, the organism resorts to the older parasympathetic system.[5]

One other distinction must be made in discussing the ANS—that between two closely related adrenal hormones or catecholamines, both of which are secreted in the adrenal gland. I mention them because they may have psychologically functional consequences. They are epinephrine and norepinephrine (sometimes called adrenalin and noradrenalin). Both have sympathetic effects, primarily by raising blood pressure. However, epinephrine acts by increasing heart rate and increasing heart output directly, while norepinephrine acts by vasal constriction and thus produces a decrease of volume, which increases heart rate. In addition, both catecholamines increase sugar levels in the bloodstream, epinephrine more effectively than norepinephrine. It is possible that ANS discharge may be differentiated in terms of the primary action of either epinephrine or norepinephrine. If that is possible—and there is no hard evidence available at present—then two kinds of sympathetic activity (epinephrine and norepinephrine dominated, respectively) may play a differential role in emotional arousal, just as sympathetic and parasympathetic discharge do. However, the psychological difference between these two sympathetic patterns is obviously going to be slight. It is mentioned primarily because there is some evidence[6] that the differential output of the two hormones may distinguish certain emotional patterns. But there is no evidence yet that these two patterns control or direct differential emotional behavior or experience.

The specific evolutionary aspect of emotional behavior and experience can be divided into two broad general areas. First, there are the preprogrammed, often species-specific behavior adaptations that function for the population of a particular species. Among these are some defensive patterns, food-gathering actions, and sexual acts. Many are considered to be, in one form or another, prime

4. Pick (1954, 1970).
5. Pick (1970).
6. Funkenstein (1956) and Brady (1967).

examples of emotional behavior, such as aggression, sexuality, and reactions to separation. A respectable ethological literature exists (e.g., in the work of Robert Hinde and Niko Tinbergen and in the early works of Konrad Lorenz) that has investigated the necessary and sufficient internal and external conditions for the appearance of such behavior in lower animals. However, little is known about the internal or external stimuli that set the conditions for such behavior in humans or about the specific action patterns that are derivative from the evolution of the species. Most of the work on human action patterns in this "emotional" area is still carried on by analogy and does not carry us significantly beyond Darwin's original speculations about emotion in animals and man. While there are exceptions—the most notable being work on attachment behavior[7]—we can only guess whether some of the conditions and behaviors seen in mammals, particularly the subhuman primates, are applicable to the human case. Thus, I can say little more than that the flight, fight, and freeze reactions under specified conditions of threat are typical of mammalian behavior. Similarly, some generalization can be built on the observation of sexual behavior in primates, and some quasi-ethological work has been done in this area on humans.[8] In any case, in the ordinary language, we describe much of this behavior as emotional because it provides the occasion for depicting individuals as fearful, loving, lustful, and so forth. However, there are other preprogrammed patterns of behavior that seem to be specific to humans, and about which we know relatively little. Among these are laughter and crying, which seem to be typical of, if not exclusive to, the human species.

We have assumed that all of these behavior patterns are necessarily "emotional" within the context of a psychological assessment of human beings. In fact, such behavior can often be seen as "cold" and unemotional. Even the peculiarly human responses of laughter and crying are often seen—and sometimes deliberately presented by actors—as devoid of "emotional" content. The same is true of some kinds of aggressive behavior, of the loving and attachment behaviors exhibited by psychopaths in pursuit of some other end, and even of sexual behavior. It can therefore be argued that there is a missing component in all of these instances; as a bridge to the second adaptive aspect of emotional behavior, we suggest that the missing component is the activation of the autonomic nervous system. The argument is that in the natural state, and particularly in subhuman species, the aggression, attachment, and sexual patterns are usually accompanied by discharge of the autonomic nervous system.

The activation of the autonomic nervous system in combination with innate behavior patterns is important because both the ANS activation and the release of the behavior pattern may occur automatically in response to the identical stimulus situation. In other words, the same functional stimuli activate the behavior pattern and the ANS arousal. These internal and external conditions act as releasers for situation-specific behavior, which has adaptive significance for the population, but they also generate physiological responses that put the organism in a

7. Bowlby (1969).
8. Masters and Johnson (1966).

state of readiness for the behavior pattern that it accompanies. Among these are the release of adrenalin and the other sympathetic and parasympathetic responses. Furthermore, it appears that it is only when the behavior is accompanied by ANS arousal that we tend to think of it as "emotional." But what is the adaptive function of this "emotional" addition?

An evolutionary analysis may first consider the functions of the autonomic nervous system without regard to any action patterns that it accompanies. Essentially, the action of the ANS can be seen as a signal system (and, if the term had not been preempted, I would call it the second signal system). In general the ANS acts as a secondary support system for initiating an evaluation of situations that require choices and actions. A particular environmental input might require a very extensive meaning analysis for an appropriate cognitive appraisal, but under some circumstances a more direct, although less informative, analysis would be more adaptive. If some event is coded quickly to provide an independent activation of the autonomic nervous system while meaning analysis is proceeding, then, regardless of the outcome of the meaning analysis, a signal (ANS arousal) will be available to the psychological system that says, "Something is going on, something needs to be done." As a secondary system, the ANS has the paradoxical advantage that it is relatively slow, and it may not respond until one to two seconds after the onset of stimulus. During that period there is extensive opportunity for the meaning analysis to proceed and for appropriate action to be initiated. However, if such action has not been initiated, then the input from the ANS (i.e., the perception of ANS activity) provides a secondary system that alerts the organism and demands additional processing. In many cases the action of the secondary system is superfluous because appropriate action was initiated long before (i.e., half a second or more before) the secondary ANS signal arrives in the perceptual system. The best example, known to most drivers, is the response to an impending accident on the road that will frequently provide an appropriate action such as stepping on the brakes within a few hundred milliseconds, but the ANS still reacts, and the well-known postemergency autonomic response will occur.

The interaction between ANS arousal and emotional reaction, on the one hand, and cognitive factors, on the other, becomes both more complicated and, at the same time, consistent with this approach if we consider the temporal parameters in neural conduction. Sensory information classically associated with painful stimuli is mainly carried by the relatively slow spinothalamic tract while, at the same time, information is also carried by the much faster dorsal columns.[9] The pathways that eventually lead to sympathetic arousal are effective even later than either of these two systems. Thus, even before some sensory evaluation and most of the ANS-arousal information is available, signals that may determine the cognitive evaluations of the situation and of the subsequent "painful" and "emotional" effects arrive at the cortex. In other words, the cognitive interpretation of the situation and of the ANS feedback may, under some circumstances,

9. Melzack (1973).

be ready before these visceral signals arrive for their own evaluation in the central nervous system.

One of the most important aspects of the signaling functions of the autonomic nervous system is evident in the case of interruption. In Chapter 8, I shall discuss extensively the interruption of plans and actions, which produces an immediate ANS reaction. The adaptive significance of that response is that it signals that an ongoing system has been interrupted. If that interruption has not been immediately perceived, it requires meaning analysis for an appropriate response.

The signaling action of the autonomic nervous system may also be construed as a mediating system. In cases in which meaning analysis is often not possible—because of the organism's inability to attend to the situation—structures may develop in which a particular action is tied to the appearance of the ANS response. The sequence of stimulus event → ANS response → action will occur. This is the pattern that has been used to explain avoidance behavior in lower mammals.[10] The two-factor theory of avoidance behavior, in which an ANS response is first "conditioned" to the experimental situation in which the animal is shocked and then serves as a mediating stimulus between the experimental situation and subsequent avoidance before the onset of the noxious stimulus, is of particular interest in the case of organisms that cannot engage in an extensive meaning analysis. In humans, elaborate sequences that use the ANS system as a mediating signal are not necessary. The analysis that a particular situation may have noxious consequences need not await the mediation of the ANS system, and avoidance can be learned relatively quickly. However, lower animals, as well as small children, do not have the elaborate cognitive apparatus available for analysis, and in that case the two-factor "theory" applies. It is more a description of the uses of the ANS system by certain species under certain conditions than a theory of avoidance behavior. Avoidance in humans can often, although clearly not always, be carried out without such an elaborate apparatus.

I can summarize my argument about the adaptive basis of arousal by focusing on the evolutionary significance of the activation of the autonomic nervous system (and, of course, the adaptive significance of having an autonomic nervous system at all).

First, the ANS functions both as an accompaniment and as a possible activator of certain action patterns. Second, activation of the ANS serves as a signal for action and colors the particular behavior it accompanies or mediates. Thus, much of the behavior that is considered emotional is seen as such only because it has ANS accompaniments. As I have indicated earlier, there are some evolutionarily significant behavior patterns that may occur without the ANS accompaniment and are then seen as "cold." It is only when accompanied by ANS discharge that they become "emotional." Conversely, as I have argued throughout, many different behavior patterns may be accompanied, by sympathetic or parasympathetic discharge and may acquire "emotional" characteristics. Under

10. Mowrer (1939).

those conditions they become more intense, are accompanied by physiological symptoms, and, because of the constriction of attention by the demands of the ANS system, often seem to be narrow, monolithic, and "irrational."

I have described here some general adaptive uses of the autonomic nervous system. In the next sections, I shall discuss in detail how ANS activity may affect attentional mechanisms and how these relations in turn affect behavioral efficiency and general perceptual processes.

Adaptive Consequences of Arousal

The dominant notion about the function and evolution of the sympathetic nervous system is the concept of homeostasis, primarily linked with W. B. Cannon's name. He described that concept unequivocally in 1930: "In order that the constancy of the internal environment may be assured, therefore, every considerable change in the outer world and every considerable move in relation to the outer world, must be attended by a rectifying process in the hidden world of the organism. The chief agency of this rectifying process . . . is the sympathetic division of the autonomic system."[11]

But Cannon's description of the homeostatic function of the sympathetic nervous system (SNS) leaves us with the uncomfortable impression of a passive organism adjusting its internal environment to external events, just as a physical thermostat does. It is more likely that the organism may react to the requirement for internal adjustment by action on the environment. These actions may change external stimulation to the point where the internal environment is restored to its previous "normal" level. We therefore assume that homeostatic action by the SNS also mobilizes action systems to act on the environment. And the first step toward such action is the analysis of the environment and of the possible actions available.

There are three developments that point to the direction of possible adaptive consequences of ANS activity and its correlates. The first of these is purely attentional.

Any environmental set of events that produces ANS activity is also the occasion for attentional activity (or focused consciousness). Research by John and Bea Lacey has shown that attentional preparatory activity is accompanied by a parasympathetic-like ANS response, specifically, cardiac deceleration.[12] We might conjecture that this deceleration in part attenuates one of the internal attention-demanding stimuli—cardiac acceleration. The less internal noise there is, the more attention the external demands are paid. However, cardiac deceleration is also correlated with fast action times; that is, the organism reacts more effectively to environmental demands, and cardiac deceleration anticipates the *perception* of the stimuli that direct behavior.[13] Cardiac deceleration is also correlated with

11. Cannon (1930).
12. Lacey and Lacey (1974) and Lacey, Kagan, Lacey, and Moss (1963). See also Coles and Duncan-Johnson (1975) and Jennings, Averill, Opton, and Lazarus (1970).
13. Higgins (1971).

the orienting response,[14] a focusing and readiness pattern.[15] The evolutionary history of the ANS[16] also seems to point toward the following: a primitive response of the ANS to demanding situations is a parasympathetic one that, while energy conserving, also increases the capability of the organism to respond to coping demands of the environmental situation (be it threat or not). This particular response may proceed at the same time that an energy-expending sympathetic activity is going on.[17]

In addition to this initial correlation of ANS activity with attention, there is a secondary mechanism of cardiac deceleration, which is a response to cardiac acceleration. Since the sympathetic response to stimulation has a relatively long latency, of the order of 1 to 1.5 seconds, this particular reaction sets in "long" after the initial attention-directing mechanism, which can occur in a few hundred milliseconds. A case can be made that the cardiac deceleration in response to afferent visceral events is a later and different response.[18] It occurs in response to increases in blood pressure, which are picked up by receptor mechanisms in the carotid sinus and other vessels. This afferently induced deceleration has the same consequences as the earlier response to attention-directing mechanisms. Here, then, is a direct parasympathetic-like response *to* sympathetic arousal that produces the kind of mechanism conducive to survival and coping that I described earlier.

The third mechanism that might produce adaptive responses guided by ANS activity is a long-range effect that suggests more effective long-term adaptive action under conditions of ANS arousal. Like the others, it also has the effect of making it more likely that the organism will, once ANS activity has set in, respond more quickly, scan the environment more effectively, and eventually respond adaptively. The major evidence in this area uses another measurement of ANS activity: the peripheral appearance of adrenalin and noradrenalin (the catecholamines).[19] This usually involves measurement of catecholamine levels in the urine. Another approach involves the infusion of catecholamines and the observation of their effect on behavior and experience. The Marañon and Schachter experiments described in Chapter 21 are two prime examples of this technique. As far as the infusion technique and the present problem of the adaptive functions of ANS activity are concerned, EEG shows activation in drowsy and sleepy animals when adrenalin is given intravenously.[20] However, such activation is not present in awake and aroused animals. This finding suggests that adrenalin produces ANS arousal, which in turn leads to environmental scanning, but does not do so when the organism is already "in contact" with the environment.

Concerning the level of peripheral catecholamines, the traditional view of ANS and catecholamine activity as "primitive" and obsolete may be mistaken;

14. Graham and Clifton (1966).
15. Sokolov (1963).
16. Pick (1970).
17. A related phenomenon is the fractionation of ANS activity reported by Lacey (1959, 1967).
18. Lacey and Lacey (1974).
19. Frankenhaeuser (1971a, 1971b, 1975).
20. Rothballer (1967).

the catecholamines, even in the modern world, play an adaptive role "by facilitating adjustment to cognitive and emotional pressures."[21] Normal individuals with relatively higher catecholamine-excretion levels perform better "in terms of speed, accuracy, and endurance" than those with lower levels.[22] In addition, good adjustment is accompanied by rapid decreases to base levels of adrenalin output after heavy mental loads have been imposed.[23] Thus, high adrenalin output and rapid return to base levels characterize good adjustment and low neuroticism. If it is true that the increased ANS activity produces automatic scanning of the environment, we might speculate not only that attention to environmental events is adaptive when events take place that automatically produce a rise in ANS activity and catecholamine levels but also that this signal from the ANS system needs to be discriminable. A constant low or high level, returning only slowly to base levels, would produce few such discriminable ANS signals to the attentive, scanning mechanisms. The quicker the return to baselines is, the more likely it is that the next event that produces catecholamine activity will be scanned and, on the average, adequately responded to with effective coping activities. Absence of "appropriate" stress responses to situations that demand attention would produce, in the long term, ineffectual adjustment to environmental demands. For example, cognitive gating of threat in the environment ("denial") might reduce the adrenalin response and the appropriate scanning, as in the "paradoxical" response, which shows decreased secretion during stress *and* poor adjustment to these cognitive and emotional stressors.[24] I conclude that there is at least suggestive evidence that a third, long-range system involves ANS activity (or adrenomedullar response) that is adaptive in making it possible for the organism to cope more adequately with environmental tasks by increasing attentive scanning activity.

AROUSAL, EFFICIENCY, AND ATTENTION

There is another line of thought that relates degree of arousal (defined autonomically) and human cognitive efficiency. The notion that there is an inverted-U-shaped relation between arousal and efficiency has existed at least since 1940.[25] Because the concept of arousal has received varied interpretations, ranging from muscle tension to activities of the reticular formation, we can just as easily relate SNS activity to efficiency. As SNS activity increases, the information-seeking activity of the organism similarly increases and thus produces more task-relevant information. As SNS arousal becomes very intense, it floods attentional mechanisms and decreases the amount of information that the organism can effectively recruit either from the environment or from its own memory store. One can also relate this effect to some of Daniel Berlyne's suggestions[26] about the

21. Frankenhaeuser (1975).
22. Frankenhaeuser (1971b).
23. Johansson and Frankenhaeuser (1973).
24. Johansson and Frankenhaeuser (1973).
25. Freeman (1940).
26. Berlyne (1960).

relation between collative variables (novelty, surprise, complexity, and incongruity), arousal, and effective thought. Conflict is an essential aspect behind the operation of these variables and is consonant with the interruption of existing cognitive structures. Novel, surprising, complex, and incongruous input or structures interrupt the execution of ongoing structures—which could be interpreted as conflict. These stimuli produce arousal (seen theoretically), whereas the accrual of new information (which brings new operative structures into play) brings arousal down again.[27] Arousal increases with interruption and decreases as the organism finds means of coping with the new interrupting information.

The finding that the interesting aspects of a situation may be mediated by its complexity is also derived from Berlyne's extensive research on collative variables.[28] Another attempt to relate attentional variables to stimulus properties is the claim that pupillary dilation is related to the pleasantness of a stimulus.[29] An extensive study[30] of these and other variables found, in the first instance, support for the hypothesis of autonomic fractionation: that parasympathetic-like (e.g., heart-rate deceleration) and sympathetic-like (e.g., pupillary dilation) responses may coexist under specifiable conditions.[31] The data suggested that attentive observation of environmental events produces pupillary dilation and cardiac deceleration, consistent with the hypotheses discussed earlier. However, unpleasantness did not produce cardiac acceleration, as some global theories of arousal, activation, and "stress" might predict. "[S]ubjects indeed can intend 'to note and detect' even when stimuli are noxious and unpleasant." In general, we can agree with the conclusion that physiological responses are not "isolated stimulus-attributes" but that autonomic activity is important in dealing with environmental demands. Thus, sociocentric notions about a world filled with objectively pleasant and unpleasant stimuli seem biologically indefensible; instead, autonomic activity responds to the informational demands of situations, reactions being dependent on coping activities as well as on "stimuli." Attention to the hedonically attractive object is supplemented by attention to potentially threatening stimuli.[32]

Finally, the correlation between autonomic activity and interest is not mediated by complexity or activation. Instead, an "attention-getting stimulus, whether simple or complex, whether conveying a sense of activity . . . or passivity . . . evokes an autonomic response-pattern characterized by pupillary dilation [sympathetic-like] and cardiac deceleration [parasympathetic-like]."[33]

In general, these various studies support the position that "automatic" reactions of the autonomic nervous system are, in the first instance, dependent on some general mechanisms such as cognitive or behavioral discrepancy or interruption, and that these may lead to cognitive and autonomic adaptations that

27. Berlyne (1960, 1965).
28. Berlyne, Craw, Salapatek, and Lewis (1963).
29. Hess (1965).
30. Libby, Lacey, and Lacey (1973).
31. Lacey (1967).
32. Hastings and Obrist (1967).
33. Libby, Lacey, and Lacey (1973).

involve attention and coping behavior. At the same time, attentional mechanisms may independently be tied to some highly specific autonomic responses.

A detailed discussion of the relation among arousal, efficiency, and attention is more appropriate to the problem of stress and will be found in Chapter 11.

The Functional Physiological Stimulus

An important distinction among types of physiological variables is the one between peripheral physiological variables in general and psychologically functional peripheral physiological variables as such. The present enterprise is primarily concerned with those inputs to the mental organization that produce emotional behavior and experience. Thus, psychologically functional physiological variables are those that can be shown to affect the mental system and to have a controlling effect over the behavior and experience in question. In particular, I am interested in those physiological variables for which it can be shown that the presence of one or more of them is necessary or sufficient for variation in some human thought or action. Physiological variables, in contrast to psychological variables, which, by definition, have known effects on behavior and experience, may be divided into four classes—restricting ourselves, of course, to autonomic and endocrine events.

1 • Psychologically functional physiological variables. This class of variables is of primary interest if we want to know what it is that determines emotion. As I shall show later, there is relatively little evidence about the differentiated action of specific variables, but it is the effect of ANS activity in general that concerns us.

2 • Psychologically nonfunctional physiological variables. Much is known about complex responses such as skin resistance to a variety of different stimuli. But at present there is no evidence that variations in skin resistance are controlling variables for psychological events or, even more generally, that skin resistance can be discriminated by the organism. Many of the autonomic responses that have been measured in emotional situations belong in this category. They are important physiological variables in that they tell us something about the body's response to certain emotional situations, but they do not, as far as is known, significantly influence emotional behavior or experience. These physiological events are correlated with behavior and experience, and they may very frequently be used as an index function, but they are not psychologically functional.

3 • Physiological functional psychological variables. Certain physiological events are, of course, determined by experiential and behavioral events. To the extent, for example, that a physiological event is an index function for behavior that precedes it, this is an important category for the investigation of behavioral-physiological interactions. In a sense, much of the physiological work on emotion falls into this category. Many of the physiological responses measured by psychophysiologists may be the result of the emotional events as well as of the environmental stimuli that give rise to them.

4 • Physiologically nonfunctional psychological variables. These events have no theoretically or practically important physiological effects and are of no particular interest in the present context.

In summary, I shall be primarily concerned with the psychologically functional physiological variables, that is, those that determine behavioral and experiential events.

There exist a host of physiological events that are correlated with behavioral events but about which we are insufficiently informed to make any causal, directive inferences. For example, subjects who find sexual stimuli disturbing show an increase in body temperature when exposed to these stimuli, whereas subjects who are particularly reactive and disturbed by aggressive stimuli show a decrease in body temperature.[34] We are unable to make any causal statement except to say that these variables are shown to covary and that further investigations are necessary to find an explanation for this covariation.

The attempt to show that different patterns of physiological responses are the determining variables for different emotional reactions and experiences has existed in psychology at least since William James's statement that the emotion is defined at least in part by the pattern of the physiological response. I have summarized these attempts in Chapter 2. It is highly unlikely that humans can discriminate slight differences in patterns of autonomic response. More important, it would have to be shown that, given the different patterns of arousal, different emotions will result. At the present time, all we can say about the different physiological patterns in different emotional situations is that they are a response either to the environmental conditions that produce differential emotions or to differential behavior.[35] Nothing in these data shows that the emotional behavior or experience is a function of the physiological pattern.

Given that there is no evidence that patterns of physiological response or autonomic discharge determine different kinds of emotions, what is the most likely psychologically functional evidence from the arousal system that controls emotional behavior and experience?

Autonomic Perception

Human beings apparently have difficulty in discriminating slight changes in physiological patterns. There is currently very little evidence about the discriminability of ANS reactions. Since we do know that there is a paucity of receptors that can pick up changes in autonomic functioning,[36] the most likely candidate for a functional autonomic stimulus is general autonomic arousal, which can, of course, vary in degree but not in discriminable pattern. I shall next examine the question whether it is likely that general autonomic arousal, varying in degree,

34. Mandler, Mandler, Kremen, and Sholiton (1961).
35. Brunswick (1924) and Landis and Hunt (1939).
36. Robbins (1983).

is a psychologically functional stimulus for emotional behavior and experience.

One demonstration of the physiological changes that can be discriminated would be to make some other behavior—some external response, for example—contingent on changes in physiological states. We made one such attempt, requiring subjects to make a discrimination that was contingent on a change in heart rate.[37] The subject was simply asked to say "fast" or "slow" whenever his heart rate changed perceptibly. The experimenter was able to provide the appropriate feedback by inspecting a cardiotachometer. Under these conditions, where the subject presumably had only changes in heart rate available as a discriminative stimulus, there was an improvement in discrimination, whether the subject determined the response onset or whether he was asked to give a response on a signal from the experimenter. Within a few hundred trials the subject was able to make 100 percent correct judgments of his heart rate. However, it turned out that what actually controlled the discrimination was not the heart rate but changes in the respiratory cycle. The more even, better-spaced, and deeper the breathing cycle is, the more pronounced are the distinctions between accelerative and decelerative phases of heart action. Thus, the subject was learning to breathe deeply and evenly and to make his fast and slow judgment on the basis of the movements of his chest cavity. In another experiment, in which a subject was not told that he was to monitor his heart rate, the sequence with which two lights went on was determined respectively by increases and decreases in the heart rate of two beats per minute or more. A subject was required to predict which of the two lights would go on. If the heart rate could be discriminated, it should have acquired control over the predictions. The subject was run for a total of 4,675 trials, and his performance never deviated significantly from chance. Our conclusion was that "discrete changes in heart rate do not easily develop into discriminated stimuli" and that the "private" stimulus conditions that control "emotional" behavior are likely to be grosser visceral changes.[38]

If minor changes in visceral patterning cannot be discriminated and if no evidence is available that the physiological patterns sometimes observed with emotional behavior in fact *precede* such emotional experiences, we may then embrace the assumption that the adequate stimulus for emotion is general gross ANS discharge.

The assumption that the perceptual system that receives input from the arousal system is insensitive may also be tested indirectly, by investigating the perception of autonomic changes in general.

One approach to this question requires studying what people are able to say about their perceived state of autonomic arousal in relation to the actual level of arousal. I summarized our data in Chapter 2, which are consistent with the summary that "self report may be an integrative variable more representative of general states of bodily activation than any single physiological variable."[39]

The relation between autonomic perception and actual autonomic dis-

37. Mandler and Kahn (1960).
38. Mandler and Kahn (1960).
39. Thayer (1970).

charge, while positive, is relatively weak. In addition, the available evidence suggests that the human organism is rather ineffective in discriminating autonomic events.[40] I have also suggested that the perception of arousal and its occurrence are not necessarily correlated and may even be disparate events. In the extreme case of autonomic imagery, perception may occur without actual stimulation, just as in visual or any other kind of imagery. Equally important is the distinction between people's reports of habitual and of situational reactions, a distinction that was subsequently codified as the difference between trait and state variables.

The degree of arousal that an individual believes to be active at a particular time thus may be a function of actual arousal or of other factors. These other factors can be purely cognitive in that the general system produces inputs to the perceptual system that indicate that a state of arousal exists when it does not. ANS arousal is not an all-or-none stimulus system. Small degrees of arousal may be perceived as more extreme or may draw increasing attention under some conditions. However, suggestive data do exist that people can be led to believe that arousal has occurred when it actually has not.

AUTONOMIC IMAGERY

I made reference earlier to the concept of imagery, which we proposed in order to understand the finding that performance sometimes varied inversely with degree of reported autonomic activity but was unrelated to actual autonomic activity.[41] We suggested then that autonomic activity may not be a necessary antecedent of autonomic perception and that autonomic perception, though initially a function of autonomic activity, may eventually become independent of autonomic events. That is, of course, not different from the imagery associated with other sensory modalities. Imagery involves the activation of some schemas of sensory patterns in the absence of environmental evidence for or input to those patterns. It is in this fashion that we can imagine seeing the Taj Mahal, hearing a familiar band or a friend's voice, feeling the touch of velvet or a cheek, or experiencing visceral arousal. In all these cases, including the autonomic one, the nature of the experience tends to be evanescent and rather pale compared with the "real thing." The latter, of course, occurs on occasions of direct activation, the former when the relevant schema is less specifically activated by conceptual, top-down processes.

Since the concept of autonomic imagery has been advanced, it has found applications to a variety of different emotional phenomena.[42] It is a helpful tool for understanding the emotional experiences in spinally injured patients[43] and for explaining the persistence of autonomically mediated behavior in sympathec-

40. Blascovich and Katkin (in press).
41. Mandler and Kremen (1958).
42. For summaries, see Clark (1982), Leventhal (1979), and Robbins (1982).
43. Hohmann (1966).

tomized animals,[44] some reactions to medication,[45] and phantom-body experiences.[46]

Clearly, autonomic imagery does not produce fully experienced emotional states, any more than auditory imagery is equivalent to hearing an orchestra. At best, the contribution of autonomic imagery produces emotional imagery. For the truly felt emotion, actual ANS arousal is a necessary condition.

Autonomic Generality

The point about the generality of visceral arousal as the starting point for emotion must be underlined. Until now I have discussed evidence that the discriminated aspects of visceral arousal probably involve a general degree of arousal, and noted that the studies that have shown different patterns have failed to show that these patterns control emotional behavior. It is, however, also true that widely different emotions show relatively few differences in physiological patterns. Here we need not go into the question of whether these patterns are antecedent to the emotional expression. If, with very different emotions, the patterns are similar, the argument can be made that it is highly unlikely the different emotions depend on different patterns. The autonomic patterns are unlikely, in this case, to have been differential antecedents to the emotional response. If the subsequent patterns show great similarity, it is unlikely that there were large differences between them before the onset of the emotional behavior and experience.

An investigation of emotional differences in patterns of visceral response showed that both sadness and mirth produce measurable visceral responses and that both of them seem to involve primarily SNS patterns.[47] Slight differences between sadness and mirth were found, which is not surprising; these states are also marked by different kinds of experiences and actions, but the data give us no clues as to any visceral differentiating states that *produce* sadness and mirth. It is more important to note that in a single experiment it has been shown that two such divergent emotional states produce similar sympathetic states of arousal. Other evidence was summarized in Chapter 2.

There is probably another reason why highly specific and discrete peripheral visceral patterning cannot serve as an adequate signal for specific emotion. The limited-capacity aspects of consciousness severely limit the kinds of patterns and certainly their discreteness, which could serve as adequate stimuli for the perception of emotion. Given the limitation to some five dimensions, with single values on each dimension it is unlikely that the kind of discrete, multifaceted patterning that would be necessary to represent the different shadings of emotions

44. Solomon and Wynne (1954).
45. Tyrer (1976).
46. Melzack and Dennis (1978).
47. Averill (1969).

can be consciously perceived and evaluated. Furthermore, if the consciousness process were preoccupied with visceral activity, it would severely restrict other cognitive factors from interacting with the production of conscious emotional states. Conversely, any nonvisceral attention would restrict visceral awareness to some few attentional chunks. Since such cognitive and environmental activity is highly likely, it is also reasonable to assume that only a small part of the limited capacity of consciousness is devoted to visceral attention. If that is the case, then the most likely source of the adequate perceptual input would be some form of a single dimension of gross visceral output.

The physiological evidence suggests that the difference between essentially similar, "negative" emotions such as fear and anger is relatively slight but that the differences between contrasting emotions, whether they are arrayed on a positive to negative continuum or whether we contrast grief and mirth, are no greater. This is additional supportive evidence for the notion that visceral patterns are unlikely to be the basis of differentiation of emotional behaviors and responses.

Autonomic Arousal and the Potentiation of Affect

Situations that arouse affect, defined merely as some evaluative state, may also be the occasions for autonomic arousal. Whether a situation is pleasant or not, whether an individual fails or succeeds, as long as there is some indication of unexpectedness or of discrepancy with expectations, there is autonomic arousal. In this connection, as far as we know, all pathological states, all mental "disturbances," are associated with such arousal. This is true of the manic individual, but also of the depressive. The external signs of inactivity of the individual in a state of depression are not linked to internal inactivity; depression, in order to be felt, requires autonomic activation.[48] The same is true of schizophrenic individuals and many others.[49]

I now turn to the evidence that autonomic arousal occurring as a function of events quite unrelated to the current state also affects the occurrence and intensity of emotional experiences.

The notion that arousal induced by conditions other than those that determine the current affective state can combine with the current evaluation to produce an emotional experience has been posited ever since the appearance of Schachter and Singer's work.[50] Typically, it has been placed in an attribution framework, that is, the cause of the arousal is assigned to the current situation.[51] That position necessitates the postulation of a need to explain or attribute the unexplained arousal. As I have argued, it is not necessary to postulate such an additional evaluative need. The existence of ANS arousal, together with some

48. See, e.g., Kelly, Brown, and Shaffer (1970) and Dawson, Schell, and Catania (1977).
49. See Zahn, Carpenter, and McGlashan (1981) for a review.
50. Schachter and Singer (1962).
51. Schachter (1971) and Zillmann (1978).

evaluative state, will produce a conscious emotional state in keeping with the current intentional state of the individual. It is the latter that determines which emotional state will be constructed, that is, used in the integration of arousal and value. In the absence of evaluative states, or in the presence of intentional states that focus on the physical symptom of the arousal, the conscious state that is constructed may not be emotional but may rather use a descriptive schema about the state of arousal.

Concerning the effect of independently manipulating the arousal and subsequent evaluative states, the notion of excitation transfer has been useful.[52] In a variety of studies, arousal engendered in one situation potentiated the degree of emotional experiences in a subsequent one. For example, the intensity of hostile behavior was shown to be a function of prior arousal induced by erotic and aggressive films, with the film that produced the highest arousal (the erotic one) having the greatest effect.[53] Similarly, prior physical exercise increased subsequent anger[54] as well as reported sexual arousal in response to an erotic film.[55] Furthermore, the degree of humorous appreciation can vary with prior erotic or disturbing experiences[56] and with degree of prior anxiety.[57] Another ingenious report in the same genre took advantage of a naturalistic situation. In one study, males were approached by an attractive female interviewer when they were either on a very fragile, anxiety-producing bridge or on one that seemed safe and sturdy. When asked to write imaginative stories, the high-arousal condition (fragile bridge) contained more sexual arousal (in the presence of the female but not a male interviewer) than did the low-arousal condition (sturdy bridge).[58] Finally, in a study on the effect of physical exercise, subjects were required to exercise or not, following which they were put into a situation that produced either positive or evaluative states (they were told they had done well on a test) or was effectively neutral. Subsequent ratings by the subjects of their university, faculty, and so forth showed that the combination of arousal and positive evaluative states produced more favorable ratings.[59]

In summary, these studies demonstrate that ANS arousal, which decays relatively slowly, will potentiate subsequent feeling states. In other words, regardless of the source of the arousal, it is used in the construction of emotional consciousness together with any evaluative states that have been induced.

I previously suggested that research showing that the injection of adrenalin by itself, without external cues, may result in negative, anxious states is neutral as far as evidence for the cognitive-arousal position is concerned.[60] It may well be relevant to an attributional, labeling position,[61] but even that is questionable.

52. Tannenbaum and Zillmann (1975) and Zillmann (1978).
53. Zillmann (1971).
54. Zillmann, Katcher, and Milavsky (1972).
55. Cantor, Zillmann, and Bryant (1975).
56. Cantor, Bryant, and Zillmann (1974).
57. Shurcliff (1968).
58. Dutton and Aron (1974).
59. Clark (1982).
60. Maslach (1979).
61. Schachter and Singer (1962).

Autonomic activity can interact with whatever evaluative state is currently active. For example, patients with an adrenomedullar tumor that increases the production of adrenalin and noradrenalin in the bloodstream often report feelings of anxiety.[62] It is not unlikely that these patients, knowing of their illness, feel helpless in their encounter with it and thus, together with the increased sympathetic activity, feel anxious. It may even be true that, in general, high levels of autonomic activity that are persistent and inescapable may give rise to evaluational states, because the individual cannot locate or identify the event that produces the autonomic activity.[63]

One final comment on the effect of arousal per se. Just as an increase in autonomic arousal should increase the probability of emotional experience, so should a decrease in arousal—assuming no change in evaluative states—decrease this probability. In the absence of experimental evidence on the subject (but see the studies on biofeedback reported in Chapter 2), we turn to anecdotal and pharmacological evidence. It is generally assumed that experienced emotions decrease in intensity when our visceral activity decreases—we "calm down." As far as pharmacological agents are concerned, it is unfortunate that most of those that have a depressing effect on the perceived arousal of autonomic activity (e.g., alcohol) also have marked effects on the central nervous system. One of the few exceptions is practolol (also propanolol), which blocks cardiac receptors (thus reducing heart action) with little attendant action on other sympathetic receptors, and very little of which enters the central nervous system. Psychiatric patients characterized by extreme anxiety showed significant improvement when administered practolol.[64] Similar agents have been used in the treatment of anxiety states[65] and may also reduce anxiety levels in nonclinical populations.[66] Thus, some emotional reactions may be regulated by a primarily peripheral management of the autonomic nervous system.

The Conditions of Autonomic Arousal

The question about the events that produce autonomic arousal pervades much of the work on emotion in general. I alluded to it before and will return to it at length in the chapters on interruption, anxiety, and even on value. The following discussion only touches on the major issues about the initiation of arousal. In the first instance it makes contact with the discussion in Chapter 5, which suggested that certain meaning analyses may lead to triggers of autonomic activation.

I shall make the distinction between releasing stimuli and functional triggers. For example, it is highly likely that a loud noise or sudden loss of support is a

62. Winkler and Smith (1972).
63. Tyrer (1976).
64. Bonn, Turner, and Hicks (1972).
65. Jefferson (1974).
66. Gottschalk, Stone, and Gleser (1974).

releasing stimulus for ANS discharge in the young infant, whereas the stimulus configuration that characterizes someone's boss is surely an acquired functional trigger and unlikely to be an innate releasing stimulus for ANS discharge.

One of the difficulties in trying to arrive at phylogenetic generalizations is that most external events and stimuli are filtered extensively through the cognitive-interpretive system. In lower animals fewer such transformations into functional stimuli take place; therefore, the functional stimulus can often be adequately described in terms of events external to the organism. However, particularly in the human, such environmental stimuli can be and are variously transformed into functionally active or nonactive stimuli; conversely, phylogenetically neutral stimuli may be transformed into functional triggers. Thus, an advantage of doing research with lower animals is that the stimulus and the constancy of its effects may be known to the observer. For humans, however, we must ask what the mechanisms might be whereby external stimuli become functional releasers. In the history of psychophysiology the central concern with ANS arousal has been within the context of classical conditioning theory. The conditionability of SNS responses has provided some of the mainstays for the demonstration of classical conditioning. Many physiological reactions, ranging from kidney secretions to the production of insulin, can be brought under the control of conditional stimuli. The mechanics of bringing visceral responses under the control of environmental stimuli are now fairly well known, but from our point of view what still needs to be specified—and still awaits a theory—is the mechanism whereby a previously innocuous stimulus becomes a stimulus for ANS response (see Chapter 3).

There exist a series of stimuli that have been identified as innate releasers of ANS activity. In most cases the interest has been in identifying stimuli that are also releasers of other behaviors, but it frequently can be assumed that ANS-arousal functions go together with such systems. For example, the species-specific responses to stress and pain[67] are presumably accompanied by ANS response. In early infancy, loss of support and high levels of stimulation also tend to be ANS releasers. Others[68] have suggested that strangeness is a source of fear and, we can assume, also a source of ANS arousal. All of these events reinforce the notion that discrepancy-interruption is the major principle that combines a variety of different sources of ANS arousal. Pain, stress, strangeness, and loss of support all involve (from different vantage points) changes in the current state of the mental system; all of them involve some disconfirmation of normal expectations, some (often rapid) change in the state of the world. I shall return to this issue in Chapter 8.

The question of how previously innocuous events become transformed into functional triggers of the ANS is, of course, a central concern of conditioning theory. As I suggested in Chapter 3, we do not have, at present, a reasonable theory that describes the representations and processes involved in this ubiquitous phenomenon. We know much about the circumstances under which con-

67. See, e.g., Bolles (1970).
68. Bowlby (1973), Hebb (1946), and Schneirla (1959).

ditioning takes place, and the suggestions for the different kinds of mechanisms and schemas that underlie different kinds of conditioning may serve as a starting point for a better understanding of the mechanisms. But even those mechanisms are inadequate to account fully for the phenomena in question.

If we were to ask how a particular individual comes to be in a state of autonomic arousal when presented with the sight of a child being nearly run over by an automobile, then we would find it difficult to describe the variety of prior conditionings that must have occurred in order for this set of events to produce a release of autonomic discharge. It is highly unlikely that the intricate concatenations of previous experiences have always been favorable in just such a way as to produce the "conditioned emotional response" that occurs. It is, in fact, the very fine-grained analyses of classical conditioning and the precise relation among unconditioned stimuli, conditioned stimuli, and unconditioned responses that these studies have shown to be necessary for the substitution paradigm to work that argue for the implausibility that those conditions are met in the "conditioning" of visceral responses in everyday life. A similar argument, with respect to instrumental or operant conditioning, has been made in relation to language learning: namely, that the conditions of language acquisition in the child are unlikely to fulfill the precise timing and topographical requirements for the optimal establishment of operant behavior.[69] None of this argues that the descriptions of classical and instrumental or respondent and operant conditioning are erroneous. The critique of classical learning theories cannot be based on a denial of their research contributions. It must be directed at the unwarranted assumption that if a particular condition produces a certain behavior, then that behavior is usually produced by identical or similar conditions.

Laboratory experiments, particularly with lower animals, provide a possible set of conditions under which the acquisition of new behavior and the substitution of new stimuli can take place. These experiments may even provide the optimal conditions under which these phenomena occur, and they demonstrate the process for exercising optimal control, not just over the behavior, but also over the mental interpretive system of the organism in question. Similarly, the control of behavior by the precise control of environmental events and the consequences contingent on certain behaviors, which has been so convincingly demonstrated by B. F. Skinner and his students, is valuable because it provides precisely the advantage of knowing what the organism is exposed to, what it is permitted to do, and what the consequences of such behaviors are likely to be. Control of behavior is a control over the instructions we give to an organism. The only instructions we can give to a nonverbal organism is through the strict control of the contingencies of reinforcement. Instructions (programming of cognitions and of plans) can be equally effective by direct communication or by the appropriate control over the input-output contingencies. The advantages of operant methods with organisms who cannot hear, may not wish to hear, or deny hearing our instructions is that they may bypass some interpretive steps and can

69. Chomsky (1959).

deal directly with the operations of the cognitive-interpretive system. The control of the behavior of animals, or of physiologically or psychologically impaired human beings, is equivalent to the proper use of instructions. Behavior therapy instructs the impaired organism in new ways of behaving, just as other individuals may be instructed by cognitive manipulation in classical psychotherapy. However, the advocates of operant methods of control do not claim—nor should they be assigned the claim—that they can describe the mechanism whereby these changes take place.

I now return to the question of how innocuous stimuli, emotionally neutral events, may be translated into functional stimuli for ANS arousal.

For lower animals, particularly those that have relatively simple cognitive-interpretive systems, it is relatively easy to specify the functional stimuli. Thus, we can describe the releasing stimuli for sexual behavior for lower species, but less and less so as we ascend the phylogenetic scale.[70] When we come to the primates, it is generally conceded that so-called cognitive factors become more and more important in determining the onset and offset of sexual behavior. The cognitive system becomes more and more effective in modifying the external stimulus. We may assume that the initiating events, or stimuli, may be practically of any character or variety but that the cognitive system converts them into functional releasing stimuli.

It does not matter what particular set of emotional behaviors we wish to put into the innate category.[71] For example, we could start with a crude distinction among rage, fear, and love[72] and translate the fear-rage distinction into the more popular and contemporary flight-fight distinction. But the events that will produce fear or rage in a human are often surprising or irrational. The person who fears and flees from events and objects that others do not fear, as in common phobias, clearly has no prewired or genetically determined fear of such objects. For example, agoraphobia, or the fear of open places, must be related to the fact that such stimuli are functionally interpreted. Similarly, the man who flies into a towering rage because somebody took his place in a queue is interpreting the stituation in a way that produces rage. In the area of sexual arousal, it is highly unlikely that handlebar mustaches have been genetically selected as releasing stimuli for female sexual arousal; instead, they may be *interpreted* as sexually arousing, just as an otherwise sexually arousing stimulus (such as a receptive cross-sex partner) may fail to arouse sexual behavior in some cases.

Two asymmetric interpretations of the effect or lack of effect of external stimuli need to be explored. In the case of the apparently neutral event that gives rise to emotional behavior, two interpretations of this transformation are possible. One is that the arousal system may be in a state of activation because of some other set of events that are extrinsic to the specific situation. For example, the man who has just been fired from his job and is in a state of autonomic arousal may react violently to being supplanted in the queue for his bus, whereas he

70. Ford and Beach (1952).
71. See Bruell (1970).
72. Watson (1928).

may not have done so had there been no prior arousal. The other possibility, the one favored by classical psychotherapists, is that the eliciting situation is reinterpreted as a threat. They then usually ask: "What are you really afraid of?" This question is posed particularly in cases of irrational aggression and irrational fear. In our example, we would ask about the meaning of being pushed out of one's place in the bus line. I will deal elsewhere with the locus of effect of different kinds of therapies; for now I am concerned only with the two possible explanations of why neutral stimuli may become functional releasing events.

In contrast to socially "neutral" stimuli, when a species-specific stimulus fails to arouse the "appropriate" emotional behavior, we assume that only one factor is operative: reinterpretation by the cognitive-interpretive system. For example, the loss of support that occurs on a roller coaster is reinterpreted by the adult to function as an innocuous or even "positive" stimulus. The possibility exists, of course, that the system is not reinterpreting the event but that it in fact fails to trigger the autonomic response or that the ANS reaction is not perceived.

Much of the discussion of the functional stimulus for ANS arousal could be translated into a discussion of the sufficient conditions for the emotional interpretation of an environmental event. Some writers have failed to make the distinction between stimuli that are ANS arousers and those that are signals for a cognitive interpretation. This frequently occurs in discussing so-called fearful stimuli or a general complex of fear without making the arousal-interpretation distinction.[73] That is perfectly appropriate when a stimulus, such as strangeness of a situation, clearly has a similar and simultaneously effective signal function both to arousal and to the cognitive-interpretive system. On the one hand, it activates the ANS because it is novel (cf. Chapter 8); on the other, it may be evaluated by the meaning analysis as theatening or fearful. But in many cases the event that gives rise to ANS arousal and the one that is interpreted at the same time not only may be two different events but may have different effects. For example, a stimulus that originally provided both ANS arousal and interpretation as an aversive negative event may be reinterpreted in one respect and not the other; it may thus lose its effectiveness as an ANS arouser and still be interpreted as aversive but produce essentially little, if any, emotional reaction. The habituation to loud noises may provide one instance of this kind of change. On the other hand, an event may still produce ANS arousal but may be cognitively reinterpreted on the basis of past experience so that it now produces a positive emotional reaction, as in the roller-coaster effect.

The discussion of the discrepancies that produce autonomic reactions belongs to a later chapter, but I shall anticipate in order to emphasize that both positive and negative events are the occasion for autonomic arousal. That argument is central to my position on emotion and on interruption. The evidence is pervasive and persuasive.[74] In brief, the most frequent cause of autonomic arousal is discrepancy-interruption, which occurs for both positive and negative states.

Examples of negatively toned situations that produce ANS arousal are obvious,

73. Bowlby (1973).
74. See Clark (1982) and Clark and Isen (1982) for reviews.

as the literature on fear, anger, and stress testifies. In addition, I have already cited evidence that arousal seems to be equally intense both for negatively and for positively toned events.[75] There is more recent evidence about the arousal function of more innocuous positive events. For example, positive remarks about an essay and a small monetary reward produce higher blood pressure than do neutral remarks and a nominal reward.[76]

The conditions that produce negative states have two effects: first, they induce some negative evaluation, and, second, they characteristically generate discrepancies, whether they produce grief (and therefore the perception of loss), anxiety (and uncertainty), fear (and threat of injury), or anger (and thwarting of a goal). Similarly, the positive conditions are also discrepant, usually invoking the incongruities of humorous situations, unexpected rewards, or (usually undeserved) praise.

75. Levi (1975) and Averill (1969).
76. Mueller and Donnerstein (1981).

7

BIOLOGY AND THE EMOTIONS

THE RELATION BETWEEN the autonomic nervous system and emotional phenomena brings us close to the broader question of the biological bases of emotion. In this chapter we will look at some general considerations about behavioral biology and evolutionary arguments, and then discuss more specifically two central concerns in a psychology of emotion: aggression and facial expression.

Behavioral biology has, for a number of reasons, concentrated on the mechanisms that deal with the evolution and genetics of very circumscribed and specific organismic functions, and those primarily in relatively simple animals. The evolution of complex animals like human beings differs from that of their simpler cousins in that the biological-behavioral system of humans has developed a wide variety of fail-safe mechanisms. The same function—on the environment and in social intercourse—can be and is subserved by several different mechanisms. The complex learning abilities of humans demonstrate the ability of the individual to achieve the same end by many different means. Likewise, some apparently "similar" ends are subserved by different mechanisms, often totally independent of each other. For example, the concept of aggression is an umbrella notion in the common language, one only loosely defined by vague ends and even vaguer means. Similarly, there are a number of ways in which food or sex can be attained. To assign genetic antecedents to all of these various means and ends is surely inappropriate. The cultural arguments against a primitive sociobiology bear witness to the large variety of arguments that would need specific genetic buttressing.

Determinism and Potential

The postulation of some unalterable aspects of emotional experience and behavior highlights a face of psychological theory that has, whether turned toward or away from the center of the science, always been a part of psychological speculation—the desire to find some biological givens, some innate aspects of human behavior and thought, some evolutionary basis for a definition of human nature. Natural selection—as exemplified in the reproductive success of individuals—is used to defend one or another human characteristic as invariant, genetically determined, and part of the biology of human nature. This tradition has most recently emerged in the guise of sociobiology.[1] Opposition to that trend cannot be based on the belief that biological evolution is irrelevant to human behavior; rather, it must rely on a principled argument about what the biological constraints on human behavior might be.[2] If the range of the target behaviors for such an argument is set very broadly, then evolutionary arguments will differ in character from those proposed for narrow ranges. Specifically, "[i]f ranges are characteristically broad, then selection may set some deeply recessed generating rules; but specific behaviors are epiphenomena of the rules, not objects of Darwinian attention in their own right."[3] Such a view of biological potential puts a different accent on human nature than does a strict biological determinism.

If one is interested in ascertaining the nature of human behavioral *potential*, one's initial steps must be both biological and psychological: biological in describing the truly narrow ranges of behavior that permit little cultural or social variation, and psychological in exploring the classes of action that have broad ranges, in order to determine what, if any, biological constraints are in fact operating. To assert the biological constraint or determination without exploring social variation is not only to put the cart before the horse but also to use an essentially lazy and intellectually unimaginative approach to complex problems. Surely, to take a very simple example of human behavior, the athletic coach who selects her team entirely on the basis of biological arguments is soon out of a job, since no program of training, diet, or exercise is expected to influence the skill determined by biology alone. In the psychology of emotion, where we know much less about biological factors, it would seem to be foolhardy to adopt a stance of determinism rather than of potentiality.

A strictly deterministic point of view sees the adaptive advantages of specific actions and behaviors arising out of the natural selection of the genetic material responsible for the adaptive behavior. An argument against such a view can deny neither that such genetic selection does take place nor that human behavior is adaptive and selected. It needs to be ascertained which behaviors are likely to be the result of genetic selection and whether adaptiveness and selection are necessarily genetic. As for the latter question, we have long been aware of the adaptiveness of human behavior that arises out of cultural selection. The reality that behaviors and actions are adaptive does not imply that they have a specific genetic basis. The very nature of human learning presupposes adaptive (natural, but not genetic) selection. Adaptiveness alone is thus not a clue to or an indicator for a genetic basis. The main difference between genetic and cultural selection is likely to be found in the range and variability of the behavior in question. Broad ranges suggest little, if any, specific genetic selection; narrow ranges point toward Darwinian rules.

1. Wilson (1975).
2. Gould (1981).
3. Gould (1981).

Another argument that sometimes is lost in the heat of genetic-environmental exchanges is the fact that certain behaviors may be the direct consequence of genetic selection without having been selected themselves. Such behaviors may even have narrow ranges. The metaphor is that of a computer built for a specific task but able to perform a variety of other functions, some of which were not even envisaged at the time of its construction.[4] Yet, surely, these new functions are determined by its design and structure. Similarly, human handwriting is determined by the design and structure of the organisms, and particularly its hand, but no one argues for the natural selection of the adaptive behavior of handwriting. Selective processes "designed" the hand long before handwriting arose and for different purposes.

What human behaviors and actions—relevant to the construction of emotion—seem to be particularly accessible to evolutionary analysis? The first and obvious candidate is the expanded function of the autonomic nervous system discussed in Chapter 6. The function of the ANS in making action on the environment more likely, rather than reacting to the environment, deserves more attention. In particular, we know little about the interaction between ANS activity and attentional behavior in organisms other than human ones. If the action of the ANS is seen not merely as homeostatic but also as drawing attention to important events, making attentional and problem-solving behavior more likely, and singling out particular events for storage and retrieval, then the evolutionary course of this system attains special interest.

There is another aspect of ANS activity that deserves biological analysis, namely, the conditions that occasion ANS arousal. As noted earlier, the usual textbook approach is to list these, without much regard to any principled account. However, such a listing of events—from tissue injury to emotional stress—would provide the kind of broad range of occurrence that should discourage genetic speculations. I have attempted to show that many of these can be brought under the rubric of discrepancy or interruption, a set of conditions that is well suited to an evolutionary history.

If it is the case that all discrepancies and interruptions produce some degree of peripheral autonomic activity, a further analysis of the evolution of the response to interruption seems at least interesting. It makes good sense that the interruption of well-organized and habitual thoughts and actions should provide a special signal to the cognitive system. In general, these suggestions contravene another popular view of emotions, one that sees them as chaotic, nonadaptive, and obsolete. Somehow the emotional side of modern life is considered to be out of step with the requirements of the modern world, an evolutionary hangover that interferes with a rational approach to our problems. In contrast, I do not believe that evolution is out of step with humankind, and since we see only an infinitesimal slice of the process, such judgments about obsolescence are unlikely to be objective. Emotional construction is an adaptive human function, as useful today as it was in prehistory.

4. The example is taken from Gould (1981).

Speculations about the mismatch between modern technology and ancient biological mechanisms are probably as pointless as are many arguments about genetic versus environmental apportionment. Psychologists in particular should be aware that just as environmentalists have inhibited the investigation of the constraints on human thought and action, so have the nativists inhibited the exploration of the development of complex behaviors. We should learn from the genetic-environmental investigations of lower animals that assignments to genetics and environment are not merely difficult but may at the present stage of knowledge be futile. For example, as simple a problem as the eye color of water shrimp cannot be subjected to simple genetic calculations. This simple animal shows the inheritance of eye color according to strictly Mendelian laws only under specific ambient temperatures, and, conversely, it is possible to postulate a genetic makeup that will make eye color appear to be entirely under environmental (temperature) controls. It would make "no sense" to assign differential weights of heredity and environment to eye color.[5] If that problem is so difficult, how much more so is an attempt to ascribe outbursts of anger, the induction of lust, or the occurrence of grief to specific genetic, adaptive, evolutionary mechanisms!

Rather than engage in speculations and in saltatory extrapolations from apes to humans or in the distribution of genetic recipes for intelligence, we might concentrate on observations and analyses of specifically human behavior and variation. Adequate psychological theories, bounded by observations, will then evolve to the point where their user will note invariances that cannot be accounted for by environmental constraints, or variabilities that speak for a plasticity in response to the environment.

In order to illustrate the complexity of the issues facing the psychology of emotion with respect to biological speculations, I have selected two behavioral syndromes for further discussion. They are aggressive behavior and facial expressions.

Aggression is important not only because it is a pervasive human preoccupation and has become a focus of genetic-environmental arguments but also because it plays a double role in the construction of emotion. I have discussed the possibilities that aggressive behavior, unmediated by conscious processing, may sometimes function as an evaluative action that colors subsequent emotional experience. We are sometimes angry because we have aggressed. More frequently, aggression occurs after the subjective experience of anger. Furthermore, aggressive behavior (however defined) is a broad-range phenomenon and is as such unlikely to be a candidate for genetic natural selection.

Facial expressions, by contrast, show relatively little variability and are therefore a likely candidate for natural-selection processes. In addition, facial expressions form a central part of some theories of fundamental emotions, and there is in fact a deceptively intimate apparent connection between emotional construction and facial messages.

5. Medawar (1977).

Aggression

Unfortunately, we cannot start with a definition of the term *aggression*, at least not with a definition that is generally acceptable. Even in the narrow sense of some behavior that threatens or inflicts injury on another person or organism, it refers to behaviors than can be evoked by a large variety of different conditions and is frequently labeled not by the behavior but by its occasions. These range from predatory aggression to parental disciplinary aggression and maternal and sexual aggression.[6] If we extend the range to behavior that is called aggressive but involves no physical threat, we are immediately presented with a plethora of possibilities in verbal aggression, in discriminatory behavior, and so forth. Exactly how the process of natural selection could have produced such varieties of actions and effective elicitors is unclear.

The argument for an innate, genetically determined tendency to "aggress" comes from two general sources. There are those who argue for an aggressive drive that, if not adequately expressed, will find alternative expression in both inter- and intraspecies aggression; there are others who simply point to the prevalence of aggression and present quasi-evolutionary arguments for its persistence. Dominant among these drive theorists are Konrad Lorenz and, in a somewhat different mode, Sigmund Freud.

Lorenz,[7] in a volume much troubled by ethnocentric conceptions, talks about aggressive drives in man and some of their possible origins but says little about the situations that are sufficient and necessary for the release of these aggressive patterns. It is obvious to the psychologist and to the anthropologist—although often not to the ethologist—that similar patterns may not be expressive of a particular drive or drive condition but may be related to different drive systems or to different cognitive structures. Thus, from an ethological point of view, hitting an object with one's fist may be interpreted as the displacement of aggressive drive, but it also may be the only way of opening a walnut.

Some of the speculations that Lorenz indulges in may be interesting, but they are not particularly useful. Saying that humans do not have much opportunity to discharge aggressive drive in interspecies competition does not help to understand specifically the social or personal conditions to which the aggressive drive is tied when it *is* expressed, nor does it help understand the expressions of that drive at a particular time. We have come a long way from postulating a unique link between frustration and aggression; we have not gone very far toward an analysis of any "instinctual" elicitation of aggressive behavior. On the other hand, we know much about the cultural and personal conditions—and they are legion—that may under various conditions produce aggressive behavior. Past research at least suggests that cognitive-experiential causes of aggression are easier to find than innate releasers or prewired patterns.

Although the same behavior may have different sources, we also know that the same sources may lead to different kinds, and very often quite antagonistic,

6. Montagu (1976).
7. Lorenz (1963).

behavior patterns. Whether we learn to channel certain cognitive structures or drives into socially acceptable patterns because of our early development or because of the operation of fear and dread, and whether we call these redirections sublimations, as Freud did, or redirected activity, as Tinbergen and Lorenz do, is not relevant; what is important is that we should be aware of the multiplicity of causes and outcomes that are operating on so-called innate behavior patterns. We know very little about the mechanisms that would lead to an adequate conceptualization of behavior that may easily be *called* instinctual.

One interesting by-product of the drive position is an attempt to understand the behavior pattern known as *laughter.* Lorenz makes the argument that laughter is "derived from aggressive behavior and still retains some of its primal motivation."[8] He sees it as the "ritualization of a redirected threatening movement" that also produces strong fellow feeling among participants and "joint aggressiveness against outsiders." Whatever the function of laughter and the origin of its releasing mechanisms, we still know very little, despite efforts from all directions of psychological thought, about the conditions under which laughter and humor will appear. In laughter many conditions other than the primitive ones that Lorenz talks about produce the same kind of behavior. One of the origins of laughter can be found in discrepancy, which produces arousal and therefore emotional response. However, what the conditions are under which this particular kind of discrepancy leads to the experience of humor instead of some other emotional content is still unclear. Olympian statements about the salutary redirection of aggression into laughter tend to obscure the search for understanding.

If stimuli other than innately programmed ones can release so-called instinctual behavior, it is equally obvious that in complexly cognitive animals such as human beings the response to "innate" releasers is not inevitable. Human beings can and do control unacceptable behavior (whether it is aggressive, sexual, or whatever), although the history of evil often obscures the ethical achievements that go counter to some of our history.

Harry Harlow and his co-workers[9] have shown how early experiences can fundamentally redirect aggression, fear, and love in the monkey. The immensely greater complexity of human mental organization suggests that problems of redirection and reinterpretation may be more important in understanding ourselves than simple analogies with primitive animals or nontechnological societies have been.

Human aggression (at least as viewed by its protectors) takes a variety of different forms; it is not—as in lower animals, which are usually posited as the prototype—either stimulus or response specific. There are no fixed action patterns in human aggression. Human aggressive responses vary widely in their topography. If, then, there is no fixed action pattern of human aggression, what is it that is innate? According to one popular alternative, it is some idea or motive or drive of aggression; this position reduces matters to some eighteenth-century notion of prior ideas divorced from the realities of life and behavior. And cer-

8. Lorenz (1963).
9. E.g., Deets, Harlow, and Harlow (1971).

tainly the notion of an evolutionary motive that energizes practically all aspects of human action would be difficult to defend on the very genetic grounds that its defenders espouse.

An examination of the use of this notion of an innate drive suggests that it has been used for purposes other than objective explanation. Consider that the instinctivist position implies that the innate drive must be seen in *all* aspects of human aggression. However, its defenders prefer to restrict the aggressive act to a physical attack on another human being, when any action or plan that harms another human should fall under their rubric. It is somewhat revealing of the Weltanschauung that motivates the instinctivists that they prefer the aggression typical of the poor and deprived but gloss over the aggression exercised by the powerful. Causing people to starve or denying them the right to join their loved ones should be aggressive actions by the definition of innate aggressive drives, although they are rarely enumerated in the instinctivist literature. Physical aggression is seen as a phenomenon of all people, but, curiously, it is found to be more prevalent among the poor and powerless. Indirect aggression by the powerful is rarely put into the same rubric. The intelligent and wealthy are somehow exempt from the ravages of our aggressive "instincts." However, if their acts are also seen as aggressive, what is it that is passed on from generation to generation among all members of the species? Would the instinctivists still endorse a genetic motive if that drive were expressed in lower-class physical aggression on the one hand and in refined laws that keep the poor in poverty and the exiles away from their homes on the other?

Once we ask about the world view that motivates the invocation of such a useful innate motive, we are tempted to conclude that the promotion of an aggressive instinct also promotes the defense of a society directed unilaterally toward competition. Competition is a close relative of aggression, and if we cannot defend the latter, maybe it will be more difficult to defend the former.[10]

A critique of the instinctivist and hydraulic models of aggression[11] has noted the self-serving aspects of these explanations and the absence of any evidence for the various energy models of aggressive behavior.[12] Aggression is seen as being similar to and consistent with the view advanced in these pages. "[A]versive experiences produce emotional arousal that can elicit a variety of behaviors, depending on the types of reactions people have learned for coping with stressful conditions."[13] Among these reactions are dependency, achievement, withdrawal, constructive problem solving, and aggression. But aggression is seen as only one possible reaction to the concatenation of aversion and arousal. I would merely add that aversive experiences are not a necessary antecedent for the emotional arousal that precedes aggression. By way of example, we need only consider pathological or commonplace sadistic behavior, which is aggressive but

10. Selg (1971).
11. Bandura (1973).
12. See also Hinde (1956).
13. Bandura (1973).

which is not necessarily preceded by aversive conditions; on the contrary, these may be typically absent.[14]

Another group of advocates of a genetic basis of human aggression is not concerned with an explanation in terms of drive, but rather argues for it on the basis of an assumed generality among other mammals, and particularly among primates, or the prevalence of aggression and warfare in human history.[15] These claims have been analyzed in great detail,[16] and little evidence has been found for the generality either among other animals or in human history. When the claim is made that territoriality, the staking out and defending of territorial "property," is at the source of aggression, its occurrence in some animal species does not justify its generalization to the human case. In fact, even in animals the observed cases of territoriality "probably represent not a single adaptation but a host of different adaptations serving different purposes for different animals."[17] And if warfare is seen as the result of some territoriality instinct, it surely does not apply to the main protagonists, the soldiers who typically show, not some continuing expression of aggression, and surely no ever-present anger, but a need to do what they are told, get it over with, and leave. Nor does it seem consistent to argue that fighting rather than fleeing is the natural human response. Flight is as "natural" a human reaction as is fight, a point of view sensitively depicted by the playwright Robert Bolt in his portrait of Sir Thomas More in *A Man for All Seasons*. Bolt has More saying at one point that "our natural part is in escaping." The notion that moral courage and physical flight are compatible is unfortunately alien to an aggressive, competitive society.

Erich Fromm[18] does posit one kind of biologically adaptive aggressive response: defensive aggression. Flight or fight actions are mobilized when "vital interests of the animal are threatened, such as food, space, the young, access to females. Basically, the aim is to remove the danger; this can be done . . . by flight, or if flight is not possible, by fighting or assuming effective threatening postures. The aim of defensive aggression is not lust for destruction, but the preservation of life." Such threats could be interpreted as interruptions of dominant and well-integrated action patterns. Given the ensuing arousal—which is likely to be intense—the emotional quality at these intensities may well bring into play learned or even "innate" systems such as flight or attack. But once the interruption has been removed, there is no remaining destructive urge, nor are the flight or fight patterns in the service of some higher destructiveness; they serve the protection of life.

Anger—the subjective emotional experience often associated with aggression—presumably occurs when there is ANS arousal and the opportunity to generate evaluative cognitions that represent the quality of anger. The latter are

14. Fromm (1973).
15. See Ardrey (1966), Morris (1967), and Wilson (1978).
16. Fromm (1973) and Montagu (1976).
17. Klopfer (1969).
18. Fromm (1973).

probably involved when goal-directed activity is blocked, when learned concatenations of circumstances bring about the desire to hurt another, or when we observe some behavior of ours that seems to have that goal. Human aggressive behavior sometimes occurs without conscious intervention. However, our perception of such behavior defines the evaluative cognitions that arise in connection with such actions and outbursts. Some of these cases seem to be amenable to a Jamesian analysis. We may well often be angry because of actual or incipient aggressive behavior. Conversely, of course, anger in most cases precedes aggressive acts.

I have argued that the case for the inevitability and generality of aggression is at least weak. This does not deny that aggression occurs frequently (too frequently) and in a variety of situations and species. The very fact that it is sometimes absent argues against some genetic code. "If innate only means possible, or even likely in certain environments, then everything we do is innate and the word has no meaning."[19] Aggression can then alternatively be seen as "one expression of a generating rule that anticipates peacefulness in other common environments."[20] What could such a generating rule be?

A common theme links practically all forms of aggression as well as the various alternative ways of coping with it. It is best described as thwarting. Aggression seems to occur when the individual involved either has been thwarted in the execution of some action or perceives that he has been thwarted. This includes purely imaginary thwartings in the case of thought processes that lead to some presumed solution of a problem, but the execution of which seems to be impossible because of some blocking agent. Thus, one is thwarted in trying to get onto a crowded bus, attempting to buy a cake but finding that the bakery just sold the last one, thinking of a tryst with an unattainable movie idol, or planning to get a raise in the face of an implacable management. Thwarting is a (usually social) occasion of interruption, which involves a specific action-related goal, which interruption in general need not involve (for example, when we are faced with an unexpected visitor or telephone call or a discrepant ending to a novel).

It is possible that in the process of natural selection a response repertory to thwarting may well have been established. It is likely to be adaptive for an organism to respond automatically to situations in which some goal-directed action fails. I shall in Chapter 8 have occasion to discuss at greater length some of the possible responses to interruption, but here I want to concentrate on one subset—the probability of persistence and increased effort. In other words, it is possible that our mammalian ancestors did go through an evolutionary process whereby effortful persistence was selected as an adaptive response to thwarting. It is the strategy most likely to succeed.

Given effortful persistence as a common heritage to thwarting, special adaptations of that original "general rule" could well have developed. We must keep in mind that other primates are the contemporary result of millions of years of

19. Gould (1981).
20. Gould (1981).

adaptive evolution. It is not true that their current modes of behavior are the precursors of ours; rather, they are the current outcome of a common ancestral mode of adaptation. It seems not unlikely that some of these strands developed aggressive, threatening (and usually defensive) behavior patterns, found in birds and other animals. However, the great differences between other animals and the human species is our plasticity and variability of behavioral expression. One of the symptoms of that plasticity, from the evolutionary point of view, might well be our ability to respond to thwarting in a variety of different ways. Whether we still possess the effortful persistence to thwarting that might be the core adaptation is not certain. It surely seems that we can even dispense with that mode and respond, quite naturally, to thwarting by avoidance and withdrawal. We do, however, share with other animals the other evolutionary heritage, the ANS response to interruption—and therefore to thwarting.

The response to thwarting and frustrating events may well be to remove the blocking agent. It is not the inevitable way of dealing with thwarting agents. Given the proper social environment, humans can be nonaggressive and loving when they reach adulthood. The Tasaday of Mindanao are a "loving, gentle people. They have no weapons, and no apparent aggressive impulses."[21] They do not speak harshly to each other; they forget themselves as individuals, even though their children seem to exhibit typical behavior toward thwarting agents. But they are taught to be different when they reach adulthood, and by then they deal with unpleasant events by turning away from them.[22] In the absence of hostile and aggressive values, they show little, if any, anger—but do show love and acceptance.

Facial Expression

If aggression is difficult to define and even more difficult to fit within the framework of genetic natural selection, the case of facial expressions is both simpler and more interesting—simpler because we can in fact find cultural universals in facial expression, and more interesting because speculations about the evolutionary, adaptive nature of these muscle movements seem to be more reasonable and more defensible.

Having rejected the idea of undefined emotional qualities, ideas, or feelings, we must deal in some detail with the unavoidable fact that a variety of facial expressions seem inevitably tied to emotional experience and behavior. The question then becomes whether these expressions express anything at all, or whether they are an important set of acts that contribute to rather than express the emotional complex.

Any discussion of facial expression must start with Darwin's painstaking investigation of the generality of emotional expression across and within species. Darwin's thesis was that just as these expressions directly externalize the lower

21. Nance (1975).
22. Montagu (1976).

animal's emotions, so they express human emotional states. He developed three general principles to explain their occurrence and particularly to address their persistence in nonadaptive contexts. After discussing Darwin's contribution, I shall return to the role of these "expressions," which not only seem to occur in direct response to "emotional" situations but also are generated in other contexts and even frequently and easily inhibited by humans.

Darwin's[23] three principles opened up major lines of thought for succeeding scientists. His principle of serviceable associated habits postulated complex actions that are "of direct or indirect" service, given certain states of mind. These habits will also occur when they "may not then be of the least use" but simply because some "state of mind" similar to the originator is present. That is, expressive movements may be indices of internal states even though they may have no adaptive significance whatsoever at the time. This principle justifies the study of expressive movements per se rather than their functional significance.

Darwin's principle of antithesis asserts that certain actions will be induced by opposing states of the mind and that these actions (or movements) may be "of no use" but will be "directly opposite in nature" to the actions and movements induced by the original state of mind. Darwin here asserts the bipolarity of certain expressive movements, an assertion that has led to the respectable tradition of seeing emotions as dimensional on such bipolar axes as pleasant-unpleasant, active-quiescent, and attending-rejecting.

Finally, his principle of the direct action of the nervous system states that certain expressive results are dependent solely on "excess nerve-force." The lack of knowledge about the nervous system at the middle of the nineteenth century prevents any unequivocal interpretation of Darwin's statement. My own reading, particularly of his examples, convinces me that in the majority of cases Darwin refers to the inevitable effects of intense ANS reactions—again a theme that is still with us today.

There are undoubtedly some few universal, unlearned, cross-cultural "emotional" expressions, primarily facial in nature. But showing the universality of facial expressions is a long way from claiming that what is universal is the expression of emotion. The misleading cue resides in the idealistic notion that the facial expressions express something "behind" them, some emotional *quale*, feeling, or idea. We can dispense with nineteenth-century psychology but still assume that there are situation-specific evolutionary remnants shown in facial expression. These facial expressions, just like other innate actions, including approach-and-withdrawal sequences, define the situation-action complex. These reactions to the environment in turn may represent emotional evaluation.

There exists a wealth of anecdotal and intuitive evidence about the reliability, detectability, variation, and change in facial expression. We all know that we can pose facial expression, that some of us are better at it than others (such as actors), and that we can suppress overt expression, even when we deeply feel some emotion. With time and experience we learn when these expressions tend

23. Darwin (1872).

to occur, when they are appropriate, and often what they mean. And they do occur early in life. Organized, nonrandom patterns of facial expressions occur as early as the third or fourth week of life.[24] But we still have much to learn about the face.

Deaf and blind children apparently must acquire "a smile, facial expression of joy, rage, agreement, protest." For example, when such a child is happy, he or she "suddenly distorts the features of his or her face into a grimace similar to our expression of pain."[25] In other words, there exists the rudimentary apparatus of using the face for communicative purposes, but these children must learn its semantics and syntax. And though the blind show the "proper" facial "emotional" expressions, they cannot act out these expressions when given the name of the emotion.[26] There is no innate connection between an idea of "hate" and baring one's teeth. Teeth are bared to specific stimuli.

The preoccupation with facial expression is not surprising, since we find so few cross-cultural constancies, particularly ones that we encounter, one way or another, in everyday experience. But this delight with finding universals should not hide the fact that we are dealing, as Darwin knew, with evolutionary *remnants*. The evidence for the universality of facial expressions is good, although not as good as some investigators would like.[27] There are strong situational and contextual determinants as to who will recognize what emotion under what circumstances. Certainly the consistency between Western stereotypes and their evaluation in non-Western nonliterate isolated cultures suggests that there is some cross-cultural constancy, and the case against those who deny such constancy[28] is quite solid. But what is it that is general to all members of the species?

In the first instance, what is general is certain facial expressions, best expressed in terms of certain muscular-action consistencies. Our facial muscles have preprogrammed consistencies, just as our leg muscles do when they make it possible for all members of the species to walk. But do they "mean" the same thing, regardless of context or situation? The interesting aspect of most of the research with facial expressions is that it usually classifies expression into some very few categories, such as anger, happiness, sadness, disgust, fear, and surprise.[29] These broad semantic categories suggest, in contrast, that many of the fine muscular patterns with which we are dealing are probably communicative acts, not expressions of some underlying palpable emotion. Nor need we assume that all facial expressions have similar origins. Some may be communicative in origin, whereas others derive from more primitive defensive reactions, such as some movements of the brow.[30] Given our evolutionary history, it is not unreasonable to assume that some broad categories of events are classified by these facial semantic cate-

24. Oster (1978).
25. Levitin (1979).
26. Dumas (1932).
27. See, e.g., Ekman (1973) and Izard (1971).
28. E.g., La Barre (1947).
29. See Ekman (1973).
30. Ekman (1979).

gories and that they may, in part, have a common history. Some situations that are "happy" are also ones that tend to elicit a smiling facial expression; some unexpected aversive events are classified as fearful, and some facial expressions are also associated with those situations. We should note, though, that a nonliterate culture in New Guinea could not distinguish surprise from fear,[31] which suggests cultural differences in adding the aversive to the surprising aspect of events.

In other words, there are certain archaic situational events that have a high probability of producing specific facial events and also have a high probability of being cognitively classified by certain "emotional" values. But surely human plasticity prevents us from saying that a particular stimulus will *always* produce a certain expression or a certain valuation. Even for nonhuman primates, the best available summary of the evidence notes, "the functional context-dependency of emotional expression is an extremely important concept, for it is only in conjunction with context that affect expressions can coordinate social interaction."

The remnants of these "expressive" characteristics occur occasionally to specific stimuli. Not only did they probably evolve as communicative acts but they may also be acquired as communicative signs. In nonhuman primates, "the appropriate contextual use of and reaction to facial behavior and its role in coordination of social interactions are highly dependent upon a normal socialization experience."[32] The development of the use and the recognition of facial expression during early childhood and the difficulty the blind have in acting out the "appropriate" expression both speak to this point in humans. In other words, humans may use facial expressions as communication devices, but they must learn exactly how and when to do so. This is a far cry from the unsupported speculation that our common experience suggests that "signs of anger act like the stickleback's red belly as a sign-stimulus for fear. . . ."[33] Any viewer of television or observer of small children can deny this "common experience."

In short, those facial expressions that seem to be emotional in character are also always evaluative; they convey important messages. To the extent that they are remnants of our species' early history, it seems reasonable to conclude that preverbal ancestors of human beings first communicated by expressions—nonverbal, to be sure, but certainly value laden. The notion that certain of these action patterns are reliably responders to environmental consistencies is not surprising. Much current belief notwithstanding, there is no evidence at all that these expressions are, even when completely spontaneous, genetically acquired messages about our internal states. They provide accurate information about pleasurable and unpleasurable judgments, but there is no direct evidence that they are always messages about emotional states.[34] Since all emotional experiences and observations consist in part of evaluative components and since it is

31. Ekman (1973).
32. Chevalier-Skolnikoff (1973).
33. Gray (1971b).
34. Ekman and Oster (1979).

primarily the evaluative aspect (not the arousal) that is obvious to the observer, we make the inductive leap that whenever we see or hear an evaluative expression, we are in the presence of some emotional event. That is probably the source of the deeply held belief that facial expressions must "express" emotions. We confuse the purely evaluative and the emotional aspects of "affects." Not only can actors "express" (show facial expressions) without feeling the requisite emotion but people can also feel an emotion without providing any expressive cues. Patients who suffer from aprosodia, the inability to use prosody in language, typically show "an inability to communicate emotions . . . through the use of facial, limb, and body gesture." But these patients do not seem to have any diminished variety or intensity of inner emotional experience.[35]

The social-communicative nature of facial expression is well expressed in the act of smiling, which, even in nonhuman primates, has a primarily communicative function, rather than that of expressing emotion.[36] The human smile, too, functions to communicate friendly contact and hostility deflection; it is strongly associated with social motivation and only erratically with emotional experience.[37]

I indicated in Chapter 2 the intimate relation between some theories of emotion and the role of facial expressions.[38] Some of these statements are bluntly unequivocal: "[A]wareness of one's facial expression *is* the emotion"[39] and "Awareness of facial activity or facial feedback is actually our awareness of the subjective experience of a specific emotion."[40] Such assertions have given rise to a number of studies in which facial expressions and their effect on emotional behavior and experience have been studied.

For example, if people are induced to "smile" or "frown" without being aware of the specific character of their expression, they will report the appropriate feelings in response to relatively innocuous pictures or cartoons. It appears that "expressive behavior mediates the quality of . . . emotional experience."[41] Expressive behavior does not follow some emotional quality; instead, the emotional quality is derived from the "expressive" behavior. As of this writing, their results are equivocal, ranging from strong support[42] to equally strong rejection[43] of the relation between facial feedback and emotion. Conclusions are hard to come by. On the one hand, one can argue that facial feedback seems to contribute little (certainly much less than does visceral feedback) to emotional experience and that facial feedback is neither necessary nor sufficient for emotional experience.[44] On the other hand, overt facial expressions "can affect the intensity

35. Ross and Mesulam (1979).
36. Hooff (1972, 1973).
37. Kraut and Johnston (1979).
38. See Ekman, Friesen, and Ellsworth (1972), Izard (1971), and Tomkins (1962).
39. Lanzetta, Cartwright-Smith, and Kleck (1976).
40. Izard (1977).
41. Laird (1974).
42. Lanzetta, Cartwright-Smith, and Kleck (1976) and Zuckerman, Klorman, Larrance, and Spiegel (1981).
43. Tourangeau and Ellsworth (1979).
44. Buck (1980).

of emotional arousal" but the evidence that "facial feedback can determine *which* emotion we experience is far more ambiguous."[45,46]

Future Rapprochements with Biology

Psychologists and popular writers have at times been somewhat facile in their use of evolutionary arguments; biologists, for their part, have often assumed that the study of human thought and behavior can be accomplished by the intensive use of armchairs and by reflection upon one's thoughts and society. By noting that aggression is behaviorally and socially not an appropriate object for biological study but that, in contrast, the reaction to thwarting and the study of facial expressions might well be such objects, we will perhaps open doors to cooperation rather than prolong arguments about lofty imponderables like environment and heredity.

New developments in Darwinian theory are worthy of special attention by psychologists. The punctuationalist proposal has challenged the gradualist tradition in Darwinian theory.[47] The argument can be briefly summarized:

> Is our world . . . primarily one of constant change (with structure as a mere incarnation of the moment), or is structure primary and constraining, with change as a "difficult" phenomenon, usually accomplished rapidly when a stable structure is stressed beyond its buffering capacity to resist and absorb?[48]

The history of psychological theory about change has been primarily gradualist; it was certainly so in the period from the British empiricists to the neobehaviorists. Whether these gradualist notions were derived from the received knowledge of dominant biological (Darwinian) thought or whether the two approaches were the result of a common social and historical process is a question still to be resolved. However, it does seem to be true that contemporary cognitive theory is more receptive to "punctuationalist" positions about change and structural adaptation. It might be useful for us to look to our biological neighbors rather than to our ancestors in searching for appropriate models both of structure and of evolution. With regard to the latter, the generalization of the punctuationalist approach to a hierarchical view of evolution[49] also deserves more attention in behavioral circles. If selection in the evolutionary process acts not only on individual organisms but also on higher-level objects such as species, we might want to reconsider some of the current speculations about the sources of human nature.

45. Ekman and Oster (1979).
46. As of 1983, one of the most knowledgeable investigators of facial expressions (Paul Ekman) told the writer that "there is obviously emotion without facial expression and facial expression without emotion."
47. Eldredge and Gould (1972).
48. Gould (1982, 383).
49. Gould (1982).

8

DISCREPANCY AND INTERRUPTION: OCCASIONS FOR EMOTIONS

IMAGINE THAT you are driving your car along a highway: as you come to a curve, you apply pressure to the brakes, but there is no resistance to your effort—your foot goes to the floorboard and the car does not slow down. Two consequences will arise almost immediately. Your autonomic nervous system will produce a high state of arousal—your heart rate will be noticeably increased, for example—and you will start thinking about alternative ways of dealing with the problem. You may at first just keep pumping the brake, doing so with more force, but then you are likely to think of other ways of slowing the car, such as using the emergency brake or shifting into a lower gear.

This sequence illustrates some of the interruption phenomena alluded to in previous chapters. The ubiquity of interruption and discrepancy will be developed in this chapter. As an introduction, the example given here also illustrates some of the mechanisms involved and the two major consequences of interruption. First, interruption is a sufficient and perhaps necessary condition for the occurrence of autonomic arousal. Second, the interruption of ongoing cognitive or behavioral activity sets the stage for changes in cognitive and action systems. In addition, in extension of these two points, we shall see that interruption may signal important changes in the environment, which often lead to altered circumstances of living and adapting.

The autonomic consequences of interruption are offered as a hypothesis, albeit one with a high degree of credibility. There is no available evidence against the hypothesis that the interruption of highly organized activities generates autonomic arousal. If it is kept in mind that the unexpected is, by definition, interruptive of ongoing cognitive activity, the general agreement that novel and unusual events generate states of arousal is relevant to this proposition. In addition, the general class of aversive events also falls into the category of disruptive (*ergo* interruptive) and unexpected occasions.

Regardless of the autonomic consequences of interruption, one of the main avenues for change in existing cognitive and action systems is undoubtedly a consequence of the failure of existing structures. An interruption occurs when a current structure fails to handle available evidence or action requirements. The adaption to the requirements of the world, "learning" in traditional terminology, occurs after interruption. Any satisfactory theory of cognitive structures must contain means whereby structures are changed whenever any ongoing cognitive or behavioral activity fails or is interrupted.

The adaptive consequences of interruption are obvious. The organism responds both with physiological preparedness and with potential cognitive and behavioral restructuring whenever interruption occurs. Or, to turn the argument around, it seems reasonable to suppose that organisms have evolved in such a way that whenever well-organized actions or plans cannot be completed (i.e., fail), two major adaptive mechanisms come into play—one physiological, the other cognitive.

Of particular interest for present purposes is the arousal function of interruption. From an evolutionary point of view, the fact that arousal comes into play whenever current activity is maladaptive can be seen to have survival value. First, arousal has preparatory flight and fight functions. These functions are of value whenever the organism is engaged in activities essential to species survival, such as food seeking, and to the protective organization of the group. Preparation for flight or fight is important when usual (well-organized) activities in these areas cannot be carried to completion. Second, the autonomic response is relevant to the role of the autonomic nervous system as an additional signal system, discussed in the preceding chapter. Increased attention and information seeking when ongoing activity is interrupted is evidently adaptive.

The term *interruption*, because of its neutral connotation and greater generality, is preferable to terms like *frustration* or *blocking*. The notion of interruption implies that an organized response is "interrupted" whenever its completion is physically blocked or temporarily delayed—for whatever reason. Examples come readily to mind: a key sticking in a lock, a pellet not found in a food cup, or a brake failing in a car; all of these are instances of interruption. We must assume in all of them that the response sequence involved actually has been organized (i.e., previously used and practiced—smoothly and frequently), that a well-defined structure exists that represents the action.

Interruptions occur not only in the realm of action but also in that of thinking and perception. In order to make that extension obvious, I have used the term *discrepancy* as synonymous with *interruption*. Perceptions that are discrepant are those that do not fit our perceptual expectations and schemas. If I open the door to a kitchen, I expect to see a stove, a refrigerator, and so forth; seeing a grandfather clock would be discrepant, it would "interrupt" the dominant expectations, the currently active schema. Similarly, if in the process of planning a vacation, I am reminded of a prior engagement on the day I am planning to leave, that new "thought" interrupts the planning activity; it is discrepant with the ongoing stream of thought.

Since most previous thought and theory related to the topic has stayed within the confines of behavior and action, most of the following discussion will deal with the interruption of organized action sequences. However, most of the discussion can easily be translated into the perceptual and problem-solving spheres.

The Consequences of Interruption

We can distinguish between general "motivational" and very specific consequences of interruption. The distinction is related to C. R. Gallistel's[1] use of the term *motivation* for higher-order nodes that organize action. "Motivational" effects of interruption are those that may produce a variety of different subsequent outcomes—depending on the situation at the time of interruption, the prior experience of the organism, and the hierarchy of action and cognitive structures that is being interrupted. Interruption may, on the other hand, produce one or more very specific responses, previously acquired and specific to the activity or sequence that has been interrupted.

A continuum of action systems and conditions ranges from conditions that elicit one and only one outcome to conditions that may elicit one or more of a family of responses or actions. Interruption, in turn, will have consequences ranging along this continuum.

In discussing the consequences of interruption, I shall follow this continuum from those cases that have relatively little variance in possible outcomes to those that seem to be motivational in the traditional sense; that is, the variance of possible outcomes is fairly large.

PERSISTENCE AND COMPLETION

I previously mentioned the inevitability of an organized response. Once initiated, it rushes to completion, and nothing external to the organism is necessary to insure the continuation of the sequence, even though external factors are crucial for its initiation.

Once an organized response has been interrupted, it is assumed that a tendency to completion persists as long as the situation remains essentially unchanged. There might at first be persisting attempts to complete the sequence despite the interruption, and in many cases such second attempts will obviously be quite successful and run off smoothly. The key may turn on the second try; ink may appear at the tip of a fountain pen. Explaining the tendency to complete or to persist is a tricky and challenging problem. We shall encounter it again later on, when I shall also present two suggestions for the origin of the tendency to complete—one cognitive, the other "emotional."

Organized sequences tend to follow the dictum "If at first you don't succeed, try again." The failure to complete a telephone connection because of faulty or interrupted dialing simply produces a return to the beginning and a second run through the sequence. Cigarette lighters often work on the second try. Thus, in the first instance, interruption of many organized sequences produces repetition.

However, even a second try may not lead to the completion of the sequence. In that case—instead of or in addition to repetition—we might find increased vigor in the completion responses.

1. Gallistel (1974).

When a key won't open a lock, the application of a little pressure sometimes produces the desired result. The same method might work when a tackle attempts to block the completion of a drive toward the goal line. Repeated and more vigorous striking of a cigarette lighter may produce a flame. The same method might produce results with a recalcitrant mule. Thus, both increased force and repetition of some part of the organized sequence might produce the end state. In none of these cases is the organized sequence appreciably altered.

It is tempting to speculate at this point that the increased vigor of response following interruption is a motivational, energizing phenomenon.[2] However, the application of increased vigor may also be a well-learned response from previous experiences with interruption.[3] I shall in a later context return to the problem of so-called motivational factors involved in completion.

RESPONSE SUBSTITUTION

Substitution involves sequence completion by other organized sequences that are more or less specific to the interrupted sequence.[4] The various factors that influence substitutability are (1) similarity between original and substitute actions, (2) contiguity of the substitute and the original goal, (3) the nature of the original goal activity, and (4) active rather than passive participation in completion.[5] In terms of Gallistel's organization of action systems, we might assume that under specified conditions, actions and behaviors subsumed under a single superordinate node are substitutable one for another.

Miller, Galanter, and Pribram[6] have discussed the problem of interruption in terms of memory storage and the load put on storage when an ongoing organized activity is interrupted. They thus explain the recall of interrupted tasks as the storage of the uncompleted portion in working memory. They suggest further that whenever an organized sequence has interchangeable parts—as in writing several letters to friends—the sequence in which the parts are executed is immaterial. However, interruption between the parts of sequence (e.g., between letters) should produce a problem of completion, just as interruption within a part (e.g., while writing a letter) should. Clearly, two organized action sequences are being interrupted: writing letters and writing a particular letter. The effect in the case of the interrupted letter should be more pronounced, but it should not be absent when only the larger, higher-order sequence is interrupted between parts. The lower in the hierarchy of action systems the interruption intervenes, the less likely it is that substitutability can occur.

The problem of substitution can, however, be posed differently. It may be that substitution involves much more than the specific consequences of a particular organized response. Kurt Lewin's theory did specify such a general principle

2. Amsel and Roussel (1952).
3. Marx (1956).
4. See the work of Lewin (1935) and his associates, and particularly Lissner (1933).
5. Deutsch (1954).
6. Miller, Galanter, and Pribram (1960).

by suggesting that substitution follows a general state of tension. I assume that whenever organisms are prevented from completing any one organized sequence, they will then tend to complete the sequence by substituting any other even minimally relevant organized sequence.

A word needs to be said first about stop rules. Any psychological theory requires some mechanism that explains the cessation of ongoing activity.[7] The completion of an organized response is obviously one stop rule; it may be the only one. The stop rule is important here because the substituted organized action, in the case of interruption, produces a new stop rule for the organism. In other words, the flow of action may be shortened or extended.

It is assumed that interruption, in the absence of situationally relevant substitutes, will result in the production of some other organized action available to the organism. Such substitution will presumably depend on two factors: the availability of organized actions in general and their relative accessibility as a function of immediately preceding events and experiences.

THE PROBLEM OF COMPLETION

Up to now I have discussed only problems involved in the completion of interrupted response sequences. I now return to the question of whether interruption produces some sort of state of tension that is dissipated by completion (vide Lewin), whether there is a completion need, or whether we can get along without an energy concept. We might think of completion as the result of a frustrated need or drive or stored-up tension. But this is not necessarily the easy way out. Consider the notion that an organism will complete an interrupted sequence, whether directly or through substitution, without invoking extraneous energy states. I would prefer to believe that the phenomena that seem to indicate greater vigor or energy are derivable from previous experiences that have produced completion by the application of force or—as I show below—from certain emotional, although not energetic, states.

Completion can be derived from the continued activation of the underlying structure of the overt organized response. If, at the time of interruption, the sequential order of the organized sequence has been laid down centrally, then the uncompleted part of the sequence will persist at the cognitive level as a plan,[8] even though interruption may disrupt the overt sequence. As soon as the blocking agent has been removed, the original overt sequence can resume where it left off, and the overt sequence will follow the isomorphic plan that represents the original action system. Such a sequence is, of course, an integral part of schema theory, and of the theory of plans, and it can easily handle the problem of substitution. The persistence of the underlying plan, which continues to be activated even though the overt action is blocked, creates the likelihood that the original plan will be completed as soon as conditions permit it.

This approach avoids the postulation of a separate completion need. Another,

7. Mandler (1962b) and Miller (1963).
8. Miller, Galanter, and Pribram (1960).

not incompatible possibility would ascribe the completion tendency to the operation of arousal, and it is generally akin to Lewin's drive theory, without, however, invoking a hypothetical drive state.

It is possible that whenever the organism is interrupted before the completion of an organized sequence, the resulting state of arousal is maintained until completion, or completion by substitution, has been achieved. If we assume that interruption frequently leads to an aversive state of distress, then we may assume that this state will persist until completion has been achieved. However, this state is one that the organism will, whenever possible, terminate, and if completion—by whatever means—terminates that state, then the emotional effects of interruption may provide an adequate explanation for the occurrence of completion tendencies. Completion of an organized sequence removes the state of distress that is usually produced by the interruption.

While this is a reasonable account that reduces the two factors to a single mechanism, I would prefer to entertain both possibilities for the time being, if for no other reason than that completion tendencies seem quite compelling when seen in the raw. There is, of course, no reason why cognitive completion tendencies, emotional consequences, and completion driven by distress cannot coexist.

Emotional Consequences of Interruption

The central postulate of the interruption hypothesis is that interruption leads to arousal that may be followed by emotional states.

The interruption of an organized response or a schema or an ongoing cognitive activity produces a state of arousal that, in the absence of completion or substitution, may develop into one or another emotional expression, depending on the occasion of the interruption. Thus, interruption may lead to expressions of fear, anger, surprise, humor, or euphoria, depending on factors *other than the interruption itself*.

There have been several theoretical suggestions about the motivational or emotional effects of interruption, all of which imply to some degree that these consequences are noxious and aversive in character. I shall return to these shortly, but first I shall present a more general statement.

In the first place it is more parsimonious to fit the emotional consequences of interruption into a general treatment of emotion than to let it stand by itself and occupy a unique position.

Second, observations of everyday behavior suggest that interruption in some cases does lead to nonaversive, pleasurable states of emotion. The prime example can be found in play behavior, particularly in that of children. Given the proper attitude or situational definition, children interrupted in the midst of organized sequences may find such interruptions pleasant, even delightful. A toddler laboriously climbing stairs may cry when suddenly snatched off them; however, she may also cry in delight when the snatching is done by a smiling parent in the spirit of play.

The conditions of interruption that lead to positive, or any other, emotional expression must be the previously acquired evaluations appropriate for these emotions. Frequently, of course, the laughing parent presents a cue that is pleasurable. Maybe more applicable to the present argument is the response to a practical joke in the adult. When the context in which a chair is pulled out from under someone is clearly playful, the response will be one of humor; but when the event occurs without such preparation, the practical joke is usually found to be not at all funny by its target. Interruptions are frequently disruptive, because they may block the activity that is most appropriate to the situation.

More important, we find different aversive emotional states in the adult, who, depending on the occasion, may react to interruption with annoyance, aggression, or withdrawal. If interruption had specific emotional consequences such diversity would be difficult to explain. Finally, even in the adult, the same interruption may result in noxious emotional states or in pleasant ones. A telephone call during dinner from a pestiferous salesman results in annoyance; a call from a friend one has not heard from in a long time may result in delight.

We should here also take note of a discussion of the inhibition of distress (see Chapter 10) that suggests the generality of the emotional sequelae of interruption.[9] Distress or anxiety may be inhibited or controlled by behavioral or situational inhibitors, and the removal or withdrawal of an inhibitor of distress may lead to distress. Thus, the child discovers early that the interruption of inhibitors, which are organized sequences, leads to distress. This process suggests one mechanism for the appearance of distress at the interruption of some organized response. It is interesting to speculate that all organized actions may act as inhibitors and that visceral arousal is a necessary consequence of the withdrawal of an inhibitor—and thus the antecedent for emotional behavior.

At this point it is appropriate to review some of the theoretical statements and empirical explorations dealing with the "emotional" effects of interruption.

EFFECTS OF INTERRUPTION

Kurt Lewin and his collaborators focused on the interruption of cognitive sequences.[10] They proposed that any intention to reach a goal produces a tension system. That tension is released when the goal is reached and, conversely, is preserved if the goal is blocked.[11] The postulation of undischarged tension led Lewin and Bluma Zeigarnik[12] to predict superior recall for interrupted activities. The major difference between the Lewinian and the present position is that we distinguish between two effects—the tendency to complete, which is present before the interruption, and an emotional response that does not emerge unless the organized response has been interrupted.

A more specific statement about the relation between interruption and emo-

9. Kessen and Mandler (1961).
10. See Butterfield (1954) for a review.
11. For the theoretical proposals, see Lewin (1935, 1940).
12. Zeigarnik (1927).

tional discharge was made by Freud in his early as well as his later theories of anxiety. In the former he postulated that anxiety was directly derivable from the damming up of libidinal energy, making particular reference to unsuccessful attempts to complete the sexual act—an interruption of organized response par excellence. This "motor" theory—akin to Lewin's—was later replaced by statements such as "Anxiety . . . seems to be a reaction to the perception of the absence of the object,"[13] which is clearly closer to the present thesis.

The first important nonmotivational statement on the emotional consequences of interruption was made in 1946 by Donald Hebb (see also Chapter 2). Hebb developed the hypothesis that "fear originated in the disruption of temporally and spatially organized cerebral activities."[14] However, his argument seems to restrict the emotional consequences of interruption to fear. I shall maintain the major thesis that interruption has as its most important consequence the innate arousal of the autonomic nervous system—that it is the prime releaser of ANS activity.

I have argued that some special consequences of interruption are likely to be highly adaptive. When organisms are engaged in well-practiced, habitual, and adaptive (i.e., well-organized) behavior, then any change in their condition or in the conditions of their surrounds that makes these organized structures maladaptive or in need of change should be signaled intensely and uniquely. In addition, the signaling function of the autonomic nervous system would be highly useful for indicating that new behavior is required, that the situation needs to be further explored, and that a variety of new and old behavior patterns may be appropriately brought into play. Sudden changes might be important for survival and should therefore be immediately attended and respond to.

There is little experimental evidence on the effects of interruption on the ANS. I have shown that the interruption of verbal material shows the expected effects. The more highly organized the material was, the stronger the ANS effect—the greater the autonomic response, regardless of whether organization was newly learned or previously acquired.[15] These studies perhaps confounded interruption with the novelty value of interruption, though I would argue that novelty is intricately related to the notion of interruption. Using pupillary dilation as a measure of arousal, one study showed that whereas arousal was *lower during* the recall of familiar (versus unfamiliar) sets of words and digits, *following* interruption the degree of arousal was *greater* for the familiar sequences.[16] Another study used the interruption of a well-organized cognitive pattern to produce arousal, and also introduced a confederate who exhibited emotional behavior.[17] The results showed the expected coaction of interruption and environmental-cognitive cues; "aroused [interrupted] subjects were generally more susceptible to the confederate's expressed mood."

13. Freud ([1926] 1975).
14. Hebb (1946).
15. Mandler (1964a).
16. Sher (1971).
17. Fry and Ogston (1971).

Probably the best set of evidence concerning the adequate conditions for ANS arousal and their relation to our concept of interruption comes from the work of Marianne Frankenhaeuser and her associates.[18] I already noted her work in connection with the relation between catecholamine secretion and environmental coping. I now turn to the conditions that produce catecholamine secretion. Conditions characterized by novelty, anticipation, unpredictability, and change usually result in a rise in adrenalin secretion.[19] More important, repeated exposure shows a decrease in adrenalin output," provided that the subject gains better control over the situation." In other words, when ongoing organized cognition or behavior is interrupted, adrenalin output increases. Adaptation occurs only when a new and adequate sequence has been found, that is, when control over the situation has been achieved.[20] Similarly, any change from a "normal" level of stimulation produces increases in adrenalin output, whether the situation involves under- or overstimulation.[21] Once again, the prevailing cognitive organization defines interruption; whether the level of stimulation is reduced or increased is unimportant, as long as it goes counter to the operating level of cognitive planning.

In summary, I list the following general principles relating interruption and arousal:

1 • Degree of organization (i.e., tightness and invariance of structure) will be reflected in degree of ANS arousal when the structure is interrupted.

2 • Degree of arousal will vary with the discrepancy between the interrupting event and the interrupted structure. Discrepancy is partly a function of the degree to which structures are available that can integrate the interrupted structure and the new event or behavior. Thus, substitute actions or thoughts available at the time of interruption may decrease arousal effects.

3 • The more highly organized behavior and plans are also more likely to be the ones that are resumed if the situation permits. Thus, while the degree of arousal may be high, it is also more likely to be short-lived under conditions of high degrees of organization and noncontinuing interruption.

INTERRUPTION OF CONSUMMATORY BEHAVIOR

I now turn to a line of inquiry restricted to the interruption of a particular set of organized responses—consummatory behavior.

The notion that the absence of an expected reward or reinforcement may have emotional consequences has been bruited about in contemporary reinforcement theories at least since 1938.[22] After a variety of attempts to develop a satisfactory theory of extinction, the notion finally became respectable in the early

18. Frankenhaeuser (1971a, 1975).
19. Frankenhaeuser (1975).
20. Frankenhaeuser and Rissler (1970).
21. Frankenhaeuser, Nordheden, Myrsten, and Post (1971).
22. Skinner (1938).

1950s, the most popular relevant concept being Abram Amsel's frustration effect.[23] His hypothesis and the data suggest that the withdrawal of reward has motivational or emotional consequences only after a particular sequence leading to consummatory behavior has been well learned. The data generally show that behavior following the interruption is enhanced (i.e., it exhibits increased vigor). In addition, the emotional consequences of nonreward (interruption) can be classically conditioned.[24] There is very little in the studies cited in Amsel's reviews[25] that is inconsistent with the position advocated here, despite the obvious gulf separating our theoretical predilections. The major differences that I would stress are as follows. First, the initial emotional consequences of interruption are visceral arousal, directly observable and measurable autonomic events that need not be reduced to the states of theoretical variables. Second, anticipatory goal reactions are not necessary or relevant in the case of well-organized response sequences. Third, the opportunities and behaviors available to the organism immediately following nonreward determine its effects. Apart from these not unimportant differences, I call on the frustration effects as weighty evidence for the general hypothesis about the arousing consequences of interruption.

Once again, we encounter the suggestion in these studies that the effect of interruption is noxious. Thus, Amsel states that fractional anticipatory frustration "operates in many respects like fear,"[26] and Mowrer talks in this connection about frustration, disappointment, and anger.[27] It may well be that the emotional effect of nonreward is usually aversive, since nonreward is negatively evaluated.

Aggressive acts are evoked by appropriate cues in the environment and supported by visceral arousal, a position consistent with my notions about the conditions for emotional behavior. More important, "if the aggressive sequence is set into operation, but completion is prevented, internal tension is induced which is channelled into whatever response happens to be under way at the time."[28] This statement suggests that the visceral arousal following interruption of an aggressive sequence acts as an additional stimulus for the support of ongoing (aggressive) behavior.

In Chapter 10 I shall discuss the emotional effects of interruption when no other relevant behavior is available. Briefly, since the onset of interruption is, by definition, unexpected and since the organism frequently has few other situationally relevant responses available or high in its repertory at the moment of interruption, it is this lack of environmental control, this "helplessness" in the face of interruption, that is responsible for the high frequency of negative affect in response to interruption. Although fear is not a necessary consequence of interruption, it is, under the conditions that we observe it in and out of the laboratory, a highly likely one. As a consequence, it should be possible to manip-

23. Amsel (1962).
24. Wagner (1963).
25. Amsel (1958, 1962).
26. Amsel (1962).
27. Mowrer (1960).
28. Berkowitz (1964).

ulate the degree of negative affect by varying the responses available to the organism immediately following the interruption.

DISRUPTION AS A CONSEQUENCE OF INTERRUPTION

Whenever an organized sequence is interrupted, we may expect the occurrence of some emotional responses. If, as often happens, this emotional eruption is incompatible with completion or continuation of the sequence, we would expect some further disruption of organized behavior to occur. If, on the other hand, the organism learns that completion is possible despite the interruption, the emotional consequences will be outweighed by the completion tendency, and recovery will, of course, be the more rapid the better organized the action. Common evidence for the disruptive effects of interruption is abundant.

At the cognitive level, the disruptive effects of interruption are commonplace. The inability of the writer or student to return to his train of thought or assignment following an interruption needs no documentation. The anxiety—or helplessness—in the absence of organized continuation in any intellectual task is well known to writers, artists, and scientists. Equally apparent are the disruptive and interfering consequences when a motor-skill sequence repeatedly fails of completion. Even a householder skilled in fixing the vacuum cleaner will show emotional disruptive effects when repeated attempts at going through the motions that "worked the last time" fail on a particular occasion.

Of particular interest to the experimental psychologist is the disruption found during extinction of previously learned responses. Extinction of an unorganized response sequence is typical in most studies where the organism is exposed to extinction immediately following the acquisition of the response. We may assume that in these cases, in which the organization of the full sequence has not yet been adequately developed, the interruption of the consummatory response produces emotional consequences in the goal box and may make the goal region aversive. Since the pregoal sequence has not yet been organized, there is no automatic running off of the sequence up to the goal box, and the behavior should soon fail to appear.

Extinction in the case of organized sequences is more complicated. Not only is the consummatory sequence interrupted in the goal region but the established organization of the behavior in the goal path inevitably brings the organism back to that goal, where it is interrupted time and again. The organism thus keeps running to a region that is becoming more and more noxious.

Resistance to extinction increases as a function of the number of trials and decreases as a function of the number of rewards in the goal.[29] The former factor presumably describes the growth of organization, which brings the animal to the goal, whereas the number (and amount) of rewards determines the intensity of the noxious emotional reaction when the consummatory response is interrupted. The aversiveness of the interruption may work backward along the goal path, but

29. Theios and Brelsford (1964).

it is pitted against the inexorable pull of the organized sequence. Thus, the organism is repeatedly brought into contact with interruption. The consequence will, in the first instance, be an active search for substitutable responses, coupled with increasing helplessness and ensuing distress as these search behaviors turn up no way to complete the sequence. Eventually—and actually fairly early in the extinction series, because of the incorporation of aversiveness in the representation of the goal path—the sequence will be abandoned. Available data support this notion that overlearned animals—compared with animals trained to mastery—tend to show a more consistent approach to the goal during early extinction trials, followed by a steeper extinction slope.[30] There should also be more searching for substitutable responses, possibly exploratory behavior, during the extinction of an organized sequence than during the extinction of a barely learned sequence.

THE ORGANIZATION OF EMOTIONAL SEQUENCES

The notion that emotional arousal—and its sequelae—may disrupt behavior should not mislead us into thinking that the emotional consequences of interruption are necessarily unorganized or disruptive. In the first place, well-learned (i.e., organized) emotional behavior will have the same characteristics of unity and organization as any other response system. A fine rage is as well organized and may even be as productive of desired consequences as the most banal and unemotional organized sequence. Well-practiced aggressive responses to well-learned objects in well-defined situations may be just another organized consequence of interruption. We must recall that the apparent lack of a "goal" does not deny the presence of organization. Organized emotions need have no "goal"; they must be freely available and have well-trodden paths.

Another possibility is that emotional arousal may become integrated into an already existing organized sequence. The best example is found in the effects of partial reinforcement. If an organism has learned a goal path well and is interrupted (i.e., nonreinforced) on some proportion of subsequent trials, final extinction will be substantially slowed; the animal will show the partial reinforcement effect.[31] If we assume that during partial training the emotional consequences of interruption become part of the organized sequence, then the early extinction trials will not be different from the partial-reinforcement trials. By that time, the structure of the sequence will consist not only of sequences that include emotional arousal as well as terminal reinforcement but also of sequences that include emotional arousal without terminal reinforcement. These latter will run off just as smoothly as the reinforced ones; the persistence found after partial reinforcement will be apparent. Since, however, the organism is hungry (i.e., organized consummatory responses are likely to occur), more and more attempts at executing these responses will be interrupted, no subsequent substitute behavior will be encountered and arousal will become more and more apparent, disorganized

30. North and Stimmel (1960, expt. 2) and Birch, Ison, and Sperling (1960).
31. Amsel (1958).

emotional consequences will appear, anxiety and helplessness will eventually be encountered, and the sequence will be disrupted. Disruption and extinction will follow.

We can speculate that prolonged partial reinforcement might lead to a preference for a partial over a continuous sequence. It is possible that after extended partial training—well beyond asymptotic levels—the pairing of arousal with reinforcement (on the reinforced trials) will produce a positive emotional response and an ensuing preference. If this turns out to be true, it will also explain the emotional appeal of gambling, just as the partial-reinforcement effect explains its persistence.

Whenever emotional behavior is controlled within specific, situational limits, it may well be organized or integrated into another sequence. When no relevant behavior—emotional or otherwise—is available to the organism, the emotional consequences of interruption will be disruptive.

In this context, all unexpected events are interruptive, even the failure of an unpleasant event to occur. If we expect to be punished and are not, interruption occurs, arousal follows, and (usually positive) emotional experience ensues. If the evaluation stays negative, the failure of a noxious event to appear will produce arousal, presumably in addition to already existing arousal. These interactions speak in part to the complexity of negative events.

THE JOYS OF COMPLETION

The completion of interrupted actions and schemas is clearly a positive event, whatever interpretation of the completion tendency one prefers. Ellen Berscheid[32] has suggested a completion hypothesis to account for a variety of different emotions that follow interruption and completion. She notes that interruptions may be unexpected but that they may, under some circumstances, facilitate rather than interfere with the completion of action sequences and plans.

Two different kinds of events fall into this category. The first involves events that unexpectedly remove or countermand some condition or knowledge that itself was previously the occasion of interruption. The joyful experience that one's injured foot is not broken, that an unpleasant relative is not coming to dinner after all, and that a feared examination will not be given are all examples from this category.

The second category involves events that make it possible, unexpectedly and often prematurely, to complete some plan on which progress has been proceeding normally. The event permits the final or goal response to occur before it had been "planned" to occur.[33] Consider the case of a piggybank dedicated to the purchase of a much desired bicycle and the interruption of that savings plan by a sudden birthday gift of a racing bicycle, or consider the expectation that one will be promoted to a better job within a year and its interruption by the sudden resignation of a colleague, which opens up a similar position prematurely. Per-

32. Berscheid (1982).
33. Berscheid (1982).

fectly reasonable and "pleasant" plans are interrupted in both cases, but the interruption produces joy as a more immediate realization of a plan is substituted for the longer-range one.

These examples not only indicate the possible positive consequences of interruptions; they also fall directly within the emotional complex. The interruptions produce pleasant consequences as well as full-fledged "emotions," since they are highly likely to be accompanied by autonomic arousal—as are all interruptions.

AN EXAMPLE OF EMOTION AND INTERRUPTION

The consequences of interruption, as enumerated here, can be shown as part of a single syndrome in the case of a child's response to the loss of his mother figure or of his familiar environment.

Bowlby has summarized the phenomenon, based largely on the work of James Robertson, who observed the behavior of two- and three-year-old children in residential nurseries or hospital wards.[34]

> In the setting described a child of fifteen to thirty months who has had a reasonably secure relationship with his mother and has not previously been parted from her will commonly show a predictable sequence of behavior. This can be broken into three phases according to what attitude to his mother is dominant. We describe these phases as those of Protest, Despair, and Detachment. Though in presenting them it is convenient to differentiate them sharply, it is to be understood that in reality each merges into the next, so that a child may be for days or weeks in a state of transition from one phase to another, or of alternation between two phases.
>
> The initial phase, that of protest, may begin immediately or may be delayed; it lasts from a few hours to a week or more. During it the young child appears acutely distressed at having lost his mother and seeks to recapture her by the full exercise of his limited resources. He will often cry loudly, shake his cot, throw himself about, and look eagerly towards any sight or sound which might prove to be his missing mother. All his behavior suggests strong expectation that she will return. Meantime he is apt to reject all alternative figures who offer to do things for him, though some children will cling desperately to a nurse.
>
> During the phase of despair, which succeeds protest, the child's preoccupation with his missing mother is still evident, though his behavior suggests increasing hopelessness. The active physical movements diminish or come to an end, and he may cry monotonously or intermittently. He is withdrawn and inactive, makes no demands on people in the environment, and appears to be in a state of deep mourning. This is a quiet stage, and sometimes, clearly erroneously, is presumed to indicate a diminution of distress.
>
> Because the child shows more interest in his surroundings, the phase of detachment which sooner or later succeeds protest and despair is often welcomed as a sign of recovery. The child no longer rejects the nurses; he accepts their care and the food and toys they bring, and may even smile and be sociable. To some this change seems satisfactory. While his mother visits, however, it can be seen that all is not well, for there is a striking absence of the behavior characteristic of the strong attachment normal at this age. So far from greeting his mother he may seem hardly to know her; so far from clinging to her he

34. The following is reprinted by the kind permission of Dr. John Bowlby (see Bowlby [1969, 27–28]).

may remain remote and apathetic; instead of tears there is a listless turning away. He seems to have lost all interest in her.

Should his stay in hospital or residential nursery be prolonged and should he, as is usual, have the experience of becoming transiently attached to a series of nurses each of whom leaves and so repeats for him the experience of the original loss of his mother, he will in time act as if neither mothering nor contact with humans had much significance for him. After a series of upsets . . . he will gradually commit himself less and less to succeeding figures and in time will stop altogether attaching himself to anyone. He will become increasingly self-centered and, instead of directing his desires and feelings towards people, will become preoccupied with material things such as sweets, toys, and food.

This description not only shows the child's reaction to interruption but also illustrates the importance of expectations in defining an interruption as well as the coping mechanisms that are available, even to the very young. The interruption of relationships in the not so young continues this tale.

INTERRUPTION AND CLOSE RELATIONSHIPS

Berscheid[35] has used interruption theory to provide an extensive, insightful, and original analysis of close relationships. She notes that the closeness of a relationship stems from the frequency, strength, and diversity of the interconnections between two individuals' sequences of life events. The sequences may be causally interconnected, so that the occurrence of an action by one is a necessary and sufficient condition for some action by the other. The organized actions of the two people are then said to be *meshed*, that is, each person facilitates and augments the other person's actions. Whenever such meshing fails, the action sequences of one or both people will be interrupted, arousal will result, and emotional experiences may follow. If a relationship is characterized by a large number of well-meshed causal interconnections, little emotion (or stress) will be observable in the normal course of events. However, such well-meshed relationships contain what Berscheid calls "hidden ticking emotional bombs." Any significant change of these relationships will result in many and extensive interruptions. Conversely, a relationship that is not closely interconnected, a "parallel" relationship, is much less likely to produce severe emotional consequences if, for example, one of the partners leaves or dies.

In other words, a relationship is defined as the causal interconnections among the chain of actions and behaviors of two individuals. Emotional events are those occasions of interruption, arousal, and evaluation in which the causal antecedents of the experiencing person's target event lie in the other person's event chain. And one's emotional investment in a relationship is defined by one's vulnerability to interruption by actions or events in the other person's event chain. Thus, a tightly meshed relationship might well appear tranquil and uneventful as the actions of the partners smoothly provide the occasions (causal antecedents) for the other's actions and behaviors. But such a relationship is potentially "emotional." A similarly tranquil appearance may be given by a nonmeshed (parallel)

35. Berscheid (1982, 1983).

relationship, in which there are few or no interconnections among the partners' actions and behaviors. The potential for emotionality in the latter relationship is, of course, minimal.

Berscheid notes that these analyses suggest important consequences: the closeness of a relationship cannot be defined in terms of the atitudes that the involved people show toward each other or by the frequency or intensity of emotions that they typically experience. Frequently intense emotional reactions can be experienced following the loss of a partner, even though the relationship itself may not have been characterized by much ongoing emotional coloring. Furthermore, global feelings of liking or disliking a situation may not represent the degree of interconnectedness, and thus may not predict emotional reactions—for example, to desertion or death. Finally, the general appraisal of a person or situation may not predict one's emotional reactions to that person. One may like or dislike a person, but how one reacts to his or her action will depend on the interconnectedness of the two lives and the conditions under which actions by the other are discrepant.

Berscheid's analyses have far-reaching implications.[35] They permit us to understand why day-to-day "feelings" of liking, or the absence of "hot" emotions, may not predict people's reactions to unexpected behavior or to the loss of a partner; they explain how automatic, daily living may erupt into rather severe emotional reactions; they provide a theoretical basis for different kinds of relationships (e.g., parallel versus meshed); and they also illuminate what Berscheid calls "the mysteries." We can now understand why obstacles to a relationship often increase passion, why a disliked person can be the occasion of "hot" (and even positive) emotion, and why well-liked persons sometimes fail to produce much emotional reaction by their absence. Interruption theory provides the guidelines for understanding emotion in social contexts, which must be studied in the "context of a person's needs, aspirations, and goals, and how another person impinges on them."[36]

COGNITIVE INTERRUPTION

Given that a particular environmental event activates a specific schema, we assume that that structure determines the individual's perception and evaluation of the environment. A new input that activates a new schema may be interrupting, if the new structure is incompatible with the old, if it contradicts the operation of the old structure, or, more generally, if it provides evidence that is not manageable (i.e., cannot be assimilated) by the existing structures.

The operation of an existing schema defines the expectation of certain events in the environment and their sequence. Turning a switch is part of the structure that includes the perception of a light going on—if it does not, the structure is interrupted. Answering the telephone, driving a car, and talking to people all involve well-established structures and serial organizations that act as "expecta-

36. Berscheid (1982).

tions" and are easily interrupted. The use of ordinary terms such as *sudden*, *unexpected*, *unlikely*, and *surprising* usually implies that an existing schema that predicted some event other than the one taking place was in operation. Even the contemplation of a dull, uniform environment is "interrupted" when there is a sudden and intense change in stimulation, whether it is a sudden shape or noise, or a drastic change in illumination.

Statements about environmental stimuli that are fear inducing because they are "strange" are best subsumed under the notion of interruption. I would thus interpret Bowlby's and Hebb's discussions of the fearful properties of strange stimuli. In addition, stranger anxiety in infants does not emerge until schemas for faces have been developed. Strangeness depends on the prior establishment of familiarity. Strange events are fearful because they are arousing; they interrupt the ongoing familiar structures, and they are interpreted as fearful, because they cannot be assimilated and no relevant action is available—a topic to which I shall return in Chapters 10 and 11.

I indicated earlier that structures may be interrupted by their own consequences as well as by external events. Consider any planning activity that is not executed but is only contemplated. At one time or another some consequence of the planned series of acts may be incompatible with the overall plan, in which case it would be interrupted. For example, we may plan to visit a friend and thus generally explore the actions to be set in motion when, in sorting through relevant memory structures, we discover an appointment, unbreakable and at the same time as the envisaged visit. Or we find that a particular plan would involve an interaction that is unpleasant or that for one or another physical or social reason cannot be executed. In all these cases, ongoing cognitive activities and their structures may lead to interruption within the mental organization without an additional input from the environment. I shall discuss this topic further in connection with guilt and anxiety.

In general, the interruption of organized behavior or operative cognitive structures is a phenomenon that has been inadequately analyzed, both empirically and theoretically. Such analyses should go hand in hand with a better understanding of the organization of plans.[37] Particular structures and particular cognitive plans form subparts of more general and, in the life of the individual, more important and more extensive cognitive structures. Thus, the interruption of a low-level plan may not produce much in the way of arousal, because the executive plan in existence at the time is a much "higher" one and because, alternatives being available, there is nothing in the interruption of the low-level plan that necessarily interrupts the higher one. For example, if one is sitting in front of a table laden with different kinds of foods, the removal of one of the dishes, even though one was in the midst of partaking from it, may not be an interruption at all of the more dominant plan of having a full meal, since we can immediately switch to another dish and continue the overriding plan of the moment. The major point is that interruption at any one point must be analyzed

37. Miller, Galanter, and Pribram (1960).

closely in terms of a hierarchy or levels of plans in order to ask which, if any of them, have been interrupted. We can assume that when all the plans, including the high-level ones, are interrupted, the degree of arousal will be intense and will produce an intense emotional reaction.

Most cognitive change involves some kind of interruption. These are essentially of two types: first, the new event that is not "expected"—that does not fit into the ongoing interpretation of the environment—and, second, the "expected" event that does not happen. While distinguishable, these two types have the same kind of interruptive structural consequences; the new event is disruptive because it occurs instead of the "expected" event, and the absence of the "expected" event implies the presence of something else that is "unexpected." In either case the ongoing cognitive activity is interrupted. At this point, coping, problem solving, and "learning" activities take place. It is apparently also at this point that the focus of consciousness is on the interruption.

In Chapter 4, I noted that consciousness has "troubleshooting" as one of its functions. Unconscious structures enter conscious constructions when they fail (i.e., when they are interrupted). This phenomenon has long been known as Claparède's law of awareness; actors become aware of automatic actions when these are disrupted or fail.[38] We assume, therefore, that one of the cognitive functions of interruption is to bring some adaptive problem into consciousness, where extensive repair work and coping activities can take place. It appears that this sometimes happens without any emotional sequelae. Thus, interruption may, under some circumstances, simply focus a problem into consciousness, and, as the problem is quickly solved, no emotional consequences follow. Only when the repair operation is not immediately successful does some emotional *quale* also enter consciousness. We shall see in Chapter 11 how this additional emotional awareness restricts attentiveness (consciousness) and may further interfere with adequate coping. In addition, however, planning for "troubleshooting" may avoid arousal altogether, since the interruption and the conscious problem solving become part of a higher-order plan. When working on a difficult problem, we expect to find one or another cognitive structure inadequate, and the ensuing "troubleshooting" becomes part of the organized sequence; no arousal occurs and no emotional consequences ensue. Once again we are reminded that it is the operative executive plan that is potentially interruptible and not necessarily any action that occurs as part of it.

The effects of interruption and discrepancy occur both for automatic and for deliberate schemas and structures. The effect itself is obviously automatic and requires no conscious participation. Whether I am walking down a flight of stairs and am interrupted by the absence of one of the steps or whether I try to remember a telephone number that is urgently needed, the effect is the same. The lack of the step and the failure to remember the telephone number will both produce an automatic interruption effect. In the case of the automatic (unconscious) walk

38. E.g., Claparède (1934).

down the steps, the interruption will immediately produce a conscious construction, whereas in the case of the inaccessible telephone number the problem is already in a conscious state. But the arousal effect will occur automatically, as soon as the interruption has occurred.

9

VALUE: SOURCE OF EMOTIONAL QUALITIES

AT VARIOUS POINTS in the preceding chapters I talked generally about sources of evaluative cognitions. These evaluations can arise out of a variety of different conditions, including the sheer completion of an interrupted task, the nature of actions, the occurrence of unacceptable discrepancies, the perception of control, and unavoidable and repeated interruptions that prevent the achievement of a goal. Just as arousal apparently has very few sources, among which interruption is the most important, so the other component of the constructed emotion—the evaluative cognition—has many different and possibly innumerable sources. In this chapter I shall attend to the various ways in which evaluations—the affective qualities—come to be constructed and to produce emotional experiences.[1] The major categories of value I shall discuss are innate preferences, personal and cultural predication, and structural value.

To start with, we must consider some terminological hurdles. How do we use such terms as *value*, *goodness*, *preference*, and *judgment*? For example, I use the term *evaluative* not only for any cognitive event that implies some *judgment* of the goodness or badness of an event but also for events that indicate some *preference* for an object or action. Clearly, two objects can both be judged as being good, but only one can be preferred to the other. I do not intend to resolve many of these issues; rather, I want—for the time being—to appeal to a fairly intuitive, consensual notion of evaluation and value. Premature precision may, in this as in many other instances, hamper rather than advance conceptual understanding. I am not looking at how events come to be labeled as good or bad, liked or disliked. On the contrary, I contend that the issue of value concerns the definition and explication of mental events that eventually come to be glossed in these valuative terms. Thus, approach, completion, and presence and absence of congruity are basic elements of value, in the way that, as I shall argue later, helplessness (in the presence of arousal) *is* anxiety.

Another hurdle involves the relation between consciousness and judgment.

1. Speculations about the sources of value are sparse and spread thinly in the psychological literature, but see some social psychological works, such as Kelvin (1969). This chapter is one attempt to view the range of possible sources.

Evaluative judgments imply, in the common understanding, a conscious state. I shall generally employ that meaning when I refer to judgments as such, that is, when they occur in the absence of specifically emotional situations. Evaluative judgments are those conscious constructions that arise when the intentional direction asks for an evaluation and nothing more; evaluative schemas are used in such constructions. However, the same schemas may be used in the construction of emotional states, when they enter into conjunction with arousal to produce holistic emotional experiences. Therefore, judgments and emotions are often based on the same underlying schema, the only difference being the kind of construction called for.

I shall return to the issue of consciousness and value later in the chapter, but for now we want to keep in mind certain distinctions whose absence confuses some problems of value and cognition. In the first instance, we need to come to grips with the confusing use of the term *affect*. It is sometimes used to refer to value, sometimes to refer to emotional states. For example, the question frequently arises what the distinction between cognition and affect is and whether the two are subserved by distinctly different mechanisms.[2] We need to recall some issues discussed in earlier chapters.

In the past, the terms *cognition* and *cognitive processes* were used to refer to conscious, thoughtlike processes. For example, in discussions about the "primacy" of affect, cognition was identified with conscious ideation.[3] Early observers asserted that affective elements move into consciousness (become conscious) before anything of the ideational elements is (consciously) perceived.[4] In making a distinction between affect and cognition, one uses a distinction between affective and ideational elements. But what seems actually to be at issue is the attainment of consciousness of likes and dislikes (i.e., values) and of descriptive (ideational) elements.

If one accepts the notion that conscious contents are constructed by cognitive processes, then it is reasonable to ask what gives rise both to the affects and to the ideas. I assume that cognitive processes are at work whenever information is processed and knowledge used or invoked. Included in that knowledge is information about preference, about liking and disliking, about good things and bad things. Final (conscious) choices or preferences are the result of (cognitive) processes that are not conscious at the time of the choice and that may, in fact, never become conscious.

All of this is more than a semantic quibble. Robert Zajonc's colorful statement that "preferences need no inferences"[5] can be rephrased to read that "*Conscious* preferences need no *conscious* inferences." Since I assume that inferences can be the result of nonconscious, theoretically postulated processes, we can refine the problem further and ask what inferred structures and processes could be responsible for judgments of value?

2. Zajonc (1980); see also Lazarus (1982).
3. Some psychologists still adhere to that usage. See, e.g., Lazarus (1982).
4. Wundt (1905).
5. Zajonc (1980).

To say that one "likes" something requires access to stored knowledge, unless one accepts the radical position that goodness is in the object. If it is true that affective-cognitive judgments appear to be made without any conscious access to other "cognitive" processes, then we must examine what it is about valuation and consciousness that produces such phenomenal characteristics. The apparent "direct" access to feelings and judgments of value is not unique to valuation; it is, as I have argued earlier, an instance of a more general characteristic of human thought.

Approaches to Value

There exist first-order approximations to the problem of "good" that have been with us for some time. The most popular solution (from the philosopher Spinoza to the contemporary behaviorists) is to explain the subjective sense of good in terms of something else—our interest, striving, wish, or approach. For example, in an attempt at a comprehensive theory of value, R. B. Perry[6] argued for the following formula:

$$x \text{ is valuable } = \text{ interest is taken in } x$$

Interest is characterized by expectancies that include not only cognitive elements but also attitudes of favoring or disfavoring the expected. A similar theme is heard in a linguistic analysis of "good" that argues that "this is what 'good' means: answering to certain interests."[7] There are two possible interpretations of "interest." An object or event may be "interesting," or it may be simply "of interest." In either case, if value is a gloss on interest, then interest must be further examined. We wish to know (from a psychological point of view) what makes events interesting or of interest. Included in such an analysis will be the psychological factors that make us favor some expected event or the realized event when it occurs. It may turn out that whatever it is that makes us attend to or seek out things is also what invests them with value.

There is an obvious distinction between the interestingness of "interest" and value. Interesting things are not always valued, and valued things are not always interesting. A square coffee cup is probably interesting without being valued, and a properly working tool like an electric drill may be valued without being particularly interesting. The arguability of a distinction between interest and value suggests the need for a more extensive analysis, to which I shall return later.

Perry also put the burden of interestingness (value) on the valuating individual when he noted that evaluative predicates refer to specific relations into which things "may enter with interested subjects." The interest here is ascribed to the subject. It is as if individuals were always ready to extend their interests to some selected objects; as if evaluative predicates were in readiness as they search for appropriate objects. In contrast, I argue that the kind of interest that is involved in value is the result of an *interactive* relation between the object and the subject.

6. Perry (1926).
7. Ziff (1960).

Only certain objects can be of interest (value) to certain subjects; people do not scan the environment ready to bestow interest (value) on deserving events.

The converse notion that positive and negative values adhere to specific stimuli is clearly incorrect. It is even incorrect when applied to such notions as pleasure and pain centers in the brain and the stimuli that activate them. A particular cranial stimulus "cannot be regarded as simply negative or positive. This property appears to depend upon its *context*, that is upon the past contingencies and the current situation in which the stimulus is presented."[8]

Evaluative judgments have often been subsumed under appraisal. Appraisal is seen as intuitive, reflexive, and automatic, though examples usually deal with inborn tendencies such as children's liking milk and disliking vinegar. However, even appraisals that require some memory of past encounters are assumed either to be based on past approach-avoidance scenarios or to invoke the good-bad judgment as somehow given. In some cases, all knowledge of good and evil is even seen as innately given.[9] Richard Lazarus and his associates use appraisal as deliberate and conscious, assuming the immediate apprehension of meaning.[10]

Researchers with the semantic differential have claimed that three general factors of evaluation, potency, and activity account for most, if not all, connotative (affective) judgments. But the evaluative factor appears to be the only truly general one. For example, in personality perception only evaluation is present in the data of all subjects. There is "little evidence for another universal dimension orthogonal to evaluation."[11]

Sources of Value

One can distinguish the following three general classes of representations that give rise to evaluative cognitions:

1 • innate sources that produce automatic approach and avoidance

2 • personal and cultural predications that are responsible for most of our learned values

3 • structural sources of two kinds—primitive preferences based on familiarity and internal relational structures

I shall discuss each of these categories separately, keeping in mind that any specific instance of evaluation is likely to contain some admixture of two or more of these sources.

INNATE VALUES

Evaluations based on apparently innate approach-avoidance tendencies no doubt exist. T. C. Schneirla[12] suggested that fundamental approach and avoid-

8. Robbins (1982).
9. Arnold (1960).
10. Lazarus, Averill, and Opton (1970) and Lazarus (1981, 1982).
11. Kim and Rosenberg (1980).
12. Schneirla (1959).

ance tendencies should be viewed as basic to positive and negative behavioral and phenomenal evaluation—a view consistent with much of the behaviorist literature, as well as with some modern views of fear and anxiety.[13] Classes of stimuli and events probably exist that act on innate structures, which in turn generate generalized approach and withdrawal tendencies.

These often species-specific dispositions are exemplified by the preference for an optimal temperature range and the rejection of extreme cold and heat, by the preference for sweet and the rejection of bitter substances, by the reaction to certain sexual stimuli, and by the retreat from looming objects. Even some of the other instances of evaluation, such as the tendency toward completion, may belong to the innate category.

These approach-withdrawal tendencies mold our early childhood experiences and extend far beyond the restricted realm in which they initially occur. They provide the basis for some personal predications when an innate preference is incorporated into the schema of previously innocuous events. Approach and withdrawal, and their phenomenal accompaniments, may well influence other derivative values. Objects may be judged in terms of memories of past approaches and avoidances. It may well be that the phenomenal experience of goodness and badness is often no more than the conscious accompaniment to (commentary on) such withdrawal and approach actions. I previously discussed the secondary schemas *about* our actions that form an important part of our cognitions of the world.[14] The representation of approaches and withdrawals, originally observed (by the self) in primitive (innate) occasions, may become the basis for generic approach and withdrawal schemas that carry with them evaluative cognitions. However, such secondary effects may be quite complex; Chapter 10 shows, for example, that the experience of pain cannot be a simple antecedent of an emotion like anxiety.

Given the discussion in Chapter 7, facial expressions come under the rubric of innate sources of value. If they are viewed as primitive remnants of communicative devices that indicate the relative attractiveness or danger of objects and events, then their very occurrence determines value orientations. Some such expressions occur without any analytic mediation, as in the response to injury and noxious smells. In any case, the occurrence of expressions influences evaluative cognitions, whatever the source of the expression.

PERSONAL AND CULTURAL PREDICATION

Culture is a powerful teacher of evaluative judgments, primarily through the vehicle of the common language. It is, for example, through the process of acculturation that we "learn" that corn is (in the United States) or is not (in France) fit for humans, that spinach is "good" for you, that shaking hands with people is or is not "proper." Such valuations are not based on an examination of an object or on an "objective" property of the event in question; rather, the value

13. Bowlby (1973).
14. See also Bem (1972).

is a predicate of the object—produced and maintained by cultural processes. Corn, for example, is said to be inedible because it is corn, not because of any particular taste or appearance.

Cultural predication is only a subset of personal predication—the individual acquisition of value attributes. Cultural predicates are those that are acquired (personally) by all or most members of a culture or society. Just as a group of people may have been told that corn is inedible, so will individuals "know" that liver tastes bad—without ever having tasted it. Personal predication makes for the celebration of differences in taste, preferences for certain kinds of heterosexual partners, enthusiasm for certain artistic periods, and so forth. Personal predication also produces phobias and philias, preoccupations and anxieties, obsessions and boredoms.

We must be careful, however, to distinguish between true predication and those values and preferences that flow from familiarity, from frequency of experience, from the novel as well as the common. Such evaluations will be discussed at length in the next section.

Personal and cultural predication arises frequently in those situations in which previously value-neutral objects and events are encountered in conjunction with value-laden occasions. Stoves that burn fingers become feared objects, photocopying machines that continuously break down become objects of frustration, songs heard together with a loved one become romantic milestones.

The usual mechanism to account for these concatenations is classical conditioning. In Chapter 3, I suggested some preliminary ways to represent the result of such conditioning in terms of novel schemas. It should be noted that mere co-occurrence does not produce a new schema. Witnessing a gruesome accident involving a small red car while dressed in a blue frock may produce future value judgments about small red cars but rarely about blue dresses. There is some evidence that such concatenations, in order to produce lasting effects, require, at least in human beings, some conscious work involving these contingencies.[15]

Predicated values also arise out of inferential processes. Typically, inferential predications occur when an object or event is classified or categorized as an instance of a more general (and valued) schema. Such inferences can range from realizing that a particular person at a party has recently been exposed to a dreaded tropical disease to very complex inferences involving attitudes and ideologies. For example, in trying to determine how to vote in a local election, one might well gather information about some local candidate, and in the course of such an investigation determine what organizations she has been associated with. No single one of these associations might produce a predication, but the individual inferences produce a particular value schema for the individual. Interacting with this schema of that person is an even more complex representation of one's social attitudes and political beliefs—one's own ideology.

The general notion that predications combine to produce unitary values is

15. Brewer (1974); see also Dawson, Schell, Beers, and Kelly (1982) for evidence of information processing during human conditioning.

generally accepted.[16] It is also applicable to emotional-affective values. For example, impression schemas are constructed from evaluative adjectives that function to a large extent as cultural predicates. These schemas influence the reactions to new events and become more easily accessible in proportion to the amount of evidence presented for a particular schema.[17]

Predications probably do not involve the "conditioning" of autonomic arousal to previously neutral events. The new schema involves the cognitive evaluation, which may, in turn, be a signal for threat or interruption, which then produces the attendant arousal. Personal and cultural predications entail the restructuring of the schema of an object or event in terms of some previously existing value. They do not of themselves create new kinds of values. The latter are created out of the innate dispositions discussed above and out of the structural evaluations detailed in the next section.

STRUCTURAL EVALUATIONS

The mental structure of an event or object, as mentally represented, gives rise to two quite distinct sources of value. The first is the appreciation of value (or beauty) based on specific relations among the features of the target event. The other, probably more primitive and certainly pervasive, is related to the familiarity of an event and our extensive previous experiences with it. It is linked to the issue of why we like what we know.

We start with the apparent distinction between descriptive and evaluative terms, sometimes also incorporated in the distinction between denotative and connotative meaning. Descriptive judgments seem to depend primarily on information that is "out there." Evaluative judgments apparently do not. We may agree that "the tree is green" but question whether "the tree is beautiful." Somewhere between those two are judgments that the tree is "old" or "sick." The value judgments seem to require something about "beautiful" that "belongs" to the speaker. Yet nothing is "good" or "beautiful" that does not have some "out there" characteristic on which we base such a judgment, and within a cultural-social group (i.e., within a group having common experiences) we can often agree on what is good and beautiful.

It appears that evaluative judgments cannot be reduced to some "objective" attributes of the object or event that is judged. If we assume that the sense of "meaning" in the natural languages is reflected in part by the relation between the representation of an event and other mental contents, then we can distinguish such "meanings" from evaluative meaning. The former might, redundantly, be called semantic meaning, which is typically handled by reference to semantic networks, feature analyses, prototypes, and so on. The latter, evaluative meaning, is apparently not dependent on such relations to other mental contents but is more properly addressed by certain internal structures of the target event;

16. Anderson (1981b).
17. Posner and Snyder (1975).

that is, specific relations *among* the features of an object are the most relevant representations.

Evaluative terms are applied to objects and events (or rather the representations of them), not on the basis of the presence or absence of their constituent features or their usual structure, but rather on the basis of a specific analysis of the structure of the event as such. For example, a tree may be called green because of the salience of its green leaves, but it is considered beautiful for reasons other than the mere presence of leaves (or a trunk or branches). The valuation is based on an appreciation of the relations among its features. A steak may taste salty because of excessive salt features, but it tastes good because of an appraisal of more than one of its features in some combination. Description and evaluation are not dichotomous; they mark the end points of a *continuum*. The "old" tree seems to be somewhat more than a description and not quite an evaluation. The continuum ranges from judgments based entirely on the presence or absence of certain features (red, hot, curved) to judgments that combine featural and structural characteristics ("That lake looks cold" or "He sounded tired") and judgments that are primarily dependent on specific structural, relational aspects of an object or event (the evaluative cognitions).

Descriptive and evaluative judgments both rely to some extent on the internal structure of the reference event. Thus, an animal is called a horse not just because it has a head, mane, tail, and legs but also because these elements occur in a particular configuration. Some aspect of these configurations is the occasion for calling a horse beautiful or not, but both kinds of judgments depend to some extent on the internal structure of the event. Clearly, the descriptive judgment applies to a wide range of possible values of variables, whereas the evaluative judgment depends on a much smaller range. However, it is not quite clear that one can draw the line between the two kinds of structural characteristics. Evaluative judgments do seem to depend primarily on the internal structure. The same features will, in different configurations, occasion the same descriptive predicate *horse*, but will give rise to two different evaluative predicates, say *beautiful* or *ugly*. Conversely, a particular configuration of features in an abstract painting may be found pleasing, and the identical configuration of different features may be equally pleasing. In the case of both the horse and the painting, it is the structure of the object, and not the presence or absence of certain features, that seems to determine its value. In other words, structure plays a very large role in evaluation and features play a relatively smaller one, whereas in description and categorization features as well as their structure have major determining functions.

Description and evaluation depend on two sets of structures—the structure of the world as it is presented to the observer and the structure of prior experiences and current expectations that reside in the mind of the observer. Most judgments depend on some event in the world and a prepared organism. In that sense descriptive (identifying) and evaluative actions are arrayed on a continuum of event-organism interactions. The mix of external (bottom-up) evidence and organism (top-down) expectations in the perception of objects and events can, of course, vary widely. Within that variation, evaluative judgments are more influenced by prior experiences and by structural relations than are descriptions or identifications. A large variety of instances satisfy the criteria for being identified as a coffee cup, an automobile, a sonnet, or a violin sonata. But very few instances satisfy the specific structural relations we demand of a comfortable coffee cup, an attractive automobile, a satisfying sonnet, or an acceptable sonata. There are specific ranges of values of features and relations among features that are the most frequently encountered for a particular class of events or objects. I wish to suggest that the objects or events that fall within those ranges will generate a primitive judgment of positive value. Other cognitive structures will guide the appearance of other kinds of evaluations, as the structural requirements of the sonata or sonnet guide our aesthetic judgments.

Although the most frequent instantiations of a particular schema will provide the basis for most of the primitive positive valuations, in some cases the general schema constrains such judgments very narrowly. The highly constrained schema of a friend's physical appearance will, for example, provide the basis for congruity or incongruity. For generic social schemas (such as cups, professors, tables, horses, and cars) a specific personal variant, the idiosyncratic experience of the event, will frequently determine the congruity that guides evaluation.

This approach has a family relation to the prototype approach to categorizations. According to Eleanor Rosch's approach to prototypes,[18] a category can be defined as the class of instances that have a certain defined relation to the categorical or class prototype. We can speculate whether social prototypes and positively valued instances show some degree of overlap. Perhaps the most frequently encountered instances of a category are also the most protoptypical ones. But this is not necessarily the case. For example, the prototypical fruit may well be the preferred fruit, but the prototypical occupation may not be the most frequently encountered one—namely, one's own.

The phenomenal experience that evaluations are somehow contributed by the "self" whereas perceptions are driven by the evidence of the environment is consistent with this interpretation of evaluative actions. To the extent that valuative judgments depend on the special subset of instances that satisfy the most frequently encountered examples, such judgments will vary from individual to individual. Descriptive and identifying actions, by the process of socialization, necessarily depend on shared elements and structures. We may differ on what we expect an acceptable plant for our living room to look like, but we do not differ on what we expect to characterize house plants in general. The structure that determines values will therefore show greater differences among people than will generally descriptive-cognitive structures.

There exist two quite distinct intellectual antecedents for a structural approach to problems of value. One is the Gestalt movement, which brought structural considerations into the mainstream of theoretical psychology—on direct com-

18. Rosch and Mervis (1975) and Rosch (1978).

petition with the then prevailing atomistic traditions. The other structuralist tradition is Piaget's, which itself derives from a longer tradition of structuralism within French intellectual history.

Piaget uses the term *assimilation* to refer to the integration of "external elements into evolving or completed structures," and *accommodation* to refer to the "modification of an assimilatory scheme or structure by the elements it assimilates."[19] Assimilation provides cognitive continuity and integration, whereas accommodation allows cognitive change. I shall shortly return to the issues raised by Piaget.

For the Gestalt movement Wolfgang Köhler presented an extensive discussion of the problem of value from the point of view of structural psychology (though he would surely have objected to this locution). He placed value within the more general notion of requiredness, which is characteristic of both the phenomenal and the physical world. The Gestalten that shape our experiences *require* certain conclusions and perceptions. Value is one instance of the recognition of requiredness. In other words, the perception of value is formed by Gestalt qualities of the world and of our perceptions. He concluded that what makes "requiredness compatible with facts" is the "observation that certain facts do not only happen or exist, but, issuing as vectors in parts of contexts, extend toward others with a quality of acceptance or rejection."[20]

Value arises out of certain structural relations (vectors), and these relations are constrained by the contexts in which they occur. Köhler notes that the world exhibits definite segregated contexts that "show properties belonging to them as contexts or systems" and that, "given the place of a part in the context, its dependent properties are determined by this position." Requiredness may change historically. Thus, a few hundred years ago "no minor chords were acceptable as conclusions of any music. . . ." That situation has changed, suggesting the subjectivity of such a requiredness. However, historical change does not provide "subjectivity in the phenomenological sense." Value seems objectively real, whether forced by historical change or not. A preference for major over minor chords is just as objectively real as the preference for sweet over bitter substances. For Köhler, both kinds of value are required by the structure of the valued events.

The Gestalt tradition has fostered extensive and creative contributions to the topic of artistic production and appreciation that are consistent with the general point of view presented here. In the field of music, Leonard Meyer presented, in 1956, the basic argument against dividing affect and cognition.[21] He also illustrated the role of expectations in aesthetic appreciation. For example, "The intellectual satisfaction which the listener derives from continually following and anticipating the composer's intentions—now, to see his expectations fulfilled, and now, to see himself agreeably mistaken. . . ."

These tangential discussions of the good and the beautiful do not imply that aesthetic judgments are based on the sorts of factors that define the primitive

19. Piaget (1970).
20. Köhler (1938).
21. Meyer (1956).

kind of value I address here. I enter the comparison only because the good and the beautiful both arise out of a structural description that emphasizes the relations within a structure. The complexities of the beautiful do, however, provide a useful bridge to the concept of interactive schemas that involve expectations, and conscious as well unconscious processes as the evidence from the surround interacts with the structures of the human mind. As Rudolf Arnheim noted, in generalizing from vision to other mental activities, "All perceiving is also thinking, all reasoning is also intuition, all observation is also invention."[22]

I have strayed from the focus of my analysis, extending my argument—for purposes of illustration—to a wide variety of evaluations, including judgments of beauty and function. I intend to concentrate next on the simple kind of evaluation that I described earlier—the preference for the familiar. The basic evaluation that I shall address depends on the simplest relational characteristics; it is embodied in the unmodified use of the word *value*, and in the pervasive ability of people to make judgments of "good" or of "liking" for all manner of objects.

The primitive judgment of positive value involves a phenomenal experience of acceptability and familiarity that arises out of the congruity between the evidence and the relational structure of the activated schema. Such an experience can occur before, or in the absence of, any awareness of the constituent characteristics of the reference event.

Whenever the analysis of an event fits an existing structural description (a schema), then the stage is set for a primitive positive evaluation. When no correspondence between schema and event is achieved—that is, when some degree of incongruity is encountered—then further mental activity will determine whether a positive or negative evaluation will ensue. In other words, the simplest (and most primitive) kinds of judgments of value arise out of the structural congruity between event and schema. More complex mental activity is required in the case of incongruity, and also for any valuative judgment that involves more than mere schematic congruity. Finally, whether a conscious judgment of value occurs at all depends on a host of factors, most of them contextual and related to the intentions of the actor and the demands of the context.

Piaget's processes of assimilation and accommodation follow the occurrence of congruity and incongruity. Both of these should, of course, be considered to represent extremes of a continuum from complete congruity (and easy assimilation) to extreme incongruity (and extensive or even unsuccessful accommodation). When schematic congruity occurs, no important structural changes will take place. On the other hand, when a fit between evidence and expectation is absent (schematic incongruity), assimilative and accommodative processes will be in evidence. I will discuss later how schematic incongruity can lead either to positive or to negative valuation. Incongruity may lead to the activation of a new schema that "fits" the new information. In this case, the cognitive activity becomes positively valued. On the other hand, incongruity may make accommodation necessary. In that case, the current expectations have been disrupted. Arousal

22. Arnheim (1974).

then sets the stage for emotional experiences, but the evaluative cognitions that accompany the arousal determine the emotional quality.

It is obviously not true that positive value arises only if there is a perfect "fit" between the evidence and expectancy (the schema). "Fitting" the evidence to our schemas is at times complex cognitive work. It will be true only rarely that the relations among the expected features and the actual ones will map exactly one onto the other. However, the general schematic system is one that not only tolerates such "noise" but is actually constructed with relatively wide bands of acceptability with respect to potential evidence. Within these bands, judgments of liking will occur if there is some reasonable fit between evidence and schema, where "reasonable" may vary from one event class to another, and also from situation to situation. In fact, the congruity-incongruity distinction is arrayed on a continuum, the mental system setting various criterial values beyond which discrepancy, for example, may be seen as intolerable. The same kind of continuity exists, of course, for the Piagetian assimilation-accommodation distinction. In the next section, I shall discuss those cases in which low levels of incongruity lead to arousal as well as to positive affect; for the present, I am concerned only with those cases in which congruity seems to be operating.

One must distinguish between congruity that leads to object identification and congruity that leads to primitive value. Congruity and assimilation of an object or event represent the classic case of object-event identification. I know that an object is a table or that somebody is cooking an omelet because the events fit certain schemas (expectations) about tables and omelets. However, whether a table is a "good" table or whether the omelet is being cooked "correctly" is clearly a different kind of judgment, even though both depend on the same underlying representations of tables and omelets. The identification of the events involves processing the features and attributes as well as their relations to each other, whereas the judgment of value is dependent primarily upon a specific relation among these features, not *that* it is a table, but how well its proportions and other traits fit my expectations. It should be kept in mind, though, that identification and valuation represent extremes of a continuum of schematic processing.

For purposes of identification, a wider band of values of variables will result in congruity than is acceptable for evaluative (relational) congruity. A table may have four legs of different lengths. Such a discrepancy falls within the bounds of acceptability for purposes of identification; but for purposes of making a judgment of positive value, the discrepancy produces incongruity. This suggests that evaluative judgments involve more cognitive effort, and at least more comparison processes, than do descriptive ones. We have accumulated reasonable evidence that this is true. People take longer to make simple judgments of "liking" familiar words and paintings than they do to make a judgment whether the letter string is a word or whether they have seen the painting before.[23]

The kind of value I have discussed is devoid of passion or fire. The most primitive values of familiarity and acceptability clearly are that; they are "cold."

23. Mandler and Shebo (1983).

Heat becomes an effective component of values once we move beyond mere schematic congruity.

What happens when the world presents evidence that is inconsistent with existing schemas? What are the consequences of schema incongruity, of an interruption of expectations and predictions? The following figure shows some of the possible outcomes consequent upon schema congruity and incongruity. The first case, on the left, is one of extreme schema congruity, an instance of the "cold" positive value discussed above. All the remaining cases assume some degree of discrepancy and arousal.

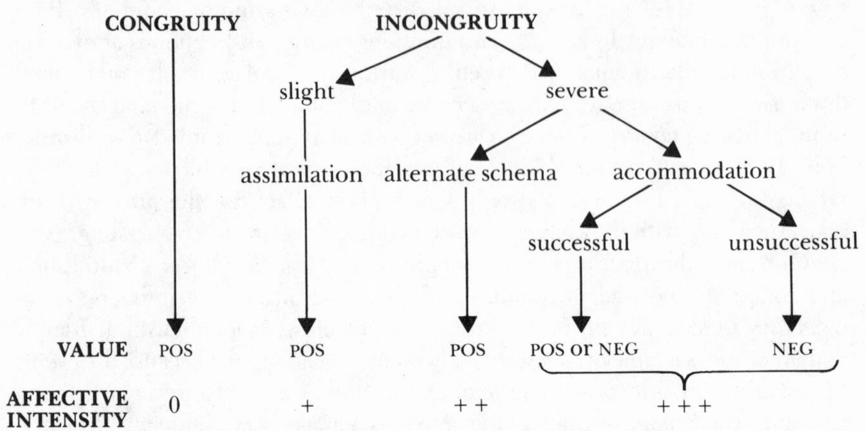

Several possible outcomes of schema congruity and incongruity in terms of both values and affective intensity. The resultant value is shown as either positive (POS) or negative (NEG). Degree of affective intensity is shown to vary from zero to + + +.

If we assume that the intensity of the emotion is a function of the degree of ANS arousal and that the latter depends to a large degree on how interrupting the eliciting event is, then emotional intensity depends on how much of a discrepancy (or incongruity) exists between what is encountered and what was expected. Assimilation results in relatively little arousal and therefore in a low degree of affective intensity. If the existing schema can incorporate the new information without any major structural changes—for example, when a new instance of a generic concept is assimilated—I would expect that there will be little disruption and, usually, a positive evaluative state. The latter will occur if for no other reason than that one of the immediate consequences of assimilation is that congruity between the world and the slightly changed schema does in fact exist. In other words, in the case of assimilation, we would expect judgments of positive value that are in fact slightly emotionally tinged. I shall return to this case in the discussion of how things become interesting; slightly incongruous events are usually interesting and positively valued. The second case in Figure 1 illustrates this concatenation. Examples that come to mind are discoveries of generalizability of previous knowledge ("That's another kind of good cake"; "I guess I can use the new variation of my old chess opening"; or "Joe doesn't look so bad without his beard").

A study[24] that sheds some light on these processes used campus stereotypes of two kinds of students (engineers and artists) and presented typical pictures of these two types with either consistent or discrepant (switched) behavioral descriptions. In general, the discrepant stimuli were liked somewhat more than the consistent ones. It is possible that the well-known physical and behavioral characteristics produced positive, humorous evaluations when they were mismatched, and presumably relatively little arousal.

If no assimilation is possible, if deep structural changes are necessary in order to accomodate the new information, then interruptions of expectation will occur, ANS arousal will be appropriately intense, and the intensity of experienced emotion will be a function of the arousal. Whether the quality of the experienced emotion will be positive or negative depends on a number of factors. Most of the time the affect will be negative, given the absence of structural congruity that could lead to a positive evaluation. More important, however, is the sense of helplessness that one may experience in the face of schematic incongruity and interruption. Other conditions of the disruptive situation may lead to other kinds of evaluative actions. If the elimination of the disruptive event is possible, the evaluative quality may well be one of hostility (and lead to aggression); if the disruption is due to the loss of a person who has played a major role in supporting one's life actions, the evaluative quality will be one of grief. On the other hand, it is possible that the meaning analysis leads to positive evaluations, for example, when one finds a long-lost friend or is given unexpected praise. The important point is that schema incongruity can lead to emotions that are positive or negative. An apposite example may be found in the positively valued concept of mastery and personal control, which indexes a situation that has been brought into conformity with the actor's expectations and intentions. In general, the quality of the emotion following incongruity will depend to a large extent on the broader evaluation of the context in which it occurs.

In the figure, I have restricted myself to relatively simple examples. The third case, from the left, illustrates a situation in which incongruity occurs, but instead of major structural changes the solution entails finding a different schema that fits the available evidence. In the simplest case, this is an occasion of delayed congruity. However, the initial discrepancy has already initiated the course of arousal, and the newly found congruity occurs within that context. The value is positive, and the arousal provides affective intensity for that positive value. At this point, it is important to note the relative time course of assimilation-accommodation and of arousal. The peripheral autonomic nervous system is relatively slow; symptoms of arousal do not occur until 1 to 2 seconds after the onset of stimulus. In contrast, the time course of schema activation and access is usually much faster, probably in the range of 300 to 1,000 msec. As a result, conditions

24. Fiske (1982).

that produce arousal (such as discrepancies) will not have autonomic consequences until some 1.5 seconds later. In the intervening time, several cognitive events can and will have occurred. As a result, incongruity will have affective consequences for some time after the cognitive discrepancy or incongruity is repaired. The conscious construction integrates the persisting arousal with the current evaluative cognition, and the resultant phenomenal affect may be intensely positive or negative, depending not on the fact of arousal but on the current state of evaluation.

The last two cases in the figure illustrate conditions in which accommodation—changes in schematic structure—is forced by the evidence in the world. If the accommodation is successful, the evaluative state may be positive or negative, depending on the relation between the newly accommodated structure and the environmental evidence. Affect will be intense. If the accommodation is unsuccessful, if the system cannot adapt to the new circumstances, then the valuative sign will most probably be negative. The unavailability of an appropriate response to the environment is likely to generate an anxiety experience.

In addition to the congruity-incongruity aspect, a number of social schemas clearly have some value built into them; they incorporate some personal or cultural predication. While our schema of houses, horses, and even persons may be less value laden, those for tornadoes, pussycats, scorpions, and chocolate cakes are clearly more so. Sometimes the source of such valuation is obvious ("Scorpions sting and may kill you"); sometimes it is not ("I feel uncomfortable in the presence of that kind of person"). In any case, these schemas act like all others; they lead to expectations that include the negative or positive value. Thus, we are as surprised by innocuous tornadoes, destructive ugly kittens, pet scorpions, and bitter chocolate cakes as by two-legged horses, houses without doors, and three-inch-high people. The incongruities produced by value-laden schemas will be just as arousing as those engendered by objects and events that are less value relevant.

Susan Fiske[25] has studied the effect of schema discrepancy and consistency on affective evaluations in cases in which the schema itself contains evaluative attributes. In these cases, personal and cultural predications have become parts of generic schemas. Fiske suggests that the affective value of a schema could be derived from piecemeal combinations of each of its individual components,[26] from the individual's past actions that lead to an inference of the target event's evaluation[27] or from the value being "classically conditioned."

In her studies, Fiske found that individuals who were consistent with her subject's preferred physical and personality characteristics produced a high degree of positive and a low degree of negative affect, whereas partial matches (physical or personality) produced positive as well as negative affect (ambivalence). A lack of consistency in both dimensions produced little positive or negative affect.[28]

25. Fiske (1982).
26. Anderson (1981a).
27. Bem (1972).
28. Fiske, Beattie, and Milberg (1981).

Value, Interest, and Familiarity

The commonsense notion of whether or not something is interesting seems to involve encounters with events that are at least slightly incongruous or discrepant. Things are usually interesting or curiosity arousing because they deviate from the usual and the expected. In other words, events that are interesting may or may not be positively valued, though, as was noted above, slight discrepancies that are easily assimilated are usually positively valued. The general topic of curiosity and arousal is one that is central to Daniel Berlyne's work.

Berlyne worked extensively on theoretical and empirical relations among arousal, effective thought, and such phenomena as novelty, surprise, complexity, and incongruity.[29] Conflict is presumed to be an essential aspect of these phenomena, and whenever it is present, it produces a hypothetical state of arousal. On the other hand, the accrual or acquisition of new information reduces the arousal.[30] With respect to evaluative judgments, "[t]here is a fair amount of work to suggest that judgments of how far stimulus objects are 'pleasing,' 'pleasant,' 'beautiful,' or 'good' reflect a common underlying . . . evaluative dimension. On the other hand, judgments of how 'interesting' objects are seem to reflect a quite different kind of evaluation. . . ."[31]

Whereas the relation among interest, familiarity, and value is most obvious with respect to structural considerations, it is also true that interest may be related to certain personal predications ("I find it more interesting to read crime stories than spy stories"). In particular, personal and cultural histories may create a greater sense of familiarity with some attributes than with others. But this again relates to the creation of schemas and their effect on phenomenal experiences of interest and familiarity.

VALUE AND FAMILIARITY

Familiarity, in the common-language sense, is obviously involved with judgments of value. In fact, the most obvious and generally accepted notion about value is that we like what we know and are familiar with, that we tend to suspect the new and the unfamiliar. The commonsense notion of familiarity seems to be very close to schematic congruity. The frequency of prior encounters with a class of events is exactly what we expect to be responsible for the construction of the relevant schema.[32] Similarly, the prior frequency of encounters is what is supposedly at the heart of familiarity.

The establishment of schemas for particular sets of objects and events is a function of the prior exposure to instances of the schematically represented event or object. The judgment of value, as derived from schematic congruity, will therefore depend on the establishment of stable schemas for the class of events

29. Berlyne (1960).
30. Berlyne (1960, 1965).
31. Berlyne (1973).
32. J. M. Mandler (1979).

that is being judged. Value, in the current primitive sense, should be related to $familiarity_1$ as discussed in Chapter 3.

A relation between a version of $familiarity_1$ and value has been demonstrated in the so-called exposure effect.[33] The exposure effect shows that, under some circumstances, increasing the sheer exposure to some events increases the probability that they will be "liked." Given that schemas probably need hundreds of exposures in order to be stably established, it is not surprising that exposure effects typically have been demonstrated not with familiar objects but rather with unfamiliar ones like Turkish words and abstract paintings that activate few existing schemas (expectations). In general, however, the effect interacts with the pre-exposure status of the judged objects. If events are rated positively before additional exposures, subsequent presentations increase their positive evaluation. If, however, they are not "liked" during the initial judgments, then increasing exposure *increases the negative evaluation.*[34] I assume that objects that are liked originally have achieved some degree of schematic congruity and that further exposures increase the schematic "fit." For objects that are initially not liked, there exists no schema congruous with the evidence presented in the test objects. In that case, the initial incongruity is only accentuated by repeated exposures to the incongruous event. Unfortunately, several of the experimental attempts to deal with this phenomenon are marred by a confusion between structural valuation and acquired predication.[35] It seems at least premature to assume that the evaluative effects of repeated exposures are directly comparable with labeling an event as negative or positive (either by providing a label or by pairing it with a culturally defined positive or negative event).

The typical recognition experiment in which individuals are asked whether a particular event is something that they have recently encountered, requires judgments of incremental familiarity, that is, $familiarity_2$. The recognition of recent occurrence, as distinct from the recognition of "knowing" the object at all, is based on an evaluation of recent renewed integration of the target event.[36] It is therefore not surprising that judgments of prior frequency of exposure (which are derived from both $familiarity_1$ and $familiarity_2$), actual prior frequency, and preference (which depends on pre-exposure familiarity as well as on subsequent exposures) are not highly correlated.[37]

If I have wandered far into the psychological landscape in this exploration, the reader should not be misled into reading more into the analysis than I have intended. The evaluative actions based on sheer familiarity are both primitive and frequently overlaid by other needs, expectations, and values of the individual. Further analyses of the many other evaluative cognitions that determine our affective lives will be needed before we can begin to understand the interactions among these mental events.

33. Zajonc (1968).
34. Brickman, Redfield, Harrison, and Crandall (1972) and Mandler and Shebo (1983).
35. Burgess and Sales (1971), Perlman and Oskamp (1971), and Zajonc, Markus, and Wilson (1974).
36. Mandler (1980a) and Mandler, Goodman, and Wilkes-Gibbs (1982).
37. Matlin (1971).

I have discussed the evaluative cognition that arises out of schematic congruity, *all other things being equal*. However, *ceteris* is very rarely *paribus*. Most of our values are complexly determined and overdetermined. We live in a flux of events that constantly changes the schemas that are being activated and used in our intercourse with the world, and that construct our phenomenal world. The value that arises out of familiarity is, in a sense, devoid of meaning; it arises entirely out of the structure of the valued event, not out of its relation to other knowledge. Most of our more complex values are dependent on the "meaning" of the valued object, on its relation to other knowledge and other valued objects and events.

The general proposition that relates increased acquaintance to positive value appears to be counterintuitive. For example, an immediate response to the notion that the old and familiar is positively valued is the thought that such events are typically dull and boring. First, we might note that the dull is not necessarily unvalued; it is certainly uninteresting, but interest and value are different dimensions. Furthermore, the search for knowledge and information instructs our mental life over and beyond the cozy ease of the familiar. For example, the continuing examination of a work of art or music may consistently violate expectations and force us to construct new and instructive views (new accommodations) of the opera, the poem, or the novel (see also Chapter 12).

Once more, I stress the multiplicity of the values that enter our daily interactions. Any schema may include structural aspects of people's and events' functions, appearances, and behaviors. Congruity implies that our expectations about such functions and behaviors have been fulfilled. Note, however, that these behaviors themselves may have cognitive value on other grounds. For example, we expect nurses to provide care, conductors to collect our tickets, aggressive colleagues to be nasty. Having adapted to—formed schemas about—these regularities, we expect their functions to be fulfilled. When they are, the world is acceptable—it is as it should be—we have obtained schema congruity and are relatively comfortable with the behavior occurring as we expected it to happen. Other schemas may, of course, be operating, like not expecting people in general to be aggressive or not having purchased a ticket for our trip. In general, however, any deviation from these schemas will produce arousal and accommodative pressures. When a nurse is uncaring or when aggressive colleagues become kind or supportive, we are faced with incongruity and arousal. What is the likely quality of the affect or emotion that will emerge? That depends on the expectation evoked by other schemas. In the case of the aggressive colleague, caring behavior frequently activates a schema that expects caring; we seek love and affection. We may therefore react positively to the new behavior, but not so in the case of the uncaring nurse whose unexpected behavior leaves us in a negative evaluative state.

How about the cases in which the familiar is apparently unpleasant? The hostile colleague may be familiar—we face him daily. However, there is no net positive value; our valuation is dominated by the negative valuation that we accord to hostility and aggression. These negative values, quite a different kind from the values based on familiarity, overwhelm the positive valuation engendered by the person's sheer familiarity. Sometimes the positive value due to familarity emerges despite some competing negative evaluation. Consider an ugly mauve couch that occupied a prominent place in one's parents' living room. Years later, the sight of that couch may well be the occasion for a positive response and subsequent nostalgic musings.

One motivation for the search for the new and for change can be found in the hierarchical character of schematic organizations. Schemas frequently serve as subgoals and subroutines for more general or abstract goals and expectations. A familiar and preferred action may cease to function as an appropriate subgoal for a more general schema and will be abandoned as other, more appropriate completions are found for the higher-order expectation. The familiar local restaurant may (perhaps because of a change of cooks) fail our expectations of having a good meal, or an old, comfortable (and liked) pair of shoes may finally be found to be beyond repair. Under those circumstances, we do act in accordance with "higher" goals and give up the liked object.

Conversely, why don't we tire of our friends? Given that negative information about people is typically granted more weight than is positive information, our continued and increased liking of our friends seems paradoxical.[38] It has been suggested that our continued affection is *in part* due to the fact that liking and disliking are not arrayed on a single dimension.

Finally, it is not true that every expectation is the result of a familiar, highly organized schema, though such schemas are clearly the basis of expectations. We frequently construct expectations and predictions of the world, but the congruity between those expectations and the subsequent evidence is not necessarily valued on structural grounds (and the positive value that accrues to congrous—successful—predictions is a somewhat different cognitive evaluation). I may expect that it will rain tomorrow, or that a friend will call, or that my favorite soccer team will lose, but these events are not expected on the basis of well-organized schemas that will produce structural value based on familiarity. On the other hand, the concept of interruption—being independent of the notion of structural value—does apply to these cases, and failures of expectations and predictions do and will frequently occasion arousal and subsequent affect.

Value—Cultural and Individual

The cultural, social, and historical aspects of knowledge are carried to a large extent by valuative judgments. The ethnocentric view of other societies and cultures has one of its origins in the reality that green trees, edible meat, warm dwellings and sexual congress are the "same" for all people, for all members of the species. Since some of the gross descriptive characteristics of the world seem to be shared by all people, the enthocentric inference assumes that all character-

38. Rodin (1978).

istics—including all or most evaluative ones—are so shared. In that view, cultural-social variation involves a "choice" of how to deal with the facts of the world, but there are no fundamental differences in the way the world *can* be perceived. Yes, trees are green, meat is nourishing, a temperature of eighteen degrees centigrade is better to live in than zero degrees, and some commonality in sexual activity is necessary for procreation. The way green trees are perceived, meat is ingested, warm houses are experienced, and sexual acts are performed depends to a large extent on the structure of the invariants "given" by the environment. But how we structure the tree, the meat, the house, and the sexual act depends on the schema that we acquire for dealing with these "given" concatenations. The distinction made here involves the extremes of the continuum, going from primarily descriptive to mainly evaluative functions of schemas; both aspects are driven by the structure of the world and by that of the prepared mind. The cultural-social difference that seems ineluctable and often incommunicable is the internal one—the evaluative outcome of the way common elements are structured in specific ways by individuals in different societies and groups. The "input" seems to be the same, but the action and thought (and, most important, the accompanying experience) depends on the way that input is structured (represented) by the experiencing individual. The kinds of relations available for such structuring depend on the cultural-social experience of the person, on the "values" that can be and are imposed on the common experience. Thus, within the same culture, but as a result of different social experiences, the evaluative structure of a green tree, a steak, a comfortable house, and a sex object-subject may differ considerably. And that difference holds beyond ties of common language and common "culture." Much of evaluation is a social phenomenon. Values are therefore not "relative" but rather the specific outcome of the social milieu that structures our experience and produces values. The idiosyncratic variations within generic schemas that determine which particular events will be congruous and which not extends from individuals to social conditions and cultures. Together with the mechanisms of cultural predication, they define value.

The schemas that determine whether an event is positively valued or not are a function of individual histories. These histories, in turn, are determined by the social mileu that structures our world and by the expectations that we learn to impose on it. The development of these schemas can be studied in a variety of psychological and social contexts; it can even be seen in the schematic representation of the memory abilities of young infants.[39]

Models of Affective Structure

Evaluative cognitions define the quality of an emotional state. I emphasize again that I do not—as some commentators have suggested—advocate a labeling theory. A particular cognition-evaluation does not provide the label for the accompanying arousal; rather, the conjunction of arousal and a particular cog-

39. See Werner and Perlmutter (1979).

nitive state produces a particular subjective state. The subjective, conscious states do, however, display family resemblances. The common language labels various sets or groups of emotional states by the emotion names that are available in that particular language, such as fear, joy, anxiety, lust, and relief. These common-language labels, and the groups of experiences that underlie or evoke them, are not haphazard groupings. For the so-called dominant or fundamental emotions, the defining cognitive states may arise from the individual's actions that define his or her evaluation of the situation. Thus, anger may involve overt or incipient action to remove the source of the initial arousal-discrepancy, and anxiety involves the futile search for appropriate thought or action; on the other hand, relief and love seem to involve primarily perceptual cognitive evaluations and reevaluations. The tendency to assign emotions to specific localized brain centers is associated with the fact that such centers when stimulated produce typical action schemas that frequently occur in emotional states (e.g., hostile aggression).[40] Similar action-based categories can be found in generalized approach (liking, wanting) and withdrawal (fear, disgust) tendencies. (See also the discussion of fundamental emotions in Chapter 2.)

The extensive common-language vocabulary that labels and describes emotions has tempted contemporary psychologists to map the cognitive-evaluative structures that underlie the common-language label system. These efforts have exhibited a wide range of sophistication, from some that claim that the specific evaluative cognition *is* the emotion, to others that search for the cognitive origins of emotional qualities and map these onto actual and possible emotional labels. Given that even the common language recognizes the fuzziness of these labels (i.e., there are different kinds of anger and fear, and these themselves shade into annoyances), such mapping cannot be precise, but the structural effort can help in spelling out some of the classes of cognitive events that lend particular qualities to emotional experiences.

The attempt to describe the basis of emotional qualities in terms of cognitions, thoughts, and actions has been made by a variety of investigators, ranging from linguists[41] to behaviorists. The current models continue the effort of other theories that demand an initial cognitive evaluation-appraisal. However, the recent models make much greater demands regarding precision and specificity.

The behaviorist suggestions frequently assume that all emotions can be defined in terms of the consequences of positive reinforcement, negative reinforcement, and the withdrawal or termination of these. Thus, positive reinforcement is related to joy, negative reinforcement to frustration and anger, whereas the termination of negative reinforcement may define joy or the emotion of relief.[42] Alternatively, the combination of appetitive and aversive operants and respondents has been used to define, in various combinations, the emotions of fear, anxiety, joy, anger, and relief.[43]

40. Panksepp (1982).
41. Wierzbicka (1972).
42. Millenson (1967).
43. Brady (1975).

I shall describe several recent models of affective cognitive structures, primarily in order to convey the flavor of the enterprise, but also to place it in the context of my point of view.

The excursions into the cognitive structure of emotions differ significantly from biological and quasi-physiological approaches. Biological approaches, and I use the term rather broadly, start with a rational reconstruction of the possible fundamental emotions, based on either evolutionary or clinical-intuitive arguments.[44] I discussed some of these theories in Chapter 2, and I will here note only that they restrict themselves to a relatively small number of emotions, and argue that other emotional states are constructed out of combinations of the fundamental states. In contrast, the cognitive structuralists start with a small set of cognitive variables, usually including goals, and then construct possible outcomes for various combinations of these cognitive states. The outcomes of these cognitive constellations are then mapped, often with some hesitation, onto the putative emotional labels of the common language. These constructions eventuate in a relatively large number of emotional or affective outcomes, ranging from a dozen or so[45] to sixteen or to as yet indeterminate larger numbers.[46]

The first model, developed by Robert Abelson,[47] has the affective experiences arise out of incompatible expectations, such that the consequences of one set of expectations interfere with those of another, a position that is another statement of the discrepancy and interruption position. Affective states are derived from a sequence in which goals lead to planned actions, which then, through some causal instrumentality, determine one or more outcomes. The addition of incompatibilities to positive or negative outcomes—incompatiblities that are the result of variations in goals, actions, and instrumentalities—illustrates different affective experiences. For example, a particular sequence of goal, action, and instrumentality leads to the expectation of a positive outcome. If, however, the actual outcome is negative, the resulting state is one of *disappointment.* Four sets of cases are presented: one set with two expected outcomes, another with an expected positive and actual negative outcome, a third set with expected negative outcomes and actual positive outcomes, and a final set with two actual outcomes in which one replaces the other. The structures result in sixteen affective states that range from guilt to joy, from luckiness to rectitude, including such states as guilt, joy, fear, and agonizing. Some of these constructions are reminiscent of the behaviorist speculations, for example, when joy is described as a positive outcome replacing one that was not positive. Such an unexpected bedfellowship is not necessarily debilitating; behaviorist and cognitive insights may in fact focus on a common reality. More restrictive is the question whether these cognitive structures exhaust possible affective states, whether they are "affective" in the common understanding of the term, and whether they in fact illuminate the construction of emotion.

44. Izard (1971), Plutchik (1970), Panksepp (1982), and Tomkins (1962).
45. Roseman (1979) and Abelson (1981).
46. Bower and Cohen (1982) and Ortony, Collins, and Clore (1982).
47. Abelson (1981).

In the first instance, the positive or negative valence of outcomes is assumed; the nature of value is not further investigated. Second, no attempt is made to introduce intensity into the scheme, and certainly not arousal. For example, is the replacement of a useless (because broken) pencil by another truly a case of joy? And what intuitive or explicit understanding of emotion or affect is appealed to when luckiness, rectitude, fear, and guilt are described as equally respectable outcomes of the formalism?

None of this argues that this kind of structural modeling is not—in itself—worthy of effort and attention. It illuminates a wide range of human goal-driven behavior. But does it go beyond that and detail the construction of emotion? All the different cognitive, and certainly the evaluative, states specified by the model are candidates for possible emotional states. Given some conditions of arousal, they may all enter into specific emotional states. Even luckiness may produce a subjective state that is highly colored by arousal. The scheme is not exhaustive, nor can any such restriction to a few cognitive variables ever be so. Does it take into account conditions that produce emotional states but that are not characterized by these specific variables? Some human action is driven by situational constraints and not by goals, and such action is just as easily subject to emotional interpretation and experience.

The attempt to describe affective structure by Andrew Ortony and his associates is much more ambitious and consequently more complex than any of the other structural models currently available.[48] It begins with a serious concern for the intensity of emotional experiences. Intensity is related to hedonic value (itself constructed out of the valence and salience of an event and its subjective importance), effort, and likelihood (expectations). Intensity is to be related, in some unspecified fashion, to arousal. I would prefer to say that such variables as salience, effort, and expectation all determine the value of any resulting discrepancy. If the likelihood of the difference between an expected and an actual event is large, if the personal salience of the event is marked, and if much effort is expended in achieving some desired future state, then the discrepancy will be large, its effect will be highly discriminable and lasting, and the resulting arousal will be very high. To the extent that these variables determine the strength of arousal, this is a much-needed effort in the direction of describing the cognitive structures that determine the degree of arousal, independently of the quality of the emotion.

On the qualitative side, the model divides the possible affective outcomes into emotion spaces, each of which is served by a subset of cognitive variables. However, all of them are to some extent marked by the occurrence of goal structures that tend toward desirable states. A *hedonic group* is characterized by the likelihood that a particular event will appear or disappear and by the valence of the state. The resulting cognitive outcome maps onto such common expressions as pleasure, disappointment, displeasure, and relief. The *state anticipation group*

48. Ortony, Collins, and Clore (1982).

deals with the interaction of realized states whose valence can be negative, positive, or neutral, and anticipated states that range over positive, unanticipated, or negative values. For example, positive anticipation and negative realized states produce disappointment; negative anticipation and positive realization generate relief. An *interpersonal action consequence group* might involve agents, patients, and experiencing persons. Agent-focused emotions assess the agent's responsibility; patient-focused emotions assess consequences for some target person, and the experiencer is the person who actually experiences the emotion. The structure of the affective states in this group requires knowledge of what the patient's state is (positive or negative), whether the agent and the experiencer are the same person, and whether the focus is on the agent or the patient. In addition, it takes into account the valence of the experiencer's attitude toward the patient. For example, outcomes may be mapped onto magnanimity when the valence of the patient's state is positive, the attitude of the experiencer toward the patient is negative, and the agent is the experiencer; blame or anger occurs when the valence of the patient's state is negative, and the agent and the experiencer are different persons. Alternatively, the interpersonal group may be restructured in terms of public or private standards. Finally, there is the *loss group*, in which the value of the lost object is physical or sentimental, and the type of loss is irrevocable or due to misplacement or to loss of opportunity. For example, grief involves the irrevocable loss of a sentimentally valued animate object.

A preliminary version of this model generates thirty-four distinct affective states. It is not all clear whether a serious effort like this will, or should, stop with that number of specifications. Just as with other cognate models, the arguments for each of the separate structural descriptions are sound and intuitively and theoretically plausible. They not only point up the potential richness of evaluative cognitions but also respond to the argument that practically any situation that eventuates in some evaluative states can become an emotional state. Such a model also poses an interesting puzzle for advocates of a system based on relatively few fundamental emotions. The "fundamental" emotions are found scattered throughout the various spaces, and nothing in this particular structure affords privileged positions for fear or distress or anger.

Another cognitive model does not spell out in detail the bridge between specific cognitive events and unique emotional states.[49] According to to this model, an event results in a cognitive interpretation to which an emotional-interpretation rule is applied, which in turn "specifies an alteration of one or more emotions." Emotions result when specific goal events in the emotional-interpretation sequence are instantiated. It is not clear whether there exists a pool of available emotions that are called for by different emotional-interpretation rules. However, it does *not* seem to be true that the particular instantiation of a goal event or some other cognitive event itself constructs the quality of the emotional experience. Emotional states are taken for granted, and their occurrence,

49. Bower and Cohen (1982).

mixture, and intensity are determined by the cognitive-interpretive sequence. At its current stage, this model does not yet specify what the set of emotional-interpretation rules might be, or how extensive or specific such rules need to be.

Joseph De Rivera's[50] structural model of the emotions is primarily concerned with interpersonal emotions. A matrix defines twenty-four distinct emotions specified by four features: "(1) whether the person . . . is the subject of the movement, (2) whether the movement is toward or away from the . . . person, (3) whether the movement alters the position of the person . . . , and (4) whether the movement occurs along the dimensions of belonging, recognition, or being." The model deals chiefly with actual or implicit movements and (unconscious) choices among the various features of the matrix. As another attempt at describing the multiplicity of human thoughts and actions that enter into the evaluative realm, the model draws our attention to the particular kinds of evaluations that are involved in interpersonal emotional experiences. However, consider Ellen Berscheid's arguments (see Chapter 8) that these *attitudinal* features may have little value in predicting or understanding interpersonal relations.

The skeptic might ask how one is to decide among these alternatives, how one is to choose from this rich menu of structural models, and what evidence will lead one to choose one or the other. I do not believe that such questions are appropriate at this time. The models' utility, and in fact their comprehensiveness, will be decided in the marketplace of ideas. The better a structural model describes the possible varieties of human emotional experience, the more likely it is to survive. For the time being, most of the models provide reasonable statements about the concatenations of cognitive variables that are possible; they map as well as can be expected onto the common language of emotion, and they usually provide possible empirical testing grounds. In their variety, these models also leave open the possibility that the same emotional label may be appropriate for more than one cognitive constellation. They illustrate the argument that simple models of simple emotions are likely to be inadequate to the task of representing the range of human emotions. Even an analysis of common usage suggests that the concept of love may have half a dozen or more separate evaluative meanings.[51]

Cultural Variation in Emotional Experience

Attempts to define the cognitive structures that determine different types and classes of emotions must face the diversity of possible emotional experiences that exist under different cultural conditions. We are all aware of the wide variety of common human actions that can be found in different cultures. We take for granted that members of different cultures like and dislike certain foods, use or reject modes of clothing, and adopt and modify interpersonal relations. We have even accepted the wide range of sexual practices that anthropologists have told

50. De Rivera (1977, 68).
51. Berscheid (in press [b]).

us about.[52] I have already discussed how cultural variation may predicate different kinds and degrees of evaluative thoughts and actions. However, it is generally believed that some emotions are human writ large and that they are necessarily transcultural; they are considered to be "biological." Even attempts to describe the cognitive structure of emotions have implied, though seldom stated explicitly, that these structures are necessary and invariant precursors of transcultural experiences. If, as I shall argue, they are not, then the relation between a particular constellation of cognitive events and a subsequent or concomitant emotional experience is not invariant; rather, it is the result of the acquisition of specific cognitive structures in specific cultural, social, and historical circumstances. The variety of emotion, then, is not only very large for the individual but also highly variable in different cultural conditions.

I shall illustrate my argument with two anthropological case histories. The first involves the Semai Senoi of West Malaysia.[53] Their outstanding emotional trait is their nonaggressiveness and their aversion for any kind of interpersonal violence. For example, over a period of fifteen years the authorities had received no reports of murder, attempted murder, or assault. Even when exposed to instances of violent aggression (e.g., atrocities committed by the Japanese army during World War II), they see these as part of the peculiar, incomprehensible deportment of the actors, not as an example of a general human characteristic. In fact, their general level of interpersonal emotionality is low, whether indexed by the absence of aggression, by the muting of mourning, or by the lack of any strong exhibitions of anger. Aggression is not, of course, an emotion—it describes an action—but the accompanying emotion supposedly is hostility or strong anger. These are absent in the Semai, and their culture is in part an argument against aggression as a general human condition.[54]

Lest one think of the Semai as an emotionally repressed people, it should be noted that they display continual and high levels of fear. This is not fear of aggression, which might suggest the lack of the latter, but fear primarily of storms and strangers, and of supernatural beings and animals, which, if insulted, might bring on disasters and dangers. Again note that the fear of offending animals does not prevent them from killing, eating, and hunting them. Fear is ever present, its expression is not considered to be a cowardly sign, and no one fails to admit fears. In other words, unlike some highly competitive cultures that encourage bravery and aggression and frown on fear, that of the Semai shows no aggression, little anger, and much socially acceptable fear. Clearly, the cognitive structures that give rise to these emotions are quite different from those that color our emotional lives.

The second example[55] comes from the Ifaluk, a Malayo-Polynesian group of Micronesia. One of their dominant emotions is *metagu*. *Metagu*, like all emotion words in Ifaluk, is described in terms of the situations that elicit it and not—

52. Luria and Rose (1979).
53. Dentan (1968).
54. Alland (1972).
55. Lutz (1983).

as such words are defined in our society—in terms of subjective states. People feel *metagu* when they go to the household of an unfamiliar family, when they are in the midst of a large group of people, when they are in circumstances in which they might encounter ghosts or sharks, or when they are canoeing in open water. When *metagu* is used, it often describes the reaction to the "justifiable anger," the moral outrage of another person of higher rank. Children and adults are expected to experience *metagu*, and the failure to do so with respect to justifiable anger is a derogation of the other person.

The similarity between *metagu* and our use of the term *anxiety* might seem striking, but the differences are important. *Metagu* is situationally defined, and it is used primarily to describe interpersonal situations. Clearly, the kind of cognitive structure that determines its evaluative flavor is not one that is obvious to a member of industrialized Western society.

It is interesting, too, that the Ifaluk, who are also typically nonaggressive, place the emotion of hate *(gasechaula)* very close to another emotion that indicates impatience, being sick and tired *(nguch)*[56]—again an unlikely result for Western societies.

If the arousal mechanism is the same for all members of the human race—a reasonable assumption—then cultural diversity indicates that the quality of emotional experience varies with the social experience of members of different cultures. As a result, models of affective structures will either have to remain ethnocentric or to look to a wider source of evidence than intuitive and clinical judgments. At the same time, some clusters of situations and actions are constrained by the nature of human existence in different cultures. Fears and joys and angers will be found in all cultures, just as nonverbal, facial messages will, but the exact nature of these emotions will be determined by the social and historical conditions of the culture and society. On the other hand, some emotions will be restricted to specific social conditions; romantic love is one example, as its history within our own culture clearly shows. Emotional commonalities and idiosyncrasies cannot be rationally posited; their postulation requires empirical and, particularly, social analyses. The study of the social development of emotions and the specification of the social conditions that favor some and discourage other affective cognitions have yet to be undertaken.

Whatever the social conditions that produce the appropriate context for a particular emotion, that emotion must still be constructed within an individual consciousness. I now turn to a discussion of the construction of emotions in consciousness.

Value and Consciousness

Consciousness involves an attempt to make phenomenal sense out of as much available data as possible. What is constructed in consciousness is a structural

56. Lutz (1982).

representation that is in keeping with the available data as well as with the task and the intentions of the moment. In fact, one cannot make a distinction between available data and the demands of the task. Instructions, sets, and other "top-down" processes, which put into motion the requirement that different kinds of structures be available, interact with other evidence available to the mental system. In the construction of the unitary experience of emotion, the major processes that contribute to that conscious structure are peripheral autonomic arousal and evaluative cognitions.

If the underlying representations that give rise to the unitary emotional consciousness are assumed to be separate for value and for arousal and if they are unified only in the process of conscious construction, evaluative structures may occur independently in judgments of value. Not only are activated evaluative structures available for conscious construction in the absence of arousal—that is, when emotional construction is unlikely—but given the appropriate set (including task, instructions, and intentions), it is usually possible to construct an evaluative judgment, separate from any emotional experience that may exist. Just as it is possible, in a state of arousal, to attend to the arousal aspect of the current emotion and, as a result, to describe one's bodily experience, so is it possible to attend to and describe one's evaluative state. Emotions like anger and ecstasy often give rise to metaphoric descriptions of the evaluative states, such as "I could strangle him" or "Being with you gives me a vision of heaven." And surely, in the absence of arousal, we are often, if not always, able to make evaluative judgments about the world around us and about our own states.

Whether the evaluative structure of an event will be used in a conscious construction or whether some more mundane representation will contribute to our current experience depends, of course, on the current demands of the situation and the self. Similarly, the "level" of representation that will be used is subject to continuous "instructions" from the world around us. To appreciate the structure of a painting, or its general beauty, or the fact that the main character "looks like Aunt Minnie" is to make a distinct use of the schemas and structures activated by the object being inspected. Just as looking across a meadow may occasion such divergent constructions as "What a beautiful landscape," "I feel at peace in this environment," "What lovely pastel colors on the flowers next to the cow," "Oh, that's heather," and "Oh, oh, that's a bull, not a cow," so it is possible to construct a variety of different experiences, descriptive and evaluative, from most objects and events. In an art museum, the more likely ones will be evaluative; in the mail room of a large institution, descriptive judgments will predominate. And, under proper conditions, we may not have access to simpler descriptive schemas but can make use of more complex evaluative structures that have also been activated, just as we may know the category of an object without knowing what it is (see Chapter 3).

Demonstrations of the apparent immediacy of affective (evaluative) judgments seem to be both persuasive and pervasive.[57] I have already argued that,

57. Zajonc (1980).

whatever the experiential appearance, some prior analytic (unconscious) endeavor will be necessary, some cognitive activity must take place as the relevant schemas are activated. The pervasiveness of affective judgments about the world around us reflects the fact that in many situations we preferentially construct evaluative experiences. We live in a world of value, in which judgments about the noxiousness, tameness, likability, horror, and beauty of the world are both important and demanded by the conditions in which we usually live. However, such demands do not tell us anything about the primacy of affect or its independence of cognitive analyses.

Finally, we need to consider the possibility that "pure" evaluative structures exist or can emerge. Are there independent schemas of goodness, evil, or beauty? Phenomenally and anecdotally, there appears to be little evidence for such a possibility. We do not seem to be able to instantiate pure beauty or describe abstract evil; we typically instantiate in terms of a specific example or define by means of illustrations. Abstract descriptions can be written, but they do not seem to be satisfactory in actual use. And yet, there is no reason why higher-order schemas that themselves abstract common features or characteristics (including relational aspects) of beautiful and evil objects should not develop, in the way other abstractions can occur as the result of regular concatenations of subsets and subsections of the schemas of physical objects. The rare cases in which people do claim that they can "think about" beauty, evil, anxiety, joy, or depression in the abstract, without any specific instantiation, may be illustrations of such schemas. Anecdotal evidence suggests that such claims are made primarily by individuals who have had extensive experience in establishing values of beauty (art experts), or evil (judges), or depression (depressive patients). It is, of course, in these cases that we would expect the high frequency of attribute concatenations that would produce new schemas at that level of abstraction.

Conclusion

Values arise from a variety of sources, and the same values may be motivated by different sources. More complexly still, different sources probably cooperate in the construction of particular evaluative cognitions. In some societies and under some conditions, personal predication and structural aspects may jointly or additively determine what is beautiful, or cultural predication and innate tendencies may together define an event as good or bad. In all cases, however, some analysis precedes the evaluative state; the information available in the environment or in the mind must be processed before a particular predication is achieved or some structural configuration is available for conscious, phenomenal experience. The problem of analysis is one even the fundamental-emotion theorists cannot escape. To determine which fundamental emotion(s) will be evoked by a particular situation, we must perceive the situation; we must go beyond the information given in the purely sensory (physical) flux. In short, the kind of analysis discussed in this chapter must eventually be a part of all theories of emotion.

This kind of analysis is, of course, only the beginning of an understanding of the representation of value. It is particularly deficient in its attention to contextual effects. These have been given only a cursory treatment and will need extensive development in the future. Just as the word or the sentence fails adequately to convey the full meaning of a written expression,[58] so the evaluative analysis of an isolated event or object fails to do justice to the complex evaluative cognitions that may arise. Value is shaped by the transactions between the individual and the world; it must therefore be understood in terms of the primarily social context in which it is formed and used.

One final emphasis. The quality of an emotional experience is determined by the mechanisms and processes that construct the relevant value; these mental contents *are* the evaluative quality. They do not need to be referred to some labeled, stored, and genetically organized emotional system (whether neural or mental).

58. Sanford and Garrod (1981).

10

ANXIETY AND EMOTION

THE REASONS FOR A SPECIAL CHAPTER ON ANXIETY are diverse and partly idiosyncratic. No other single topic within the domain of emotion has been the focus of as much attention and dispute during the past century. Poets have decried and celebrated anxiety's pervasive effects on the human condition. Theorists have made anxiety the central concept of their attempts at understanding the human mind, or they have felt unfulfilled if their theory has not adequately handled "the problem of anxiety." Philosophers have argued about the meaning of anxiety. Experimentalists have attacked and defended dozens of attempts to measure, produce, and avoid it. A book about emotion should at least illustrate some of the theoretical sallies in the direction of anxiety.

I myself have been preoccupied with the problem of anxiety for a third of a century. I shall start with a review of three major positions on anxiety and some comments about the problem of measurement. That is followed by a critique of received opinion about the sources of anxiety, coupled with a new look at its possible elicitors and inhibitors, which William Kessen and I developed some years ago in a break with traditional concepts. In the final sections of this chapter, I bring these developments forward and place them in the context of the present volume.

There is no single problem of anxiety. Different theorists and different experimental investigators have tackled various aspects of a broad complex of phenomena, all of them summarized under the conceptual category of anxiety. Anxiety has variously been considered as a phenomenal state of the human organism, as a physiological syndrome, and as a theoretical construct invoked to account for defensive behavior, the avoidance of noxious events, and neurotic symptoms.

The role of anxiety in the study of personality has been peculiarly a child of the past century. The eighteenth- and nineteenth-century precursors of modern psychology were above all concerned with the rational aspects of human personality development, and it was not until the work of Alexander Bain[1] that motivational concepts became important in speculations about complex human

1. Bain ([1859] 1899).

behavior. Thus, with the exception of such forerunners of modern existential philosophy and psychology as Søren Kierkegaard,[2] few thinkers paid much attention to the problem of anxiety.

However, negative, aversive, and unpleasant emotions have preoccupied many modern thinkers. Anxiety was not only considered the negative emotion par excellence, but, even apart from its prototypical status as a negative emotion, it became generally the central emotional concept of many theoretical treatments in psychology. Anxiety *was* emotion.

The following schema briefly recapitulates the various theoretical and empirical topics that have collectively come to be known as the problem of anxiety.

Three general rubrics describe various emphases within the problem of anxiety: causal, organismic-hypothetical, and behavioral and experiential conditions. Although this triad can be conceptually delimited, there are, as will be obvious, borderline problems that defy any such simple categorization.

In the first instance, there has been a continuing interest in the conditions that give rise to the anxiety phenomenon. Practically all workers in the field have, at one time or another, been concerned with the stimulus that elicits anxiety. What is it in the environment that gives rise to the experience of anxiety or to the behavior that is symptomatic of anxiety? With the notable exception of the existentialists and some psychoanalytic writers, those who have considered these conditions have usually viewed anxiety as an acquired emotion, rarely found until the organism has gone through some learning experiences. As an acquired emotion, it is often distinguished from the fear aroused by a threatening or noxious event, and it is usually reserved for those learned conditions that signal or cue the impending occurrence of some threat to the integrity of the organism.

The second set of conditions that is subsumed under the problem of anxiety is the hypothesized or observable state of the organism. A theoretical purist can easily postulate the anxiety state as a theoretical device with explanatory functions only, but most notions about the phenomenon have assumed some physiological or specifically autonomic arousal state. Those who have taken a position in this matter have usually assumed that the experience of anxiety is accompanied by some measurable level of SNS discharge. Although there has been some speculation about whether this discharge shows a specific pattern for the emotion of anxiety, it has generally been assumed that while the discharge may be specific to the individual, it is likely not to be specific to the emotion. Unfortunately, the autonomic processes involved have frequently been ignored, and, though some state of the organism has been postulated, its empirical referents have not necessarily been investigated. This position is particularly true of the concept of anxiety used by learning theorists in the United States. Even they, however, have at times spoken about the internal cues associated with the anxiety state.

The experiential or behavioral aspects of anxiety have been given the widest variety of definition and emphasis. The subjective experience of anxiety is acces-

2. Kierkegaard ([1844] 1957).

sible primarily through the report of the experiencing individual, and one major group of anxiety theorists, the existentialists, has concerned itself primarily with the experiential correlates.

In addition to what anxious human beings say about themselves, the problem of anxiety deals with the effect of the various antecedent and physiological states on practically all aspects of their behavior. Apart from the effect of anxiety on neurotic or other pathological behavior, anxiety has been studied as it affects early learning, child rearing, adult acquisition of normal aversions and apprehensions, motor behavior, complex problem solving, and so forth. Anxiety has also been defined in terms of expressive behavior, general level of activity, and a whole class of diagnostic behavioral and physiological symptoms.

These three general classes of variables provide an overview of the extent of the problem of anxiety, but they are hardly mutually exclusive. Quite understandably, different writers on the problem have stressed the importance of different aspects of this triad. When learning theorists deal with anxiety, they are dealing primarily with antecedent-consequent relations; when existentialists speak of anxiety, they are concerned primarily with the experience of anxiety and only remotely with the antecedent conditions of learning.

With these general considerations in mind, I move to a brief exposition of three major theoretical positions.

Theoretical Positions

PSYCHOANALYTIC THEORY

Whereas much has been written about the development of and changes in the psychoanalytic concept of anxiety, the major position, even after several decades, remains Freud's own set of statements. Nothing better attests to the complexity of the problem of anxiety than Freud's struggle to build an adequate theory of anxiety. In no other area did he change his point of view as dramatically as he did in that of the origins and mechanisms of anxiety. In fact, he presented two theories.

Freud's early theory of anxiety,[3] generally stated in 1917, was relatively straightforward and part of the energy system of psychoanalytic theory. Anxiety was defined as transformed libido. The transformation occurs as a result of repression, which distorts, displaces, or generally dams up the libido associated with instinctual impulses. This transformation-of-libido or "damming-up" theory of anxiety suggests that whenever the organism is prevented from carrying out an instinctually motivated act, whether by repression or by some prevention of gratification, anxiety will ensue. Such anxiety may then serve as a motive for a symptom that in turn functions to terminate or prevent the subsequent occurrence of anxiety. This theory was amended in 1926 when Freud published *Inhi-*

3. Freud ([1916–17] 1975).

bitions, Symptoms, and Anxiety. The new position was restated in the *New Introductory Lectures on Psychoanalysis*, in 1933, and remained his final statement on anxiety.

The second theory reversed the relation between repression and anxiety. Although Freud tended to maintain the possibility of both kinds of relations, the second theory added the possibility that repression occurs *because* of the experience of anxiety. To Freud, this was the more important possibility. In this context, anxiety becomes a signal from the ego. Whenever real or potential danger is detected by the ego, this perception gives rise to anxiety and mobilizes the defensive apparatus, including, of course, repression. Thus, because of the impending danger from unacceptable or dangerous impulses, the unpleasantness of anxiety produces repression, which leads the organism out of danger.

Central in both of Freud's theories of anxiety is the notion of the avoidance of overstimulation. Whether libido is dammed up by the failure to execute some instinctual act or whether the ego signals impending stimulation that cannot be adequately handled, anxiety always anticipates an impending situation for which no adequate coping mechanism is available. The ultimate unpleasantness is overstimulation, including pain, and in both theories anxiety signals or anticipates this prototypical state. Thus, Freud derives anxiety from the prototype of overstimulation. Such a derivation is necessary at least for the second theory, which presupposes cognitive, perceptual actions on the part of the ego. Here anxiety is learned; it is acquired as a function of past experience. It is in this sense that the psychoanalytic theory of anxiety, including its several revisions, has never abandoned the first theory, which describes the development of "automatic" anxiety. In the second theory, anxiety is derived from "automatic" anxiety; in the first, all anxiety is "automatic."

The origin of "automatic" anxiety is traced by Freud to the very earliest period of life: the birth trauma and the immediate period thereafter. His emphasis on the helpless infant and on the birth trauma as the origin of the anxiety state sets him apart from Rank,[4] who sees the birth trauma as the sole source of anxiety.

For Freud,[5] the experience of anxiety has three aspects: (1) a specific feeling of unpleasantness, (2) efferent or discharge phenomena, and (3) the organism's perception of these discharge phenomena. In other words, the perception of autonomic arousal is associated with a specific feeling of unpleasantness. As to the primitive occasions for this anxiety experience, Freud is frequently hazy. Although he sometimes considers the predisposition toward anxiety a genetic mechanism, at other times he considers anxiety as arising from separation from the mother, castration fears, and other early experiences. He regards the specific unpleasant experience of the anxiety state as derived from the first experience of overstimulation at the time of birth. The birth experience "involves just such a concatenation of painful feelings, of discharges and excitation, and of bodily

4. Rank ([1924] 1952).
5. Freud ([1926] 1975).

sensations, as to have become a prototype for all occasions on which life is endangered, ever after to be reproduced again in us as the dread or 'anxiety' condition."[6]

Some of the discussions that have arisen out of several interpretations of Freud's theory of anxiety have confused the specific experience of anxiety derived from the physiological makeup of the organism and the birth trauma. The conditions that produce or threaten unmanageable discharge are, in addition to the birth trauma, separation or loss of the mother, with the attendant threat of overstimulation caused by uncontrollable impulses and threats, and castration fears with similar consequences. The organism inherits or learns the affect at birth; other specific conditions that elicit it are added later on in early life. On this basis, it is reasonable to claim "that all anxiety has as its core what Freud has called 'free floating anxiety.' "[7]

In this context, the various types of fears or anxieties that Freud discusses are not different in their initial source but, instead, differ in the specific conditions that give rise to them. They are fear, in which anxiety is directly related to a specific object; objective anxiety (*Realangst*), which is the reaction to an external danger and which is considered to be not only a useful but also a necessary function; and neurotic anxiety, in which the anxiety is out of proportion to the real danger and frequently is related to unacceptable instinctual impulses and unconscious conflicts.

Freud's notion that anxiety is brought about when the ego receives those external or internal cues that signal helplessness or inability to cope with environmental or intrapsychic threats is mirrored in the statement that basic anxiety is "the feeling a child has of being isolated and helpless in a potentially hostile world."[8]

The psychoanalytic position not only treats anxiety as essential for the adequate handling of a realistically threatening environment; it also relates anxiety to the development of neurotic behavior. Whereas Freud sees the basic anxiety mechanisms in early separation and castration fears, the "cultural" psychoanalysts stress the social environment at large. All of them, however, related anxiety to the inability to cope with a situation that threatens to overwhelm, and to the absence of adequate acts to deal with environmental or intrapsychic events. As Freud later formulated it, "anxiety . . . seems to be a reaction to the perception of the absence of the object (e.g., goal)."[9] With the object absent, no action is possible and helplessness (i.e. anxiety) ensues.

LEARNING THEORY

The theoretical position taken by most representatives of modern learning or behavior theory is generally derived from the work of I. P. Pavlov and J. B.

6. Freud ([1916–17] 1975).
7. Kubie (1941).
8. Horney (1945).
9. Freud (1926).

Watson. The role of anxiety for learning theory is to explain the nature and consequences of punishment.[10] In the case of punishment, the application of a painful or noxious event following the performance of a response inhibits or interferes with the performance of that response on subsequent occasions. Similarly, when an organism avoids a situation, it is, through the operation of some mediating mechanism, precluding the occurrence of a noxious or painful event. The nature of this mediating mechanism, learning theorists contend, is what is commonly called fear or anxiety.

The conditioning model states that a previously neutral event or stimulus (the conditioned stimulus, or CS), when paired with an unconditioned stimulus (US), which produces a noxious state such as pain, will elicit a conditioned response (CR) after a suitable number of pairings. This conditioned response is commonly called fear. In a typical experimental situation, an animal might be placed in a white box with a door leading to a black box. The floor of the white box is electrified, and the animal receives a shock (US), which becomes associated with the white box (CS). If the animal is then permitted to escape from the shock through the door to the black box, it will eventually run from the white box to the black box before the application of shock. Learning theorists assert that the fear (CR) conditioned to the white box (CS) motivates subsequent activity. The reduction of the fear—by escape from the CS—produces avoidance of the original noxious unconditioned stimulus. Fear—or anxiety—is viewed as a secondary or acquired drive established by classical conditioning.

Whether avoidance learning is achieved by the mediating effect of the conditioned fear or ascribed to conditioned aversive stimuli,[11] the question is still open as to the necessary characteristics of the original, unconditioned, noxious, or aversive stimulus. In one of the early statements on conditioned fear,[12] it was suggested that fear was the conditioned form of the pain response. However, we shall see shortly that pain cannot be a necessary condition for the establishment of anxiety. A more general statement about the nature of acquired drives such as fear[13] extended the class of unconditioned stimuli adequate for fear conditioning to essentially all noxious stimuli. O. Hobart Mowrer[14] came close to a psychoanalytic position when he expressed essential agreement with the position that fear is a psychological warning of impending discomfort. However, work with experimental animals usually centered on painful stimuli has failed to establish unequivocally that fear can be conditioned on the onset of other discomforting primary drives or USs.

The above evidence becomes important when we consider not only the antecedent conditions for the establishment of fear, which the learning theorists relate to the conditioning paradigm, but also the nature of the mediating response (the CR). Some studies have shown that the development of the anxiety or fear state

10. Mowrer (1960).
11. Schoenfeld (1950).
12. Mowrer (1939).
13. Miller (1951).
14. Mowrer (1960).

in animals depends on an adequately functioning autonomic nervous system.[15] It follows from this that fear or anxiety can be conditioned only if the unconditional stimulus is also one that produces sympathetic or general autonomic effects. To the extent that a learning-theory position assumes autonomic responses correlated with the fear state, it also suggests that fear necessarily derives only from those primary conditions that are autonomically arousing. In essence, the threat of discomfort, a rise in primary drives, or overstimulation in general can be prototypes for anxiety only if these conditions have autonomic components. However, this does not seem to be true for states such as hunger and thirst.

As far as the consequences of conditioned fear are concerned, there seems to be general agreement that they fall into two broad classes. In the first class, fear and anxiety operate as secondary drives and exhibit all the usual properties of drives, serving as motives for the establishment of new behavior. When fear acts as a drive, new responses are reinforced by the reduction of that drive. This response-produced drive is the major emphasis that learning theory has placed on fear or anxiety. In the second class, the conditioned fear response or the conditioned emotional response (CER) may, in a variety of situations, interfere with or suppress ongoing behavior. In this sense, it is not different from the general anxiety concept of the psychoanalysts in that behavioral anxiety or preoccupation with anxiety may be incompatible with other behavior or thoughts required from the organism in a particular situation.

EXISTENTIALIST THEORY

The emergence of existentialism from a purely philosophical school to an important influence on psychology was a phenomenon of the mid-twentieth century. What existentialist thinking has done for psychology is not so much to present it with a new theory in the tradition of well-defined deductive positions as to provide it with a wealth of ideas and challenges to conventional wisdom. Although a variety of different positions and schools can be discerned within the movement, the existential exposition on anxiety has remained essentially unchanged since Kierkegaard's pathbreaking formulation, published nearly 150 years ago.[16] Kierkegaard's central concept of human development and human maturity was freedom. Freedom is related to man's ability to become aware of the wide range of possibility in life; possibility in that sense is not statically present in his environment but is created and developed by man. Freedom implies the existence and awareness of possibility.

Anxiety is intimately tied up with the existence of possibility and potential freedom. The very consideration of possibility brings with it the experience of anxiety. Whenever we consider possibilities and potential courses of action, we are faced with anxiety. Whenever the individual attempts to carry any possibility into action, anxiety is a necessary accompaniment, and growth toward freedom

15. E.g., Wynne and Solomon (1955).
16. Kierkegaard (1844); see also Sartre ([1943] 1956).

means the ability to experience and tolerate the anxiety that necessarily comes with the consideration of possibility. In modern terms, any situation requiring choice involves the experience of anxiety; therefore, for the existentialist, the antecedents of anxiety are, in a sense, the very nature of human existence in a world in which choice exists.

Kierkegaard endows even the newborn child with an unavoidable and necessary prototypical state of anxiety. However, since the child is originally in what Kierkegaard calls a "state of innocence," a state in which it is not yet aware of its specific possibilities, anxiety, too, is one that is general but without content. Possibility exists, but it is a possibility of action in general, not of specific choices. The peculiarly human problem of development faces the child as it becomes aware of both itself and its environment. Possibility and actualization become specific, and anxiety appears at each point where the development and individuation of the child progress; at each point a new choice of possibilities must be faced, and anxiety must be confronted anew.

The consequences of this notion of anxiety are that as we develop, we are continuously confronted with the unpleasant experience of anxiety and with the problem of mature development in the face of it. It is not only unavoidable; it is, Kierkegaard maintains, actually sought out. "Anxiety is an alien power which lays hold of an individual, and yet one cannot tear oneself away, nor has the will to do so; for one fears, but what one fears one desires. Anxiety then makes the individual impotent."[17] Since anxiety is unavoidable and must be encountered if we are to grow as human beings, all attempts at avoiding the experience of anxiety either are futile or result in a constricted, uncreative, and unrealistic mode of life. Only by facing the experience of anxiety can we truly become actualized human beings and face the reality of human existence.

Kierkegaard also makes a clear distinction between fear and anxiety. Fear involves a specific object that is feared and avoided, whereas anxiety is independent of the object and, furthermore, is a necessary attribute of all choice and possibility.

The importance of Kierkegaard, and of the existentialist development in general, is in the assertion—found inter alia in some psychoanalytic writings—that anxiety is not primarily a learned experience derived from past encounters with painful environmental events, but is a naturally occurring initial state of the organism. We may actually be born with anxiety instead of learning it through experience. While existentialism has not produced any clear definitions of anxiety apart from appealing to an assumed common phenomenology, it has raised important questions both about the general problem of anxiety and, in the field of psychotherapy, about the proper treatment for the conditions that show pathological effects of anxiety. Clearly, a therapeutic attitude that considers anxiety as a normal state is radically different from one that stresses the avoidance of primary and secondary traumata.

17. Kierkegaard (1844).

The Measurement of Anxiety

Over the past several decades, a large body of research has been devoted specifically to anxiety. This rash of experimental investigations was, in the first instance, instigated by the development of the so-called anxiety scales. The most widely used and influential of these is the Manifest Anxiety Scale, developed by Janet Taylor Spence.[18] The Test Anxiety Questionnaire developed by Mandler and Sarason has also been used extensively.[19]

The Manifest Anxiety Scale was originally developed to test some of the implications of the anxiety-drive concept. It was expected that individuals who had high anxiety scores would exhibit a more elevated drive level than individuals with less anxiety, since anxiety is—within this theoretical position—considered to be a secondary, or acquired, drive. In keeping with that theory, individuals scoring high on this scale acquire conditioned responses based on aversive (but not nonaversive) unconditioned stimuli much more rapidly than individuals scoring low on the scale.

A further prediction was that individuals with high anxiety should perform better on simple tasks than on complex ones but that individuals with little anxiety should perform better on complex tasks.[20]

Whereas the Manifest Anxiety Scale concentrated on the drive aspects of anxiety, the Test Anxiety Questionnaire was concerned more specifically with interfering responses generated by the anxiety state. It addresses the experience of anxiety in test or examination situations. The hypothesis suggested that the more an individual tends to report the occurrence of anxietylike experiences on a questionnaire, the more likely it is that these will occur in any situation that involves examination or test pressures such as potential success or failure and time limits. Here, too, the predictions about the interfering nature of anxiety in complex situations have in general been borne out.

Correlational studies of the two scales have shown a low positive relation, but the Manifest Anxiety Scale seems to tap more general characteristics of the individual, whereas the Test Anxiety Questionnaire is more sensitive to situational cues.

I shall argue in the following paragraphs that anxiety (as a trait) is generally a cognitive variable. It summarizes habitual interpretations and appraisals of the world. However, the disappointingly low correlations that personality measures generate with criterion variables[21] suggest that evaluations of individual consistencies in appraisal are best directed at quite specific situations.

The first questions that need to be raised are the following: What are the effects of instructions on subjects? To what extent do subjects instruct themselves about a task? What is the interaction between what the experimenter tells sub-

18. Taylor (1953).
19. Mandler and Sarason (1952).
20. Taylor (1956).
21. Cf. Mischel (1968).

jects about a task or situation and what they tell themselves about that task? Instructions and self-instructions are a mode of selecting structures and programs, of selectively tuning the system as to what it will or will not do and what strategies it will use to process the information given. Instructions are not always, and may not even be frequently, contained in the verbal instructions to the subjects; they are communicated by the structure and form of the task.

Anxiety scales are a method of measuring the self-instructional tendencies of our subjects. They tell us about subjects' habitual tendencies in response to the instructions they find implicit in a variety of performance-oriented tasks. We have a method of looking at the interaction of what we tell subjects and what they tell themselves about a situation. In other words, self-instructions may program one approach to the task, one way of handling it, while the experimenter's instructions may suggest another way or may reinforce or counteract the self-instructional tendency.

I am assuming that high-anxious subjects tell themselves that the appropriate (not necessarily useful or adaptive) behavior in a testlike situation consists of observing their own behavior, examining their failures, ruminating about their responses and emotional reactions, and thinking about standards set by themselves or by the performance of others. Low-anxious subjects, on the other hand, give themselves few such instructions—they do not even think about them as possibilities—and may, instead, orient their behavior and cognitions toward the specific requirements of the task, excluding extraneous ideations, analyzing appropriate task-oriented behavior, and so forth.

Given the fact that high-anxiety subjects have self-instructions that are self-deprecating, interfering, and failure inducing, under what conditions are those instructions operative? High-test-anxious subjects give themselves instructions about the test situations that say: This is a task in which I will do badly, this is a task in which I will have difficulties, this is a task in which I am going to be upset. As soon as the subjects then find themselves in a test situation, these instructions are let loose and interfere with performance under certain conditions. But, under what conditions can we persuade a subject to turn off these self-instructions?

Reassurance counteracts the self-deprecating, interfering self-instructions of the high-anxiety subjects. It provides instructions at variance with the self-instructions. Reassurance has the opposite effect for the low-anxiety subjects. Low-anxiety subjects do not generate and do not think about making self-deprecating, interfering responses in the test situation. However, reassurance instructions suggest to them that it might be possible to think that way. It is difficult to tell people *not* to think about something. The effect is usually the opposite of the one desired; the instructions suggest specific cognitions. I believe this is also what happens with the low-anxiety subjects. They are told: This is the place where you might consider worrying. High-anxiety subjects do not need to be told that; they are already worrying, and they may in fact be reassured.

In other words, the instructions tell high-anxiety subjects something they already know—that they will do poorly in complex tasks. At the same time, these instructions tell low-anxiety subjects something they do *not* know—that they, too, are likely to do poorly.

We might regard test-anxiety scales not as "measures of anxiety in testing situations" but as test-relevant self-instruction scales that measure individual differences in the manner in which people instruct themselves about their appraisal of and response to testing situations.

Such a perspective on paper-and-pencil "anxiety" tests in terms of task-relevant perceptions and actions generates no fundamentally new insights. Self-oriented, task-irrelevant reactions to "anxiety" are deleterious to performance (see also the discussion in Chapter 11),[22] but "arousal appears to bear no *consistent* relationship to performance" (my italics), while self-referential "worry" is attention demanding and detracts from available attention processes.[22] An attentional emphasis focuses on how people use their available time, on what they are thinking about, and the "degree of arousal is irrelevant unless the subject is attending to his arousal." In sum, anxiety scales and, specifically, test-anxiety scales, are indicators of the way people handle their interpretation of arousal, its initiators, and their current situation.

Anxiety, Pain, and Inhibition

We have seen that theories of anxiety have been developed from evidence as diverse as the avoidance behavior of animals and the symptomatic behavior of human neurotics; the language of these theories ranges from that of existentialism to that of learning theory. For all the differences in detail, however, some similarity is evident in the approaches of different theorists to the problem of anxiety.[23]

We shall examine the proposition that these theoretical communalities do not fully encompass available data about human and animal distress, and we shall then go on to present several theoretical propositions that supplement current theories of anxiety.

Briefly, the following shared characteristics of contemporary theories of anxiety can be noted. First, an archetypical event or class of events exists that evokes anxiety primitively, innately, or congenitally. For Freud, this original inciter is overstimulation; for Mowrer, it is pain; for Miller, the "innate fear reaction"; for Rank, the birth trauma; for Selye, stress; for the existentialists, the very fact of being human and alive.[24] The second commonality in theories about anxiety is the postulation that, somehow, the response to the archetypical event is transferred to previously innocuous events—events either in the external environment or in the action of the organism. The typical assumption is that this association takes place with the contiguous occurrence of trauma and neutral events, although the students of human learning have been more detailed than this in discussing

22. Wine (1971).
23. The section on anxiety, pain, and inhibition is adapted in part from Kessen and Mandler (1961).

the conditioning of fear.[24] Finally, it is assumed that the events terminating or reducing anxiety are closely related to the events that evoke it. Thus, the primitive danger of overstimulation is controlled by a reduction in the level of stimulation; similarly, the "fear" of electric shock is reduced by moving away from events associated with shock, presumably in inverse analogue to the model of hunger and thirst, in which a deficit of some substance (deprivation) is repaired by its replacement (eating or drinking).

These common elements of present-day conceptions of anxiety—the archetypical evoker, the mechanism for association to previously neutral events, and the parallel state of the elicitation and the reduction of anxiety—have produced discernible biases in contemporary psychology. In theory, in research, and apparently in therapy, the problem of anxiety has come to be, on the one hand, largely a problem of trauma (i.e., what events set off the anxiety) and, on the other, largely a problem of flight (i.e., what responses will lead away from the inciting event). In what follows, we shall discuss the place of the "trauma" or "archetype" notion by examining in detail the best candidate for the role of primary primitive evoker of anxiety—pain—and then go on to consider a position that is alternative to, but not necessarily incompatible with, the common elements of anxiety theory sketched out here.

We shall defend the position—coming to be widely held in American psychology—that a theory of anxiety based solely on pain as an archetypical precondition is untenable. The evidence at hand suggests two conclusions: first, that pain is not a necessary condition for the development of anxiety and avoidance behavior and, second, that when pain is apparently a sufficient condition for the development of anxiety, a variety of factors are at work rather than a single, innate link.

Three areas of evidence support the conclusion that anxiety can occur even when pain does not occur. First, there are the external events other than pain that arouse—without prior experience of association with pain—behavior that bears the marks of distress or anxiety. Of particular interest to our argument in the next section are the startle and distress responses of the newborn human infant to loud noise or to loss of support.[25] Among animals, escape, avoidance, and species-appropriate signs of distress to nonpainful events have been reported in abundance by ethologists; the mobbing of chaffinches at the appearance of an owl is an example.[26] Unless a severe twist is given to the behavioral interpretation of "anxiety," these cases, among others, stand against the Original Pain principle.

More striking as a demonstration of the separability of pain and anxiety is the behavior of human beings afflicted with congenital analgesia. This apparently inherited syndrome consists typically of a complete absence of pain sensitivity, despite an otherwise normal registration of the environment. A review of some thirty cases shows the severely debilitating effects of the absence of pain mecha-

24. E.g., Dollard and Miller (1950).
25. Peiper (1956) and Watson (1919).
26. Hinde (1954).

nisms.[27] The patients were usually mutilated during childhood; undiscovered fractures and scarred tongues and limbs are among the injuries found. Although these patients fail to develop specific adaptive avoidance behavior in the face of many injuries and noxious situations, anxiety toward other (nonpainful) events always seems to develop normally. The conclusion applied to one such case can be generalized to all observed cases of congenital analgesia: "Anxiety plays a motivating role in determining certain aspects of the patient's behavior."[28] In brief, the development of anxiety and avoidance behavior is not halted by the absence of pain sensitivity, even though the avoidance of normally painful events is missing.

The foregoing two points have shown that distress will develop in the absence of pain. A third collection of evidence supports the assertion of the disjunction without conclusively demonstrating the absence of an association with pain, but the data, when seen all in a row, strongly indict an exclusive commitment to a pain-traumatic theory of anxiety. I refer here to the evidence in Chapter 8 that anxiety or discomfort may occur when highly practiced and well-organized responses are interrupted. It is at least difficult to fit these cases into a theory of anxiety that depends primitively on pain or any other archetypical trauma.

If it can be agreed that pain is not a necessary condition for the development of anxiety, another question arises. To what degree or in what fashion is pain a sufficient antecedent condition for the development of anxiety? The skeptical answer that appears to be warranted by the evidence is that the relation between pain and anxiety is rarely simple or obvious and, furthermore, that attention to the distinction between pain as a sensory event and the distress reaction that usually, but not always, accompanies pain may clarify the complexity somewhat.[29] We shall only summarize what seem to be legitimate supports for the two-or-more-factor theory of pain and then move on to a more extended treatment of the nature of distress.

There is some, although admittedly very little, evidence that the appearance of discomfort with painful stimulation requires early experience of an as yet unknown character. Puppies raised in a restricted environment showed indifference to stimulation painful to normal dogs and great difficulty in learning to avoid objects associated with pain.[30] These observations are of crucial importance to speculations about anxiety, and they warrant replication and extension. In human infants, there is a striking temporal difference between the first "defensive" response to painful stimulation (withdrawal or startle) and the second "distressful" response (crying, increased motility, and so on). The first response has a latency of 0.2 seconds while the second response has a latency as high as 5 to 7 seconds.[31]

A similar separability of what might be called cognitive pain and distress

27. Fanconi and Ferrazzini (1957).
28. West and Farber (1961).
29. See Barber (1959), Melzack and Wall (1965), and Melzack (1973).
30. Melzack and Scott (1957).
31. Peiper (1956).

occurs in some cases of prefrontal surgical interference to deal with intractable pain. "When prefrontal leucotomy alleviates intractable pain it does not necessarily elevate the pain threshold or alter 'the sensation of pain' . . . [Furthermore,] with few, if any, exceptions, investigators report that the 'sensation' or 'perception' of pain is practically unaltered by any of these procedures."[32]

Noxious painful stimulation has wide cortical effects and argues against a neurology of pain based exclusively on specific pain pathways or pain areas, a position developed in fine theoretical detail by Melzack and his associates.[33] The discomfort-pain association seems to depend on extensive cortical organization—in the words of the present argument, on the experience of pain and discomfort.

During the past decade, the discovery of endorphins has vastly influenced our view of pain mechanisms. Endorphins are endogenous substances in the central nervous system that have analgesic properties similar to those of the opiates. Pain experiences can be modulated by environmental activations of endorphins, and these mechanisms occur in parallel with modulating systems that are activated by the environment, but they are not mediated by endorphins.[34]

The death of pain as original in all anxiety does not rule out alternative formulations of the traumatic or archetypical variety.[35] One alternative, which will be explored here, is to examine a postulation of anxiety that is independent not only of pain but also of any archetypical traumatic event.

FUNDAMENTAL DISTRESS

A nontraumatic theory of the sources of anxiety can be defended, and anxiety may be reduced or terminated by devices other than escape from and avoidance of threat. These alternative formulations are proposed as supplements to, rather than as substitutes for, the archetypical theories of anxiety.

The schematic model suggested for the occurrence of anxiety—as distinct from the classical model of the organism fleeing the associations of pain—uses the cyclical distress of the human newborn. There may be antecedent events that could account for the crying and increased activity we recognize as distressful in the young infant (e.g., food privation and shifts in temperature), but it is not necessary to specify or even to assume such a specific antecedent event. It is a defensible proposition that the strong bent of the archetypical formulations to study those conditions of distress for which a specific evoker could be discerned seriously limits the range of proper investigation. The distress of the human newborn, as obviously "anxious" as a rat in a shuttle box, can be taken as an example of human anxiety and as a starting point for changes in speculations about human emotion, regardless of the absence of known or well-guessed "unconditioned" archetypical evokers. More than that, this modification sug-

32. Barber (1959).
33. E.g., Melzack (1973).
34. Watkins and Mayer (1982).
35. Solomon and Brush (1956).

gests that there are cases in which the old and respected saw about anxiety as the conditioned form of the stimulus-specific fear reaction may be misleading; that is, there may be interesting cases in which a stimulus-specific fear (as indicated by flight or avoidance) may be better understood as a conditioned form of primitive anxiety or *fundamental distress*.[36]

To see anxiety as fundamental distress is to raise the ghosts of the dispute between James and Cannon. Let us take a further theoretical step and suggest that the crucial event in fundamental distress is the perception or afferent effect of variable and intense autonomic, visceral activity. This is, of course, a rough restatement of James's position. Most of Cannon's counterarguments are not relevant here, but his major argument that emotional reactions take place with a latency far shorter than that of autonomic reactions deserves particular attention. To recapitulate some arguments from Chapter 6, the delayed emotional response of infants, as well as the variable, badly organized reactions of infants, suggests just such a delayed emotional mechanism as Cannon ascribes to James. If we assume further that these visceral reactions are eventually represented centrally as autonomic imagery, then the ascription of a developmental shift from a Jamesian to a Cannonic mechanism becomes plausible. As I noted earlier, the argument that visceral discomfort may become centrally represented does not imply that the vicsceral response will not thereafter occur; the postulation of central representation is required to explain the adult's quick and efficient reaction to threatening events. However, given the rapid removal from the situation of threat, the "postthreat" visceral response may not occur. A closely related argument is that "although the James-Lange type of theory provides a useful basis for studying the early ontogeny of mammals, . . . a Cannon-type theory of higher-center control is *indispensable* for later stages of perceptual and motivational development. If ontogeny progresses well, specialized patterns of [approach] and [withdrawal] . . . , or their combinations, perceptually controlled, often short-circuit or modify the early viscerally dominated versions."[37]

One final comment on the nature of distress is warranted. It is not assumed that the distress reaction is usually terminated suddenly by the occurrence of an escape or an avoidance response. Instead, we assume that, except in a few laboratory situations, the distress reaction is reverberatory in character. Particular events or responses do not terminate the anxiety immediately; moreover, the distress reaction will serve as a signal for further distress. Depending on partially understood environmental and organismic conditions, these reverberations will augment the initial anxiety or gradually diminish and disappear.[38]

In short, fundamental distress is held to be a state of discomfort, unease, or anxiety that bears no clear or necessary relation to a specific antecedent event (archetypical evoker). The model or "ideal case" of fundamental distress is held to be the recurrent distress of the human newborn. It remains to examine the

36. Auersperg (1958).
37. Schneirla (1959).
38. See Mednick (1958).

occasions of the reduction or termination of anxiety and the relation of such occasions to fundamental distress.

The second departure from conventional views of anxiety has to do with the techniques for the reduction or termination of anxiety. In addition to the classical mechanisms of escape and avoidance of danger, the operation of *specific inhibitors* brings anxiety under control (i.e., diminishes or removes it). Before moving on to a discussion of the inhibitory mechanism, however, we must consider a point implicit in the foregoing treatment. The undifferentiated discomfort of the infant that we have taken as an example of fundamental distress may accompany particular conditions of need or drive; that is, the newborn may be hungry *and* distressed, thirsty *and* distressed, cold *and* distressed, and so on. With the removal of the privation or drive, the distress may disappear, but this reduction by the repair of a deficit—which is formally equivalent to escape from danger—is not of primary interest in the present discussion. Instead, our concern is with those responses of the organism and events in the environment that inhibit distress—regardless of their relation to a specifiable need, drive, or privation.

Anecdotal evidence of the operation of congenital inhibitors of anxiety in infants abounds, but there has been relatively little systematic exploration of these inhibitors in the newborn human or animal. Two empirical studies illustrate the character of the inhibitory mechanisms; one is based on a response of the infant, the other on a particular pattern in the environment. Research by William Kessen and his associates has shown that infant distress, as indicated by crying and hyperactivity, is dramatically reduced by the occurrence of empty (i.e., nonnutritive) sucking as early as the fourth day of life. The performance of the congenital sucking response on a rubber nipple stuffed with cloth brings the newborn to a condition of motor and vocal quiescence. Thus, sucking appears to fit the pattern of the congenital inhibitor of distress or, more broadly, of anxiety. Also, the hungry infant, during the first days of life, with little or no experience of feeding, will quiet when given breast or bottle, even though it is unlikely that its hunger has been reduced during the first several sucking responses.

The second instance of distress inhibition derives from research with infant monkeys, which, when distressed, whether by a frightful artificial Monster Rhesus or in the routine cycle of discomfort, seek out a situation—the experimental "mother"—that inhibits the distress.[39] Beyond doubt, a complex environmental event terminates a condition of the animal that meets our usual criteria for the presence of anxiety; this event bears no obvious relation to physiological privation or deficit.

There are undoubtedly several congenital or early-developed inhibitors of distress that have not received adequate empirical examination; the quieting effects of rocking and the response of the two-month-old infant to the adult face come to mind. A strong presumptive case can be made for the operation of a class of such distress terminators that do not depend on escape from or avoidance of a

39. Harlow (1958).

specific evoker of distress for their effects. One group of inhibitors of distress appears to be characterized by rhythmic periodicity: regular sounds, rocking, the nodding of the head of the adult, and so on. Investigation of the relation of this class of events to visceral rhythms would lead to increased precision in speculations about fundamental distress. It is interesting to speculate in this connection that distress is related to inhibition as sympathetic is related to parasympathetic activation.

There is a further aspect of the problem of distress inhibition that will illustrate the relation of fundamental distress and its inhibitors to anxiety of the archetypical variety. If distress is under control by the operation of an inhibitor, what is the effect of withdrawing the inhibitor? What, in other words, are the consequences of disinhibition of distress? For the occurrences of some inhibitors (e.g., rocking the hungry and distressful infant), it seems that disinhibition "releases" or "reinstates" the distress. For others (e.g., sucking on the hands until asleep), the withdrawal of the inhibitor does not result in the recurrence of distress.

The following proposals can be made to deal with this kind of disjunction. Archetypical evokers (e.g., pain, hunger) are accompanied by or lead to distress. This distress can usually be reduced in two distinct ways: by the action of a specific inhibitor that reduces distress but does not necessarily affect the primitive evoker; or by changes acting directly on the level of the primitive evokers. The best example of mechanisms working together in nonlaboratory settings is nutritive sucking. The infant's *sucking* inhibits the fundamental distress accompanying hunger; at a slower rate, the ingestion of food "shuts off" the source of distress. These two mechanisms for the reduction of distress or anxiety are profitably kept separate in psychological theory.

The separation of distress reduction by specific inhibition and distress reduction by changes in archetypical evokers can be defended on other grounds as well. As noted earlier, much infantile (and later) distress is of a periodic variety without obvious relation to specific environmental evokers. Specific inhibitors may tide the organism over the peaks of these distress cycles, whatever their source, until some other occurrence (e.g., the onset of sleep) results in a more stable reduction of the level of organismic disturbance.

It is reasonable to assume that the inhibitory mechanism under discussion is not limited to the operation of primitive inhibitors early in development. Instead, events associated with inhibitors may, under appropriate circumstances, acquire learned or secondary inhibitory properties. Under this proposal it can be maintained that the immediate "satisfying" effects of food may be ascribable to its association with the inhibition of distress by eating, rather than the other way around.

With the foregoing reservations in view, we would argue, finally, that among the earliest differentiations the child makes are those that have to do with the handling of distress. Whether in regard to fundamental distress or in regard to distress set off by specific environmental events, much of early infant behavior can be related to the management of discomfort or unease. Furthermore, it is probably in these connections that the infant first learns about the consequences of the interruption of organized response sequences or expectations. Just as it has been assumed that secondary inhibitors of distress can be developed, so it is assumed that learned signals of disinhibition (i.e., the reinstatement of distress at the withdrawal of an inhibitor) can be developed over the course of infancy (e.g., in separation anxiety). It is tempting to speculate that tendencies in the older organism to be active[40] may be related to the repeated arousal of distress as a consequence of the withdrawal or omission of a well-entrenched inhibitor of anxiety. In other words, the interruption of well-established behavior sequences may lead to anxiety, and their continuation may ward it off.

Anxiety, then, is not only the result of a trauma that must be fled; it is also a condition of distress that can be met by the action of specific inhibitors. Whereas, for the young child, only a limited repertory of events and behaviors is available that will inhibit or control the basic state of distress, any organized activity in the older child and in an adult will do so, and any organized activity serves to ward off the state of distress. Trusted companions and our relations with them are important inhibitors of anxiety in adults as well as in children—separation anxiety can be with us throughout the life span.[41] Whenever the organism is not able to draw on some behavior, act, or companion that controls the environment (i.e., in a condition of helplessness, unable to control stimulation or environmental input in general), anxiety will ensue.

This view is consistent with the psychoanalytic tenets on overstimulation and Freud's statement that anxiety is related to the loss of the object. When overstimulation threatens or when no object (goal) is present, the organism has no behavior available to it and cannot act. As far as the existentialist position is concerned, the state of anxiety occurs whenever the individual has no way of coping with environmental demands—has, in other words, no way of confronting possibility, no way of overcoming the anxiety that goes with possibility and freedom. Finally, the noxious, painful unconditioned stimulus of learning theory typically is an event that is unmanageable, represents overstimulation, and disrupts ongoing behavior. When the organism does find a way of coping with this situation by escape, this escape behavior is the way of overcoming helplessness vis-à-vis the noxious stimulus, and it will appear on a signal (the conditioned stimulus) before the occurrence of the unconditioned stimulus.

Fundamental distress, from this position, involves a general and variable state of arousal in the absence of well-developed organized actions or plans—the state of infancy. However, unlearned organized actions do exist, such as sucking, and these can—at a very early stage—inhibit fundamental distress. The effect of sucking on arousal (and emotion) may in fact be more general, since it also reduces an infant's positive, pleasurable excitation to a condition of relaxation.[42] Thus, the very occurrence of organized behavior preempts the occurrence of arousal and distress. In the adult, organized action and thought is the norm, not

40. Exemplified in the concepts of *Funktionslust* (Bühler, 1930) and "competence motivation" (White, 1959).
41. See Bowlby (1973).
42. Bruner (1980).

the exception. I turn, therefore, to the relation between arousal and the specific conditions that generate phenomenal anxiety.

Anxiety and Interruption

In Chapter 8, I discussed the arousing consequences of the interuruption of plans or actions. What are the occasions that turn the arousal engendered by interruption into distress or anxiety? The emotion of choice is anxiety when the environment or the thought processes and, as a result, the onset or offset of visceral arousal are not under control of the organism. Thus, when no response is available whereby the interruption can be terminated, the emotion to be expected is anxiety, distress, or fear. Anxiety should appear when the organism, interrupted in the midst of well-organized action sequences or in the execution of a well-developed plan, has no alternative behavior available to it. The inability to complete a sequence and the unavailability of alternative completion sequences produce helplessness, a plan or action sequence that has been initiated but that cannot be completed; the organism does not "know" what to do. The lack of adequate sequences and the absence of purposeful behavior define the disorganized organism. Helplessness and disorganization *are* anxiety.

The major consequences of interruption and the absence of relevant or suitable strategies will be continuing visceral arousal and the disruption of any other ongoing behavior sequences. One reason for the disorganized aspect of anxiety-dominated behavior is that with interruption and arousal a search for relevant substitutable behaviors is initiated. As long as such a search—seen often as inefficient attempts at initiating a variety of different actions—is unsuccessful, and as long as the sequence is incomplete, further arousal will continue, more disorganization will result, and the typical picture of interference caused by anxiety will emerge. I have already pointed out how the discovery of some apparently satisfactory substitute acts may control the arousal. Such acts, when nonadaptive, are usually called neurotic symptoms and are frequently illustrated by obsessive-compulsive behavior.

It is appropriate here to return to the distinction between fear and anxiety in order to appreciate two related views on anxiety and helplessness. In a critique of the attempts to distinguish fear from anxiety, or real from neurotic anxiety, John Bowlby has pointed out that fears usually do have a reasonable basis, both on theoretical and on clinical grounds. He reminds us that "reality" is "never more than some schematic representation of the world that happens to be favored by a particular social group at a particular time in history."[43] Similarly, the reality of fears and anxieties are socially and historically determined. It is, of course, this truism that often leads to the discovery of emotional "problems" among the poor—based on the definition of social reality by the powerful. Bowlby points out that the reality of dangers in the world is in the eye of the beholder.

43. Bowlby (1970, 1973).

It is not in the definition by governments or established professional groups. Given that the personal environment defines the reality of dangers, Bowlby concludes that to confine the term *anxiety* to those conditions in which threat is "realistically" absent might be to define the term out of existence.

For Bowlby, what is feared includes "not only the *presence*, actual or imminent, of certain sorts of situation but *absence*, actual or imminent, of certain other sorts of situation."[44] His own work has stressed that a principal source of fear is "simply the strangeness of a situation."[45] Bowlby suggests that the term *anxiety* seems appropriate for the feeling tone that "accompanies impeded approach or threatened separation." The similarity between his formulation and the current one is obvious. I would add, however, that the term *anxiety* is probably most appropriate when the approach is impeded or the separation threatened *and* no readily apparent substitute is available; it is then that interruption issues into helplessness and anxiety.

A similar view of anxiety dependent on cognitive interpretations has been proposed by A. T. Beck. He notes that cognitive factors may outweigh "realistic external stresses." Again, the danger is real because the individual so interprets the situation. This interpretation of danger, together with an underestimation of one's coping capacity, produces "high levels of anxiety and autonomic arousal."[46] Beck adds that the cognition of arousal is also read as danger by the cognitive system and thus produces a spiraling anxiety effect. For Beck, one's evaluation of coping ability (comparable to Lazarus's position) is an important contributor to anxiety. The evaluation of being able to produce situationally relevant actions will determine the degree to which one interprets a situation as being productive of helplessness. If no coping actions are in sight, the situation is necessarily interpreted as one in which no relevant actions are, or even might be, available, and helplessness results.

Any situation that interrupts, or threatens the interruption of, organized response sequences and that does not offer alternative plans or actions to the organism will be anxiety producing.[47] There is some evidence that some plans and cognitive structures may be temporally quite flexible, that is, that the organism plans for *what* will happen relatively independently of *when* it will occur.[48] Such flexibility applies particularly to real-life sources of interruption. In this section we discuss two such instances: guilt and social factors in anxiety production.

Anxious guilt may be seen as an instance of the effects of interruption. Guilty persons feel anxious about some past action, real or imagined. Usually, of course, they cannot undo what they have done. Attempts to begin a sequence leading to the undoing of the previously committed act are invariably interrupted by the situational fact that the consequences of the act are in the past. We can atone,

44. Bowlby (1970).
45. Bowlby (1973); see also Schneirla (1959).
46. Beck (1972).
47. The following section has been adapted in part from Mandler and Watson (1966).
48. Elliott (1966).

but we cannot undo. The cognitive sequence that would lead to the undoing of some act is, in reality-oriented persons, inevitably interrupted by the knowledge that the act is in the past and cannot be undone.

We often teach children that they should be good and do no wrong. It follows that certain cognitive sequences, such as the plan to right the wrongs that we have committed, will be well organized. Furthermore, such sequences will be organized so that there are very few substitutions that can be performed if the original sequence is interrupted. The knowledge that one has committed some wrong, therefore, should activate the sequence to right the wrong, but, if the act is in the past and cannot be righted, then the cognitive sequence will be interrupted. Short of reversing time, the wrong act usually cannot be undone; there are no substitutes, and the consequences of the act are often unchangeable. Thus, the guilty person is continually instigating a sequence to undo what cannot be undone and is therefore continually interrupted in this sequence, yet has no alternative response available following interruption. This is the prototypical situation for anxiety.

The only difference between the emotions of anxiety and guilt may be the situational variables that lead us to label the two situations differently. Such an analysis would explain two of the aspects of guilt. The guilty person ruminates on guilt, which we would describe as persistent attempts to complete a sequence of undoing. But the guilty person may feel better after confession or making amends, possible substitutes for undoing. There are social variables that determine the degree to which confession or ways of making amends are available and the degree of their accepted relevancy as alternative responses. A Catholic child, for example, is likely to be taught that confession is a socially acceptable substitute for the interrupted cognitive sequence leading to undoing. Confession enables the guilty person to complete a substitute sequence.

The consequence of confession may seem paradoxical: though it enables guilty individuals to complete at least some cognitive sequences, it leads to punishment as often as to forgiveness. The paradox vanishes, however, if we view the punishment that may follow confession as the completion of a sequence instead of as a peculiar or even masochistic goal. Confession feels good, whether it leads to punishment or to forgiveness, because it leads somewhere; in particular, it enables the human to complete organized sequences that were often unsuccessfully initiated before. The assumption that people seek goals often leads us to posit situations in which the goals sought are distinctly unpleasant. By not making this assumption, but by postulating that we seek to complete organized sequences, we resolve the paradox.

The relation between guilt and social variables raises the general question of the relation between social factors and anxiety or psychopathology.[49] In considerations of the influence of social or cultural factors in psychopathology, a number of different problems have been noted. One of these is the question of how social or cultural factors influence the production of anxiety or other symptoms.

49. See, e.g., Averill (1980).

Symptom formation might occur when some objectively inappropriate response systems are used in the completion of an interrupted sequence.

Social and cultural variables can influence the anxiety of the members of the society by (a) inculcating organized sequences or plans that have a high probability of interruption, (b) interrupting organized sequences for various reasons, (c) not providing alternative responses to follow such interruption, and (d) providing only inappropriate alternative sequences.

A society inculcates organized sequences with a high probability of interruption when, for example, it teaches a high degree of "achievement motivation" to a large number of the members of the society but offers only a limited number of social positions that gratify the achievement motive. In other words, a numbrr of the members of the society develop well-organized plans leading to success, but the society does not provide a relatively equal number of social positions through which the organized sequence can be completed. Social pressures provide almost continual interruption of organized sequences to success for all but the fortunate few.

Societies or groups often interrupt the organized sequences of their members for a number of reasons. For example, it may be efficient from the group's point of view for most of its members to possess plans leading to positions of social power in that it guarantees sufficient competition that the most promising gain power. However, once any given group has arranged itself into some power structure and achieved its goals, the group may not allow its members to continue attempts at the exercise of power. Thus, the group would interrupt the organized sequences leading to power that are attempted by those who continue to strive for it.

A group or society, then, can inculcate organized sequences and, at the same time, provide for their interruption. Furthermore, the society may not provide substitute behavior to follow the interruption. There may be, for example, no socially acceptable substitute for success, even though not all members of a society have an opportunity to achieve success. In our society, ethnic minorities are exposed to many communications that would lead to the development of plans leading to the achievement of social power. At the same time, they are denied access to social poisitions through which they could complete the necessary actions and are provided with few socially acceptable substitutes.

Last, a society, group, or culture may provide substitute responses that are either inappropriate to whatever organized sequences are interrupted or that serve to interrupt other organized sequences. Becoming the town's best garbage collector is probably at best only a partial substitute for an interrupted sequence leading to social recognition. Becoming a juvenile deliquent may enable a youngster to complete certain plans, but it is likely to lead to the interruption of others. Membership in groups that have unclear goals, or unclear paths for attaining the goals, produces unpleasant emotional states among the group members.[50] Unclear communication procedures, inefficient work flow, and vague power channels

50. Raven and Rietsma (1957).

produce a type of social disorganization most likely to interrupt response sequences and to fail to offer alternate responses following the interruption.

Social or cultural variables can determine both how much control one has over potential interruption and what one can do if interruption occurs. If individuals have a good deal of control over situations, they are much less likely to be interrupted. Furthermore, "control" implies that relevant alternative responses are available. We suggest that any social system can be analyzed in terms of (1) the degree to which it inculcates or presses for the completion of sequences that are in fact often interrupted, (2) the degree of control that it allows over potential interruption, and (3) the range and availability of alternative responses that it offers.

It might be useful to engage in such an analysis of our society, its promises and failures to fulfill those promises, its egalitarian pretensions and failures to act on them, and its educational programs and their shortcomings in order to understand the degree of emotional reaction that this society can engender, particularly among those who have been taught to take its social and political plans seriously but who find them lacking when they meet the larger world. It should not be surprising that this kind of discrepancy may provide a conjunction of arousal and cultural cues toward violence that leads to anger, to aggression, and, too often, to hopelessness.

We have been speaking primarily of situational determinants of anxiety. Obviously, any dichotomy between situational and individual determinants of anxiety is a false one, but we may vary the emphasis. Here we want to pay more attention to the individual. Some theorists have spoken about the anxiety of schizophrenics, and, of the several theories of schizophrenia, one seems particularly relevant to the notions that we have advanced here. That is the idea of the double-bind communication to which some schizophrenics are supposedly subjected.[51] Briefly, the idea is that communications from important others, such as the mother, are within themselves contradictory. If we assume that the intent of certain communications is to set the recipient into action, then we can see that the communication activates some organized sequence on the part of the recipient. A double bind, however, would be one that, as soon as it has activated some organized sequence, interrupts it. Completion is not allowed, for example, when the child is told: "Love me, but don't touch me." It is not surprising that such communications develop a great deal of anxiety, since the organized sequences that they could execute are almost continually being activated and then interrupted. Any conflictful situation, of course, can be seen as one that both activates and interrupts response sequences.

Given that socially induced acts, produced by the double-bind communications, are anxiety producing, it is also not surprising that the individual will develop idiosyncratic, often socially irrelevant, acts that *can* be completed. Schizophrenic behavior then becomes an admirable substitute for the acts demanded and interrupted by the social milieu.

51. Bateson, Jackson, Haley, and Weakland (1956) and Weakland (1960).

I have mentioned the necessity of evaluating an individual's cognitive appraisal of a situation in order to determine the threatening or stressful aspects of the situation. Richard Lazarus and his colleagues[52] have shown that by altering a subject's cognitive appraisal of a situation (e.g., viewing a disturbing movie of a subincision rite from the stance of anthropological detachment or from that of a simple spectator) it is possible to alter the subject's emotional responses to produce less anxiety. Alternative responses can be executed when subjects are confronted with the anxiety-provoking movie. Subjects identify with the people in the film, and identification can be seen as a shared set of cognitions or plans. The subjects would like to escape from the potentially painful situation, but the sequence of escape is interrupted by the constraints of the psychological experiments. Various sets of sound tracks provide the subjects with alternative responses (i.e., psychological escape), and thus their anxiety level is lowered.

Work with surgical patients demonstrates that the expectation of a future threatening event—postoperative pain—lessons anxiety-producing characteristics.[53] At least at the cognitive level, it is possible for the human organism to incorporate the expectation of pain into a plan. The patients who expected pain were not rendered helpless, since any distress could be a cue for the thought "Things are going as planned." Hence there would be little interruption and arousal.

In these studies, subjects were provided with some control over interruption. Defense mechanisms can also be construed as attempts to control interruption. These are either responses that avoid interruption or alternative responses that follow interruption.

The idea of control over interruption is somewhat similar to the idea of competence.[54] Competence as a personality variable is the degree of control an individual can exercise over the environment. A sense of competence is presumably generated by the individual's felt control in executing organized response sequences. The term *competence* can be defined as the individual's ability to avoid interruption or, if interrupted, to provide alternative responses that aid in the completion of the interrupted sequence. Related is the notion of frustration tolerance, which can be defined as the ability to delay responding after interruption until an appropriate substitute response can be found. It is quite obvious that individuals vary in their ability to delay[55] and in their ability to find or learn appropriate alternative responses.

One further variable is the appraised degree of control over the environment. The locus-of-control scale[56] differentiates individuals according to the degree to which they appraise themselves or the environment to be in control of the occurrence of reinforcement. In terms appropriate to interruption theory: the degree to which persons consider themselves in control of reinforcing events should be

52. Lazarus and Alfert (1964) and Lazarus, Speisman, Mordkoff, and Davison (1962).
53. Janis (1958) and Leventhal (1982).
54. White (1959).
55. Mischel and Metzner (1962).
56. Rotter, Seeman, and Liverant (1962).

highly correlated with their appraised degree of control over interruption. Since a high degree of appraised control over interruption is presumably based on the individuals' history of successful attempts to cope with interruption, they would presumably be rendered less anxious by any present interruption, since they would have a repertory of available alternative responses and would also be more likely to search for substitute responses when confronted with interruption.

The problem of personal control involves the establishment of cognitive plans that are consistent with the realities of the world—not an easy task. As the term *personal control* suggests, it is a highly individual phenomenon; we believe that we have personal control of the world around us when we plan for what is likely to happen, whether we "control" the events or not. Planning to encounter a traffic jam on the way home may give me an illusion that I am in control of the local traffic. In fact, its nonoccurrence may be disappointing—interrupting. "The stress-inducing or stress-reducing properties of personal control depend upon the *meaning* of the control response for the individual; and what lends a response meaning is largely the context in which it is imbedded."[57] That the illusion of control can have powerful effects has been demonstrated in experiments showing that the perceived painfulness of shock varied with the perceived control over its occurrence. Equally interesting and consistent with the complexity of the problem was the finding that individuals who typically view themselves as being in control over their environs showed differentially greater anxiety about the shock over which they had no control. "Magnitude or intensity of stimulation is less important than contextual variables such as the belief that one has little control over stimulus occurrence."[58]

Anxiety, Helplessness, and Hopelessness

I can now summarize the question of the ontogeny of anxiety. The cyclical distress of the human newborn may be the basis for the original experience of anxiety. Fundamental distress is to be viewed as a state of discomfort, unease, or anxiety that bears no clear or necessary relation to a specific antecedent event. One of the mechanisms to bring such anxiety under control is the operation of specific inhibitors. These inhibitors control distress regardless of their relation to a specifiable need, drive, or privation. Among such possible inhibitors are sucking and rocking. Furthermore, although the inhibitor operates to control the distress, the withdrawal of such an inhibitor might reinstate it. Finally, not only innate inhibitors but later-acquired organized behavior may have the same function of anxiety and distress inhibition.

One particular set of cognitive and environmental conditions that turns arousal into anxiety is a general state of helplessness, or the unavailability of task- or situation-relevant plans or actions. In a state of arousal the organism that has no relevant behavior available and continues to seek situationally or cognitively

57. Averill (1973).
58. Glass, Singer, Leonard, Krantz, Cohen, and Cummings (1973).

appropriate behavior is "helpless" and may also be considered, in terms of the common language, to be in a state of anxiety. Thus, helplessness is defined not by an objective situation but by the organism and its repertory of actions.

The conditions that control distress and the conditions that produce it are not necessarily correlated—they may be independent. In that sense, I reject a view of anxiety that speaks of anxiety reduction or escape from fear or similar symmetric propositions. Variables that control the onset of a process or behavior need not be the same ones that control its offset.[59]

The interruption of plans or behavior is only *one* of the conditions that frequently lead to states of helplessness. When interruption leads to arousal and when no appropriate behavior is available, either to substitute for the original plan or to find alternative ways to the original goal, then we have one typical state of anxiety. Interruption is sufficient for arousal and emotion to occur. Furthermore, it will lead to helplessness if and only if no adequate continuation behavior or substitute is available. Interruption is particularly relevant to helplessness because it may lead independently to disorganization or the absence of appropriate organized behavior.

This kind of theoretical point of view avoids any prior judgment about the adaptive value of a particular set of behaviors. Organized behavior need not be "relevant" or "valuable"; it will serve to inhibit or control anxiety as long as it is organized or a well-organized plan exists.

I turn to an illustration, a brief clinical description of the consequences of interruption in its purest form.[60]

D. is a nine-year-old boy referred to the Clinic because of failure in school and distractable behavior. Psychometric testing revealed an IQ of about 120, a normal neurological examination, a borderline EEG, and negative pediatric examination. The mother volunteered the following history and comments (the quotations are hers). When he was a baby he would bang his head when he got "interrupted." "When he gets interrupted you can expect an explosion." He becomes "frustrated terribly when he is doing something and you ask him to do something [else]." He then stamps his feet, cries, and protests with behavior resembling a temper tantrum. "Our family is not on much of a schedule; maybe he would be better off if he knows what's coming." "He can't seem to stand the exuberance and fun behavior of the family at home." When the noise or activity going on at home reaches a certain point he may go out and ride his bicycle to get away from it. Whenever the teacher talks to him in any angry voice or there is a "tense atmosphere," he withdraws; "he tunes you out" and acts as if he did not hear and did not understand anything that is being said to him. At these times he apparently cannot understand even simple directions. Those are the essential and basic facts of this history.

This boy is a distractable, nervous, but bright and attentive-appearing boy who relates readily, and initially interrupts me and his mother during the interview. He responded quickly to my setting limits. During my subsequent interview with him alone he was attentive, coherent, much better organized and readily understood all of my questions.

To comment on this boy I think most psychiatrists would diagnose him as borderline childhood schizophrenia; the catastrophic reaction (complete disorganization and with-

59. Cf. Deutsch (1960).

60. The following summary was made available to me by Dr. Gordon D. Jensen.

drawal under stress) is apparent. However, I do not feel that this is a very satisfactory diagnostic classification. Instead, I conceptualize his most serious problems as a disorganization of thinking provoked by stress, but, more particularly, a *deficient ability* to maintain or carry out a cognitive plan when experiencing interruption or environmental disorganization.

I have demonstrated another extreme case of helplessness in a series of animal experiments.[61] These studies showed that severe behavioral disturbances can be produced in animals when they are given extinction trials, but are not hungry (i.e., when they have been satiated). Given a well-organized response sequence (maze running), the absence of both consummatory response (food) and the drive state (hunger) places the organism in a situation in which neither completion nor substitute behaviors (food searching) are available. The result is behavioral disorganization and distress. These experiments also demonstrate that distress and helplessness are not necessarily dependent on the avoidance of or escape from traumatic or noxious events.

These extreme cases of helplessness and reactions to it lead us to consider another extreme case of helplessness—namely, hopelessness. Helplessness is, in a sense, an immediate reaction to the situation and is somewhat stimulus bound. The person does not know what to do in this particular situation. However, we can assume that if this builds up over a variety of situations, we might get to a generalized feeling of not knowing what to do in any situation, which is parallel to hopelessness. Hopelessness may also arise with repeated failures (noncompletions) of a single identifiable plan. However, this apparently occurs only if that plan has a high degree of salience, as in occupational efforts. It remains unclear why these kinds of situations lead into true depression, characterized typically by the effect of hopelessness, in some individuals and not in others. The concept of hopelessness and the generalized notion of not being able to complete a sequence or find an acceptable alternative or substitute for it must be related to the notion of self-esteem. If self-esteem is low, then the likelihood of finding such a substitute—the likelihood of finding a way out of the helpless situation—will be judged to be very low. If it is judged to be very low, then there may be much less searching for acceptable alternative organized plans or behaviors. Or, possibly, in cases of low self-esteem, the slightest interruption of an organized sequence is interpreted as being a final one, a reaction not unusual in persons who are either low in self-esteem or depressed. There usually occurs a special sensitivity to any signal of failure (interruption). Thus, the depressive state can be subsumed as a further extension of the notion of anxiety and helplessness. At the same time, it should be acknowledged that this discussion covers only a part of the various symptoms and etiologies subsumed under the label of depression.[62]

Contact should also be made with psychoanalytic notions of the relation between guilt and depression. I discussed previously the question of anxiety and guilt, in the context of the interruption sequence, and noted that the guilty

61. See Mandler and Watson (1966) and Mandler (1972b).
62. See Beck (1967).

ruminate on their guilt. Generalized helplessness or hopelessness and depression might arise exactly out of such continual attempts at undoing.

Let me go one step further in my investigation of hopelessness and look at the long-range consequences of a continual state of not being able to undo the wrong we have done (real or imagined) and of being faced with a state of low self-esteem that generates plans that are incapable of being completed or overestimates slight interruptions as final ones. Eventually, we become immobilized in a truly fundamental state of helplessness, unable to move, but continually subjected to an extremely painful state of anxiety or distress that is unrelieved by any kind of organized behavior. The hopeless, depressed person is then left with one final, organized act, and that is the one of self-destruction—an act that seems to make rational sense, because it is designed to put an end to the state of continuing helplessness that nothing seems to be capable of relieving.

The intensity of true depressive reaction must be related to equally intensive cognitive and actions structures that are being interrupted. In primates, the blockage of tasks that are important for species survival leads to anger and, if the blockage is prolonged, to depression.[63] The prolongation is *necessary* in order to generalize from helplessness to hopelessness.

The notion of helplessness has also been introduced in a similar context by M. S. P. Seligman and his associates.[64] I adopted the term *helplessness* specifically as an analogue to the analysis of anxiety. This development led to the use of the term *hopelessness* to describe helplessness transsituationally, and related to the symptoms and experience of depression.

Seligman and his co-workers introduced the term *learned helplessness* to refer to the acquisition of a cognitive state that follows the perception that the termination of a noxious state is independent of the organism's behavior. Under these circumstances, the probability of responding is perceived as being independent of escape and thus produces little incentive for initiating any response. As a matter of fact, it is assumed that this sequence of events reduces the "probability of doing anything active."[65,66] From this position, Seligman generalized that learned helplessness was at the basis of human depression. I use the term *helplessness* for situational anxiety, and *hopelessness* for generalized depression, which Seligman calls learned helplessness.

The underlying notion in the learned-helplessness position was that the person learns that he or she is helpless to influence outcomes. A later formulation incorporated attribution theory into the learned-helplessness notion.[67] Helplessness may be attributed to a universal state of affairs, in which neither the individual nor anyone else could have affected that state of affairs, or to personal helplessness, in which the individual alone is helpless to change the course of events. The latter is clearly more likely to lead to depression, changes in self-

63. Hamburg, Hamburg, and Barchas (1975).
64. Seligman and Maier (1967) and Maier, Seligman, and Solomon (1969).
65. Maier, Seligman, and Solomon (1969).
66. Seligman (1972).
67. Abramson, Seligman, and Teasdale (1978).

esteem, and so on. Other attributions determine the range of events over which helplessness functions, as well as the temporal consistency and stability of the attributed helplessness. These extensions are useful additons to our knowledge of the kind of cognitive structure that determine the evaluative valences of different kinds of helplessness and hopelessness.

There is one major difference between this approach and mine. I am particularly concerned with the availability of relevant actions. Whenever a search for appropriate actions indicates that, because of past experience or the generalized evaluation of personal competence, no actions are available that will achieve desirable ends, then helplessness or hopelessness will result. These means and ends need not be associated with the avoidance of aversive events; they may just as well relate to the unattainability of desirable states.

Because of the pervasiveness of anxiety, the intense interest in its manifestations seems well justified. Human beings are imperfect, and their imperfections often bring them into situations in which they are helpless, unable to cope; the result is anxiety. How this helplessness frequently interferes with adequate functioning will be illustrated in the next chapter.

11

STRESS AND EMOTION

IN THE PRECEDING CHAPTER, I dealt with one aspect of the emotional domain that is generally considered deleterious and unpleasant. However, the discussion of anxiety was devoted primarily to its definition and theoretical status and to the conditions that determine its occurrence. Another widely accepted notion about anxiety is that it interferes with effective functioning,in particular with thought and with problem solving. Those effects will be dealt with here. Specifically, what are the mechanisms whereby emotions in general affect, interfere with, and sometimes even assist and focus human thought and action? In the most extreme form, these effects fall under the rubric of stress, and I shall concentrate on that topic in order to illustrate the more general problem.

In the common language the term *anxiety* is a model of precision when compared with the term *stress*. At least we seem to agree that anxiety is something that people "have," that they experience. Stress, by contrast, seems to refer to things that people are exposed to, that they are "under" (experience?), but in general it seems to be a characteristic of situations. My dictionary tells me that *stress* refers to "condition of things compelling or characterized by strained effort," to a "strain upon bodily organ or mental power," or to an "Overpowering pressure of some adverse force or influence." The latter two definitions appear to be closest to the sense of the word *stress* that psychologists try to convey. Stress involves conditions that have some effect on body and mind. What conditions? What effects? Once again I shy away from an attempt to answer the question "What is stress?" And again I choose to describe a set of psychological conditions that will, to a large extent, satisfy the common definition.

In fact, no new devices, no new definitions, are needed. What we have to do is use our framework to account for the effects that are usually ascribed to stress. These are essentially twofold: first, the effects of stress on thought,or—to be more precise—the kinds of variables that seem to have very specific, often deleterious effects on the processing of information; and, second, the long-term effects of being exposed to stressful situations—in other words, the effect of life stress on bodily and mental functioning.

In the short-term case, stress is associated with high levels of autonomic arousal and, usually, with a negative evaluation of the arousing conditions. I say "usually" because there are some positive conditions that produce the same characteristics as do the negative ones, intense preoccupation with desired (animate or inanimate) states or objects being one obvious example. In contrast to anxiety, in which the major defining characteristic is a cognitive one—that is, the state of helplessness—stress refers primarily to situations that evoke a high level of arousal, usually in the presence of noxious evaluations.

Lest the stress situation be considered primarily one defined by physiological variables, it must be noted that the psychological aspects in the initiation of stress depend on the interpretation of the situation in such a way that it *does* in fact provide the occasion for high levels of arousal. As we shall see, and to no one's surprise, these occasions are interruptions and discrepancies. However, in stress situations more than in most others, we are frequently dealing with peremptory events, with those that demand conscious capacity over and above any expectations or attentional strategies. In the stress situation the inevitable arousal in response to loud noises, bright light, intense tissue stimulation (pain), and similar events overrides any psychological preparation of the individual and demands conscious capacity.

In the long-term effects of stress, we are dealing once again with a situation dominated by autonomic arousal. But here the effect is one not of intensity but of repeated and unavoidably recurring arousal. Life stress and the recurrence of arousal are not primarily associated with noxious events; both pleasant and unpleasant situations may induce cumulative life stress. Nor are we dealing with any peremptory situations; the stress of life is part of the everyday life of people—not restricted to unusual events or unusually salient ones.

Short-term Effect of Stress: Stress and Thought

We need to specify the kinds of events that are to be included under "thought processes." Traditionally, thought processes have been seen as coextensive with the contents of consciousness. I have emphasized that "thought" processes can be found in both the conscious and the nonconscious mode, that they refer to any and all varieties of complex transformations performed on environmental inputs as well as to intermediate products of the information-processing chain. When I discuss stress and thought I shall be concerned to a large extent with an interaction of stress with *conscious* thought.

As we saw in Chapter 4, the notion that conscious capacity is limited is by no means new. But the use of this view to explain interfering and capacity-limiting events (such as stress) is relatively recent. One influential model assumes that the amount of available capacity varies with arousal (theoretically rather than autonomically defined).[1] Spare capacity is defined as the amount of capac-

1. Kahneman (1973).

ity that remains after most of the capacity available has been supplied to the primary task at hand. I shall argue that the definition of a "primary" task is at least difficult and that the amount of capacity available for any task facing the individual is a function of other tasks and other capacity-demanding inputs with which some fixed limit of capacity must be shared.

I shall summarize some of the major characteristics of conscious operations, in particular how and why they function in problem solving and memory tasks. The first set of characteristics deals with consciousness during problem solving in the broad sense, and we review when and why particular conscious structures are developed, or when it is that conscious processes are both useful and necessary.

Certain events—among them intense stimuli and, most important for the present discussion, internal physiological events such as autonomic nervous system (ANS) activity—claim and preoccupy some part of the limited-capacity system, and other cognitive functions will suffer, that is, they will be displaced from conscious processing, and problem-solving activities will be impaired. Particularly during the interruption or failure of ongoing interactions with the world, signals from both the external and the internal world will demand conscious representation.

In order to assess the interaction of stress and consciousness, we need to review when conscious processes are most obvious. First of all, they are evident in the construction and integration of mental and action structures. Essentially this refers to the use of consciousness in the learning process. Thoughts and actions are typically conscious before they became well integrated and subsequently automatic. For example, learning to drive a car is a conscious process, but the skilled driver acts automatically and unconsciously.

Second, conscious processes are active during the exercise of choices and judgments, particularly with respect to the action requirements of the environment. These choices, often novel ones, require the consideration of possible outcomes and consequences and frequently involve "covert trial and error."

Third, many automatic structures become "conscious" when they fail in their functions, when a habitual way of acting fails or when a thought process cannot be brought to an appropriate concluson. The experienced driver becomes "aware" of where she is and what she is doing when something new and different happens—when a near miss, a police car, or an unexpected traffic light is suddenly registered. The troubleshooting function of consciousness permits repair on unconscious and automatic structures, and subsequent choice from among other alternatives.

Conscious processes also enter into both the storage and the retrieval mechanisms of memory. While it is commonplace to note that what is not attended to cannot be remembered, it is less clear exactly how consciousness and memorial processes interact. Is consciousness both necessary and sufficient at the time of both storage and retrieval? For example, there is evidence that retrieval is made possible by cues that may not have been encoded or attended to at times of storage.[2] However, all that needs to be noted for present purposes is the conditions under which conscious processes obviously interact with memory, so that we can note later how stress interacts with those conditions.

Storage mechanisms that involve consciousness are those in which attention is clearly paid to ongoing contexts within which some to-be-remembered events take place. In a sense all conscious current commentary on ongoing environmental events and activities produces some storable structures that may be used for later retrieval and that, conversely, may be interfered with under conditions of stress. We often construct some retrieval structures specifically for the purpose of later use, as when we note: "I must remember that John passed his examination and congratulate him the next time I see him."

At the retrieval end many memory-search processes, particularly those involving complex searches, require conscious processing. Among these are the search processes that involve the generation of possible retrieval candidates ("His name started with an *F*. What was it?") and specifically search processes that are usually preceded by Wh . . . questions: "Where did I leave my watch?" "What is his name?" "When am I supposed to be in his office?"

I shall argue that the most important effect of stresses on thought processes is that they interfere specifically with the smooth operation of these conscious cogitations and cognitions. What exactly interferes with these processes?

We start with a psychological, rather than a physiological, definition of stress. One of the difficulties with "objective" definitions of stressors has been the absence of the cognitive mediators. "Emotional arousal" is one of the most ubiquitous reactions, common to a great many situations that are considered stressful.[3] However, these emotional responses depend on psychological interpretive mechanisms. The major consequence of such an interpretation or appraisal is the activation of a stress reaction that is psychologically functional, that is the perception of intense ANS activity, particularly of sympathetic activation. Thus, a situation is defined as stressful if and when the interpretive-cognitive activities of the organism transform the input in such a way that a peceptible internal change results. I shall confine myself here to the effect of perceptible intense autonomic activity, and I shall not consider problems of the "milder" stresses or venture any fine-grained analysis of the limited-capacity system.[4]

It is also possible to consider other reactions, such as hormonal release, that would have perceptible effects, as well as conditions under which some physiological activity occurs without direct cognitive interpretations. Stress responses (physiologically defined) do and can occur even when no "emotional" arousal is observed.[5] If they do and if they are perceived by the organism, then they properly belong under the rubric of thought and stress.

If there is a class of psychologically defined stressors, then its best representation can be found in the collection of interruption, disrupting, and discrepant events. They have two important characteristics that cover the common notion

2. Anderson and Pichert (1978).
3. Mason (1975).
4. For such analyses, see Broadbent (1971).
5. Selye (1956, 1975).

of stress: first, they demand conscious capacity, and, second, they give rise to autonomic arousal. There are irrelevant thought processes that may not in fact be disrupting. The student studying for his exams who finds himself daydreaming about totally unrelated events is, of course, interfering with the desired (or boring) task at hand. However, it is only when other thoughts actively interrupt ongoing activity that we are dealing with *emotional* effects that have interfering properties. Similarly, a high fever may prevent a student from studying, but here again we are dealing with the interfering effects of physiological events that are not in themselves *psychological* stressors, though—as I have already noted—the results do come under the topic of thought and stress.

Stress—defined as an interruption—can also have the effect of increasing attention to central or crucial events in the environment. Under these circumstances, the stressful situation produces highly adaptive reactions and improves the coping capability of the organism. On the other hand, autonomic activity may act as "noise" in the cognitive system. If the individual attends to these internal events, then less focal attention is available for other task-directed and coping activities. To the extent, therefore, that autonomic activity is past the point of alerting the individual, continuing autonomic arousal will be consciously registered and will interfere with ongoing cognitive efficiency. In that sense, autonomic activity becomes "noise."

The conditions that produce the "stress" are the primary causes of the autonomic "noise." As such, they may be considered noxious (e.g., interpreted negatively) by the individual and therefore subject to some effort aimed at their removal. For example, during the performance of some skill or task, continuous comments from a co-worker or loud noises may be interpreted as stressful. As a result, some effort, involving conscious capacity, might be made to remove these noxious conditions. Attempts at avoiding the stressful conditions are a "secondary task" that interferes with the primary task engaged by the individual.[6]

In short, the problem of stress is twofold: the internal autonomic signals and the conditions that generate those signals both require some conscious capacity, and thereby interfere with the performance of some target task or skill.

I now turn to the specific application of these general theoretical considerations to problems of stress and thought. I shall start with a rather ancient but still serviceable notion embodied in the Yerkes-Dodson law, which describes the relation between efficiency and stress (or stimulation). I will then bring that view into contact with modern concepts and consider some current evidence on the effect of stress and autonomic activity on attention and consciousness. From that vantage point I shall then deal with the more general relation between thought, consciousness, and stress.

COGNITIVE EFFICIENCY

I have assumed that the effect of physically or environmentally defined stressors depends on their analysis as threats and stresses. There are, of course, stres-

6. Hamilton (1975).

sors that demand a stressful "interpretation" or that automatically produce stress reactions (particularly ANS reactions). When such a demand or effect is obvious, we need not speak complexly about cognitive interpretations but can talk directly about stressor effects. Among these are inescapably painful (because extremely intense) stimuli, such as electric shock. The advantage of being able to talk about stressors rather than about interpreted stresses and threats is that it enables us to make contact with an older (frequently behaviorist) literature that defined stresses exclusively in terms of environmental, physical variables. Perhaps the oldest and single most important finding in that tradition is enshrined in the Yerkes-Dodson law. Robert Yerkes and J. D. Dodson discovered that whereas performance on an easy discrimination task improved with increasing shock intensity, performance on a difficult task was worse with weak and strong shocks and optimal with intermediate-level shocks. This curvilinear relation represents the Yerkes-Dodson law.[7]

Further evidence was supplied by G. L. Freeman, who confirmed an inverted-U-shaped relation between arousal and cognitive efficiency.[8] This statement was important because it set the stage for several decades of preoccupation with the rather vague concept of arousal, specifically with arousal as a theoretical entity rather than as a measurable and observable set of events that occupy conscious capacity. Indices of arousal have varied widely, from general muscular activity to SNS activity and to activity of the reticular activating system. In the process it has been pointed out that there is no single unitary and useful concept of arousal.[9] I shall restrict myself to the stress- or threat-induced effects of peripheral ANS activity; and I shall consequently use the terms *autonomic activity* and *autonomic arousal* interchangeably (see also Chapter 6).

The next step in the evolving understanding of the U-shaped function that related performance, efficiency, and cognitive competence to arousal was Easterbrook's cue-utilization hypothesis.[10] J. A. Easterbrook concluded that "the number of cues utilized in any situation tends to become smaller with increase in emotion." Since he equated emotion with emotional drive, the extension to arousal was frequently made. Furthermore, Easterbrook related the restricted utilization of cues to changes in attention, but without providing mechanisms for the restriction in attention due to emotion or arousal.

I can now return to my initial discussion of the effects of autonomic arousal on limited conscious capacity. Given the presence of attention-demanding occurrences, it is to be expected that with increasing autonomic activity the number of events (cues) that can share conscious attention will be limited. Easterbrook noted that in some cases restrictions in attention (and effective cues) may improve cognitive efficiency. Clearly, when the excluded cues are irrelevant to the thought processes at hand, efficiency will be improved, but when a task requires attention to a wide range of cues, then the narrowing of attention will have deleterious effects.

7. Yerkes and Dodson (1908).
8. Freeman (1940).
9. See Lacey (1967).
10. Easterbrook (1959).

What cannot be maintained is that there exists some specific "law" relating efficiency to arousal. What affects the relation between efficiency and stress involves the effects of specific stressors, an approach to arousal that assigns it definable properties rather than global unspecified effects, a knowledge of the requirements of the task, and, finally, knowledge about the individual's perception of the task and the ensuing stress. Such an analysis focuses on the interaction between different stressors and the componential requirements of a task.[11]

Stress may be experienced in the most innocuous situations. Whether trying to open a door that is stuck, to fill out a complicated bureaucratic form, or to assemble a child's toy, most of us have experienced states of high stress in these, and similar, situations. Repeated attempts to open the door, to follow instructions, or to fit part A between parts B and C may fail, autonomic arousal then increases, irrelevant ideation ("Those idiots, incompetents, and fools!!!"), and panic-like behavior may ensue. Each failure is an interrupted sequence, and each interruption further potentiates autonomic arousal.

The notion that such sequences have attention-narrowing consequences is not new, witness, for example, the conclusion that "emotional states, such as anxiety, panic, and orgasm . . . produce a . . . narrowing of attention. . . . [A] correlation between narrowed attention and central sympathomimetic activity is demonstrated."[12] Similarly, the tendency to engage in task-irrelevant behavior is well known. Consider the psychological problem of panic in deep-sea diving, which has been described as "a strong, fearful perception by an individual that he is out of control, that he is not capable of coping with the situation in which he finds himself, leading to behaviors that not only do not solve the problem posed by the danger but actually may work directly against such solution."[13]

The best analysis and summary of the available evidence on cognitive efficiency in dangerous environments has been presented by Alan Baddeley:[14]

> [It] appears that one way in which danger affects performance is through its influence on the subject's breadth of attention. A dangerous situation will tend to increase the level of arousal which in turn will focus the subject's attention more narrowly on those aspects of the situation he considers most important. If the task he is performing is regarded by him as most important, then performance will tend to improve; if on the other hand it is regarded as peripheral to some other activity, such as avoiding danger, then performance will deteriorate. With experience, subjects appear to inhibit anxiety in the danger situation and hence reduce the degree of impairment. We still do not know what mechanisms mediate the effect of arousal on the distribution of attention, or what is involved in the process of adaptation to fear.

The evidence for Baddeley's conclusion comes from a variety of sources, which I shall review briefly, together with other, more recent evidence. First, equal degrees of nitrogen narcosis (which results when air is breathed at its highest pressure) produced different impairments in efficiency, depending on whether

11. Hockey and MacLean (1981).
12. Callaway and Dembo (1958).
13. Bachrach (1970).
14. Baddeley (1972).

the test was conducted in the open sea or in a pressure-chamber situation.[15] The greater impairment in the more realistic situation could be ascribed only to the greater degree of danger perceived by the subjects. In addition, more anxious subjects were more easily influenced, and impaired, by the increased "danger" of the more realistic situations.

Given these observations, can we say that the perception of danger behaves like "arousal," can it be subsumed under the cue-utilization hypothesis of Easterbrook? For example, an increase in noise improves the performance on centrally attended stimuli at the expense of peripheral ones.[16] Although some of these results may be questioned on procedural grounds,[17] another study makes the same point more persuasively. Arousal not only impairs attention to peripheral cues but also narrows the range of cues processed by systematically "reducing responsiveness to those aspects of the situation which initially attract a lesser degree of attentional focus."[18] This loss is actually due to a diminution in subjects' sensitivity, and arousal affects the capacity limitation directly.

The bridge to the danger situation was provided by a demonstration of the same diminution of attention to peripheral stimuli in a task simulating danger.[19] Experimental subjects showed both increased autonomic activity and the decrease in attention to peripheral stimuli, but no decrement in the performance of a central task.

Thus, the conclusion holds that stress has effects very similar to those of noise in reducing attentional capacity and narrowing it to central tasks. We can assume that what is perceived as psychologically "central" will be determined by the initial attention assigned to it. What is at first maximally attended to is central; whatever receives less attention is perceived as "peripheral" and will suffer the greater loss of attention under stress. Whenever the target task is "central," increased autonomic arousal may well improve performance. That point was made clearly by Baddeley and subsequently adumbrated by an attack on the notion that noise necessarily interferes with efficiency.[20]

Whereas most of the earlier studies of the effect of noise on human performance used relatively high levels of noise (95 decibels or greater), recent studies have indicated that these effects can also be obtained with moderate levels. Levels of noise found in the home or office (70 to 90 db) affect efficiency, such effects are especially likely to be found when "one measures the allocation of effort between two or more activities," and the nature of these effects seems to be related to a general state of reactivity or arousal.[21]

Finally, we must deal with the observation that experienced subjects show few or none of the deleterious effects of stress (envioronmentally defined). First, we note again that stress must be *subjectively* defined. For the experienced sub-

15. Baddeley (1971).
16. Hockey (1970).
17. Poulton (1976a).
18. Bacon (1974).
19. Weltman, Smith, and Egstrom (1971).
20. Poulton (1976b).
21. Broadbent (1981).

ject the perception of objectively defined stress must necessarily be different from that shown by the naïve observer. Apart from what is perceived or judged to be stressful, the effect of the stressor differs radically for experienced and inexperienced subjects. For example, one finds increased efficiency before a parachute jump as a function of previous jumping experience.[22] Similarly, novice jumpers have a high pulse rate before a jump, which drops to a normal level upon landing, whereas the experienced jumpers show the reverse effect.[23] The same lack of stress responses has been found among highly trained astronauts and has been explained in the same fashion.[24]

The effect of experience must be related to the proposition that autonomic arousal is linked to the interruption of ongoing behavior, plans, and expectations and that stress occurs when no available action or thought structures are available to handle the situation. Astronauts, for example, are trained to have response sequences, plans, and problem-solving strategies available for all imaginable emergencies. An emergency then ceases to be one; it is another routine situation, by definition not unexpected—and not stressful. Conversely, the novice parachutist ruminates on possible outcomes, none of which he is able to handle, emergencies that he either imagines or remembers and for which no action structures are available. At the end of the jump, this interruptive effect, interrupting thoughts about the successful completion of the jump, is eliminated—the original plan (to complete the jump successfully) has been achieved. At the more speculative level, one might assume that for the experienced parachutist who enjoys the jump (both emotionally and cognitively) the completion interrupts that enjoyment, or even elation—more concretely, it terminates a complete and competent action structure. Relevant confirming reports are available anecdotally from sky divers who cannot wait to go up again for the next jump.

As far as Baddeley's final question about the mechanisms that mediate the effect of arousal on attention is concerned, I have provided such a mechanism. Autonomic arousal narrows attention in two ways: first, automatically by the direct action of the autonomic nervous system and, second, indirectly by occupying some of the limited capacity of attention-consciousness and thereby limiting the remaining available attentional capacity to those events or stimuli that have originally been perceived as "central."[25]

COPING WITH STRESS

Stress may result in cognitive processes that draw attention to centrally important aspects of the environment. Such efforts are often described as relevant to the mastery of stress, to our ability to control a particular situation. The term *mastery* refers to our perception that the events in our personal world may be brought under our control. I suggested earlier that this sense of control or mastery may

22. Hammerton and Tickner (1967).
23. Epstein and Fenz (1965).
24. Mandler (1967).
25. Bacon (1974).

be important not so much because it directly affects our actions but because it colors the cognitive interpretation of our world. It is generally considered "good" to be in control of our world, and when the world is appraised as "good" the emotional tone will be positive. Something that frightens us may become amusing when we have a sense of mastery, even though our actual control of the situation has not changed. What has changed is the relevance of the event to our ongoing plans; if they are seen as relevant and as impeding (interrupting) ongoing action, they may become frightening. If they are seen as irrelevant, or impeding only in the short term, they may become amusing and tolerable. When a friend and colleague criticizes our work, the remark is often seen as constructive and leading to mastery, whereas the identical remark from a supervisor may easily appear threatening. The objective absence of control is not necessarily seen as negative; just consider the enjoyment some people experience on a roller coaster. It is the subjective sense of control that is important rather than the objective control of the environment.

There is no doubt that the sense of mastery in many cases reduces the deleterious effects of stress and alleviates the subjective sense of emotional disturbance. I assume that this effect may occur under two conditions.

First, any action directly related to the threatening, interrupting situation or event may change that event and reduce its threatening, that is, interrupting, effect. In that case an action by the individual has changed the situation from one that is arousing (and interpreted as threatening) to a nonarousing one, and thereby removed its threatening aspects.

Second, without changing any of its objective aspects, a situation may be reinterpreted in such a way that the events are not perceived as interrupting any more. The overall structure or plan under which the situation and events are perceived is changed significantly to remove its interrupting aspect or to view the interruptive events as beneficial. In the latter case, the autonomic arousal will persist but will be positively interpreted. The roller coaster seen as a joyful situation that will terminate when planned (at the end of its run) will thus become nonfrightening. The other kind of event, the cognitive removal of interruptive aspects, occurs less frequently. Consider the case of the student who has received his graded examination paper with a grade of 66 percent. She had hoped (planned) to get at least a 75 percent grade, in order to pass the course. These plans have been disrupted; she is in a state of autonomic arousal—negatively interrupted. Then she notices a slip of paper appended to the examination which says that the examination was unusually difficult and that 66 percent will be recorded as a passing grade. The same event has now been reinterpreted; its interruptive, as well as negative, aspect has been removed.

This discussion leads once again to the general topic of coping, appraisal, and reappraisal. I previously indicated the contribution to this problem by Richard Lazarus and his colleagues.[26] They have also addressed the issue of mastery and stress.[27] Why does activity as such apparently have the capacity to lower

26. Lazarus (1975) and Folkman, Schaefer, and Lazarus (1979).
27. Gal and Lazarus (1975).

stress reactions. R. Gal and Lazarus distinguish between threat-related and non-threat-related activities. The former lower stress reactions because they provide a feeling of control or mastery. In the case of non-threat-related activities, however, their effect derives from the fact that they distract or divert attention from threat. It is this latter explanation that should be added to the account I have given here. In some cases of threat, some restriction of attention may reduce the perception of both the threatening event as well as the internal autonomic activity. However, activity as such is not stress reducing in all cases. In panic situations, for example, continuing interrupted activity not only fails to reduce the experience of stress but usually increments it. In general, the question of mastery and control, as well as of the effects of activity as such, requires detailed analyses of the task, the perceived situation, and the general structures that guide thought and action at each point in time.

How does the mastery of threat and the effect of interpreted threat influence the efficiency of the performance of complex intellectual tasks? Here we come close to observing the outcomes of complex thought processes directly, and at the same time addressing a topic of some practical importance. Specifically, we are concerned with the effect of perceived threat on the performance of testlike tasks.

The major research strategy has been to select individuals who report (on paper-and-pencil tests) high and low degrees of anxiety or concern about test situations. These test-anxiety scales were described in the preceding chapter. I assume that the high-anxious subjects tell themselves that appropriate behavior in a test situation consists of observing their own behavior, of examining their failures, whereas low-anxious individuals orient their behavior and cognitions toward the specific requirements of the task.

In our original study[28] we noted not only that high-anxious individuals performed worse on intelligence tasks but also that the absence of any further instructions was most beneficial for the high-anxiety people. On the other hand, instructions telling subjects that they failed were most helpful for low-anxious individuals. In a subsequent study, I. G. Sarason found that high-anxious subjects solved anagrams more efficiently than did low-anxious individuals when the situation was nonthreatening, that is, when they were instructed that they were not expected to finish all the anagrams, because they were very difficult and harder than usual. When the subjects were told that the task was directly related to one's intelligence level and that they should finish easily if they were of average intelligence, the low-anxious individuals performed significantly better than the high-anxious ones.[29]

We conclude that many people bring stress into a situation, just as the situation brings out their stress potential. Both a potentially threatened individual and a properly interpretable situation are needed to produce the stress reaction. That reaction, in turn, presumably takes two forms: first, the individual ruminates—thinks—about the irrelevant aspects of the task, including his own state,

28. Mandler and Sarason (1952).
29. Sarason (1961).

performance, and reactions; and, second, the threat interpretation produces autonomic activity that is in itself attention demanding. Both of these sets of internal events then vie for the limited capacity and thereby reduce the conscious capacity available for thought processes that the task itself requires.

THE STRANGE AND THE UNUSUAL

In this section, I want to explore some further aspects of the events that are usually called stressful, including the question of how they come to be stressful.

For most people the strange, the unusual, and the unexpected are generally stressful events. Clearly, this kind of common-language usage refers to exactly the kinds of events that are interruptive. Several writers have also emphasized the importance of the strange and the unusual. Bowlby has sensitively described the general problem of fear and its ontogeny, in the framework of his attachment theory.[30] Others have ascribed the occurrence of fear to perceptual discrepancies.[31] Both expositions assume that fear of the strange does not occur until after familiarity and expectations have been developed. Stranger anxiety in infants does not occur until schemas for faces have been developed. Chimpanzees are terrorized by detached parts of chimp bodies only after they have experienced intact bodies. Thus, the strange is interruptive because the schemas that are evoked in and by a particular situation are violated; the strange is unassimilable. However, apart from the violation of specific expectations by the strange and the unusual, there is another characteristic of human cognition that produces fearful (arousing and negatively interpreted) conditions. In the presence of events and perceptions that are new—that is, for which no current schemas are appropriate—the individual will search for an appropriate way to interpret the surround, will undertake a meaning analysis. Given the essentially novel characteristic of the situaton, no such appropriate structure will be found, but in the process each attempted structure fails of environmental support and is thus interrupted. This unavailability of appropriate response or action alternatives, this helplessness in the face of the environment, defines the quality of anxiety.

Shifting to intrapsychic stressful events, we will consider first the condition under which ongoing cognitive structures are interrupted by their own consequences. Consider some plan that is not executed but is examined. If a consequence of this plan is discovered to be incompatible with some other, maybe hierarchically higher, plan, or with some expected environmental condition, then we are once again confronted with an interruption, an intrapsychic cognitive one. These thought processes will lead to arousal just as an external event will. For example, planning to attend the theater and then remembering a previous engagement at the same time will lead to stress and coping activities.

Recall the discussion in Chapter 8 of the hierarchical structure of plans and cognitive structures.[32] The stress produced by the interruption of a particular plan

30. Bowlby (1969).
31. Hebb (1946).
32. Miller, Galanter, and Pribram (1960).

will vary with the number of other plans (subordinate and superordinate to the interrupted one) that are disrupted at the same time. For example, the interruption of a low-level plan ("I want to have eggs for breakfast, but there aren't any in the house") may not be too arousing and stressful, because a higher one is not affected ("I want to have breakfast—and might as well eat some cereal"). The important point to be noted is that any interruptive event must be analyzed in terms of the level of plans and relevant hierarchies that are involved. Thus, when all levels of plans are threatened (cannot be completed) by some event, the degree of autonomic arousal will be intense and the stress most severe.

Action structures and intrapsychic cognitive structures may both be interrupted for one of two reasons: the failure of an expected event or sequence to occur, or the occurrence of something unexpected. Both of these situations involve interruption and autonomic arousal and usually, in the kind of situation considered in this chapter, are interpreted as negative and unpleasant. In either case, the interruption of a current cognitive structure automatically focuses consciousness on that structure and on the interruptive event or thought. One of the functions of consciousness is to become the arena for troubleshooting when conscious or unconscious structures fail. When such "snapping into consciousness" takes place, the field of focal attention will be narrowed, and, under many circumstances, other ongoing activity will be impaired because of the restricted amount of conscious capacity that remains available. However, it should be noted that much troubleshooting will occur without any stressing sequelae. When working on a complex problem, we often expect to find one or more structures to be inadequate for the solution of the problem at hand. In that case, the operative executive plan "expects" interruptions, and the expected does not lead to autonomic arousal. Expected interruptions of this kind will be innocuous only if they are not perceived as being destructive of the executive plan. The anxious individual, in contrast, who "expects" to fail, will perceive these interruptions as being fatal or at least deleterious to the goal at hand.

PROBLEM SOLVING, MEMORY, AND STRESS

How is stress likely to affect the efficiency of memory and its component mechanisms? It is generally agreed that the degree of elaboration of an event will determine how efficiently it is stored and how easily it can be retrieved.[33] These elaborative operations are typically performed in the conscious state of the target structure. Both integrative (intrastructural) and elaborative (interstructural) requirements make demands on conscious capacity and thereby delimit the amount of storage possible under various circumstances.

Given these assumptions about memory, storage, and retrieval, the restriction of conscious capacity that occurs as a function of stress should have obvious effects on memory functions. Not only will events be less elaborately coded under conditions of stress (we remember fewer things that occurred while we were

33. Craik and Lockhart (1972), Craik and Tulving (1975), and Mandler (1979a).

under stress, and less well), but also—with central focusing during stress—we should remember a few salient events that occurred under stress extremely well. Anecdotal evidence, at least, bears this out. Similarly, one would expect that retrieval under stress should show similar characteristics and also that the stressful occurrence may provide additional retrieval cues.

Unfortunately, little experimental evidence is available on the effects of stress on complex storage and retrieval processes. What data there are tend to be rather dated and simply make the point that stress (frequently defined as failure) impairs memory. Much of that evidence was collected under behaviorist paradigms and therefore tends to emphasize drive-performance interactions and to pay little heed to underlying cognitive processes. The only set of extensive data concerns the effect of stress on short-term memory and shows that practically any kind of stress, failure experience, or uncontrollable noise will impair short-term memory retrieval. Since short-term memory is to some degree coextensive with span of attention or consciousness, such a finding is not surprising and adds little to our understanding of more complex processes. To the extent that short-term memory experiments require the holding in consciousness (or working memory) of the to-be-remembered material, we would naturally expect that any set of events that makes demands on the limited processing capacity will at the same time interfere with these short-term "storage" processes.

If the experimental literature on stress and memory fails to respond to the need to examine underlying cognitive processes, experimental work on stress and problem solving unfortunately fails equally. Lay people and psychologists have known for some time that under stress the thought processes involved in problem solving demonstrate the kind of narrowing and stereotyping that the present analysis would lead us to expect. If much of problem solving involves the manipulation—in consciousness—of alternatives, choices, probable and possible outcomes and consequences, and alternative goals, then the production of internal "noise" of stress and autonomic arousal should—and does—interfere with such processes. Thought processes become narrowed in the sense that only the available alternatives are considered and that no conscious capacity is available to consider new alternatives. In the same sense, thought becomes stereotyped and habitual. Conversely, the possibility of bringing in new strategies and considering their possible effect is reduced—thought becomes repetitive and unelaborated. In a sense, the restriction on memorial elaboration refers to the very same elaboration that is restricted during problem solving under stress. We saw examples of these consequences in the discussion of the available data on the question of central and peripheral processing under stress.

What are needed are some fine-grained experimental analyses of these processes during problem solving. How and when does the introduction of stress (however produced or defined) restrict the available alternatives? Which processes are suppressed or removed from consciousness and in what order? Does the very inability to solve a problem because of stress potentiate further stress reactions because of the interruptive process of the failure to solve a problem? How is hypothesis sampling affected by stress conditions? Under what circumstances can the focusing that occurs under stress become beneficial? How does attention to centrally relevant problems under stress promote more efficient problem solving? The research potential is indeed great, but our preoccupation with the unstressed mind has restricted experimental work on these problems.

Long-term Effects of Stress: Life Stress

I have discussed immediate effects of stress specifically on thought and action. But stress can also be cumulative. What are the long-term consequences of stress on the health and effective functioning of the individual? These-long term effects cumulate not only from the kinds of stress situations just discussed but also from repeated stresses experienced in the course of daily living. Such events are stressful to the extent that they are discrepant or interrupting, and their cumulative impact is due to the direct action of repeated sympathetic arousal on the physiological system.

LIFE STRESS AND INTERRUPTION

Any event in the life of an individual will generate ANS arousal if and when the world changes in such a way that expected outcomes no longer occur or are no longer possible. Any change in the life of the individual in which the expected no longer happens is potentially stressful. The definition of what can be or is expected must be seen as very broad. It ranges from the place where one expects to find one's toothpaste in the morning to the items that are usually on the menu of the restaurant where one eats lunch, the people one encounters in the workplace, the friends with whom one goes bowling, and the spouse with whom one shares daily experiences.

The relevance of a life event is not defined by how much one likes or dislikes it or by whether one classifies a particular event as important or not. The crucial feature of a life event and its changes is the degree to which the changes are discrepant with one's expectations, the degree to which the new state of the world is subjectively perceived as different from the normal, modal one.

The determination whether an event of everyday life is a potentially stressful one will depend to a large extent on the kind of analysis that Ellen Berscheid[34] has developed for close relationships (see Chapter 8). An action or thought is subject to interruption chiefly if it is meshed with other actions and with events in the life of the individual. Berscheid's analysis can be extended to the work situation, to the family environment in general, and to practically all aspects of the person's life. When a colleague is fired from his job, the degree to which that event is interruptive for others will depend on the interactions one has with that colleague in the work situation. A promotion will be interruptive to the extent that it involves the individual in tasks that she has not previously undertaken, produces a perceptible change in her earning power, and so on. In short,

34. Berscheid (1983).

life events will be cumulatively stressful to the extent that they are interconnected with one's daily life.

THE EFFECTS OF STRESS

How does life stress, as seen from this vantage point, affect the long-range welfare of the individual? An initial analysis will require us to know something about the individual's schemas that represent important life situations, to know the expectations that are elicited by the world and the interactions with it. Potentially stressful situations must be analyzed in terms of the interconnectedness of the individual's life with situational demands and with other people. If we assume that interruptions are a sufficient (and possibly necessary) condition for the activation of ANS activity, then clearly repeated life stresses will increase the individual's general level of arousal. Such arousal is likely to have three general consequences.

First of all, in the short run, continuing autonomic arousal will interfere with the effectiveness of the individual's intellective functioning. Extensive and continuing autonomic arousal has as one of its consequences conscious preoccupation with such arousal and with the causes of the interruption. Furthermore, the limited capacity of human consciousness will entail constriction of thought, stereotyping of plans, limitation of creative problem solving, and general interference with efficient cognitive functioning (see above).

Second, the continual arousal of ANS activity is likely to overload the system, to require extraordinary cardiac activity, and to be responsible for general deleterious effects on cardiac and visceral functions.[35]

Third, a body of evidence is accumulating that the catecholamines interfere with the immune system.[36] Although it is true that the hormonal system itself is complex and not completely understood, the conclusion seems by now established that continuing high levels of epinephrine have immunosuppressive effects and make the individual more vulnerable to illness.[37]

The current concern with life stress and the intensive empirical attack on the attendant phenomena can be dated back to the appearance of the Social Readjustment Rating Scale (SRRS).[38] That scale has been the basis for variant versions and has undergone changes in content, wording, and scoring procedures;[39] other scales have been developed with similar intent and content.[40] The general conclusion is that retrospective studies show a reasonably high correlation between current illness and prior life stresses but that prospective studies are much less promising; many people who have been exposed to the life stresses listed in the various scales do not display any illness or disturbance. Also, individuals with a

35. Eliot (1974, 1979) and Dembroski, Weiss, and Shields (1978).
36. Solomon and Amkraut (1983).
37. Bourne, Lichtenstein, Melmon, Henney, Weinstein, and Shearer (1974) and Rogers, Dubey, and Reich (1979).
38. The scale was originally developed by Holmes and Rahe (1967).
39. Rahe (1979).
40. Dohrenwend, Krasnoff, Askenasy, and Dohrenwend (1978).

history of depression, for example, are more sensitive to the deleterious effects of life stress than the normal population is. Finally, social support seems to have some, though often a very weak, role in softening the impact of life stresses.[41]

Even a cursory examination of the life stresses listed in the various questionnaires and inventories shows that they are all consistent with the basic tenets of interruption theory. The events listed are life events in which a usual situation is changed, in which novel events are encountered, and in which the new life situation is discrepant vis-à-vis the old. In fact, the questions are frequently posed in terms of "changes" in the life situation. Equally consistent with interruption theory is the fact that positive as well as negative changes are listed and that the positive events are often given greater weight than the negative ones. It must be remembered, however, that weights for the items on the scales are typically determined by having people rate the degree of adjustment and coping necessary to deal with the target events. As various commentators have noted, this does not indicate how the individual who is being rated by such a scale can or does cope with the actual event. It is therefore misleading to consider the scales to be objective (veridical) measures of life stress. Even though the population at large may consider some event to be difficult to deal with, the individual involved may not find it difficult. Beyond such considerations, it is important to be wary of the intro- or retrospective reports of individuals concerning either their current state or their prior experiences. Reports of such experiences or of current sensitivities are frequently shaped more by beliefs and hypotheses than by veridical perceptions.[42]

In discussing the low prospective utility of these scales, we should not ask how "the majority of individuals tolerate their recent life change experiences and remain healthy" or state that "new research needs to be done in the area of systematic quantification of subjects' stress tolerance characteristics."[43] Rather than talking about the tolerance for events that are assumed to be equally stressful for all people, we must ask which events are actually effective stresses *for the individual*. If the event is not stressful, no tolerance is required. Remember the analyses by Berscheid, that seemingly equal relationships may in fact hide quite different degrees of potential for interruption. Rather than seeking complex new models that integrate social, psychological, and physiological aspects, we should look at particular events and determine their potential stressfulness in terms of their interruptive potential.

One of the most impressive programs of research on the relation between stress and autonomic (endocrine) functions has been carried out over many years by Marianne Frankenhaeuser at the University of Stockholm. She emphasizes that neuroendocrine responses reflect the emotional impact of the psychosocial environment on the person, which "is determined by his or her cognitive appraisal of stimuli and events."[44] Conditions that are "perceived as deviating from those

41. For a review and summaries, see Rahe (1979), Rahe and Arthur (1978), Silver and Wortman (1980), and Wallston, Alagna, DeVellis, and DeVellis (1981).
42. Nisbett and Wilson (1977).
43. Rahe (1979).
44. Frankenhaeuser (1979).

to which the person is accustomed will induce a change in adrenalin output, whereas stimuli and events that are perceived as part of the familiar environment will not affect secretion. Novelty, change, challenge, and anticipation may be considered key components in the psychosocial conditions triggering the adrenal-medullary response." I shall summarize here only a few immediately pertinent results from the Frankenhaeuser laboratory.

Several studies have shown that deviations from the level of stimulation that the individual expects will lead to increased adrenalin output. For example, both a monotonous vigilance task and a complex reaction-time task produce adrenalin levels higher than that produced by a situation that matches the average complexity of a normal environment. However, when the situation is subjectively restructured so that people perceive themselves to be able to exercise control over the environment, then the adrenalin output is determined by degree of perceived control.[45] In terms of my formulation, interruption is determined by subjective expectancies, and when control is perceived as being exercised over the situation, it becomes more predictable and less interrupting, and therefore less effective in terms of autonomic arousal. Similarly, commuters who entered a crowded train (where seat selection was difficult) showed higher adrenalin levels than those entering the train when it was less crowded and when seat selection was more under their control, that is, the length and the duration of the trip were not the determiners of adrenalin—perceived control was.[46] Another series of studies in the workplace indicates that highly constricted, machine-paced work and repetitive, physically constrained work in which the pace is outside the worker's control contribute to high and continuing levels of adrenalin output.[47]

On the question of the relation between health and stress, Frankenhaeuser notes that the cardiovascular system may be adversely affected if "periods of high secretion [of catecholamines] are prolonged or repeated frequently." Data from her laboratory show that individuals whose adrenalin response returns quickly to baseline after stress are psychologically better balanced and more efficient than are "slow decreasers." Frankenhaeuser suggests that the coronary-prone, Type A behavior pattern may be related to "low flexibility in physiological arousal relative to situational demands."

The work of T. M. Dembroski and his associates has shown consistently higher heart rates in response to competitive and social challenges among Type A than among Type B individuals.[48] Type A individuals, who have been shown to be at risk for coronary heart disease, are characterized by excessive activity, competitiveness, hostility, and a sense of urgency. Type A persons show cardiac-rate resting levels indistinguishable from those of Type B persons, but their heart-rate variability is greater; they also respond with significantly greater increases in heart rate to a speeded-up task;[49] and they show "significantly greater cardiovas-

45. Frankenhaeuser and Rissler (1970).
46. Singer, Lundberg, and Frankenhaeuser (1978); see also Lundberg (1976).
47. Frankenhaeuser (1979).
48. Dembroski (1981).
49. Dembroski, MacDougall, and Shields (1977).

cular changes indicative of sympathetic ANS arousal than Type B individuals.[50] From the point of view of interruption theory, Type A individuals are more likely to perceive their performance on these tasks as less than required and therefore discrepant with their expectations. These discrepancies produce SNS activity, which in turn is responsible for lasting changes in and the deterioration of the cardiovascular system.

David McClelland and his associates have reported some interesting results obtained within a different framework—namely, the study of individuals high in need for power (*n* Power).[51] Individuals high in *n* Power are defined by the fact that they write imaginative stories about their having an impact on others by aggression; they also play more competitive sports and generally try to increase their impact on others. Subjects were selected in whom such characteristics were also associated with high scores on inhibition, as well as with high scores on items from the Holmes and Rahe scale, which indicated stresses in the power-achievement areas. These individuals showed higher adrenalin excretion rates and a lower concentration of immunoglobulin A as well as more frequent reports of illnesses than did all other subjects not characterized by this triple identification. The authors conclude that a "strong need for Power, if it is inhibited and stressed, leads to chronic sympathetic overactivity which has an immunosuppressive effect," which in turn leads to a greater susceptibility to illness.[52] Additional evidence can be found in a study of college students who participated in a competitive TV-tennis game. Those subjects "who responded during the contest with extreme increases in heart rate and diastolic blood pressure were significantly more likely to have frequent minor illnesses than those responding with moderate or low increases."[53]

In terms of my formulation, the need for power is indexed by a set of habitual reactions to and actions in a variety of situations. Individuals have, in a sense, a script or schema, which determines how they are to deal with certain situations that require aggressive and power-defined social interactions. When these actions are blocked by the environment (as indicated by the power stress measures) or when they are inhibited intrapsychically from being executed, then interruptive events occur that leads to ANS arousal.

A more general effect of life stress (and interruption) is found in the medical histories of relatives of persons who have recently died. Here the mortality rate is several times greater than among the members of a control group who do not have recently deceased family members. It also appears that after the death of a spouse, remarriage protects against the excess mortality rate in men.[54]

Two other features of stress need to be considered. I have assumed, in keeping with the available evidence, that positive discrepancies have autonomic effects

50. Dembroski, MacDougall, Shields, Pettito, and Lushene (1978); see also Jorgensen and Houston (1981).
51. McClelland, Floor, Davidson, and Saron (1980), McClelland and Jemmott (1980), and Jemmott, Borysenko, Borysenko, McClelland, Chapman, Meyer, and Benson (1981).
52. McClelland, Floor, Davidson, and Saron (1980).
53. Dembroski, MacDougall, Slaats, Eliot, and Buell (1981).
54. Temoshok, Zegans, and Van Dyke (1983).

similar to negative discrepancies. However, there is some evidence that the *qualitative* aspects of some positive states have very specific effects on a wide variety of adaptive activities. Alice Isen and her collaborators[55] have concluded on the basis of extensive evidence that people who are feeling happy show pronounced effects on the way they deal with their environment. They "reduce the complexity of decision situations and the difficulty of tasks . . . by adopting the simplest strategy possible, considering the fewest number of alternatives possible, and doing little or no checking of information, hypotheses, and tentative conclusions." I assume that such states of bliss involve little preparation for interruptions, probably have a low level of arousal, and show little narrowing of attention in the interplay with the environment. They should also be quite susceptible to the effects of stress and interruption.

If happy people seem to take the world as it is, the most extreme case of apparent passivity occurs at the other end of the emotional continuum when resignation sets in. Hans Selye[56] has suggested that repeated and high levels of stress may exhaust the autonomic nervous system such that little or no arousal can occur. The psychological equivalent is found in some cases of apparently depressed people who make no effort to interact with a usually hopeless world. They show little emotional reaction, and their subjective state is one of resignation—lack of action, thought, and emotion.

We have seen that stress is not just a burden our environment imposes on us but also an internal or external event that needs to be interpreted by our mental apparatus. Given the nature of that interpretation and our reactions to it, the consequences may vary from mild annoyance to severe incapacity, and they may even include improved coping with the environment.

55. Isen, Means, Patrick, and Nowicki (1982).
56. Selye (1956, 1975).

12

IMPLICATIONS AND EXTENSIONS

THIS CHAPTER DEALS WITH the implications of the cognitive-arousal view of emotions for a number of different topics. I start with some ideas about aspects of early development that might influence the growth of emotions. The next section deals with an area that gained the concentrated interest of psychologists only recently—the interplay between emotions and memory. I then turn to a discussion of problems of change, particularly therapeutic efforts, and a look at personality variables that are of importance to the occurrence and experience of emotions and memory. The next section deals with sexual, lustful feelings as a special case of emotion, and I end with speculations about the origins of some aesthetic experiences and of personal creativity.

The Development of Emotion

The emotions of the child (and the adult) are constructed in the process of development. The construction will to a large extent depend on the individual's cognitive development, on the way he or she learns to construct the world, the individual reality. There are some primitive emotional reactions that can appear prior to extensive cognitive development. Fearlike reactions may be constructed out of autonomic reactions and unlearned resonses to the environment. Still, these primitive emotions during early stages of development are often dissimilar from the adult emotion. For example, in the adult the category of emotions classified as fear usually has some quite specific cognitive content. In any case, I shall concentrate on the acquired rather than the innate aspects of emotional experience. Thus, I shall assume that in many, if not most, cases, emotional development depends on the cognitive development of the individual. Although there are issues in the development of visceral responsivity, we will see that even these depend in many instances on cognitive evaluative processes.

The distinction between cognitive and emotional development is an artificial one, because emotional development (if it is to be considered separately at all) is a function of cognitive development. It is true that much of the work on cognitive development has dealt with issues of intellective, problem-solving, and language functioning, and many of the insights gained from a knowledge of those processes have relatively little bearing on emotional functioning. Still, the development of the evaluative perception of the world, the construction of the social world, and the acquisition of evaluative categories all presumably proceed in a fashion similar to the development of spatiotemporal perception, the construction of physical objects, and the acquisition of semantic categories. The differentiation of complex emotional states should go hand in hand with cognitive development and differentiation.

I will focus on those aspects of development that are directly relevant to the construction of emotion. Because it is not my intention to review the literature on these topics, the following discussion in no way implies that some (or all) of these questions have not been previously addressed; many of them have. My intent is to indicate those areas of investigation and potential knowledge that are specifically relevant to the point of view expressed in these pages.

THE DEVELOPMENT OF COGNITIVE-EVALUATIVE PROCESSES

If limited-capacity consciousness is the arena for emotional experience, then one of the first questions that arises concerns the change in conscious capacity with age—assuming any change indeed occurs. Currently there are two major theories, one holding that capacity changes over ontogeny and the other that the apparent developmental changes are a function of the increasing ability of the organism to organize and structure mental products (and pari passu the presentation of the external world). If—as I tend to believe—the latter interpretation is correct, then the organization of autonomic perception and evaluative cognitions, as well as actions, will significantly change conscious contents during the course of development. At least the anecdotal evidence suggests that adults can think about, or keep in mind, more disparate events at any one time than the young child can. The apparent lack of continuing attentiveness on the part of some children may be one symptom of the relative capacity of conscious attention. Better packaging (chunking) of information seems to be one result of cognitive growth, but increased skill in time sharing may also be involved. How well that capacity is used in general will determine the extent to which emotional states interfere, for example, with other ongoing thought and action. Given some built-in automatic structures and the vast array of cognitive structures still to be developed, the interesting problem is this: What characteristics of the child and of the environment determine the growth of automaticity, the utilization of limited-capacity consciousness, and—consequently—the development of emotional experience?

The cognitive evaluation of the world is an important determiner not only of the kinds of complex emotions that the individual can and will experience but also of the specific emotions that any particular event is likely to elicit. One of the central cultural influences on the pervasive, and the individual, emotions concerns the frequency with which certain emotions are encountered in a culture or society, as well as the distribution of their intensities. The values, categories, and schemas that encode a particular societal structure (culture) will determine in part how and when anxiety, grief, depression, and fear will be experienced. Developmental studies of how the problem of helplessness is handled, of how people deal with the absence of significant others, of the cognitive manipulation of pain, and of the expression of feeling in the presence of the unexpected, address problems of the noxious emotions. Similar questions about the context of early problem solving, of the categorization of parent figures, of play and the interactions with peers, of giving and receiving comfort, and of attitudes toward sexual stimulation will enlighten us about the development of the positive emotions.

In order to understand the development of the emotions, we need to know how the child comes to construct systems of values. How does the categorization of values develop? To what extent are the categories of the common language accepted during socialization without conflict, and when does conflict between value structures and the message of the common language arise? How do variations in the semantic, syntactic, and pragmatic aspects of the home language affect values and the categories imposed on the world? More generally, we must become more alert to the evaluative structures imposed on the emotional life of the child (and the adult) by the prevailing value structures of the society in which people construct their emotions. For example, television viewing of violence in a violent culture should have emotional consequences quite different from those to be expected in a cooperative nonviolent culture.

The importance of currently available structures leads us to the problem of interruption in the very young child. The newborn infant presumably has few cognitive and action structures available, although we have come to reject fairly universally the *tabula rasa* view of the newborn. Both cognitive and action structures exist in the newborn in rudimentary ways. This view is represented in the corpus of Piaget's contribution.[1]

However, given the primitive form of these infantile structures, we would expect a more labile organism, subject to influences other than the immediate interruption. Alan Sroufe and his co-workers[2] have demonstrated this point in their studies of emotional development in infants. In general, they assume that novel, incongruous stimuli will, within a positive context such as the home, produce positive, smiling, and reaching actions and that negative contexts will produce crying and avoidance. The amount of discrepancy will by itself not predict the nature of the affect.[3] Instead—and this is completely consistent with the theme of my discussion—discrepancy determines the amount of attention and "tension" and the magnitude of the affect, whereas the direction of the affect is largely a function of context. Novelty, such as the approach of a stranger, and

1. See also Kessen (1965), for a historical view.
2. Sroufe and Wunsch (1972) and Sroufe, Waters, and Matas (1974).
3. Sroufe, Waters, and Matas (1974); see also Berlyne (1960) and Kagan (1971).

different contexts are relatively ineffective for the younger (six-month-old) infant, but with the development of familiar schemas and "cognitive sophistication," contexts become more and more important. The novel situation will then elicit both approach and avoidance tendencies, and the effect generated will be determined by contextual features such as setting, the sequence of environmental events, familiarization, and the duration of the event. An important step in determining the development of emotional expression in response to interruption (discrepancy or novelty) must be the study of the development of sensitivity to contextual factors. Similarly, the determinants and development of laughter in children show that laughter follows, first, from arousal contingent on the experience of unexpected stimuli and, second, from an evaluation that the stimulus is safe or inconsequential.[4] Clearly, such an evaluation is easier for a cognitively sophisticated organism than for a newborn.

PSYCHOANALYTIC THEORY AND EMOTIONAL DEVELOPMENT

If the cognitive-interpretive system is our primary means of lending meaning to our world, then the early aspects of its development must be important for its future functioning. We assume that, without further intervention, the schemas, pathways, pointers, and other connections within the system are maintained from childhood on and become the central skeletal framework on which the adult system is developed. The notion that the meaning of the adult world is a function of early infantile development is, of course, at the heart of psychoanalytic theory. Freud assumed that there are three major systems that produce arousal (or cathexis) and that can, depending on the course of the child's history, receive varying kinds of mental interpretations. These are the oral or alimentary system, the anal or elimination system, and the genital or sexual system. These systems are not the only ones that develop specific arousal-characterization conjunctions of importance for later life. Two others might be the management of pain and of sleep or sleep deprivation. The general point that needs to be made is that arousal associated with oral, anal, genital, pain, or sleep management will make various aspects of these activities pleasant or unpleasant, depending on the attendant interpretation of the environment. We may assume that any event that, coupled with arousal, produces relief from distress or achievement of pleasant states will become effective as a positive characterization of the environment. Thus, any event that signals relief from subjective or psychological hunger, any signal that produces release from either prior or subsequent unpleasantness associated with urination or defecation, any signal that is associated with pleasurable sexual excitement, any event that signals relief from pain, or any signal that is associated with the termination of sleep deprivation—any of these may become, for the child, a positive characterization of the environment, available for emotional or affective interpretation.

Freud taught the important lesson that some events and some of their inter-

4. Rothbart (1973).

pretations and transformations that are perfectly acceptable during childhood may, during adulthood, not lead to the same pleasurable, unconflicted outcomes. It is at this point that Freud introduced the notion of repression. Similarly, anxiety may signal the unpleasant consequences of previously pleasant trains of thought and action. The anticipation that a particular plan of action may not be completed serves as a stimulus both for autonomic discharge and for the unpleasant affect of helplessness or anxiety.

The difference between the early and the late systems of cognition and meaning analysis is, in Freud's terms, in part the difference between the primary and the secondary process. The secondary process is concerned with much of the reality that surrounds adults, the complex transformations and plans necessary to achieve the satisfaction of their needs, and the events that will produce positive rather than negative emotional consequences. Freud gave the appearance of the primary process the character of irrational thought and behavior. It is irrational in the sense that it does not follow the rational reality imposed on it. However, the implication of psychoanalytic theory that the only way to undo the destructive effects of repressed thought processes is by a restructuring of cognitions through reinterpretation and replanning is not inevitable; the forming of new pathways is not always necessary. There is no reason why behavior therapy, for example, may not lift the noncompletion tendency by demonstrating that the completion of a particular sequence does not necessarily lead to disastrous consequences. Typically, this is done by small incremental steps, the first of which may not be anxiety arousing (i.e., conflictful) at all, and thus slowly removing the repression. Such a procedure may lead to the removal of phobias without inquiring about the aspects of the system that produced them. Nor is it necessary that such removal of the symptom bring on a new one, unless the repression that produced the symptom also operates on parts of the cognitive system that affect other aspects of action systems. If it does not, behavior therapy should be just as effective as psychoanalytic therapy, and may even be more so.

Another way of talking about the early experience and its importance for later development, or to make the distinction between the primary and the secondary process, is to consider infancy the time when certain innate action systems are first activated and are given their characterization in terms of attendant environmental events. At the first occurrence of certain actions,—including, of course, consummatory responses such as drinking and eating—the functional releasing stimuli for those action systems are registered and encoded. The occasions for eating (and, in parallel, those for going hungry) or the occasions for elimination are loosely defined by the evolutionary background of the organism. What specific stimuli or interpretations will be encoded with the release of the consummatory or terminal responses depends on early experiences.

More generally, early experiences establish the central interpretive basis for subsequent encounters with the environment and its effect on innate arousal or action mechanisms. These initial interpretations of environmental releasers are in a sense "automatic" since they are often identical with, and at least similar to, automatically released action patterns. This is most visible in lower animals but presumably occurs to some extent in humans. It can be hidden by the very rapid development, even in the infant, of complex information processing and rudimentary planning, such that the consequences of particular inputs can be evaluated and alternative actions taken in light of the "reality" of the environment. This use of the reality principle through complex cognitive transformations gives rise to the secondary process.

The last example again stresses both the importance and the impotence of our instinctual biological makeup. On the one hand, we are reminded of our evolutionary heritage; on the other, we note the ubiquitous role of our sociocultural-economic status, which directs our cognitions and may channel, exacerbate, or deny the expression of instinctual patterns. What is seen as frightening and aggressive, loving and sexual, warm and reassuring, may be influenced by similar evolutionary products, but it will be vastly different, depending on our cognitive-cultural history. Our perception of society changes with its structure, culture, and economic conditions. Social and historical understanding is more likely to lead to human understanding than ethological analogies are, just as the analysis of individual cognitions will lead to a better comprehension of individuals than the appeal to immutable early-childhood experiences will.

Questions about cognitive development are central to affective development, and the two may not in fact be distinguishable.[5] But there is an area of development that is not cognitive and that may be equally important in the developing emotions—that is, the emergence of autonomic functions.

THE DEVELOPMENT OF AUTONOMIC-VISCERAL FUNCTIONS

If the perception of autonomic nervous system (ANS) activity is necessary for the experience of "hot" emotions, then the development of such perception becomes part of the emotional development. And central to the role of peripheral autonomic responses is the implication that global arousal must be perceived in order to be "emotionally" effective. The perception of internal autonomic events, just like the perception of spatial and temporal events in the environment, depends on the acquisition of perceptual structures that govern what is perceived and what is perceivable. At present we know very little about the early development of the perception of autonomic events. We know that the autonomic activity of the newborn is immensely variable. That variation often occurs independently of external events. It seems reasonable to assume that the first steps toward building stable perceptual structures occur during this period. Of particular interest would be the development of individual thresholds for the perception of visceral arousal, since high and low thresholds for such perception may be one of the bases for the development of sociopathic and anxiety-neurotic response patterns, respectively (see below).

The interaction of visceral regulatory systems with early cognitive (and emotional) development deserves serious attention. In the very young child (as some-

5. See also Berscheid (in press [a]).

times in the adult), attention to arousing events is delayed until the autonomic nervous system has reacted (with a latency of one to two seconds or more). Detailed studies of the time course of this reaction and its development toward the generally much quicker adult response seem most important for an understanding of the development of emotional reactions in children. More generally, how do children learn to take advantage of the alerting function of the visceral system?

Related questions address the problem of the sympathetic-parasympathetic balance and the source of temperamental differences. Individuals differ in the relative balance between reactions of the sympathetic and parasympathetic nervous systems. Are these differences preset, or are they influenced by environmental events during development? Are they related to temperamental differences, which seem to be relatively innate in origin? Specifically, are differences in temperament (speed, attention, reactivity) related to physiological activity, to differences in differential attention and scanning of the world, or to both? What is their developmental course?

The resolution of some of these questions about cognitive and autonomic development will not only lead to a better understanding of emotional development in childhood but also provide a better basis for understanding the operation of evaluation and of autonomic perception in the adult. For example, both the relative richness of evaluative schemas and the sensitivity to arousal will determine how the adult reacts to and experiences emotional situations.

Emotion and Memory

A generally accepted intuitive notion holds that the way we feel determines what we do and remember and also influences what we take in and pay attention to. The evidence from a variety of experiments bears out that intuition.[6] To summarize rather selectively: when people are made to feel good, they will look on other people more positively[7] and also feel better about goods that they have purchased;[8] they will evaluate ambiguous scenes more positively[9] and do the same with ambiguous facial expressions;[10] and they will help others.[11] Similar (and opposite) effects, though with greater variability, are found when people are made to feel bad.

Research[12] on hypnotic induction of mood states (such as happy and sad) showed a state-dependent memory; people recalled more events (whether laboratory-induced or natural personal occurrences) when the moods during acquisition and recall were the same than when they were different.[13] Induced moods

6. Bower (1981), Clark and Isen (1982), and Isen, Means, Patrick, and Nowicki (1982).
7. Gouaux (1971).
8. Isen, Shalker, Clark, and Karp (1978).
9. Isen and Shalker (1977).
10. Schiffenbauer (1974).
11. Isen (1970), Isen and Levin (1972).
12. Bower (1981), Bower and Cohen (1982).
13. E.g., Bower, Gilligan, and Monteiro (1981).

also influenced fantasies, associations and judgments, and they increased attention to events congruent with the induced mood. But mood induction during recall alone did not selectively produce better recall of mood-congruent facts; recall was affected only by the congruence between the subjects' mood during acquisition and their mood during recall.[14]

A variety of hypotheses try to explain these phenomena. Gordon Bower and his colleagues[15] suggest that the data and ancillary observations favor a selective-reminding hypothesis for the recall phenomena. When an episode at the time of acquisition reminds the individual of personal, related events, he or she is more likely to attend to and remember the target episode. However, the selective-reminding hypothesis, though probably correct for sheer recall data, does not adequately account for the wealth of other data on social facilitation, personal preferences, and so on. Another hypothesis, also partially correct, is the intensity hypothesis,[16] which assumes that the intensity of the emotion at the time of the experience determines how well the event is remembered. I discussed another aspect of this proposal in Chapter 11; focusing during stress may under different circumstances increase or decrease attention to the various events taking place at the time, depending on the centrality of the target event. It is also true that specific tests for memory show retrograde effects on memory when the emotional experience is extreme; a shocking event decreases memory for the details of the surrounding events.[17] Most of these cases are probably best viewed from the perspective of a narrowed cognitive (conscious) capacity that does not permit processing of noncentral events.

Explanations of the facilitations produced by the gentler feeling states have focused on an activation account that implicates stored "feelings" or "moods" that are aroused and that are related to other relevant memory contents. I shall explore such an explanation, but first note that it is unlikely that any single hypothesis either can or should account for the memory-emotion effects. It is likely that all of the various hypotheses, under some circumstances, are adequate explanations of the observed effects. Selective reminding, intensity, and specific feeling activation can easily operate side by side.

The major hypothesis that has been advanced regarding the effect of feeling and mood states on cognition and behavior postulates the existence of "pure" feeling entities in the underlying mental representation.[18] The general assumption is that "descriptions of emotional events feed excitation into the corresponding emotion node"[19] or that "some nodes represent feeling tone" and that memories "which are closely associated" with such a node form a mental category.[20] Though this is rarely stated specifically, these nodes are assumed to be given in the mental armamentarium. Even when cognitive conditions for their activation are postu-

14. Bower, Gilligan, and Monteiro (1981).
15. Bower, Monteiro, and Gilligan (1978).
16. Dutta and Kanungo (1975).
17. Loftus and Burns (1982).
18. Bower (1981), Isen, Shalker, Clark, and Karp (1978), and Clark and Isen (1982).
19. Bower (1981).
20. Clark and Isen (1982).

lated, the existence of the nodes themselves is assumed.[21] In other words, these nodes function just as the emotions do in fundamental-emotion theories. For a constructivist position, the cognitive conditions themselves are likely to determine the emotional quality, and we will examine possible ways in which such nodes, schemas, or categories could be established.

First of all, the major source of emotional induction used in these studies is evaluative. Certain classes of evaluative cognitions exist that activate associated states, behaviors, and cognitions. The term *feeling* or *mood*, used so often in these studies, suggests that little arousal is involved, though certainly under some conditions true emotional states are produced. Therefore, we need to find a mechanism by which generic evaluative cognitions can be represented in mental structures in such a way that their activation will spread to structures representing thoughts and behaviors not initially activated. We need not worry too much about accompanying arousal. In fact, I doubt whether proposals that suggest that arousal (or arousal imagery) may also be implicated in mood induction are viable.[22] Without the appropriate evaluative states, autonomic arousal does not produce emotional states; the structures that represent arousal do not, when activated, provide any spreading activation to evaluations or to any feelings or emotions as such.

There are various ways in which we can accommodate the findings about the arousal of behaviors and memories through the induction of moods. The way in which selective reminding is handled is fairly obvious. Schemas that represent certain past experiences are activated, and either the accompanying moods are part of these activated schemas or the experience itself, possibly because of some discrepant or interrupting consequences, produces the feeling state. However, in the absence of phenomena like selective reminding, we need to find some way in which the occurrence of an evaluation (mood, feeling) will activate other relevant structures.

One possibility that immediately comes to mind is that the abstract (generic) evaluative structures, which I discussed earlier, may be implicated. I suggested that the frequent occurrence of certain cognitions that constitute a particular value will themselves form a new generic structure. Given its rather abstract nature, such a schema will typically be activated when its various elements are activated, that is, when it is instantiated. This is consistent with the experimental evidence that moods are best instantiated when people are asked to imagine specific mood-relevant experiences. Another possibility is that schemas of events and objects that have some evaluative cognitions incorporated in their structure (see Chapter 9) provide the bridge that joins various experiences, so that when an experience that includes a particular evaluation is activated, the fact that this feature is also a member of other schemas will serve to spread of activation. It is likely, though, that the activation of a single feature will not be sufficient to activate an entirely different schema; other similarities between the two will be

21. Bower and Cohen (1982).
22. Clark (1982).

needed. At present, there is little evidence indicating how the spread of activation from experiences and moods (evaluations) to other experiences (more or less related) works.

Changing Mental Structures

One of the consequences of a distinction between "conscious" and "unconscious" processing is a possible difference in the kind of changes that may be brought about in the cognitive and action systems. We often require hypotheses about the structure of our thoughts and actions, and the testing and retesting of such hypotheses. This process of testing and examining possible hypotheses takes place primarily in consciousness. It is only when a hypothesis or "theory" about a particular mental structure is "correct," in the sense that it makes adequate predictions about the outcomes of those structures, that it might be possible to manipulate those structures. To effect changes in human action, we must generate some plausible explanations of its cognitive and environmental antecedents. Consciousness plays an important part in this external manipulation by others (whether they are psychotherapists, friends, or prison wardens). In any case, *hypotheses* about cognitive structures occur in consciousness, and, once the consequences of these cognitive structures are evaluated, it becomes possible to consider potential new structures and new consequences.

Acquisition and loss, or learning and forgetting, are not symmetric processes. The notion of symmetry has a long history in psychology. It used to be thought that the events that instigate a particular drive state and those that reduce it are symmetrical, or that the conditions that produce the learning of some behavior and those that produce its forgetting or unlearning are isomorphic and complementary. Theory and research, in the motivational area as well as in learning and psychotherapy,[23] suggest that turning a particular process on and turning it off may rely on two completely different mechanisms.

Central to the symmetry notion has been the relation between the acquisition and the extinction of behavior, which has been ascribed to reinforcement and its absence, respectively. At the same time, it has been obvious that though a response that is not reinforced may be inaccessible in the future, this does not necessarily entail that it has been lost or unlearned. This issue is complex, but it is introduced as an illustration of the complexities that we face when dealing with the acquisition, change, or loss of mental structures.

A particular mental schema structures a set of environmental events so that they bring about certain behavioral outcomes. When, in the course of everyday life or as a result of deliberate intervention, these structures are changed so that the same event now leads to a new outcome, several possibilities exist as to how this may happen. First, the old structure may be changed to a new structure, such that the new structure leads to a new outcome. When that happens, the old structure may still be available and, in fact, both old and new products may

23. Deutsch (1960) and Costello (1970).

occur. Thus, we may learn that a particular park can be appreciated for its lovely flowers and need not be evaluated entirely in terms of poignant memories of unrequited love. Second, a new action outcome may be assimilated into the old structure—in which case the old outcome is not available any more. For example, a student may come to address her old professor by his first name. The cognition of respect and love would be essentially unchanged, but it would assimilate "Peter" instead of "Professor Pan" as one of its behavioral outcomes. Finally, a new structure with a new outcome may be developed—and the old structure is changed or deleted so as not to be accessible any more. A patient might learn to reevaluate his interactions with women. Instead of the perception of threat and consequent avoidance, he now perceives acceptance and warmth and behaves accordingly.

Since the differences between the old and the new outcomes may be differences between emotional reactions and nonemotional ones, the process of such change is of some interest. I am concerned with processes whereby old structures change into new ones and with the fate of the old structure under those circumstances. In some cases of behavior therapy, the replacement of old with new outcomes while maintaining the old structure is of interest, although in many cases that structure may change.

Ulric Neisser,[24] following Piaget's notions of assimilation and accommodation, described three kinds of structural changes: *absorption*, where new structures are developed that contain effectively all of the old structures; *displacement*, where the old and new structure continue to "exist side by side"; and *integration*, where new structures—at a more comprehensive level—still contain parts of the old. I shall deal illustratively with some of these processes.

The change of a mental structure is dependent on the history and evaluation of the old structure and on the development and value of the new structure, just as if they were theories of the individual's behavior. It is fairly clear that the acquisition of new structures that do not interfere significantly with existing ones is a problem different from that of *replacing* existing ones with new ones. For example, if a child learns a particular structure for the manipulation of algebraic symbols (i.e., she learns algebra), very little in the way of existing structures needs to be replaced. In such a case, it appears that the individual may often be given a verbal program for those structures that, given the appropriate translations of the verbal symbols, may be applied to the material manipulated, and a slow development of a new structure takes place, unimpeded by old structures. One interesting aspect of the acquisition of new structures is the difference between telling people what a structure ought to be and letting them manipulate the objects or symbols that are to be structured—the distinction between classical instructional and discovery methods.[25]

The establishment of a new structure is like the establishment of a new theory in science—hypotheses are applied to a given body of data. The parallel also extends to the current existence of old structures, current theories that must be

24. Neisser (1962).
25. Bruner (1961).

replaced by new ones. This replacement occurs as it does *historically* in the development of science, not the way it necessarily occurs for the individual scientist. It consists of a partly deductive, partly inductive process, in which new hypotheses about the structure of the individual's behavior and experience are generated and tested. The process involves asking questions about the whys and hows of one's actions. Given an existing old structure that handles the data base, although it may have unwanted outcomes, as in the case of neurotic behavior, the replacement is relatively slow. New cognitive structures are evaluated and tested with possible actions and their consequences. New behavior may be attempted in order to check its satisfactory fit to the new structure. This is what is generally known as "working through" or "experiencing" in the therapeutic situation. Individuals develop new hypotheses about the structures that mediate their behavior; they try out these hypotheses against experience and may use some of these structures to generate new behaviors in whole or in part. In the process, the structure of the new "theory" about inputs and desired outputs is slowly developed, tested, and established. This may be done in daily life, and is probably done in many cases without the benefit of clergy, therapists, or friends. It may also be the case that the information necessary to produce the new structure is available but that the conceptual work has not been done. This is one of those cases in which a therapist may tell a patient: "Consider what you have done, look at what you're doing, examine the relation between these various things that have happened, discover that outcomes have always been of a particular kind; doesn't it make sense that the following hypothesis adequately accounts for your experiences and your behavior?" A new theory or structure may then be created. A similar case may occur when an individual, given a new hypothesis, generates the data from her experience, from her memory of herself, and finds that many things that have happened in the past fit the new hypothesis, which may then be tested and established.

In none of these cases does it appear to be necessary that the old structure is changed at all. It is just replaced by a new one. The "residual" old structures may become the basis for some types of fantasy experience.[26]

The creation of new structures replacing old ones describes much of what occurs in behavior therapy. By contrast, classical dynamic theorists have always maintained that the old structures are "still there" and that, even though the old behavior may not occur, these old structures may "show up" in other unwanted behavior.[27]

Under what conditions *are* the old structures deleted, absorbed, or integrated? An aspect of insight therapy consists of an examination of what the old structure is—what is my old "theory"? In that case it is necessary to examine one's thought and action and to determine what theories, or structures, adequately explain the current link between inputs and behavior. Insight therapy and the extensive processes of psychoanalysis require an investigation of the current experience *and* an examination of hypotheses that will fit it. These hypotheses, or old structures, may be changed by changing parts of the old structures into

26. Rosenbaum (1972).
27. See, e.g., Weitzman (1971).

new ones. When old structures are changed to new ones, they are "brought into consciousness"; by continually developing and testing hypotheses, one makes them available to consciousness. The "making conscious" of old "unconscious" processes entails the development of hypotheses and testing them; the development of new structures goes through the same process.

Many unsuccessful cases of psychotherapy are those in which structures or theories are developed that are appealing (i.e., sound useful) but are, in fact, nonworking. The use of bad theories that explain only an inadequate part of the data is not unknown in science, and scientists hold on to those just as jealously as individuals hold on to pseudoexplanations of their own behavior.

This conception raises questions of insight into personal motivation. Clearly, if we want to know why we have done something, we need to know about the structure that leads to a particular action system. We may have available an "explanation" of our "motive"—a secondary structure "about the action" that has access to conscious experience. What is its relation to the structure that actually leads to action? We might believe that a particular structure is "responsible" for a certain action when, in fact, some other "unconscious" structure brings about the action.

In general we say that people have "insight" into their actions when the structures that lead to action and those that lead to a conscious state are isomorphic. Other variations are interesting exercises in the vagaries of human insight and delusion.

The question of insight into personal motivation is important in the context of psychotherapy, because it is well known that informing patients what their "underlying" motives are is of no particular use in modifying their behavior. When a psychotherapist infers what the structure is that leads to a particular kind of action and then tells the patient, her "telling the patient" is not equivalent to the patient's inspection of the cognitive system. In some unusual circumstances, this input may be checked against the actual action structure; it may be found to be similar, and insight may be gained. However, since the verbal formulations of the therapist tend to deviate considerably from the structure that mediates a particular action, that situation is unlikely. It is necessary to encourage the patient to test and elaborate on what the structures might be that mediate certain actions. If these hypotheses are correct (i.e., if he is developing the appropriate hypotheses about that particular structure), then it is likely that he would be able to interfere with and change it. In other words, by "knowing and using" these structures, first insight might be developed, and change can then follow. Changes will occur to the extent to which the patient can use the experience and action system as a private laboratory for generating and testing hypotheses. Once again, cognitive structures are changed and generated by action.

THE PSYCHOTHERAPY OF EVERYDAY LIFE

One of the maxims of contemporary psychology holds that behavior can often best be understood by looking at the extremes, by investigating the causes and cures of abnormal cases. That point of view is reasonable and has been very useful, but the complementary case has often been ignored and should also be considered. Specifically, what can we learn about abnormal behavior by studying the common or normal case? To illustrate, let us look at some normal phobias that are amenable to intervention without any extensive therapeutic apparatus or intensive treatment of the patient.

Consider the traveler who has been told that she must under no circumstances drink any water in Slobovia. She is given detailed and gory descriptions of the consequences of any transgression. Her behavior is clearly phobic as we observe her in Slobovia. She avoids water like the plague, rinses the top of soft-drink bottles with distilled water, refuses to eat fruits and vegetables that might have been rinsed in the local water, and even eyes beer with suspicion if it is of local production. We might assume that curing the poor woman of her phobia would involve either extensive psychotherapy, to discover the unconscious motives that have imbued water with some special symbolic significance, or extensive sessions with a behavior therapist, during which she slowly deals with Slobovian water by first just thinking about it and, finally, after extensive work, taking a sip. Such are the consequences of thinking about normal behavior in terms of an abnormal model. In fact, many cases similar to that of our unfortunate traveler can usually be cured in one session, which is never considered to be therapeutic in the psychological sense, nor does it involve much expenditure of effort or funds. Any authoritative statement from somebody whose opinion she respects (e.g., her physician or a local resident whom she has known for many years) declaring Slobovian water to be perfectly safe or actually better than the water she has been drinking all her life immediately cures the phobia, with hardly any remnant of the phobic behavior or any fear that the "underlying conflict" will reappear in some other context.

The lesson to be drawn from this example—and there are numerous others in everyday life, is simple: there exist many programs and structures that are available to consciousness and addressable in ordinary language. Being available and being capable of unequivocal statement, they apparently are easily changed and either removed or suppressed. There is nothing new about the existence of such programs. A variety of different plans and structures are continually being changed without any great difficulty; they include simple things like driving to a particular location, or complicated ones like understanding social relations and who talks to whom and why. The insight provided by our example is that the same kinds of programs apparently exist for abnormal and for superficially maladaptive behavior and that we should consider how structures that underlie "true" maladaptive behavior may be affected; some simple interventions may often be quite useful.

The difference between the "true" phobia and that of our example is, of course, that the real phobic cannot usually be treated with a simple instruction from an authoritative source. The question then is, Why not? The psychoanalytic answer—one quite appropriate from our point of view—is obvious: the structures that underlie phobic behaviors are not available to consciousness, cannot be spoken, and therefore are not amenable to change by simple instructions.

The obvious answer is to make these programs as available to consciousness as is the program of our Slobovian traveler.

I have indicated two general ways in which structures that are not available to consciousness, and therefore not available to immediate testing, may be changed. One system invokes laborious methods of hypothesis testing and of determining what the underlying structures are; the other involves building new structures and circumventing the unpalatable consequences of the existing structures. The latter is often described as the major goal of behavior therapy. It is useful at this point to spend some more time on an analysis of what happens when the methods of operant conditioning are used in the alleviation of unwanted symptoms.

The methods developed in the conditioning laboratory and used so effectively in the management of both lower animals and some human situations are unequivocal in developing structures between inputs and outputs. They allow little variance in behavior, and they are invariant with respect to the specific means-ends relations of the given situation. Operant conditioning techniques, in particular, have been especially useful in demonstrating these characteristics. Data from Skinner boxes are clean and easily repeatable and permit insight into the behavior of a single animal. Any conditioning technique, whether operant or Pavlovian or whatever, builds up mental structures (see Chapter 3). When the method that develops such structures is equivocal, it will take much longer for the organism to develop a stable structure that has a specified outcome. I can tell somebody to put a pencil on the table and be fairly sure that his behavior will be easily predictable; I can achieve the same result by operant reinforcement techniques. It just takes longer. However, in an organism that cannot use language, because it is either not human or not quite fully grown human, as in the case of the very young child, I have no better way of communicating what the proper means-end structure is than using operant conditioning techniques.

Thus, we can view operant conditioning and shaping techniques as ways of instructing the organism about new structures (designed, for example, to avoid unpleasant consequences). The operant methods—and, by analogy, the methods used by behavior therapists and behavior modifiers—are ways of instructing organisms that either cannot talk or cannot speak about the programs that we wish to change. The former situation applies to rats and infants, the latter to the phobic patient. We can thus speak a program to be used or we can teach it. Or, to turn B. F. Skinner's viewpoint around, operant conditioning may be used as a shortcut when language is not available.

Personality, Pathology, and Individual Differences

In this section I shall examine a variety of topics as they relate to emotion, specifically: How are differences among individuals generated, personality patterns initiated, and extreme (or abnormal) emotional states or action patterns produced?

Most theories of maladjustment, psychopathology, and personality deal with anxiety in one way or another as a central concept. If anxiety, helplessness, and distress can be deduced from the interruption notion by coupling emotional arousal with the unavailability of relevant or substitute actions, a variety of speculations in the field of psychopathology and personality theory emerge.

The idea that reactions to interruption or frustration are central to personality development is not new in psychology.[28] The emphasis on the consequences of interruption, however, permits us to look afresh at some classical problems.

Among the important consequences of interruption—from the point of view of psychopathology—are those that do and those that do not provide substitutable behavior. Any highly organized sequence that is interrupted and that does not then lead to some substitute completion will result in anxiety, here engendered by helplessness and the absence of an appropriate organized action. In this view, free-floating anxiety does not stem from the generalization of the anxiety response from some initial traumatic association; instead, anxiety is conditional on the absence of appropriate environmental stimuli and associated actions.

Symptom formation might occur when some objectively inappropriate response systems are used in the completion of the interrupted sequence. Just as in psychoanalytic theory, and in keeping with the inhibition model of anxiety that Kessen and I have advocated,[29] the symptom protects the organism from the appearance of anxiety because it avoids the deleterious effects of interruption. But, instead of asking what satisfaction of what need has been frustrated, I would suggest that we investigate the specific "goal path" that has been diverted, goal and path being given equal weight.

This suggests that therapeutic efforts should deal equally with acceptable substitute completions (not necessarily including the original "goal"), with a change of path that might bypass the interruption, with removal of the environmental or intrapsychic blocking agent, and with actual achievement of the original goal path. Such a conceptual approach indicates that both behavior therapy[30] and depth therapy may contribute to the alleviation of symptom and anxiety, that these approaches are complementary rather than mutually exclusive.

Therapy, then, may successfully tackle the problem of maladaptive behavior from any one of a variety of vantage points, and the opposing claims of different schools of psychotherapy may express mainly preferences for attacking one or another facet of the problem. It may be important for the therapist to determine the locus in the sequence where an attack offers the most likely signs of success. Depending on whether the goal path should be retained, whether plans need replacing, or whether some other intervention seems most promising, different therapeutic techniques might be indicated. But first the therapist might usefully consider what it is that has been interrupted.

For illustrative purposes, I will cite some quite different but relevant examples from the literature. Work on so-called fixated behavior[31] has found that the

28. See Rosenzweig (1944).
29. Kessen and Mandler (1961).
30. E.g., Wolpe (1958) and Kanfer and Phillips (1970).
31. Maier (1949).

most successful method for breaking the "fixation" consists of guiding the animals to the new response sequence or forcing the performance of the consummatory response, from which the new organized sequence can then be built up.

In a different context, consider the symptomatology of acute grief, the emotional behavior following the "sudden cessation of social interaction."[32] The management of these reactions stresses the importance of "finding new patterns of rewarding interaction." It is not necessarily the affectionate nature of the interaction with the deceased but rather its intensity and frequency, the degree of meshing, that determines the severity of the grief reaction. Grief is an important emotional consequence of interruption; a review of the nature and significance of grief concluded that grief "comprises a sterotyped set of psychological and physiological reactions of biological origin."[33] It is not necessary to ascribe a specific innate role to the emotion of grief, as in making the distinction between mourning (behavior determined by particular social and learned factors) and grief (considered to be of biological origin). The extreme degrees of disruption and interruption occasioned by the loss of a loved member of one's social environment are adequate to explain the appearance of grief. In particular, in groups that are socially cohesive and in which cohesiveness has become a factor in their survival, increasing numbers of plans and structures exist that incorporate particular individuals. Thus, the more elaborate the cognitive structures that need particular individuals for their execution are, the more complex the interruptive and disruptive reactions to loss will be.[34] How intense the effect of such a loss can be is seen in the high levels of anxiety, sometimes approaching panic, that characterize grief.[35]

A final word about frustration tolerance. What the organism does in the face of interruption depends on previous experiences with interruption situations. Freud[36] argued that the ability to delay gratification (completion) marks the triumph of the reality principle, or rationality. Given an interrupted sequence of behavior, the ability to delay—the tendency not to employ the immediately available substitutes or completions—simply makes it more likely that, as the situation changes, more appropriate substitutions will become more probable. The ability to delay following an interruption provides a wider choice of possible substitute actions. Thus, the problem of frustration tolerance becomes the problem of being able to "hold" in the face of mounting arousal and distress. Similar to a learned tendency to delay, learned tendencies to remove the tension brought about by interruption may exist. But here I am back in the mainstream of personality theory, and the readers can complete this sequence according to their own theoretical predilections.

The problem of individual differences in emotional dispositions or emotional reactions is complex; at present, there is no description of personality dimensions

32. Lindemann (1944).
33. Averill (1968).
34. See Berscheid (1982, 1983) and Berscheid, Gangestad, and Kulakowski (in press [a]).
35. Parkes (1972).
36. Freud ([1911] 1975).

that goes beyond the suggestive or that leads to reasonable predictive and explanatory systems. The fact that most personality evaluations and scales available today have relatively little descriptive and explanatory value[37] suggests two possible conclusions. One is that the highly variable nature of early experiences and child-rearing practices (and the resulting cognitive interpretations of the environment) makes it unlikely that simple dimensions can be found that will account for a reasonable number of the differences in individual behavior. The second possibility is that there are no overriding innate, biological characteristics that characterize individuals over and above the large degree of variance introduced by cognitive interpretations, which are developed by their early and later experiences.

In a sense, the emotional system we have described is a system of individual differences, of emotional experiences that are, to a large extent, idiosyncratic. Short of knowing the biological inheritance of individuals and their complete history, it is essentially impossible to predict their reactions to specific situations. This is not a counsel of despair; instead it is a general statement that scientific systems are not designed and do not intend to predict the behavior of objects or systems, which are unique combinations of innumerable variables.

Two possible strategies for finding significant individual variation are available to us. One of them is to describe some general sensitivities to environmental events that may characterize an individual's emotional reaction and that may allow some prediction; the other is to discover whether, within a particular culture or society, there are preferred cognitive systems that will predict differences in emotional response. The former approach leads to the construction of personality scales. The second is represented by the psychoanalytic approach, which suggests that there are major sources of cognitive interpretations that lead to the functional release of emotional reactions, and that these major sources are few in number and related to specific complexes of early childhood experiences.

PERSONALITY SCALES

As far as paper-and-pencil personality tests are concerned, I suggested in Chapter 10 that answers to questions on a personality questionnaire indicate predilections toward interpreting a set of situations in a particular way. The scales provide one index (and only one out of a range of possible ways of measuring cognitive structures) of the manner in which events are functionally interpreted. Thus, individuals scoring high on a text-anxiety scale interpret test situations as threatening, interrupting. These situations are reinterpreted and become functional arousers for the autonomic nervous system. If this says that pencil-and-paper tests tell us only what people "think" about situations, it is probably correct but should not be dismissed lightly. The way in which a person thinks about a situation tells us how it is evaluated and appraised; in short, it shows what struc-

37. Mischel (1968).

tures are used to transform the situation into the kind of stimuli with which the action and arousal systems must eventually deal.

H. J. Eysenck[38] has interpreted two major dimensions of personality tests, which he calls introversion-extroversion (I-E) and neuroticism (N), in terms of conditionability (for the I-E dimension) and emotionality (for the N dimension). Relative to the variables that address the two-factor theory of emotion, the I-E dimension may describe the degree of arousal in response to arousal signals, or it may be related to the perception of arousal or to the interpretation of signals as being relevant to arousal. It seems unlikely that differential levels of arousals account for the I-E dimension unless it can be shown that all kinds of arousal signals, whether they are aversive or not (including both fearful and joyful situations), elicit the same, idiosyncratic degree of arousal for a given person. However, differences in arousal along the I-E dimension occur only for aversive signals.[39] With a single arousal system the individual differences must be found in the interpretation of the environment and in the differential likelihood that individuals will see the world as threatening or not. Once they see it as threatening, the arousal system comes into effect. If I-E is, in fact, indexed by a greater degree of conditionability, specifically to threatening stimuli, or by a greater sensitivity to punishment or frustration, then it seems unlikely that either the arousal system or the perception of arousal is involved; instead, we are probably dealing with a perceptual-cognitive phenomenon. If that is true, it is possible that the N dimension accounts for differences in arousal. Clearly, whether we call that dimension "emotionality" or "sensitivity to reinforcers," individual differences in the degree of arousal would produce differences in the degree of emotionality and in the differential sensitivity to reinforcement. Thus both a positive and a negative reinforcement, interpreted appropriately, would produce arousal, the effect of which would be attenuated or amplified by the individual's arousal system and its tendency to be activated.

To summarize, we assume that Eysenck's introversion-extroversion dimension orders individuals according to their tendency to interpret events as threatening, punishing, or frustrating, whereas the neuroticism dimension orders people according to differential degrees of arousal.

Personality scales and the measurement of personality types vary in the degree of abstractness of the concepts they employ and in the generality of the predictions they make. Anxiety scales deal with the experience of anxiety in specific situations; psychoanalytic theory claims pervasive effects of personality types in practically all aspects of human endeavors.

It is central to the psychoanalytic theory of personality constellations that specific emotional structures are developed very early in life in respect to the major modes of mastering the environment in the oral, anal, and genital areas. Schemas are built up that give meaning to the environment in relation to these early concepts, whether they are part of emotional structures or not. It is assumed,

38. E.g., Eysenck (1967).
39. Gray (1970).

for example, that a very high-level abstract "oral" schema becomes related not only to modes of taking in food but also to attitudes toward and ideas about supplies of love and support, to uses of the oral apparatus in speaking and communicating, and to a variety of other minor ways of expressing oral concerns. It is similarly argued that anal-retentive attitudes relate to other abstract schemas (e.g., to problems of money management). However, the more abstract and higher in the hierarchy a concept is, the more diffuse its expressions at the lowest levels of specific everyday concepts and uses will be. Thus, in order to show that one's attitude toward savings banks is related to a thirty-year-old schema at the "anal" abstract level, one must postulate extensive and complex networks of schemas. The more abstract the emotional structure is, the more diffuse its manifestations will be, the less consistent the behavior that it is supposed to predict, and the fewer the hard data with which to support it. On the other hand, the lower (or more concrete) a particular emotional structure is, the easier it is to demonstrate its applicability to very specific situations and very specific behavior, the more likely its expression in a limited set of behaviors, and the easier the marshaling of data in its support. As a corollary, the more diffuse the evidence and the manifestations of a higher-order abstract structure are, the less likely it is to be immediately obvious in the day-to-day life of the individual, and the more difficult it will be to intervene—that is, to change the unwanted relation between the abstract notion and the emotional expression.

Schema theory supports the possibility of the broad abstract personality structures that psychoanalytic theory assumes, but at the same time it implies that their function is going to be of less importance than that of structures that are at a lower level of abstraction and generality and of more immediate relevance to the life of the individual. Thus, the conclusion that situational factors frequently override personality dispositions should not be surprising.

Finally, the restriction of these abstract structures to oral, anal, and genital events has seriously hampered the development of a useful psychoanalytic taxonomy of personality types. By limiting the number of types to three or four or five, we are forced into an unnecessarily restrictive classification. There should be no reason to exclude other abstract schemas, dealing with equally important events, that may be at the same level of abstraction and importance as the ones suggested by Freud. Among these, as I suggested earlier, are the management of pain, problems of cold and hunger, the management of sleep, the relation to violence and aggression, and many others. These abstract syndromes will vary in importance as a function of the individual's background, his social class, and his specific experiences. The systems developed by Freud for a middle-class, turn-of-the-century society and its syndromes may not be appropriate today for classes other than the ones with which he dealt.

PSYCHOPATHY

Individual differences in the sensitivity or lability of the autonomic nervous system may be, as was suggested earlier, of great relevance in emotional development and expression. In a provocative paper on the origins and functions of the psychopathic personality, Stanley Schachter and Bibb Latané[40] proposed that psychopaths or sociopaths are constitutionally adrenalin sensitive and have at the same time learned to ignore their autonomic reactions. Psychopaths are more responsive to adrenalin (i.e., they show stronger ANS reactions to adrenalin injections), but they also show less emotion, which suggests that they ignore their autonomic reactions. I have put forward some possible mechanisms during the early learning of autonomic perception that are relevant both to the antecedents of psychopathic personality structures and to the development of emotion-sensitive, possibly neurotic, personality structures.

> If . . . the psychopath grows up in an environment that either ignores, punishes, or indiscriminately reinforces emotional responses that occur with autonomic stimulation, he will learn not to discriminate his autonomic stimuli. We assume that he has learned to ignore normal levels of arousal. However, there will be some occasions when the psychopath's physiological stimuli are so intense that they cannot be ignored, and emotional responses will in fact occur. It also appears that even the psychopath likes to "feel" every now and then. Now, if he can only distinguish high levels of stimulation then, by definition, his threshold for emotional responsiveness is very high; low levels or autonomic stimulation which drive the emotional behavior of the normal are not effective for the psychopath. If—as I believe—the normal has to learn to keep his autonomic level relatively low in order not to be in a constant state of emotional upheaval, then the psychopath needs not learn to keep his autonomic level low. His autonomic stimuli can operate—in response to external stimulation or not—at a much higher level than they do in the normal, and without producing continuous upheaval. What I am suggesting is that while the normal learns to be adrenalin- or stimulation-insensitive in order to be able to remain calm, the psychopath handles the problem by just not noticing the stimulation. But then high levels of autonomic arousal will occur more frequently in the psychopath than in the normal. Thus, the "ignoring" mechanism can produce both high levels of autonomic response and low levels of emotion. The psychopath may in fact be more sensitive (autonomically) to emotional stimuli in the environment since he—or at least some psychopaths—in fact seeks levels of autonomic stimulation high enough to produce emotion (the "kick-seeker"). Similarly, the normal who has not learned to keep levels of autonomic stimulation at low levels becomes an anxiety neurotic, continuously exposed to autonomic levels above his threshold.[41]

Stuart Valins followed up this suggestion in offering the hypothesis that "although the psychopath experiences and perceives his bodily changes, he ignores them in the sense of not utilizing them as cues when evaluating emotional situations."[42] Psychopathic subjects were unaffected by a procedure that misinformed them about the actual heart rate they were experiencing, whereas normal subjects used this heart-rate feedback as a cue for evaluating emotional stimuli. Similarly, psychopathic subjects were unable to "produce" galvanic skin responses, which normal subjects could do.[43] Thus the psychopaths do tend to ignore auto-

40. Schachter and Latané (1964).
41. Mandler (1964b).
42. Valins (1970).
43. Stern and Kaplan (1967).

nomic feedback and also are less able to influence their ANS reactions. On the other hand, no systematic data are available to indicate that they may seek autonomic stimulation—that is, stimulation at levels well above that produced in the normal individual.

The hypothesis states that psychopaths fail to respond to the moral imperative of their autonomic response and thus display antisocial behavior. They also may seek the emotional stimulation that they lack and thus enter into and produce situations that are more deviant than the ones that normals usually seek out or generate.

EMOTIONAL INVOLVEMENT

It is a truism to say that a situation becomes emotionally important to the extent that one feels personally involved or feels that the situation is personally relevant. This is not an explanatory statement, but it asserts that there are mechanisms whereby innocuous situations become personally important or relevant. One might seek an explanation by considering a particular example and seeing how the degree of personal involvement changes as various aspects of the situation change. Consider a range of situations in which the same event displays significant differences and different emphases.

The general event of a child's being run over by an automobile may come to our attention from our reading a brief notice in an out-of-town newspaper, from a similar notice in the local paper referring to a nearby street corner, from that same notice referring to the child of a neighbor, from our actually seeing it happen to a child we know, and, in the extreme case, from our being the child involved in such an accident. The degree of emotional involvement clearly increases from an initial nonemotional, intellectual taking-in of the information to personal terror, fear, and grief.

The degree of personal involvement can be measured by the degree to which the situation concerned permits us to see ourselves as participants in the events or scene described or imagined. Descriptions and experiences of complex events are often represented as images, as representations that are manipulable within the cognitive system. One asks: To what extent can I put myself as an actor into that situation? Such an operation on or transformation of an image from one involving other people to one involving the self is relatively simple, when one of the actors could be the self. The example I have used requires that the image of the accident be made "relevant" to the individual by the establishment of a relation between some of the actors in the image and the perceiver. The injections of the self into the image may take a variety of forms; consider two major ones. One of them makes the child involved a child of the perceiver; the other puts the perceiver in the role of the driver of the car. Which projection of the self the individual will engage in is a function of his or her previous experiences and history. However, it seems to be fairly clear that putting the self into the image and carrying out the actions involved produces certain consequences that may in turn be functional stimuli for arousal. Thus, the loss of a child or having caused the death of a child leads to an outcome that produces arousal and thus emotional response and involvement.

Another example, more useful because it demonstrates some of the other mechanisms involved in the use of central images, can be found in the area of human sexuality. An account of homosexual behavior may vary in its emotional consequences to the degree to which the situation described is one in which the self may reasonably be a participant. Such an evaluation will vary with a description of the scene involved, the circumstances under which it takes place ("Are these circumstances in which the self may in fact ever appear?"), and the reality aspects of the situation. Clearly, there may also be repressive consequences for some of the outcomes, once the self has been put into the image. The very notion of seeing onself in a homosexual situation may, on the basis of past history, range from very pleasurable to highly frightening. In the latter case, a repressive mechanism or such classic mechanisms as denial ("I don't even see the situation as a homosexual one") may be operating. One of the reasons why bad pornography is frequently sexually nonarousing is that the descriptions of the situations are so ludicrous and unrealistic that people find it very difficult to imagine themselves as participants.

Finally, since there is good evidence that individuals vary in their use of visual imagery, how might these differences affect emotional functioning? Our own research[44] suggests that individuals who prefer visual codes tend to be concrete; that is, they see situations as presented and do not generalize to the generic case as easily as those who use verbal codes. Therefore, high-imagery individuals who tend to generate visual images of a particular scene are more likely to see it in its specific context, rather than as an example of a more general (and less threatening?) situation. They are also more likely to be tied to the immediate emotional demands of that situation. Concreteness and emotionality may go hand in hand. Relations among differences in electrical activity of the brain, imagery, and personality types suggest that visualizers may be hypersensitive and that verbalizers are calm and even tempered.[45]

Sex—A Different Emotion?

Until now we have discussed the arousal involved in emotional states as if it were of a piece—general autonomic, usually sympathetic arousal, which is perceived globally and integrated with cognitive signals. But there is one arousal system that is significantly different from the primarily sympathetic system that I have discussed up until now. In the discussion of the autonomic nervous system, I made the distinction between sympathetic and parasympathetic arousal. I noted that these two systems tend to be complementary and to act in concert rather

44. Hollenberg (1970), Stewart (1965), and Anderson (1973).
45. McFarlane-Smith (1964).

than being alternate ways of responding. It is also likely, in terms of their function, that these two systems have different evolutionary significances and histories.

If all the usual kinds of emotions, such as love, hate, fear, and euphoria, are determined by the coaction of sympathetic arousal and cognitive interpretations—how about sexual arousal? Sexual arousal seems above all to involve the perception of visceral arousal, which is, at least intuitively and ancedotally, different from the perception of general emotional arousal in the other emotions cited.

The parasympathetic nervous system plays a significant role during sexual arousal. The initial phases of sexual activity and of arousal tend to be dominated by parasympathetic-nervous-system responses, but, as sexual activity proceeds, sympathetic activity becomes more important, until it overshadows parasympathetic activity completely at the time of orgasm.[46] The available data[47] on physiological measures of sexual arousal tend to support the importance of parasympathetic arousal in the immediate response to sexual stimulation. Such visceral responses as tumescence, vasodilation, genital secretions, and rhythmic muscular movements constitute a cluster of responses that are uniquely characteristic of sexual arousal and sexual responses. In particular, the occurrences of tumescence and of vaginal lubrication, which are parasympathetically innervated, are not only characteristics of sexual arousal but—and this is important from the present point of view—obviously and uniquely subject to differential internal perception and thus play psychologically functional roles. On the other hand, massive sympathetic arousal is typical of the later phases of sexual arousal and plays the same role, in the emotions produced and felt, as sympathetic arousal does for all the various emotional states considered so far.

The effect of drugs on sexual arousal is also a case in point. Drugs that tend to depress SNS activity interfere with the phases of sexual activity, for example, ejaculation. By contrast, drugs that inhibit parasympathetic activity may inhibit early features, such as erection.

The data on sexual arousal, outside of specific stimulation during and preceding sexual activity, are relatively inconclusive,[48] but it could be argued that one of the distinctions we need to make in the discussion of emotional states is, in the case of sexual arousal, determined by differential autonomic arousal. Sexual stimuli may thus be considered to differ from other stimuli in that they produce parasympathetic arousal, a specific perceptual syndrome following such arousal, and structures that are specifically related to sexual and lustful emotion.

Some interesting conjectures arise concerning the interaction between these two emotional systems. "The possibility that sympathetic dominance may inhibit arousal and facilitate ejaculation may explain why sexual anxiety may be expressed in an inability to attain or maintain an erection, *or* premature ejaculation. Assuming that anxiety creates a state of heightened autonomic arousal these

46. See, e.g., Wenger, Jones, and Jones (1956).
47, 48. Zuckerman (1971).

effects would follow."[49] Thus, we may speculate that the sympathetically dominated emotions may actually interfere with the initial phase of sexual arousal. Although sympathetic arousal does not interfere with erection during the orgasmic phase, it does inhibit erection during the early phases. The interaction between sympathetic and parasympathetic systems is complex, but what is more important is that the interference of the sympathetic emotions with sexual arousal need not be restricted to anxiety.

If we are correct in assuming that the majority of all emotional states depend on autonomic arousal that is primarily sympathetic, then any such state, given the appropriate environmental events, should in principle interfere with the early parasympathetic phases of sexual arousal.

In contrast, and consistent with the current point of view, romantic love falls into the general continuum of the sympathetically aroused emotions.[50] Among the conditions that produce romantic love is the "unexpected realization that another is able and willing to help one fulfill one's most cherished plans and hopes."[51] In terms of Berscheid's concept of meshed relationships, romantic love is frequently seen as an extension of the self to encompass the actions, wishes, and feelings of the other. Clearly, a variety of evaluative cognitions produce love emotions, and all of them are associated with SNS arousal.

What is the relation between sexual arousal (lust) and romantic love? The contrast between the sympathetic arousal in love and the parasympathetic character of early sexual arousal prompts the interesting prediction that intensive romantic love during the early stages of sexual arousal may effectively interfere with adequate erection and lubrication, both important concomitants of sexual behavior and experience. An excess of romantic love may interfere with sexual performance. This conjunction is not as farfetched as it may sound. Anecdotal evidence abounds about cases of impotence and frigidity on the wedding night. The disjunction between love and lust is often carefully avoided in Western society (at least it is verbally denounced), but in the individual experience it may, in fact, be an important factor. For example, the excessive demands made on women in our society to display romantic love may be one of the factors that lead to an increase in frigidity and lack of sexual arousal.

Even more interesting is a speculation about the structures that relate cognitive interpretations to lust and/or love. Consider the condition in which a structure relates sympathetic arousal to sexual objects, or one that relates parasympathetic arousal and genital feelings to nonsexual objects. If we are to "love" and not lust after certain individuals, this might inhibit sexual response. On the other hand, the sexual response may in turn be specifically related to the significant persons whom one does not, cannot, or should not love. The twentieth century might not offer the best examples for some of these concatenations, although they may exist in individuals just as they may have existed for large

49. Zuckerman (1971).
50. Berscheid and Walster (1974, 1978) and Berscheid (in press [b]).
51. Berscheid (1982).

sections of the society in the nineteenth century. Then, the middle class in Western society was frequently taught that love emotions were to be expressed toward members of the same class, whereas lust emotions were reserved for others. Whether it was the Victorian gentleman who reserved his lust for women outside his connubial relationship, or whether the Victorian lady was able to express her lustful emotions only with gamekeepers, the examples illustrate our general argument. Sexual structures that reserve the lust emotion to very specific cognitive objects, whether they are prostitutes or husbands, conversely produce an inhibition of lust and sexuality toward others. At the same time, the emotion of love is necessarily restricted to a different set of individuals. When the occasions and persons that produce love and those that produce lust are different, difficulties in both sexual arousal and interpersonal relations will result.

Another consequence of this dissociation can be seen in the effects of drugs such as tranquilizers and alcohol, which will vary with the particular emotion (love or lust) that is evoked. Alcohol can act as a depressant for either parasympathetic or sympathetic arousal and thus may have rather differential effects. If it suppresses anxiety, it encourages lustful sexual behavior; if it suppresses sexual arousal, it obviously does not. Which of the two systems will be more sensitive to the intervention of drugs will depend on the biological and psychological history of the individual.

Our argument about love and lust applies equally to other emotions that may be aroused in sexual contexts. It is not my purpose to explore the wide range of sexual deviations from the norm that could be fitted into the current framework. I am thinking primarily about the kinds of events and people that may arouse sympathetic responses within the sexual sphere or the kind of nonsexual objects that may have become part of the structure of sexual, parasympathetic arousal. Perversities come in at least two flavors.

Consider the example of sexual masochism. The salient features of emotion (inputs from sensory systems, arousal, and cognitive processes) determine the experience of pain just as they determine the experience of other emotions.[52] To a very large extent, the motivational-affective dimension of pain is influenced by cognitive activity. The noxious experience of pain is derived in part from early experiences with so-called painful stimuli—for example, in the evaluation of the source of the painful stimuli or the seriousness of the injury that they produce. It is therefore not surprising that under some circumstances the sensory aspects of "painful" stimuli may be redirected or restructured by sensory-motivational-cognitive systems that imbue these events with positive effects. The basic feature of masochism is not that all so-called painful stimuli become pleasurable but that "painful" stimuli, under certain conditions, are interpreted as pleasurable. It is not unlikely that early experiences with painful stimuli that occurred in relation to a loving parent may, under certain conditions, produce the interpretation of a painful stimulus as pleasurable. Two consequences may then follow. First, the events and cognitions that are present at the time of such pleasurable

52. Melzack and Casey (1968, 1970) and Melzack and Wall (1965).

interpretations of pain may also be occasions for other kinds of emotional experiences. For example, the cognitive interpretation of the individual who inflicts the pleasurable pain may also be an interpretation that leads to sexual excitement. Under those circumstances there will be a conjunction between pleasurable pain and sexual arousal—to the point that the painful event becomes interpreted in terms of sexual arousal, possibly accompanied by a unique mixture of sympathetic and parasympathetic arousals. The second consequence refers to the difficulty of modifying this complex syndrome. The individual knows that under other circumstances the painful stimuli do, in fact, give rise to noxious and aversive experiences and "prefers" the positive interpretation whenever possible. At the same time, the conjunction between the painful stimulus and the pleasurable sexual experience further reinforces the utility of the masochistic structure. Thus, the masochistic individual will most reluctantly change the interpretive structures because abandonment may lead to noxious experiences and because it also involves the loss of pleasant sexual experiences. A structure that avoids noxious experiences and leads to pleasurable experiences at the same time should be more difficult to change than a structure that does only one or the other.

As another example, consider romantic jealousy. Jealousy is typically described as a compound emotion, particularly by writers committed to the existence of fundamental emotions. A review of the various concatenations that have been proposed reveals at least eight different combinations of different basic emotions, ranging from anger and fear to hate and aggression and to aggression, depression, and envy. However, jealousy can be described in terms of situational-cognitive events and defined "by the potential, or actual, loss of a loved one, or a mate, to a real or imagined rival."[53] Like so many other emotions, romantic jealousy then becomes an emotion sui generis, and we need not consider the various components that one or the other combinatory recipe describes. To be sure, resemblances to other emotions, such as anger, will be found because of the similarities between the cognitive evaluations, but that is not a reason to deprive jealousy of an independent status.

The potential for interruption and discrepancies is obvious from the definition given above. Again within the context of the meshed nature of close relationships, the real or imagined interactions between the loved one and the rival produce real or imagined interruptions.[54] Even some of the more bizarre variations in jealousy—when, for example, a rival is needed in order to create a scenario that defeats the rival—fit well into the general framework. In addition, individual predisposition to jealousy should arise out of particular views of the world or the self. A world seen as being full of predatory male or female rivals, or a self-image that sees the self as continuously vulnerable to intervention by unwanted others, will predispose the individual to jealous outbursts. Just as some of us carry our heart on our sleeve, so others flaunt their jealousies.

53. Hupka (1981).
54. Berscheid (1982).

Speculations about Aesthetics and Creativity

One of the possible difficulties with an arousal-cognitive interpretation of emotion is that it seems to fail to account for the tones of positive emotional feeling that occur in aesthetic appreciation. The degree of emotional involvement on hearing a piece of music, seeing an outstanding piece of art, or appreciating a new and masterly recipe seems to have very little to do with arousal. Although it is highly likely that there is a degree of arousal during such aesthetic appreciation, it becomes difficult to specify the functional stimulus for such arousal. It is unlikely that the particular configurations used by Beethoven, Rembrandt, or Rodin have innate releasing qualities. Much as some philosophers of aesthetics have argued for an immediate appreciation of the beautiful in music and art, it is unlikely from a biological or psychological point of view that such preformed structures do in fact exist in the human organism.

It is more likely that the arousal function of a piece of art can be derived from an interaction between it and the viewing, listening, and tasting individual. The probable source for the arousal can be found in certain structures that have been built up in relation to works of art. These structures may vary in the degree to which they anticipate the artistic event, that is, the degree to which the actual event does or does not conform to (and therefore interrupt or disrupt) the structure. The best-known attempt in this direction is the notion of the adaptation level and deviations from it. For example, it has been suggested that the confirmation of expectations with a low probability leads to negative affect, the confirmation of expectations with medium probabilities leads to positive affect, and the confirmation of expectations with high probability leads to boredom,[55] or that the degree of competition between incompatible response tendencies or expectations determines the degree of emotional tension.[56] These are just some examples of theories that eventually come to grips with the informational content of a stimulus complex and its relation to affective reactions. Another interpretation of the relation between the information content of a work of art and its emotional effect holds that the degree of activation (arousal) varies with the discrepancy between stimulation and anticipation.[57] The intensity of an anticipation is a monotonically increasing function of the objective conditional probability of a particular stimulus in the appropriate context. The relation between the informational content of a stimulus sequence and the degree of activation released by the perception of a sequence is consistent with the present position that when an event conforms with certain mental structures, no disruption or interruption will occur and that therefore no arousal will take place.

We can assume, together with a variety of aesthetic theorists, that the complexity of a work of art generates further and finer differentiations of its content. The greater the informational content, the greater the possibility of new inter-

55. McClelland (1951).
56. Berlyne (1960).
57. Werbik (1971).

pretations and new differentiations. Thus, we would expect that the aesthetically meaningful experience (i.e., meaningful in the emotional sense) will be related to continual attempts at analysis. These analyses will, by definition, be discrepant with previously developed structures that involve that work of art. It is this continuing analysis and new appreciation and reappreciation of a work of art that produces the discrepancy, then the arousal, and finally the affective reaction. It has been shown that the amount of artistic training one has is related to one's affective response to a work of art. The popular song that permits few new interpretations quickly loses its affective content, just as the less complex and less "interesting" work of art quickly loses its emotional impact.

The cognitive constituents that produce some of the positive emotions in appreciating a work of art are the achievement of a new interpretation, a new view of the aesthetic object, and the development of new mental structures. On the other hand, there must be cases in which the arousal that goes with a work of art would also produce negative emotional reactions. This is most frequently seen in the response to the radically new or revolutionary art form. Presumably, in these cases, no structures are available that can handle, interpret, or analyze the work of art that is presented. When an attempt is made to analyze a stimulus complex and when that attempt is unsuccessful because no structures are available, the conditions for anxiety and helplessness will have been met. Thus, the new art form, whether it is Beethoven's in his time or Picasso's in his, is frequently responded to as being unpleasant and negative. With education and experience, structures are developed that can assimilate this material, and the emotional reaction changes from negative to positive.

The appreciation of art may be related to problems of creativity and originality and their sources in early development. It can be argued that the creative and original individual not only must be able to create new forms and structures in the world but must also have certain emotional characteristics. First, such an individual should be able to tolerate the emotions engendered when the new structure, the new work of art, or the new theory is produced; and, second, as a corollary, such emotional situations should be attractive. The perception of the new structure, the interruption of the old, and their emotional consequences must be positive, desirable cognitive interpretations.

I have entertained a hypothesis about creativity that has two aspects, neither of which is necessarily new. First, the creative work, whether in art or in science, requires an act of destruction of the existing forms and structures. The artist who breaks new paths in the forms of musical or visual expression and the scientist who proposes a new theory both know that by that very act they are destroying or at least undermining existing structures—structures that have been accepted by their colleagues and by society at large. Thus, the creative individual must be able to tolerate and even to seek out the destructive consequences of the creation. In a sense, that destruction must not be "aggressive" in the normal sense of intending to hurt someone but, instead, must be seen as neutral, vis-à-vis the other artists and scientists, and destructive only of ideas in the service of creating new structures. If it is seen as destructive of people, it will (and should) frequently (although clearly not always) have negative aversive characteristics and may inhibit the creative effort.

Second, it appears that creative individuals very frequently have a cross-sex parent who has been thwarted or frustrated in some artistic or intellectual endeavor. Under certain circumstances this frustration may be seen in the same-sex parent, but not typically so. In a sense the cross-sex parent and the child exemplify Rank's distinction between two kinds of nonconformist: the parent as the thwarted nonconformist and the child as the creative one.[58]

If we assume that there is a relatively high degree of emotional contact between a child and the cross-sex parent—by appealing, for example, to the latent or manifest romantic and sexual attraction between the two[59]—then we can expect that the positive emotional ties between the child and the cross-sex parent will color their relationships. I am suggesting that the parent "lives out" his or her thwarted ambitions by driving, encouraging, and motivating the child toward ever new and different achievements. No particular stage of development is adequate; a higher level and a better one must be reached. Thus, just as the child reaches a stable structure in relation to intellectual, artistic, or scientific endeavors, the parent interferes directly by producing a new structure that is to supplement it, a new level of achievement that is to be attained. In the context in which positive emotional ties between parent and child are already present, the disruption of existing structures is added, and the achievement of new structures becomes a positively viewed and positively valued objective. The change of old structures becomes a positive "destructive" goal rather than a negative aggressive one directed against others, and this creative change is viewed as positive and desirable. Arousal (whether "sexual" or not) is provided by the parent and by the disruption of old patterns; positive evaluation is derived both from the parent and from the achievement of new structures. Some of the empirical literature about creative persons supports the general notions of increased nonconformity, ability to accept destructiveness, and the kind of parent-child relationships suggested here.[60]

In summary, then, the creative act, being both destructive and productive of new structures, is learned during early life as a desirable and acceptable way of interacting with the environment. In contrast, the uncreative individual may shy away from the destruction of existing structures because it is seen as aggressive, or the arousal produced in the denial or disruption of old structures cannot be tolerated, because such arousal is accompanied by negative rather than positive cognitive appraisals.

It is appropriate in this context to return to some of the things stated and implied in Chapter 7. If the context of early childhood interactions colors the emerging emotional tone of creativity, how much more does the prevailing character of society affect that interaction? It is the character of the society that determines the cognitive evaluations of feelings and actions. Regardless of the parent-

58. E.g., Rank (1932).
59. Mandler (1963).
60. MacKinnon (1962) and Barron (1968).

child interaction, the values of society are a prior condition. The ability to tolerate the destruction of the old and to see it as creative instead of aggressive depends in the first instance on the social values that inform both creativity and aggression. Thus, a society that directs creative acts toward competition and personal achievement, that equates competition and aggression, and that rewards creativity but also competitive, aggressive achievements will tend to undermine the free creative act that—ideally—can see the change of the old in the positive light of personal and social achievement rather than as an additional sign of interpersonal aggressive competition.

I would like to end on that note. When all has been said about mental processes, we can return to the importance of the social conditions under which they operate, to the recognition that life and society determine consciousness, not vice versa.

REFERENCES

Abelson, R. P. 1981. Constraints, construal, and cognitive science. Paper presented at the Third Annual Cognitive Science Conference, Berkeley, California, August.

Abramson, L. Y., M. E. P. Seligman, and J. D. Teasdale. 1978. Learned helplessness in humans: Critique and reformulation. *Journal of Abnormal Psychology* 87:49–74.

Adrian, E. D. 1966. Consciousness. In *Brain and conscious experience*, edited by J. C. Eccles. New York: Springer.

Alland, A., Jr. 1972. *The human imperative*. New York: Columbia University Press.

Amsel, A. 1958. The role of frustrative nonreward in noncontinuous reward situations. *Psychological Bulletin* 53:102–19.

Amsel, A. 1962. Frustrative nonreward in partial reinforcement and discrimination learning. *Psychological Review* 69:306–28.

Amsel, A., and J. S. Roussel. 1952. Motivational properties of frustration: I. Effect on a running response of the addition of frustration to the motivational complex. *Journal of Experimental Psychology* 43:363–68.

Anderson, N. H. 1981a. Integration theory applied to cognitive responses and attitudes. In *Cognitive responses in persuasion*, edited by R. M. Petty, T. M. Ostrom, and T. C. Brock. Hillsdale, N.J.: Erlbaum.

Anderson, N. H. 1981b. *Foundations of information integration theory*. New York: Academic Press.

Anderson, R. E. 1973. Individual differences in the use of imaginal processing. Ph.D. diss., University of California, San Diego.

Anderson, R. C., and J. W. Pichert. 1978. Recall of previously unrecallable information following a shift in perspective. *Journal of Verbal Learning and Verbal Behavior* 17:1–12.

Angier, R. P. 1927. The conflict theory of emotion. *American Journal of Psychology* 39:390–401.

Annau, Z., and L. J. Kamin. 1961. The conditioned emotional response as a function of the intensity of the US. *Journal of Comparative and Physiological Psychology* 54:428–32.

Ardrey, R. 1966. *The territorial imperative*. New York: Atheneum.

Armstrong, S. L., L. R. Gleitman, and H. Gleitman. 1983. What some concepts might not be. *Cognition* 13:263–308.

Arnheim, R. 1974. *Art and visual perception: A psychology of the creative eye—The new version*. Berkeley: University of California Press.

Arnold, M. B. 1960. *Emotion and personality*. Vols. 1 and 2. New York: Columbia University Press.

Arnold, M. B., ed. 1970a. *Feelings and emotions: The Loyola Symposium*. New York: Academic Press.

Arnold, M. B. 1970b. Perennial problems in the field of emotion. In *Feelings and emotion*, edited by M. B. Arnold. New York: Academic Press.

Auersperg, A. P. 1958. Vom Werden der Angst. *Nervenarzt* 29:193–201.

Averill, J. R. 1968. Grief: Its nature and significance. *Psychological Bulletin* 70:721–48.

Averill, J. R. 1969. Autonomic response patterns during sadness and mirth. *Psychophysiology* 5:399–414.

Averill, J. R. 1973. Personal control over aversive stimuli and its relationship to stress. *Psychological Bulletin* 80:286–303.

Averill, J. R. 1980. A constructivist view of emotion. In *Theories of emotion*, edited by R. Plutchik and H. Kellerman. New York: Academic Press.

Ax, A. F. 1953. The physiological differentiation of fear and anger in humans. *Psychosomatic Medicine* 15:433–42.

Bachrach, A. J. 1970. Diving behavior. In *Human performance and scuba diving*. Chicago: Athletic Institute.

Bacon, S. J. 1974. Arousal and the range of cue utilization. *Journal of Experimental Psychology* 102:81–87.

Baddeley, A. D. 1971. Diver performance. In *Underwater science*, edited by J. D. Woods and J. N. Lythgoe. London: Oxford University Press.

Baddeley, A. D. 1972. Selective attention and performance in dangerous environments. *British Journal of Psychology* 63:537–46.

Bain, A. [1859] 1899. *The emotions and the will*. 4th ed. London: Longmans.

Bandura, A. 1973. Social learning theory of aggression. In *The control of aggression*, edited by J. F. Knutson. Chicago: Aldine.

Barber, T. X. 1959. Toward a theory of pain: Relief of chronic pain by prefrontal leucotomy, opiates, placebos, and hypnosis. *Psychological Bulletin* 56:430–60.

Barron, F. 1968. *Creativity and personal freedom*. Princeton, N.J.: Van Nostrand.

Bartlett, F. C. 1932. *Remembering*. Cambridge: Cambridge University Press.

Bateson, G., D. D. Jackson, J. Haley, and J. Weakland. 1956. Toward a theory of schizophrenia. *Behavioral Science* 1:251–64.

Baum, M. 1970. Extinction of avoidance responses through response prevention (flooding). *Psychological Bulletin* 74:276–84.

Beck, A. T. 1967. *Depression*. New York: Hoeber.

Beck, A. T. 1972. Cognition, anxiety, and psychophysiological disorders. In *Anxiety: Current trends in theory and research*, edited by C. D. Spielberger. Vol. 2. New York: Academic Press.

Bem, D. J. 1967. Self-perception: An alternative interpretation of cognitive dissonance phenomena. *Psychological Review* 74:183–200.

Bem, D. J. 1972. Self-perception theory. In *Advances in experimental social psychology*, edited by L. Berkowitz. New York: Academic Press.

Berkowitz, L. 1964. Aggressive cues in aggressive behavior and hostility catharsis. *Psychological Review* 71:104–22.

Berlyne, D. E. 1960. *Conflict, arousal and curiosity*. New York: McGraw-Hill.

Berlyne, D. E. 1965. *Structure and direction in thinking*. New York: Wiley.

Berlyne, D. E. 1973. The vicissitudes of aplopathematic and thelematoscopic pneumatology (or The hydrography of hedonism). In *Pleasure, reward, preference*, edited by D. E. Berlyne and K. B. Madsen. New York: Academic Press.

Berlyne, D. E., M. A. Craw, P. H. Salapatek, and J. L. Lewis. 1963. Novelty, complexity, incongruity, extrinsic motivation and the G.S.R. *Journal of Experimental Psychology* 66:560–67.

Berscheid, E. 1982. Attraction and emotion in interpersonal relationships. In *Affect and cognition: The Seventeenth Annual Carnegie Symposium on Cognition*, edited by M. S. Clark and S. T. Fiske. Hillsdale, N.J.: Erlbaum.

Berscheid, E. 1983. Emotion. In *Close relationships*, edited by H. H. Kelley, E. Berscheid, A. Christensen, J. Harvey, T. Huston, G. Levinger, E. McClintock, A. Peplau, and D. R. Peterson. San Francisco: Freeman.

Berscheid, E. In press (a). Emotional experience in close relationships: Implications for child development. In *The effects of early relationships on children's socioemotional development*, edited by Z. Rubin and W. Hartup. New York: Cambridge University Press.

Berscheid, E. In press (b). Interpersonal attraction. In *Handbook of social psychology*, edited by G. Lindzey and E. Aronson. 3d ed. Reading, Mass.: Addison-Wesley.

Berscheid, E., S. J. Gangestad, and D. Kulakowski. In press (a). Emotion in close relationships: Implications for relationship counselling. In *Handbook of counselling psychology*, edited by S. D. Brown and R. W. Lent. New York: Wiley.

Berscheid, E., and E. Walster. 1974. A little bit about love. In *Foundations of interpersonal attraction*, edited by T. L. Huston. New York: Academic Press.

Berscheid, E., and E. Walster. 1978. *Interpersonal attraction*. 2d ed. Reading, Mass.: Addison-Wesley.

Birch, D., J. R. Ison, and S. E. Sperling. 1960. Reversal learning under single stimulus presentation. *Journal of Experimental Psychology* 60:36–40.

Blascovich, J., and E. S. Katkin. In press. Arousal-based social behaviors as a function of individual differences in visceral perception. *Review of Personality and Social Psychology.*

Bolles, R. C. 1970. Species-specific defense reactions and avoidance learning. *Psychological Review* 77:32–48.

Bonn, J. A., P. Turner, and D. C. Hicks. 1972. Beta-adrenergic receptor blockade with practolol in treatment of anxiety. *Lancet* 1:814–15.

Borkovec, T. D. 1976. Physiological and cognitive processes in the regulation of fear. In *Consciousness and self-regulation: Advances in research*, edited by G. E. Schwartz and D. Shapiro. New York: Plenum.

Borkovec, T. D., and G. T. O'Brien. 1977. The relationship of autonomic perception and its manipulation to the maintenance and reduction of fear. *Journal of Abnormal Psychology* 86:163–71.

Bourne, H. R., L. M. Lichtenstein, R. L. Melmon, C. S. Henney, Y. Weinstein, and G. M. Shearer. 1974. Modulation of inflammation and immunity by cyclic AMP. *Science* 184:19–28.

Bower, G. H. 1981. Mood and memory. *American Psychologist* 36:129–48.

Bower, G. H., and P. Cohen. 1982. Emotional influences in memory and thinking: Data and theory. In *Affect and cognition: The Seventeenth Annual Carnegie Symposium on Cognition*, edited by M. S. Clark and S. T. Fiske. Hillsdale, N.J.: Erlbaum.

Bower, G. H., S. G. Gilligan, and K. P. Monteiro. 1981. Selectivity of learning caused by affective states. *Journal of Experimental Psychology: General* 110:451–73.

Bower, G. H., K. P. Monteiro, and S. G. Gilligan. 1978. Emotional mood as a context of learning and recall. *Journal of Verbal Learning and Verbal Behavior* 17:573–85.

Bowlby, J. 1969. *Attachment and loss.* Vol. 1. *Attachment.* London: Hogarth Press and Institute of Psychoanalysis.

Bowlby, J. 1973. *Attachment and loss.* Vol. 2. *Separation.* London: Hogarth Press and Institute of Psychoanalysis.

Bowlby, J. 1979. Reasonable fear and natural fear. *International Journal of Psychiatry* 9:79–88.

Brady, J. V. 1967. Emotion and sensitivity of psychoendocrine systems. In *Neurophysiology and emotion*, edited by D. C. Glass. New York: Rockefeller University Press and Russell Sage Foundation.

Brady, J. V. 1975. Toward a behavioral biology of emotion. In *Emotions: Their parameters and measurement*, edited by L. Levi. New York: Raven Press.

Brewer, W. F. 1974. There is no convincing evidence for operant and classical conditioning in humans. In *Cognition and symbolic processes*, edited by W. B. Weimer and D. S. Palermo. Hillsdale, N.J.: Erlbaum.

Brickman, P., J. Redfield, A. A. Harrison, and R. Crandall. 1972. Drive and predisposition as factors in the attitudinal effects of mere exposure. *Journal of Experimental Social Psychology* 8:31–44.

Broadbent, D. E. 1958. *Perception and communication.* London: Pergamon Press.

Broadbent, D. E. 1971. *Decision and stress.* New York: Academic Press.

Broadbent, D. E. 1981. The effects of moderate levels of noise on human performance. In *Hearing research and theory*, edited by J. V. Tobias and E. D. Schubert. New York: Academic Press.

Bruell, J. H. 1970. Heritability of emotional behavior. In *Physiological correlates of emotion*, edited by P. Black. New York: Academic Press.

Bruner, J. S. 1961. Human problem solving. *Harvard Educational Review* 31:21–32.

Bruner, J. S. 1975. From communication to language—A psychological perspective. *Cognition* 3:255–78.

Bruner, J. S. 1980. Personal communication.

Brunswick, D. 1924. The effects of emotional stimuli on the gastro-intestinal zone. *Journal of Comparative Physiology* 4:19–79, 225–87.

Buck, R. 1980. Nonverbal behavior and the theory of emotions: The facial feedback hypothesis. *Journal of Personality and Social Psychology* 38:811–24.

Bühler, K. 1930. *The mental development of the child.* New York: Harcourt, Brace.

Burgess, T. D. G., II, and S. M. Sales. 1971. Attitudinal effects of "mere exposure": A reevaluation. *Journal of Experimental Social Psychology* 7:461–72.

Butterfield, E. C. 1954. The interruption of tasks: Methodological, factual, and theoretical issues. *Psychological Bulletin* 62:309–22.

Callaway, E., III, and D. Dembo. 1958. Narrowed attention: A psychological phenomenon that accompanies a certain physiological change. *AMA Archives of Neurology and Psychiatry* 79:74–90.

Candland, D. K., J. P. Fell, E. Keen, A. I. Leshner, R. Plutchik, and R. M. Tarpy. 1977. *Emotion*. Monterey, Calif.: Brooks Cole.

Cannon, W. B. 1914. The interrelations of emotions as suggested by recent physiological researches. *American Journal of Psychology* 25:256–82.

Cannon, W. B. 1927. The James-Lange theory of emotions: A critical examination and an alternative theory. *American Journal of Psychology* 39:106–24.

Cannon, W. B. 1929. *Bodily changes in pain, hunger, fear and rage.* 2d ed. New York: Appleton-Century-Crofts.

Cannon, W. B. 1930. The Linacre lecture on the autonomic nervous system: An interpretation. *Lancet* 218:1109–15.

Cantor, J. R., J. Bryant, and D. Zillmann. 1974. Enhancement of humor appreciation by transferred excitation. *Journal of Personality and Social Psychology* 30:812–21.

Cantor, J. R., D. Zillmann, and J. Bryant. 1975. Enhancement of experienced sexual arousal in response to erotic stimuli through misattribution of unrelated residual excitation. *Journal of Personality and Social Psychology* 2:69–75.

Chevalier-Skolnikoff, S. 1973. Facial expression of emotion in nonhuman primates. In *Darwin and facial expression*, edited by P. Ekman. New York: Academic Press.

Chomsky, N. 1959. Review of B. F. Skinner's *Verbal behavior. Language* 35:26–58.

Claparède, E. 1934. *La genèse de l'hypothèse*. Geneva: Kundig.

Clark, M. S. 1982. A role for arousal in the link between feeling states, judgments and behavior. In *Affect and cognition: The Seventeenth Annual Carnegie Symposium on Cognition*, edited by M. S. Clark and S. T. Fiske. Hillsdale, N.J.: Erlbaum.

Clark, M. S., and A. M. Isen. 1982. Toward understanding the relationship between feeling states and social behavior. In *Cognitive social psychology*, edited by A. H. Hastorf and A. M. Isen. New York: Elsevier North Holland.

Coles, M. G. H., and C. C. Duncan-Johnson. 1975. Cardiac activity and information processing: The effects of stimulus significance, and detection and response requirements. *Journal of Experimental Psychology: Human Perception and Performance* 1:418–28.

Collins, A. M., and E. F. Loftus. 1975. A spreading activation theory of semantic processing. *Psychological Review* 82:407–28.

Costello, C. G. 1970. Dissimilarities between conditioned avoidance responses and phobias. *Psychological Review* 77:250–54.

Craik, F. I. M., and R. S. Lockhart. 1972. Levels of processing: A framework for memory research. *Journal of Verbal Learning and Verbal Behavior* 11:671–84.

Craik, F. I. M., and E. Tulving. 1975. Depth of processing and the retention of words in episodic memory. *Journal of Experimental Psychology: General* 104:268–94.

Craik, F. I. M., and M. J. Watkins. 1973. The role of rehearsal in short-term memory. *Journal of Verbal Learning and Verbal Behavior* 12:599–607.

D'Andrade, R. 1982. A folk model of the mind. Unpublished manuscript, University of California, San Diego.

Darwin, C. 1872. *The expression of the emotions in man and animals.* London: John Murray.

Dawson, M. E., A. M. Schell, J. R. Beers, and A. Kelly. 1982. Allocation of cognitive processing capacity during human autonomic classical conditioning. *Journal of Experimental Psychology: General* 111:273–95.

Dawson, M. E., A. M. Schell, and J. J. Catania. 1977. Autonomic correlates of depression and clinical improvement following electroconvulsive shock therapy. *Psychophysiology* 14:569–78.

Dean, P. 1971. Organizational structure and retrieval processes in long-term memory. Ph.D. diss., University of California, San Diego.

Deets, A. C., H. F. Harlow, and M. K. Harlow. 1971. Development of aggression in primates. Paper presented at AAAS meetings, December.

Dembroski, T. M. 1981. Environmentally induced cardiovascular response in Type A and B individuals. *Perspectives on behavioral medicine.* New York: Academic Press.

Dembroski, T. M., J. M. MacDougall, and J. L. Shields. 1977. Physiological reactions challenge in persons evidencing the Type A coronary-prone behavior pattern. *Journal of Human Stress* 3(3):2–9.

Dembroski, T. M., J. M. MacDougall, J. L. Shields, J. Pettito, and R. Lushene. 1978. Components of the Type A coronary-prone behavior pattern and cardiovascular responses to psychomotor performance challenge. *Journal of Behavioral Medicine* 1:159–76.

Dembroski, T. M., J. M. MacDougall, S. Slaats, R. S. Eliot, and J. C. Buell. 1981. Challenge-induced cardiovascular response as a predictor of minor illnesses. *Journal of Human Stress* 7 (4):2–5.

Dembroski, T. M., S. M. Weiss, and J. L. Shields, eds. 1978. *Coronary-prone behavior*. New York: Springer.

Dempster, F. N. 1981. Memory span: Sources of individual and developmental differences. *Psychological Bulletin* 89:63–100.

Dentan, R. K. 1968. *The Semai, a nonviolent people of Malaya*. New York: Holt, Rinehart and Winston.

De Rivera, J. 1977. *A structural theory of the emotions*. New York: International Universities Press.

Deutsch, D. 1981. The octave illusion and auditory perceptual integration. In *Hearing research and theory*, edited by J. V. Tobias and E. D. Schubert. Vol. 1. New York: Academic Press.

Deutsch, J. A., and D. Deutsch. 1963. Attention: Some theoretical considerations. *Psychological Review* 70:80–90.

Deutsch, J. A. 1960. *The structural basis of behavior*. Chicago: University of Chicago Press.

Deutsch, M. 1954. Field theory in social psychology. In *Handbook of Social Psychology*, edited by G. Lindzey. Vol. 1. Cambridge, Mass.: Addison-Wesley.

Dewey, J. 1894. The theory of emotion: I. Emotional attitudes. *Psychological Review* 1:553–69.

Dewey, J. 1895. The theory of emotion: II. The significance of emotions. *Psychological Review* 2:13–32.

Dillon, R. F., and J. Person. 1981. Bibliography of eye-movement research, 1976–1980. *Catalog of Selected Documents in Psychology* 11:49.

Dixon, N. F. 1971. *Subliminal perception: The nature of a controversy*. London: McGraw-Hill.

Dohrenwend, B. S., L. Krasnoff, A. R. Askenasy, and B. P. Dohrenwend. 1978. Exemplification of a method for scaling life events: The PERI life events scale. *Journal of Health and Social Behavior* 19:205–29.

Dollard, J., and N. E. Miller. 1950. *Personality and psychotherapy*. New York: McGraw-Hill.

Duffy, E. 1962. *Activation and behavior*. New York: Wiley.

Dumas, G. 1932. La mimique des aveugles. *Bulletin de l'Académie de Medicine* 107:607–10.

Dunlap, K., ed. 1922. *The emotions*, by C. G. Lange and W. James. Baltimore: Williams and Wilkins.

Dutta, S., and R. N. Kanungo. 1975. *Affect and memory: a reformulation*. Oxford, England: Pergamon Press.

Dutton, D., and A. Aron. 1974. Some evidence for heightened sexual attraction under conditions of high anxiety. *Journal of Personality and Social Psychology* 30:510–17.

Easterbrook, J. A. 1959. The effect of emotion on cue utilization and the organization of behavior. *Psychological Review* 66:183–201.

Ekman, P. 1973. Cross-cultural studies of facial expression. In *Darwin and facial expression*, edited by P. Ekman. New York: Academic Press.

Ekman, P. 1979. About brows: emotional and conversational signals. In *Human ethology*, edited by M. von Cranach, K. Foppa, W. Lepenies, and D. Ploog. Cambridge: Cambridge University Press.

Ekman, P., W. V. Friesen, and P. Ellsworth. 1972. *Emotion in the human face*. New York: Pergamon Press.

Ekman, P., and H. Oster. 1979. Facial expressions of emotion. *Annual Review of Psychology* 30:527–54.

Eldredge, N., and S. J. Gould. 1972. Punctuated equilibria: An alternative to phyletic gradualism. In *Models in paleobiology*, edited by T. J. M. Schopf. New York: Freeman, Cooper.

Eliot, R. S., ed. 1974. *Stress and the heart*. Mt. Kisco, N.Y.: Futura.

Eliot, R. S. 1979. *Stress and the major cardiovascular disorders*. Mt. Kisco, N.Y.: Futura.

Elliott, R. 1966. Effects of uncertainty about the nature and advent of a noxious stimulus (shock) upon heartrate. *Journal of Personality and Social Psychology* 3:353–56.

Epstein, S., and W. D. Fenz. 1965. Steepness of approach and avoidance gradients in humans as a function of experience: Theory and experiment. *Journal of Experimental Psychology* 70:1–13.

Ericsson, K. A., and H. Simon. 1980. Verbal reports as data. *Psychological Review* 87:215–51.

Eysenck, H. J. 1967. *The biological basis of personality*. Springfield, Ill.: Charles C. Thomas.

Fanconi, G., and F. Ferrazzini. 1957. Kongenitale Analgie: Kongenitale generalisierte Schmerzindifferenz. *Helvetica Paediatrica Acta* 12:79–115.

Fiske, S. T. 1982. Schema-triggered affect: Applications to social perception. In *Affect and cognition: The Seventeenth Annual Carnegie Symposium on Cognition*, edited by M. S. Clark and S. T. Fiske. Hillsdale, N.J.: Erlbaum.

Fiske, S. T., A. E. Beattie, and S. J. Milberg. 1981. Schema-triggered affect: Cognitive schemas and affective matches in the initiation of close relationships. Unpublished manuscript, Carnegie-Mellon University.

Folkman, S., C. Schaefer, and R. S. Lazarus. 1979. Cognitive processes as mediators of stress and coping. In *Human stress and cognition: An information processing approach*, edited by V. Hamilton and D. M. Warburton. London: Wiley.

Ford, C. S., and F. A. Beach. 1952. *Patterns of sexual behavior*. New York: Harper.

Foulkes, D. 1966. *The psychology of sleep*. New York: Scribners.

Fowler, C. A., G. Wolford, R. Slade, and L. Tassinary. 1981. Lexical access with and without awareness. *Journal of Experimental Psychology: General* 110:341–62.

Fraisse, P. 1968. Les émotions. In *Traité de psychologie expérimentale*, edited by P. Fraisse and J. Piaget. Vol. 5. Paris: Presses Universitaires.

Frankenhaeuser, M. 1971a. Behavior and circulating catecholamines. *Brain research* 31:241–62.

Frankenhaeuser, M. 1971b. Experimental approaches to the study of human behavior as related to neuroendocrine functions. In *Society, stress, and disease*, edited by L. Levi. Vol. 1. London: Oxford University Press.

Frankenhaeuser, M. 1975. Experimental approaches to the study of catecholamines and emotion. In *Emotions: Their parameters and measurement*, edited by L. Levi. New York: Raven Press.

Frankenhaeuser, M. 1979. Psychoneuroendocrine approaches to the study of emotion as related to stress and coping. In *Nebraska symposium on motivation: 1978*, edited by H. E. Howe and R. A. Dienstbier. Lincoln: University of Nebraska Press.

Frankenhaeuser, M., B. Nordheden, A.-L. Myrsten, and B. Post. 1971. Psychophysiological reactions to understimulation and overstimulation. *Acta Psychologia* 35:298–308.

Frankenhaeuser, M., and P. Pàtkai. 1965. Interindividual differences in catecholamine excretion during stress. *Scandinavian Journal of Psychology* 6:117–23.

Frankenhaeuser, M., and A. Rissler. 1970. Effects of punishment on catecholamine release and efficiency of performance. *Psychopharmacologia* 17:378–90.

Franks, J. J., and J. D. Bransford. 1971. Abstraction of visual patterns. *Journal of Experimental Psychology* 90:65–74.

Freeman, G. L. 1940. The relationship between performance level and bodily activity level. *Journal of Experimental Psychology* 26:602–8.

Freud, S. [1900] 1975. *The interpretation of dreams*. Vols. 4 and 5 of *The standard edition of the complete psychological works of Sigmund Freud*. London: Hogarth Press.

Freud, S. [1911] 1975. *Formulations regarding the two principles of mental functioning*. Vol. 12 of *The standard edition of the complete psychological works of Sigmund Freud*. London: Hogarth Press.

Freud, S. [1915] 1975. *The unconscious*. Vol. 14 of *The standard edition of the complete psychological works of Sigmund Freud*. London: Hogarth Press.

Freud, S. [1916–17] 1975. *Introductory lectures on psychoanalysis*. Vols. 15 and 16 of *The standard edition of the complete psychological works of Sigmund Freud*. London: Hogarth Press.

Freud, S. [1926] 1975. *Inhibitions, symptoms, and anxiety*. Vol. 20 of *The standard edition of the complete psychological works of Sigmund Freud*. London: Hogarth Press.

Friedman, A. 1979. Framing pictures: The role of knowledge in automatized encoding and memory for gist. *Journal of Experimental Psychology: General* 108:316–55.

Fromm, E. 1973. *The anatomy of human destructiveness*. New York: Holt, Rinehart and Winston.

Fry, P. S., and D. G. Ogston. 1971. Emotion as a function of the labeling of interruption produced arousal. *Psychonomic Science* 24:153–54.

Funkenstein, D. H. 1956. Norepinephrine-like and epinephrine-like substances in relation to human behavior. *Journal of Mental Diseases* 124:58–68.

Gal, R., and R. S. Lazarus. 1975. The role of activity in anticipating and confronting stressful situations. *Journal of Human Stress* 1 (4):4–20.

Gallistel, C. R. 1974. Motivation as central organizing process: The psychophysical approach to its functional and neurophysiological analysis. In *Nebraska symposium on motivation: 1974*, edited by J. K. Cole and T. B. Sonderegger. Lincoln, Neb.: University of Nebraska Press.

Gallistel, C. R. 1980. *The organization of action: A new synthesis*. Hillsdale, N.J.: Erlbaum.

Gardiner, H. M., R. C. Metcalf, and J. G. Beebe-Center. 1937. *Feeling and emotion: A history of theories*. New York: American Book Co.

Garner, W. R. 1962. *Uncertainty and structure as psychological concepts.* New York: Wiley.
Garner, W. R. 1974. *The processing of information and structure.* Hillsdale: N.J.: Erlbaum.
Gentner, D. R., J. Grudin, S. Larochelle, D. A. Norman, and D. E. Rumelhart. 1982. Studies of typing from the LNR typing research group. Technical Report no. 111, Center for Human Information Processing, University of California, San Diego, September.
Gentner, D., and A. Stevens, eds. 1982. *Mental models.* Hillsdale, N.J.: Erlbaum.
Glass, D., J. E. Singer, H. S. Leonard, D. Krantz, S. Cohen, and H. Cummings. 1973. Perceived control of aversive stimulation and the reduction of stress responses. *Journal of Personality* 41:577–95.
Gottschalk, L. A., W. N. Stone, and G. C. Gleser. 1974. Peripheral versus central mechanisms accounting for antianxiety effects of propanolol. *Psychosomatic Medicine* 36:47–55.
Gouaux, C. 1971. Induced affective states and interpersonal attraction. *Journal of Personality and Social Psychology* 20:37–43.
Gould, S. J. 1981. *The mismeasure of man.* New York: Norton.
Gould, S. J. 1982. Darwinism and the expansion of evolutionary theory. *Science* 216:380–87.
Graesser, A. C., II, and G. Mandler. 1978. Limited processing capacity constrains the storage of unrelated sets of words and retrieval from natural categories. *Journal of Experimental Psychology: Human Learning and Memory* 4:86–100.
Graf, P., G. Mandler, and P. Haden. 1982. Simulating amnesic symptoms in normal subjects. *Science* 218:1243–44.
Graf, P., L. R. Squire, and G. Mandler. In press. The information that amnesic patients do not forget. *Journal of Experimental Psychology: Learning, Memory, and Cognition.*
Graham, F. K., and R. K. Clifton. 1966. Heart rate changes as a component of the orienting response. *Psychological Bulletin* 65:305–20.
Gray, J. A. 1970. The psychophysiological basis of introversion-extraversion. *Behavior Research and Therapy* 8:249–66.
Gray, J. A. 1971a. The mind-brain identity theory as a scientific hypothesis. *Philosophical Quarterly* 21:247–52.
Gray, J. A. 1971b. *The psychology of fear and stress.* London: World University Library.
Hamburg, D., B. Hamburg, and J. Barchas. 1975. Anger and depression: Current psychobiological approaches. In *Emotions: Their parameters and measurement*, edited by L. Levi. New York: Raven Press.
Hamilton, V. 1975. Socialization anxiety and information processing: A capacity model of anxiety-induced performance deficits. In *Stress and anxiety*, edited by I. G. Sarason and C. D. Spielberger. Vol. 2. Washington, D.C.: Hemisphere.
Hamilton, W. 1859. *Lectures on metaphysics and logic.* Vol. 1. Edinburgh: Blackwood.
Hammerton, M., and A. H. Tickner. 1967. Tracking under stress. *Medical Research Council Report*, No. APRC 67/CS 10 (A).
Harlow, H. F. 1958. The nature of love. *American Psychologist* 13:673–85.
Hasher, L., and R. T. Zacks. 1979. Automatic and effortful processes in memory. *Journal of Experimental Psychology: General* 108:356–88.
Hastings, S. E., and P. A. Obrist. 1967. Heart rate during conditioning in humans: Effect of varying the interstimulus (CS-UCS) interval. *Journal of Experimental Psychology* 74:431–42.
Hebb, D. O. 1946. On the nature of fear. *Psychological Review* 53:259–76.
Hebb, D. O. 1949. *The organization of behavior.* New York: Wiley.
Heider, F. 1958. *The psychology of interpersonal relations.* New York: Wiley.
Herbart, J. F. 1816. *Lehrbuch zur Psychologie.* Königsberg and Leipzig: A. W. Unzer.
Hess, E. H. 1965. Attitude and pupil size. *Scientific American* 212:46–54.
Higgins, J. D. 1971. Set and uncertainty as factors influencing anticipatory cardiovascular responding in humans. *Journal of Comparative and Physiological Psychology* 74:272–83.
Hinde, R. A. 1954. Changes in responsiveness to a constant stimulus. *British Journal of Animal Behavior* 2:41–55.
Hinde, R. A. 1956. Ethological models and the concept of "drive." *British Journal of the Philosophy of Science* 6:321–31.
Hinton, G. E. 1981. The role of spatial working memory in shape perception. In *Proceedings of the Third Annual Conference of the Cognitive Science Society.* Berkeley, Calif.
Hinton, G. E., and J. A. Anderson, eds. 1981. *Parallel models of associative memory.* Hillsdale, N.J.: Erlbaum.
Hochberg, J. 1981. On cognition in perception: Perceptual coupling and unconscious inference. *Cognition* 10:127–34.

Hockey, G. R. J. 1970. Effect of loud noise on attentional selectivity. *Quarterly Journal of Experimental Psychology* 22:28–36.

Hockey, R., and A. MacLean. 1981. State changes and the temporal patterning of component resources. In *Attention and performance IX*, edited by A. D. Baddeley and J. Long. Hillsdale, N.J.: Erlbaum.

Hohmann, G. W. 1966. Some effects of spinal cord lesions on experienced emotional feelings. *Psychophysiology* 3:143–56.

Hollenberg, C. K. 1970. Function of visual imagery in the learning and concept formation in children. *Child Development* 41:1003–5.

Holmes, T. H., and R. H. Rahe. 1967. The social readjustment rating scale. *Journal for Psychosomatic Research* 11:213–19.

Hooff, J. A. R. A. M. 1972. A comparative approach to the phylogeny of laughter and smiling. In *Non-verbal communication*, edited by R. A. Hinde. Cambridge: Cambridge University Press.

Hooff, J. A. R. A. M. 1973. A structural analysis of the social behavior of a semicaptive group of chimpanzees. In *Social communication and movement*, edited by M. von Cranach and I. Vine. New York: Academic Press.

Horney, K. 1945. *Our inner conflicts: A constructive theory of neurosis*. New York: Norton.

Hunt, J. McV., M. W. Cole, and E. S. Reis. 1958. Situational cues distinguishing anger, fear, and sorrow. *American Journal of Psychology* 71:136–51.

Hunt, W. A.. 1941. Recent developments in the field of emotion. *Psychological Bulletin* 38:249–76.

Hupka, R. P. 1981. Cultural determinants of jealousy. *Alternative Lifestyles* 4:310–56.

Husserl, E. 1931. *Ideas: General introduction to pure phenomenology*. New York: Macmillan.

Intraub, H. 1981. Identification and processing of briefly glimpsed visual scenes. In *Eye movements: Cognition and visual perception*, edited by D. F. Fisher, R. A. Monty, and J. W. Senders. Hillsdale, N.J.: Erlbaum.

Isen, A. M. 1970. Success, failure, attention and reaction to others: The warm glow of success. *Journal of Personality and Social Psychology* 15:294–301.

Isen, A. M., and P. F. Levin. 1972. The effect of feeling good on helping: Cookies and kindness. *Journal of Personality and Social Psychology* 21:384–88.

Isen, A. M., B. Means, R. Patrick, and G. Nowicki. 1982. Some factors influencing decision-making strategy and risk-taking. In *Affect and cognition: The Seventeenth Annual Carnegie Symposium on Cognition*, edited by M. S. Clark and S. T. Fiske. Hillsdale, N.J.: Erlbaum.

Isen, A. M., and T. E. Shalker. 1977. Do you "Accentuate the positive, eliminate the negative?" when you are in a good mood? Unpublished manuscript, University of Maryland, Baltimore County.

Isen, A. M., T. Shalker, M. Clark, and L. Karp. 1978. Affect, accessibility of material in memory, and behavior: A cognitive loop? *Journal of Personality and Social Psychology* 36:1–12.

Izard, C. E. 1971. *The face of emotion*. New York: Appleton-Century-Crofts.

Izard, C. E. 1977. *Human emotions*. New York: Plenum Press.

Izard, C. E., and S. Buechler. 1980. Aspects of consciousness and personality in terms of differential emotion theory. In *Theories of emotion*, edited by R. Plutchik and H. Kellerman. New York: Academic Press.

James, W. 1884. What is an emotion? *Mind* 9:188–205.

James, W. 1890. *The principles of psychology*. New York: Holt.

James, W. 1894. The physical basis of emotion. *Psychological Review* 1:516–29.

Janis, I. L. 1958. *Psychological stress*. New York: Wiley.

Jasnos, T. M., and K. L. Hakmiller. 1975. Some effects of lesion level and emotional cues on affective expression in spinal cord patients. *Psychological Reports* 37:859–70.

Jefferson, J. W. 1974. Beta-adrenergic receptor blocking drugs in psychiatry. *Archives of General Psychiatry* 31:681–91.

Jemmott, J. B., M. Borysenko, J. Borysenko, D. C. McClelland, R. Chapman, D. Meyer, and H. Benson. 1981. Stress, power motivation, and immunity. Unpublished manuscript.

Jennings, J. R., J. R. Averill, E. M. Opton, and R. S. Lazarus. 1970. Some parameters of heart rate change: Perceptual versus motor task requirements, noxiousness, and uncertainty. *Psychophysiology* 7:194–212.

Johansson, G., and M. Frankenhaeuser. 1973. Temporal factors in sympathoadrenomedullary activity following acute behavioral activation. *Journal of Biological Psychology* 1:67–77.

Jorgensen, R. S., and B. K. Houston. 1981. The Type A behavior pattern, sex differences, and cardiovascular response to and recovery from stress. *Motivation and Emotion* 5:201–14.

Kagan, J. 1971. *Change and continuity in infancy*. New York: Wiley.

Kahneman, D. 1973. *Attention and effort*. Englewood Cliffs, N.J.: Prentice-Hall.

Kamin, L. J. 1969. Predictability, surprise, attention and conditioning. In *Punishment and aversive behavior*, edited by B. A. Campbell and R. M. Church. New York: Appleton-Century-Crofts.

Kanfer, F. H. and J. S. Phillips. 1970. *Learning foundations of behavior theory*. New York: Wiley.

Kant, I. [1781] 1929. *Critique of pure reason*. Translated by N. Kemp Smith. London: Macmillan.

Kantor, J. R. 1921. An attempt toward a naturalistic description of emotion. *Psychological Review* 2:19–42, 120–40.

Kaufman, E. L., M. W. Lord, T. W. Reese, and J. Volkmann. 1949. The discrimination of visual number. *American Journal of Psychology* 62:498–525.

Kelley, H. 1967. Attribution theory in social psychology. In *Nebraska symposium on motivation: 1967*, edited by D. Levine. Lincoln, Neb.: University of Nebraska Press.

Kelly, D., C. C. Brown, and J. W. Shaffer. 1970. A comparison of physiological and psychological measurements on anxiety patients and normals. *Psychophysiology* 6:429–41.

Kelvin, P. 1969. *The bases of social behaviour*. London: Holt, Rinehart and Winston.

Kessen, W. 1965. *The child*. New York: Wiley.

Kessen, W. 1971. Early cognitive development: Hot or cold? In *Cognitive development and epistemology*, edited by T. Mischel. New York: Academic Press.

Kessen, W., and G. Mandler. 1961. Anxiety, pain, and the inhibition of distress. *Psychological Review* 68:396–404.

Kierkegaard, S. A. [1844] 1957. *The concept of dread*. 2d ed. Princeton, N.J.: Princeton University Press.

Kim, M. P., and S. Rosenberg. 1980. Comparison of two structural models of implicit personality theory. *Journal of Personality and Social Psychology* 38:375–89.

Klopfer, P. H. 1969. *Habitats and territories*. New York: Basic Books.

Knapp, D. 1979. Automatization in child language acquisition. Ph.D. diss., University of California, San Diego.

Köhler, W. 1938. *The place of value in a world of facts*. New York: Liveright.

Kraut, R. E., and R. E. Johnston. 1979. Social and emotional messages of smiling: An ethological approach. *Journal of Personality and Social Psychology* 37:1539–53.

Kubie, L. S. 1941. A physiological approach to the concept of anxiety. *Psychosomatic Medicine* 3:263–76.

La Barre, W. 1947. The cultural basis of emotions and gestures. *Journal of Personality* 16:49–68.

LaBerge, D. 1974. Acquisition of automatic processing in perceptual and associative learning. In *Attention and performance* V, edited by P. M. A. Rabbitt and S. Dornic. London: Academic Press.

LaBerge, D. 1982. Measuring the size of the attention spotlight. Talk given at the Center for Human Information Processing, University of California, San Diego, January.

Lacey, B. C., and J. I. Lacey. 1974. Studies of heart rate and other bodily processes in sensorimotor behavior. In *Cardiovascular psychophysiology: Current mechanisms, biofeedback and methodology*, edited by P. A. Obrist, A. Black, J. Brener, and L. DiCara. Chicago: Aldine-Atherton.

Lacey, J. I. 1959. Psychophysiological approaches to the evaluation of psychotherapeutic process and outcome. In *Research in psychotherapy*, edited by E. A. Rubenstein and M. B. Parloff. Washington, D.C.: American Psychological Association.

Lacey, J. I. 1967. Somatic response patterning and stress: Some revisions of activation theory. In *Psychological stress: Issues in research*, edited by M. H. Appley and R. Trumbull. New York: Appleton-Century-Crofts.

Lacey, J. I., J. Kagan, B. C. Lacey, and H. A. Moss. 1963. The visceral level: Situational determinants and behavioral correlates of autonomic response patterns. *Expression of the emotions in man*, edited by P. H. Knapp. New York: International University Press.

Laird, J. D. 1974. Self-attribution of emotion: The effects of expressive behavior on the quality of emotional experience. *Journal of Personality and Social Psychology* 29:475–86.

Landis, C., and W. A. Hunt. 1939. *The startle pattern*. New York: Farrar.

Lange, C. 1885. *Om Sindsbevaegelser*. Copenhagen.

Lanzetta, J. T., J. Cartwright-Smith, and R. E. Kleck. 1976. Effects of nonverbal dissimulation on emotional experience and autonomic arousal. *Journal of Personality and Social Psychology* 33:354–70.

Lashley, K. S. 1923. The behavioristic interpretation of consciousness. *Psychological Review* 30:237–72, 329–53.

Lazarus, R. S. 1968. Emotions and adaptation: Conceptual and empirical relations. In *Nebraska symposium on motivation: 1968*, edited by W. J. Arnold. Lincoln, Neb.: University of Nebraska Press.

Lazarus, R. S. 1975. The self-regulation of emotion. In *Emotions: Their parameters and measurement*, edited by L. Levi. New York: Raven Press.

Lazarus, R. S. 1981. A cognitivist's reply to Zajonc on emotion and cognition. *American Psychologist* 36:222–23.

Lazarus, R. S. 1982. Thoughts on the relations between emotion and cognition. *American Psychologist* 37:1019–24.

Lazarus, R. S., and E. Alfert. 1964. Short-circuiting of threat by experimentally altering cognitive appraisal. *Journal of Abnormal and Social Psychology* 69:195–205.

Lazarus, R. S., J. R. Averill, and E. M. Opton, Jr. 1970. Toward a cognitive theory of emotion. In *Feeling and emotion*, edited by M. B. Arnold. New York: Academic Press.

Lazarus, R. S., A. D. Kanner, and S. Folkman. 1980. Emotions: A cognitive-phenomenological analysis. In *Theories of emotion*, edited by R. Plutchik and H. Kellerman. New York: Academic Press.

Lazarus, R. S., J. C. Speisman, A. M.. Mordkoff, and L. A. Davison. 1962. A laboratory study of psychological stress produced by a motion picture film. *Psychological Monographs* 76: (Whole no. 553).

Leventhal, H. 1979. A perceptual-motor processing model of emotion. In *Advances in the study of communication and affect*. Vol. 5. *Perception of emotion in self and others*, edited by P. Pliner, K. R. Blankstein, and I. M. Spigel. New York: Plenum Press.

Leventhal, H. 1982. The integration of emotion and cognition: A view from the perceptual-motor theory of emotion. In *Affect and Cognition: The Seventeenth Annual Carnegie Symposium on Cognition*, edited by M. S. Clark and S. T. Fiske. Hillsdale, N.J.: Erlbaum.

Levi, L., ed. 1975. *Emotions: Their parameters and measurement*. New York: Raven Press.

Levi-Montalcini, R., and P. W. Angeletti. 1961. Biological properties of a nerve growth promoting protein and its antiserum. In *Regional neurochemistry*, edited by S. S. Kety and J. Elkes. New York: Pergamon.

Levitin, K. 1979. The best path to man: A report from a children's home. *Soviet Psychology* 18:3–66.

Lewin, K. 1935. *A dynamic theory of personality*. New York: McGraw-Hill.

Lewin, K. 1940. Formalization and progress in psychology. *University of Iowa Studies in Child Welfare* 16 (3):9–42.

Libby, W. L., Jr., B. C. Lacey, and J. I. Lacey. 1973. Pupillary and cardiac activity during visual attention. *Psychophysiology* 10:270–94.

Lindemann, E. 1944. Symptomatology and management of acute grief. *American Journal of Psychiatry* 101:141–48.

Lissner, K. 1933. Die Entspannung von Bedürfnissen durch Ersatzhandlungen. *Psychologische Forschung* 18:27–89.

Loftus, E. F., and T. E. Burns. 1982. Mental shock can produce retrograde amnesia. *Memory and Cognition* 10:318–23.

Lorenz, K. 1963. *On aggression*. London: Methuen.

Luce, R. D. 1959. *Individual choice behavior: A theoretical analysis*. New York: Wiley.

Lundberg, U. 1976. Urban commuting: Crowdedness and catecholamine excretion. *Journal of Human Stress* 2 (3):26–32.

Luria, A. K. 1971. Towards the problem of the historical nature of psychological processes. *International Journal of Psychology* 6:259–72.

Luria, Z., and M. D. Rose. 1979. *Psychology of human sexuality*. New York: Wiley.

Lutz, C. 1982. The domain of emotion words on Ifaluk. *American Ethnologist* 9:113–28.

Lutz, C. 1983. Parental goals, ethnopsychology, and the acquisition of emotional meaning. *Ethos* 11: in press.

MacCurdy, J. T. 1925. *The psychology of emotion*. London: Kegan Paul, Trench, Trubner.

MacKinnon, D. W. 1962. The nature and nurture of creative talent. *American Psychologist* 17:484–95.

Macnamara, J. 1972. Cognitive basis of language learning in infants. *Psychological Review* 79:1–13.

Maier, N. R. F. 1949. *Frustration: The study of behavior without a goal*. New York: McGraw-Hill.

Maier, S. F., M. E. P. Seligman, and R. L. Solomon. 1969. Pavlovian fear conditioning and learned helplessness. In *Punishment and aversive behavior*, edited by B. A. Campbell and R. M. Church. New York: Appleton-Century-Crofts.

Mandler, G. 1962a. From association to structure. *Psychological Review* 69:415–27.

Mandler, G. 1962b. Emotion. In *New directions in psychology*, by R. W. Brown, E. Galanter, E. H. Hess, and G. Mandler. New York: Holt.

Mandler, G. 1963. Parent and child in the development of the Oedipus complex. *Journal of Nervous and Mental Diseases* 136:227–35.

Mandler, G. 1964a. The interruption of behavior. In *Nebraska symposium on motivation: 1964*, edited by D. Levine. Lincoln, Neb.: University of Nebraska Press.

Mandler, G. 1964b. Comments on Dr. Schachter's and Dr. Latané's paper. In *Nebraska symposium on motivation: 1964*, edited by D. Levine. Lincoln, Neb.: University of Nebraska Press.

Mandler, G. 1967. Invited commentary. In *Psychological stress*, edited by M. H. Appley and R. Trumbull. New York: Appleton-Century-Crofts.

Mandler, G. 1969. Acceptance of things past and present: A look at the mind and the brain. In *William James: Unfinished business*, edited by R. B. McLeod. Washington, D.C.: American Psychological Association.

Mandler, G. 1972a. Comments. In *Anxiety: Current trends in theory and research*, edited by C. D. Spielberger. New York: Academic Press.

Mandler, G. 1972b. Helplessness: Theory and research in anxiety. In *Anxiety: Current trends in theory and research*, edited by C. D. Spielberger. Vol. 2. New York: Academic Press.

Mandler, G. 1975a. Memory storage and retrieval: Some limits on the reach of attention and consciousness. In *Attention and Performance* V, edited by P. M. A. Rabbitt and S. Dornic. London: Academic Press.

Mandler, G. 1975b. Consciousness: Respectable, useful, and probably necessary. In *Information processing and cognition: The Loyola symposium*, edited by R. Solso. Hillsdale, N.J.: Erlbaum.

Mandler, G. 1975c. *Mind and emotion*. New York: Wiley.

Mandler, G. 1979a. Organization and repetition: Organizational principles with special reference to rote learning. In *Perspectives on memory research*, edited by L.-G. Nilsson. Hillsdale, N.J.: Erlbaum.

Mandler, G. 1979b. Emotion. In *The first century of experimental psychology*, edited by E. Hearst. Hillsdale, N.J.: Erlbaum.

Mandler, G. 1979c. Thought processes, consciousness, and stress. In *Human stress and cognition: An information processing approach*, edited by V. Hamilton and D. M. Warburton. London: Wiley.

Mandler, G. 1980a. Recognizing: The judgment of previous occurrence. *Psychological Review* 87:252–71.

Mandler, G. 1980b. The generation of emotion: A psychological theory. In *Theories of emotion*, edited by R. Plutchik and H. Kellerman. New York: Academic Press.

Mandler, G. 1981a. The recognition of previous encounters. *American Scientist* 69:211–18.

Mandler, G. 1981b. What is cognitive psychology? What isn't? Invited address to the Division of Philosophical Psychology, American Psychological Association, Los Angeles, August.

Mandler, G. 1982a. The structure of value: Accounting for taste. In *Affect and cognition: The Seventeenth Annual Carnegie Symposium on Cognition*, edited by M. S. Clark and S. T. Fiske. Hillsdale, N.J.: Erlbaum.

Mandler, G. 1982b. The integration and elaboration of memory structures. In *Cognitive research in psychology*, edited by F. Klix, J. Hoffmann, and E. van der Meer. Amsterdam: North Holland.

Mandler, G. 1982c. Stress and thought processes. In *Handbook of Stress*, edited by L. Goldberger and S. Breznitz. New York: Free Press/Macmillan.

Mandler, G. 1983. Emotion and stress: A view from cognitive psychology. In *Emotions in health and illness: Foundations of clinical practice*, edited by L. Temoshok, L. S. Zegans, and C. Van Dyke. New York: Grune and Stratton.

Mandler, G., G. O. Goodman, and D. Wilkes-Gibbs. 1982. The word frequency paradox in recognition. *Memory and Cognition* 10:33–42.

Mandler, G., and M. Kahn. 1960. Discrimination of changes in heart rate: Two unsuccessful attempts. *Journal for the Experimental Analysis of Behavior* 3:21–25.

Mandler, G., and W. Kessen. 1959. *The language of psychology*. New York: Wiley.

Mandler, G., and W. Kessen. 1974. The appearance of free will. In *Philosophy of psychology*, edited by S. C. Brown. London: Macmillan.

Mandler, G., and I. Kremen. 1958. Autonomic feedback: A correlational study. *Journal of Personality* 26:388–99. (Erratum, 1960, 28, 545).

Mandler, G., and C. K. Kuhlman. 1961. Proactive and retroactive effects of overlearning. *Journal of Experimental Psychology* 61:76–81.

Mandler, G., J. M. Mandler, I. Kremen, and R. D. Sholiton. 1961. The response to threat: Relations among verbal and physiological indices. *Psychological Monographs* 75: (Whole no. 513).

Mandler, G., J. M. Mandler, and E. T. Uviller. 1958. Autonomic feedback: The perception of autonomic activity. *Journal of Abnormal and Social Psychology* 56:367–73.

Mandler, G., and S. B. Sarason. 1952. A study of anxiety and learning. *Journal of Abnormal and Social Psychology* 47:166–73.

Mandler, G., and B. J. Shebo. 1982. Subitizing: An analysis of its component processes. *Journal of Experimental Psychology: General* 111:1–22.

Mandler, G., and B. J. Shebo. 1983. Knowing and liking. *Motivation and Emotion* 7:125–44.

Mandler, G., and D. L. Watson. 1966. Anxiety and the interruption of behavior. In *Anxiety and behavior*, edited by C. D. Spielberger. New York: Academic Press.

Mandler, J. M. 1979. Categorical and schematic organization in memory. In *Memory organization and structure*, edited by C. R. Puff. New York: Academic Press.

Mandler, J. M. 1983. Representation. In *Cognitive development*, edited by J. H. Flavell and E. M. Markman. Vol. 3 of *Handbook of child psychology*, edited by P. Mussen. 4th ed. New York: Wiley.

Mandler, J. M., and G. Mandler. 1974. Good guys vs. bad guys: The subject-object dichotomy. *Journal of Humanistic Psychology* 14:63–87.

Marañon, G. 1924. Contribution à l'étude de l'action émotive de l'adrénaline. *Revue Française d'Endocrinologie* 2:301–25.

Marcel, A. J. 1983a. Conscious and unconscious perception: Experiments on visual masking and word recognition. *Cognitive Psychology* 15:197–237.

Marcel, A. J. 1983b. Conscious and unconscious perception: An approach to the relations between phenomenal experience and perceptual processes. *Cognitive Psychology* 15:238–300.

Marx, M. H. 1956. Some relations between frustration and drive. In *Nebraska symposium on motivation:* 1956, edited by M. R. Jones. Lincoln, Neb.: University of Nebraska Press.

Maslach, C. 1979. Negative emotional biasing of unexplained arousal. *Journal of Personality and Social Psychology* 37:953–69.

Mason, J. W. 1975. A historical view of the stress field. *Journal of Human Stress* 1 (1):6–12; (2):22–36.

Masters, W. H., and V. E. Johnson. 1966. *Human sexual response*. New York: Little, Brown.

Matlin, M. W. 1971. Response competition, recognition, and affect. *Journal of Personality and Social Psychology* 19:295–300.

McClelland, D. C. 1951. *Personality*. New York: Sloane.

McClelland, D. C., E. Floor, R. J. Davidson, and C. Saron. 1980. Stressed power motivation, sympathetic activation, immune function, and illness. *Journal of Human Stress* 6 (2):11–19.

McClelland, D. C., and J. B. Jemmott, III. 1980. Power motivation, stress and physical illness. *Journal of Human Stress* 6 (4):6–15.

McClelland, J. L., and D. E. Rumelhart. 1981. An interactive activation model of context effects in letter perception: Part I. An account of basic findings. *Psychological Review* 88:375–407.

McFarlane-Smith, I. 1964. *Spatial ability*. London: University of London Press.

Medawar, P. B. 1977. Unnatural science. *New York Review of Books* 24:13–18.

Mednick, S. A. 1958. A learning theory approach to research in schizophrenia. *Psychological Bulletin* 55:316–27.

Melzack, R. 1973. *The puzzle of pain*. New York: Basic Books.

Melzack, R., and K. L. Casey. 1968. Sensory, motivational, and central control of pain: A new conceptual model. In *The skin sense*, edited by D. L. Kenshalo. Springfield, Ill.: Charles Thomas.

Melzack, R., and K. L. Casey. 1970. The affective dimension of pain. In *Feelings and emotions*, edited by M. B. Arnold. New York: Academic Press.

Melzack, R., and S. C. Dennis. 1978. Neurophysiological foundations of pain. In *The psychology of pain*, edited by R. A. Sternbach. New York: Raven Press.

Melzack, R., and T. H. Scott. 1957. The effects of early experience on the response to pain. *Journal of Comparative Psychology* 50:155–61.

Melzack, R., and P. D. Wall. 1965. Pain mechanisms: A new theory. *Science* 150:971–79.

Meyer, L. B. 1956. *Emotion and meaning in music*. Chicago: University of Chicago Press.

Meyer, D. E., and R. W. Schvaneveldt. 1976. Meaning, memory structure, and mental process. In *The structure of human memory*, edited by C. N. Cofer. San Francisco: Freeman.

Millenson, J. R. 1967. *Principles of behavioral analysis*. New York: Collier/Macmillan.

Miller, G. A. 1956. The magical number seven, plus or minus two: Some limits on our capacity for processing information. *Psychological Review* 63:81–97.

Miller, G. A. 1962. *Psychology: The science of mental life*. New York: Harper & Row.

Miller, G. A., E. H. Galanter, and K. Pribram. 1960. *Plans and the structure of behavior.* New York: Holt.

Miller, N. E. 1951. Learnable drives and rewards. In *Handbook of experimental psychology*, edited by S. S. Stevens. New York: Wiley.

Miller, N. E. 1963. Same reflections on the law of effect produce a new alternative to drive reduction. In *Nebraska symposium on motivation: 1963*, edited by M. R. Jones. Lincoln, Neb.: University of Nebraska Press.

Miller, N. E. 1969. Learning of visceral and glandular responses. *Science* 163:434–45.

Minsky, M. 1975. A framework for representing knowledge. In *The psychology of computer vision*, edited by P. H. Winston. New York: McGraw-Hill.

Mischel, W. 1968. *Personality and assessment.* New York: Wiley.

Mischel, W., and R. Metzner. 1962. Preference for delayed reward as a function of age, intelligence, and length of delay interval. *Journal of Abnormal and Social Psychology* 64:425–31.

Montagu, A. 1976. *The nature of human aggression.* New York: Oxford University Press.

Morris, D. 1967. *The naked ape.* New York: McGraw-Hill.

Mowrer, O. H. 1939. Stimulus-response analysis of anxiety and its role as a reinforcing agent. *Psychological Review* 46:553–65.

Mowrer, O. H. 1947. On the dual nature of learning: A reinterpretation of "conditioning" and "problem solving." *Harvard Educational Review* 17:102–48.

Mowrer, O. H. 1960. *Learning theory and behavior.* New York: Wiley.

Mueller, C. W., and E. Donnerstein. 1981. Film-facilitated arousal and prosocial behavior. *Journal of Experimental Social Psychology* 17:31–41.

Murdock, B. B., Jr. 1961. The retention of individual terms. *Journal of Experimental Psychology* 62:618–25.

Nance, J. 1975. *The gentle Tasaday.* New York: Harcourt Brace Jovanovich.

Natsoulas, T. 1970. Concerning introspective "knowledge." *Psychological Bulletin* 73:89–111.

Natsoulas, T. 1977. Consciousness: Consideration of an inferential hypothesis. *Journal for the Theory of Social Behavior* 7:29–39.

Neely, J. H. 1977. Semantic priming and retrieval from lexical memory: Roles of inhibitionless spreading activation and limited-capacity attention. *Journal of Experimental Psychology: General* 106:226–54.

Neisser, U. 1962. Cultural and cognitive discontinuity. In *Anthropology and human behavior*, edited by T. E. Gladwin and W. Sturtevant. Washington, D.C.: Anthropological Society of Washington.

Neisser, U. 1967. *Cognitive Psychology.* New York: Appleton-Century-Crofts.

Newell, A., and H. Simon. 1972. *Human problem solving.* Englewood Cliffs, N.J.: Prentice-Hall.

Nisbett, R. E., and T. D. Wilson. 1977. Telling more than we can know: Verbal reports on mental processes. *Psychological Review* 84:231–59.

Norman, D. A. 1973. Learning and remembering: A tutorial preview. In *Attention and performance IV*, edited by S. Kornblum. New York: Academic Press.

Norman, D. A. 1982. Some observations on mental models. In *Mental models*, edited by D. Gentner and A. Stevens. Hillsdale, N.J.: Erlbaum.

Norman, D. A., and D. G. Bobrow. 1975. On data-limited and resource-limited processes. *Cognitive Psychology* 7:44–64.

Norman, D. A., and D. E. Rumelhart. In press. Representation in memory. In *Handbook of Experimental Psychology*, edited by R. C. Atkinson, R. J. Herrnstein, G. Lindzey, and R. D. Luce. New York: Wiley.

Norman, D. A., and T. Shallice. 1980. Attention to action: Willed and automatic control of behavior. CHIP Technical Report no. 99, Center for Human Information Processing, University of California, San Diego, December.

North, A. J., and D. T. Stimmel, 1960. Extinction of an instrumental response following a large number of reinforcements. *Psychological Reports* 6:227–34.

Nowlis, V., and H. H. Nowlis. 1956. The description and analysis of mood. *Annals of the New York Academy of Science* 65:345–55.

Obrist, P. A., J. R. Sutterer, and J. L. Howard. 1972. Preparatory cardiac changes: A psychobiological approach. In *Classical conditioning II*, edited by A. H. Black and W. F. Prokasy. New York: Appleton-Century-Crofts.

Ornstein, R. E. 1969. *On the experience of time.* Harmondsworth: Penguin.

Ornstein, R. E. 1972. *The psychology of consciousness.* San Francisco: Freeman.

Ortony, A., A. Collins, and G. L. Clore. 1982. Principia pathematica. Unpublished manuscript.

Osgood, C. E., G. J. Suci, and P. H. Tannenbaum. 1957. *The measurement of meaning*. Urbana: University of Illinois Press.

Oster, H. 1978. Facial expression and affect development. In *The development of affect*, edited by M. Lewis and L. A. Rosenblum. New York: Plenum.

Panksepp, J. 1982. Toward a general psychobiological theory of emotions. *Behavioral and Brain Sciences* 5:407–22.

Parker, R. E. 1977. The encoding of information in complex pictures. Ph.D. diss., University of California, San Diego.

Parkes, C. M. 1972. *Bereavement: Studies of grief in adult life*. New York: International Universities Press.

Paulhan, F. 1887. *Les phénomènes affectifs et les lois de leur apparition*. Paris: F. Alcan.

Paulhan, F. 1930. *The laws of feeling*. Translated by C. K. Ogden. London: Kegan Paul, Trench, Trubner.

Peiper, A. 1956. *Die Eigenart der kindlichen Hirntätigkeit*. 2d ed. Leipzig: Thieme.

Perlman, D., and S. Oskamp. 1971. The effects of picture content and exposure frequency on evaluation of negroes and whites. *Journal of Experimental Social Psychology* 7:503–14.

Perry, R. B. 1926. *General theory of value: Its meaning and basic principles construed in terms of interest*. Cambridge: Harvard University Press.

Peters, R. S. 1969. Motivation, emotion, and the conceptual schemes of common sense. In *Human action*, edited by T. Mischel. New York: Academic Press.

Piaget, J. 1953. *The origin of intelligence in the child*. London: Routledge and Kegan Paul.

Piaget, J. 1970. Piaget's theory. In *Carmichael's Manual of child psychology*, edited by P. Mussen. 3d ed. Vol. 1. New York: Wiley.

Piaget, J. 1971. *Insights and illusions of philosophy*. London: Routledge and Kegan Paul.

Piaget, J., and B. Inhelder. 1969. *The psychology of the child*. New York: Basic Books.

Pick, J. 1954. The evolution of homeostasis: The phylogenetic development of the regulation of bodily and mental activities by the autonomic nervous system. *Proceedings of the American Philosophical Society*, 298–303.

Pick, J. 1970. *The autonomic nervous system*. Philadelphia: Lippincott.

Plutchik, R. 1962. *The emotions: Facts, theories and a new model*. New York: Random House.

Plutchik, R. 1970. Emotions, evolution, and adaptive processes. In *Feelings and emotions*, edited by M. B. Arnold. New York: Academic Press.

Plutchik, R. 1977. Cognitions in the service of emotions: An evolutionary perspective. In *Emotion*, edited by D. K. Candland, J. P. Fell, E. Keen, A. I. Leshner, R. Plutchik, and R. M. Tarpy. Monterey, Calif.: Brooks Cole.

Pollard, P. 1982. Human reasoning: Some possible effects of availability. *Cognition* 12:65–96.

Posner, M. I. 1967. Short term memory systems in human information processing. *Acta Psychologia* 27:267–84.

Posner, M. I., and S. J. Boies. 1971. Components of attention. *Psychological Review* 78:391–408.

Posner, M. I., and S. W. Keele. 1970. Time and space as measures of mental operations. Paper presented at the Annual Meeting of the American Psychological Association, Miami Beach, September.

Posner, M. I., and R. M. Klein. 1973. On the functions of consciousness. In *Attention and performance IV*, edited by S. Kornblum. New York: Academic Press.

Posner, M. I., and C. R. R. Snyder. 1975. Attention and cognitive control. In *Information processing and cognition: The Loyola symposium*, edited by R. Solso. Potomac, Md.: Erlbaum.

Posner, M. I., and R. E. Warren. 1972. Traces, concepts and conscious constructions. In *Coding processes in human memory*, edited by A. W. Melton and E. Martin. Washington, D.C.: Winston.

Poulton, E. C. 1976a. Continuous noise interferes with work by masking auditory feedback and inner speech. *Applied Ergonomics* 7:79–84.

Poulton, E. C. 1976b. Arousing environmental stresses can improve performance, whatever people say. *Aviation, Space, and Environmental Medicine* 47:1193–204.

Rahe, R. H. 1979. Life change events and mental illness: An overview. *Journal of Human Stress* 5 (3):2–10.

Rahe, R. H., and R. J. Arthur. 1978. Life change and illness studies: Past history and future directions. *Journal of Human Stress* 4 (1):3–15.

Rank, O. 1932. *Art and artist: Creative urge and personality development*. New York: Knopf.

Rank, O. [1924] 1952. *The trauma of birth*. New York: Brunner.

Rapaport, D. [1942] 1961. Emotions and memory. *Menninger Clinic Monograph Series*, no. 2. New York: Wiley.

Raven, B. H., and J. Rietsma. 1957. The effects of varied clarity of group goal and group path upon the individual and his relation to his group. *Human Relations* 10:29–45.

Rescorla, R. A. 1967. Pavlovian conditioning and its proper control procedures. *Psychological Review* 74:71–80.

Rescorla, R. A., and R. L. Solomon. 1967. Two-process learning theory: Relations between Pavlovian conditioning and instrumental learning. *Psychological Review* 74:151–82.

Reymert, M. L., ed. 1928. *Feelings and emotions: The Wittenberg symposium*. Worcester, Mass.: Clark University Press.

Reymert, M. L., ed. 1950. *Feelings and emotions: The Mooseheart symposium*. New York: McGraw-Hill.

Robbins, T. W. 1983. The neuropsychology of emotion. In *The handbook of psychiatry*, edited by M. Shepherd and O. L. Zangwill. Vol. 1. Cambridge: Cambridge University Press.

Rodin, M. J. 1978. Liking and disliking: Sketch of an alternative view. *Personality and Social Psychology Bulletin* 4:473–78.

Rogers, M. P., D. Dubey, and P. Reich. 1979. The influence of the psyche and the brain on immunity and susceptibility to disease: A critical review. *Psychosomatic Medicine* 41:147–67.

Rosch, E. 1975. Cognitive representations of semantic categories. *Journal of Experimental Psychology: General* 104:192–233.

Rosch, E. 1978. Principles of categorization. In *Cognition and categorization*, edited by E. Rosch and B. B. Lloyd. Hillsdale, N.J.: Erlbaum.

Rosch, E., and C. Mervis. 1975. Family resemblances: Studies in the internal structure of categories. *Cognitive Psychology* 7:573–605.

Roseman, I. 1979. Cognitive aspects of emotion and emotional behavior. Paper presented at the convention of the American Psychological Association, New York, August.

Rosenbaum, D. A. 1972. The theory of cognitive residues: A new view of fantasy. *Psychological Review* 79:471–86.

Rosenzweig, S. 1944. An outline of frustration theory. In *Personality and the behavior disorders*, edited by J. McV. Hunt. New York: Ronald.

Ross, E. D., and M.-M. Mesulam. 1979. Dominant language functions of the right hemisphere. Prosody and emotional gesturing. *Archives of Neurology* 36:144–48.

Rothballer, A. B. 1967. Aggression, defense and neurohumors. In *Aggression and defense: Neural mechanisms and social patterns*. (Brain function, vol. 5) edited by C. D. Clemente and D. B. Lindsley. Los Angeles: University of California Press.

Rothbart, M. K. 1973. Laughter in young children. *Psychological Bulletin* 80:247–56.

Rotter, J. B., M. R. Seeman, and S. Liverant. 1962. Internal versus external control of reinforcement: A major variable in behavior theory. In *Decisions, values and groups*, edited by N. F. Washburne. Vol. 2. London: Pergamon Press.

Rozin, P., and J. W. Kalat. 1971. Specific hungers and poison avoidance as adaptive specializations of learning. *Psychological Review* 78:459–86.

Ruckmick, C. A. 1936. *The psychology of feeling and emotion*. New York: McGraw-Hill.

Rumelhart, D. E. 1980. Schemata: The building blocks of cognition. In *Theoretical issues in reading comprehension*, edited by R. Spiro, B. Bruce, and W. Brewer. Hillsdale, N.J.: Erlbaum.

Rumelhart, D. E., G. E. Hinton, and J. L. McClelland. In preparation. *Parallel distributed processing in cognition*.

Rumelhart, D. E., and A. Ortony. 1978. The representation of knowledge in memory. In *Schooling and the acquisition of knowledge*, edited by R. C. Anderson, R. J. Spiro, and W. E. Montague. Hillsdale, N.J.: Erlbaum.

Ryle, G. 1949. *The concept of mind*. London: Hutchison.

Sanford, A. J., and S. C. Garrod. 1981. *Understanding written language*. Chichester, England: Wiley.

Sarason, I. G. 1961. The effects of anxiety and threat on the solution of a difficult task. *Journal of Abnormal and Social Psychology* 62:165–68.

Sartre, J.-P. [1943] 1956. *Being and nothingness: An essay on phenomenological ontology*. New York: Philosophical Library.

Schachtel, E. G. 1959. *Metamorphosis*. New York: Basic Books.

Schachter, S. 1970. The assumption of identity and peripheralist-centralist controversies in motivation and emotion. In *Feelings and emotion*, edited by M. B. Arnold. New York: Academic Press.

Schachter, S. 1971. *Emotion, obesity, and crime.* New York: Academic Press.

Schachter, S., and B. Latané. 1964. Crime, cognition and the autonomic nervous system. In *Nebraska symposium on motivation:* 1964, edited by D. Levin. Lincoln, Neb.: University of Nebraska Press.

Schachter, S., and J. E. Singer. 1962. Cognitive, social and physiological determinants of emotional state. *Psychological Review* 69:379–99.

Schank, R., and R. Abelson. 1977. *Scripts, plans, goals and understanding: An inquiry into human knowledge structures.* Hillsdale, N.J.: Erlbaum.

Schiffenbauer, A. 1974. Effect of observer's emotional state on judgments of the emotional state of others. *Journal of Personality and Social Psychology* 30:31–35.

Schneirla, T. C. 1959. An evolutionary and developmental theory of biphasic processes underlying approach and withdrawal. In *Nebraska symposium on motivation:* 1959, edited by M. R. Jones. Lincoln, Neb.: University of Nebraska Press.

Schoenfeld, N. 1950. An experimental approach to anxiety, escape and avoidance behavior. In *Anxiety*, edited by P. H. Hoch and J. Zubin. New York: Grune.

Schwartz, B., and H. Lacey. 1982. *Behaviorism, science, and human nature.* New York: Norton.

Scott, J. P. 1958. *Animal behavior.* Chicago: University of Chicago Press.

Selg, H., ed. 1971. *Zur Aggression verdammt? Psychologische Ansätze einer Friedensforschung.* Stuttgart: W. Kohlhammer.

Seligman, M. E. P. 1972. Depression and learned helplessness. Paper presented at the American Psychological Association meetings, Hawaii.

Seligman, M. E. P. 1975. *Helplessness: On depression, development, and death.* San Francisco: Freeman.

Seligman, M. E. P., and S. F. Maier. 1967. Failure to escape traumatic shock. *Journal of Experimental Psychology* 74:1–9.

Selye, H. 1956. *The stress of life.* New York: McGraw-Hill.

Selye, H. 1975. Confusion and controversy in the stress field. *Journal of Human Stress* 1 (2):37–44.

Sergi, G. 1896. Sulla nuova teoria della emozioni. *Rivista di Sociologica* 3:23–38.

Shallice, T. 1972. Dual functions of consciousness. *Psychological Review* 79:383–93.

Sher, M. A. 1971. Pupillary dilation before and after interruption of familiar and unfamiliar sequences. *Journal of Personality and Social Psychology* 20:281–86.

Sherrington, C. S. 1900. Experiments on the value of vascular and visceral factors for the genesis of emotion. *Proceedings of the Royal Society of London* 66:390–403.

Shiffrin, R. M., and W. Schneider. 1977. Controlled and automatic human information processing: II. Perceptual learning, automatic attending, and a general theory. *Psychological Review* 84:127–90.

Shurcliff, A. 1968. Judged humor, arousal, and the relief theory. *Journal of Personality and Social Psychology* 8:360–63.

Silver, R. L., and C. B. Wortman. 1980. Coping with undesirable life event. In *Human helplessness: Theory and applications*, edited by J. Gaber and M. E. P. Seligman. New York: Academic Press.

Simon, H. A. 1967. Motivational and emotional controls of cognition. *Psychological Review* 74:29–39.

Singer, J. E., U. Lundberg, and M. Frankenhaeuser. 1978. Stress on the train: A study of urban commuting. In *Advances in environmental psychology*, edited by A. Baum, J. E. Singer, and S. Valins. Vol. 1. Hillsdale, N.J.: Erlbaum.

Sirota, A. D., G. E. Schwartz, and D. Shapiro. 1974. Voluntary control of human heart rate: Effect on reaction to aversive stimulation. *Journal of Abnormal Psychology* 83:261–67.

Sirota, A., G. E. Schwartz, and D. Shapiro. 1976. Voluntary control of human heart rate: Effect on reaction to aversive stimulation: A replication and extension. *Journal of Abnormal Psychology* 85:473–77.

Skinner, B. F. 1938. *The behavior of organisms.* New York: Appleton-Century-Crofts.

Skinner, B. F. 1957. *Verbal behavior.* New York: Appleton-Century-Crofts.

Sokolov, E. N. 1963. *Perception and the conditioned reflex.* New York: Macmillan.

Solomon, G. F., and A. F. Amkraut. 1983. Emotions, immunity and disease. In *Emotions in health and illness: Foundations of clinical practice*, edited by L. Temoshok, L. S. Zegans, and C. Van Dyke. New York: Grune and Stratton.

Solomon, R. L., and E. S. Brush. 1956. Experimentally derived conceptions of anxiety and aversion. In *Nebraska symposium on motivation:* 1956, edited by M. R. Jones. Lincoln, Neb.: University of Nebraska Press.

Solomon, R. L., and L. C. Wynne. 1954. Traumatic avoidance learning: The principle of anxiety conservation and partial irreversibility. *Psychological Review* 61:353–85.

Sroufe, L. A., E. Waters, and L. Matas. 1974. Contextual determinants of infant affective responses. In *Origins of fear*, edited by M. Lewis and G. Rosenblum. New York: Wiley.

Sroufe, L. A., and J. P. Wunsch. 1972. The development of laughter in the first year of life. *Child Development* 43:1326–44.

Staddon, J. E. R., and V. L. Simmelhag. 1971. The "superstition" experiment: A reexamination of its implications for the principles of adaptive behavior. *Psychological Review* 78:3–43.

Stern, R. M., and B. E. Kaplan. 1967. Galvanic skin response: Voluntary control and externalization. *Journal of Psychosomatic Research* 10:349–53.

Stewart, J. C. 1965. An experimental investigation of imagery. Ph.D. diss., University of Toronto.

Sutherland, A. 1898. *The origin and growth of the moral instinct*. London: Longmans, Green.

Sutherland, N. S., and N. J. Mackintosh. 1971. *Mechanism of animal discrimination learning*. New York: Academic Press.

Tannenbaum, P. H., and D. Zillmann. 1975. Emotional arousal in the facilitation of aggression through communication. *Advances in Experimental Social Psychology* 8:149–92.

Taylor, J. A. 1953. A personality scale of manifest anxiety. *Journal of Abnormal and Social Psychology* 48:285–90.

Taylor, J. A. 1956. Drive theory and manifest anxiety. *Psychological Bulletin* 53:303–20.

Temoshok, L., L. S. Zegans, and C. Van Dyke, eds. 1983. *Emotions in health and illness: Foundations of clinical practice*. New York: Grune and Stratton.

Thatcher, R. W., and E. R. John. 1977. *Foundations of cognitive processes*. Hillsdale, N.J.: Erlbaum.

Thayer, R. E. 1970. Activation states as assessed by verbal report and four psychophysiological variables. *Psychophysiology* 7:86–94.

Theios, J., and J. Brelsford. 1964. Overlearning-extinction effect as an incentive phenomenon. *Journal of Experimental Psychology* 67:463–67.

Tinbergen, N. 1951. *The study of instinct*. Oxford: Oxford University Press.

Titchener, E. B. 1896. *An outline of psychology*. New York: Macmillan.

Tomkins, S. 1962, 1963. *Affect, imagery, and consciousness*. Vol. 1. *The positive affects*. Vol. 2. *The negative affects*. New York: Springer.

Tomkins, S. S. 1980. Affect as amplification: Some modifications in theory. In *Theories of emotion*, edited by R. Plutchik and H. Kellerman. New York: Academic Press.

Tomkins, S. S. 1981. The quest for primary motives: Biography and autobiography of an idea. *Journal of Personality and Social Psychology* 41:306–29.

Tourangeau, R., and P. C. Ellsworth. 1979. The role of facial response in the experience of emotion. *Journal of Personality and Social Psychology* 37:1519–31.

Treisman, A. M. 1964. Verbal cues, language and meaning in selective attention. *American Journal of Psychology* 77:206–18.

Treisman, A. 1969. Strategies and models of selective attention. *Psychological Review* 76:282–99.

Treisman, A. M., and G. Gelade. 1980. A feature-integration theory of attention. *Cognitive Psychology* 12:97–136.

Treisman, A., and H. Schmidt. 1982. Illusory conjunctions in the perception of objects. *Cognitive Psychology* 14:107–41.

Tversky, A. 1972. Elimination by aspects: A theory of choice. *Psychological Review* 79:281–99.

Tversky, A., and A. Kahneman. 1973. Availability: A heuristic for judging frequency and probability. *Cognitive Psychology* 5:207–32.

Tyrer, P. J. 1976. *The role of bodily feelings in anxiety*. Maudsley Monographs. London: Oxford University Press.

Valins, S. 1966. Cognitive effects of false heart-rate feedback. *Journal of Personality and Social Psychology* 4:400–408.

Valins, S. 1970. The perception and labeling of bodily changes as determinants of emotional behavior. In *Physiological correlates of emotion*, edited by P. Black. New York: Academic Press.

Valins, S., and A. A. Ray. 1967. Effects of cognitive desensitization on avoidance behavior. *Journal of Personality and Social Psychology* 7:345–50.

Von Holst, E. V. 1939. Die relative Koordination als Phänomen und als Methode zentralnervöser Funktionsanalyse. *Ergebnisse der Psychologie* 42:228–306.

Vygotsky, L. S. 1962. *Thought and language*. Cambridge, Mass.: M.I.T. Press.

Wagner, A. R. 1963. Conditioned frustration as a learned drive. *Journal of Experimental Psychology* 66:142–48.

Wallston, B. S., S. W. Alagna, B. M. DeVellis, and R. F. DeVellis. 1981. Social support and physical health. Unpublished manuscript.

Warrington, E. K. 1975. The selective impairment of semantic memory. *Quarterly Journal of Experimental Psychology* 27:635–57.

Watkins, L. R., and D. J. Mayer. 1982. Organization of endogenous opiate and nonopiate pain control systems. *Science* 216:1185–92.

Watson, J. B. 1919. *Psychology from the stand-point of a behaviorist*. Philadelphia: Lippincott.

Watson, J. B. 1928. *Psychological care of infant and child*. New York: Norton.

Weakland, J. H. 1960. The "double-bind" hypothesis of schizophrenia and three-party interaction. In *The etiology of schizophrenia*, edited by D. Jackson. New York: Basic Books.

Weiss, P. 1941. Self-differentiation of the basic patterns of coordination. *Comparative Psychology Monographs* 17 (4).

Weitzman, B. 1971. A reply to Wolpe. *Psychological Review* 78:352–53.

Weltman, G., J. E. Smith, and G. H. Egstrom. 1971. Perceptual narrowing during simulated pressure-chamber exposure. *Human Factors* 13:99–107.

Wenger, M. A., F. N. Jones, and M. H. Jones. 1956. *Physiological psychology*. New York: Holt.

Wenzel, B. M. 1972. Immunosympathectomy and behavior. In *Immunosympathectomy*, edited by G. Steiner and E. Schonbaum. Amsterdam: Elsevier.

Werbik, H. 1971. *Informationsgehalt und emotionale Wirkung von Musik*. Mainz: B. Schott.

Werner, J. S., and M. Perlmutter. 1979. Development of visual memory in infants. In *Advances in child development and behavior*, edited by H. W. Reese and L. P. Lipsitt. Vol. 14. New York: Academic Press.

West, L. J., and I. E. Farber. 1961. The role of pain in emotional development. Unpublished report, University of Oklahoma Medical School.

White, R. W. 1959. Motivation reconsidered: The concept of competence. *Psychological Review* 66:297–333.

Wierzbicka, A. 1972. Emotions. In *Semantic primitives*, by A. Wierzbicka. Frankfurt: Athenäum.

Wilensky, R. 1982. Points: A theory of the structure of stories in memory. In *Strategies for natural language processing*, edited by W. G. Lehnert and M. H. Ringle. Hillsdale, N.J.: Erlbaum.

Wilson, E. O. 1975. *Sociobiology*. Cambridge: Harvard University Press.

Wilson, E. O. 1978. *On human nature*. Cambridge: Harvard University Press.

Wine, J. 1971. Test anxiety and direction of attention. *Psychological Bulletin* 76:92–104.

Winkler, H., and A. D. Smith. 1972. Phaeochromocytoma and other catecholamine producing tumors. In *Catecholamines*, edited by H. Blashko and E. Mascholl. Berlin: Springer.

Wolf, S., and H. G. Wolff. 1943. *Human gastric function*. New York: Oxford University Press.

Wolpe, J. 1958. *Psychotherapy by reciprocal inhibition*. Stanford: Stanford University Press.

Woodward, A. E., R. A. Bjork, and R. H. Jongeward, Jr. 1973. Recall and recognition as a function of primary rehearsal. *Journal of Verbal Learning and Verbal Behavior* 12:608–17.

Woodworth, R. S. 1938. *Experimental psychology*. New York: Holt.

Wundt, W. 1891. Zur Lehre von den Gemüthsbewegungen. *Philosophische Studien* 6:335–93.

Wundt, W. 1905. *Grundriss der Psychologie*. Leipzig: Wilhelm Engelmann.

Wynne, L. C., and R. L. Solomon. 1955. Traumatic avoidance learning: Acquisition and extinction in dogs deprived of normal peripheral autonomic function. *Genetic Psychology Monographs* 52:241–84.

Yerkes, R. M., and J. D. Dodson. 1908. The relation of strength of stimulus to rapidity of habit-formation. *Journal of Comparative and Neurological Psychology* 18:459–82.

Zahn, T. P., W. T. Carpenter, and T. H. McGlashan. 1981. Autonomic nervous system activity in acute schizophrenia. I. Method and comparison with normal controls. *Archives of General Psychiatry* 38:251–58.

Zajonc, R. B. 1968. Attitudinal effects of mere exposure. *Journal of Personality and Social Psychology Monograph* 9, no. 2, pt. 2:1–28.

Zajonc, R. B. 1980. Feeling and thinking: Preferences need no inferences. *American Psychologist* 35:151–75.

Zajonc, R. B., H. Markus, and W. R. Wilson. 1974. Exposure effects and associative learning. *Journal of Experimental Social Psychology* 10:248–63.

Zeigarnik, B. 1927. Das Behalten erledigter und unerledigter Handlungen. *Psychologische Forschung* 9:1–85.

Ziff, P. 1960. *Semantic analysis*. Ithaca, N.Y.: Cornell University Press.

Zillmann, D. 1971. Excitation transfer in communication-mediated aggressive behavior. *Journal of Experimental Social Psychology* 7:419–34.

Zillmann, D. 1978. Attribution and misattribution of excitatory reactions. In *New directions in attribution research*, edited by J. H. Harvey, W. Ickes, and R. F. Kidd. Vol. 2. Hillsdale, N.J.: Erlbaum.

Zillmann, D., A. H. Katcher, and B. Milavsky. 1972. Excitation transfer from physical exercise to subsequent aggressive behavior. *Journal of Experimental Social Psychology* 8:247–59.

Zuckerman, M. 1971. Physiological measures of sexual arousal in the human. *Psychological Bulletin* 75:297–29.

Zuckerman, M., R. Klorman, D. T. Larrance, and N. H. Spiegel. 1981. Facial, autonomic, and subjective components of emotion: The facial feedback hypothesis versus the externalizer-internalizer dimension. *Journal of Personality and Social Psychology* 41:929–44.

NAME INDEX

SUBJECT INDEX